Your Literacy Standards Companion at a Glance

Indexes Cross-Referencing Your State Standards with the Common Core appear at the front of the book.

Specific strands and standards are listed for each state.

Each state and grade level is listed at the top for easy reference.

The gist of each standard is succinctly summarized.

This column shows where to find instructional guidance for each standard.

Indexes Cross-Referencing Your State Standards

Alaska, Kindergarten

Alaska Strand/Standard	Focus of Alaska Standard	For More Information
Reading Literature		
RL.1	Ask and answer questions about a text using key details	R1 pp. 6–11
RL.2	Retell familiar stories, using key details	R2 pp. 12–17
RL.3	Identify characters, settings, and major events in a story	R3 pp. 18–23
RL.4	Ask and answer questions about unknown words in a text	R4 pp. 24–29
RL.5	Identify common types of text (e.g., storybooks, poems)	R5 pp. 30–35
RL.6	Name the author and illustrator of a story and describe the role of each	R6 pp. 36–41
RL.7	Describe the relationship between the illustrations and the story in which they appear	R7 pp. 42–47
RL.8	NA	
RL.9	Compare and contrast the characters in familiar stories	R9 pp. 54–59
RL.10	Actively engage in reading activities with purpose and understanding	R10 pp. 60–65
Reading Informational Text		
RI.1	Ask and answer questions about information in a text, using key details	R1 pp. 6–11
RI.2	Identify the main topic and retell key details of a text	R2 pp. 12–17
RI.3	Describe the connection between two individuals, events, ideas, or pieces of information in a text	R3 pp. 18–23
RI.4	Ask and answer questions about unknown words in a text	R4 pp. 24–29
RI.5	Identify the front cover, back cover, and title page of a book	R5 pp. 30–35
RI.6	Name the author and illustrator of a text and describe the role of each	R6 pp. 36–41
RI.7	Describe the relationship between visual images and the text in which they appear	R7 pp. 42–47
RI.8	Identify the opinions an author states in a text	R8 pp. 48–53
RI.9	Identify basic similarities and differences between two texts on the same topic	R9 pp. 54–59
RI.10	Actively engage in reading informational text with purpose and understanding	R10 pp. 60–65
Reading Foundational Skills		
RF.1	Print Concepts: Demonstrate understanding of the organization and basic features of print	RF1 pp. 72–77
RF.2	Phonological Awareness: Demonstrate understanding of spoken words, syllables, and sounds (phonemes)	RF2 pp. 78–83
RF.3	Phonics: Know and apply grade-level phonics and word analysis skills in decoding words	RF3 pp. 84–89
RF.4	Fluency: Read level-appropriate texts with purpose and understanding	RF4 pp. 90–95
Writing		
W.1	Use a combination of drawing, dictating, and writing to compose opinion pieces	W1 pp. 100–105
W.2	Use a combination of drawing, dictating, and writing to compose informative/explanatory texts	W2 pp. 106–111
W.3	Use a combination of drawing, dictating, and writing to narrate a single event or several loosely linked events and provide a reaction to what happened	W3 pp. 112–117
W.4	NA	
W.5	Respond to questions and add details to strengthen writing as needed	W5 pp. 118–123

(Continued)

Alaska Strand/Standard	Focus of Alaska Standard	For More Information
Writing		
W.6	Explore a variety of digital tools to produce and publish writing	W6 pp. 124–129
W.7	Participate in shared research and writing projects	W7 pp. 130–135
W.8	Recall information from experiences or gather information from provided sources to answer a question	W8 pp. 136–141
W.9	NA	
W.10	NA	
Speaking and Listening		
SL.1	Participate in collaborative conversations with diverse partners about topics and texts in small and larger groups	SL1 pp. 146–151
SL.2	Ask and answer questions about key details to confirm understanding of a topic	SL2 pp. 152–157
SL.3	Ask and answer questions in order to seek help, get information, or clarify something that is not understood	SL3 pp. 158–163
SL.4	Describe familiar people, places, things, and events	SL4 pp. 164–169
SL.5	Add drawings or other visual displays to descriptions to provide additional detail	SL5 pp. 170–175
SL.6	Speak audibly and express thoughts, ideas, feelings, and ideas clearly in complete sentences when appropriate to task and situation	SL6 pp. 176–181
Language		
L.1	Demonstrate command of the conventions of standard English grammar and usage when writing or speaking	L1 pp. 186–191
L.2	Demonstrate command of the conventions of standard English capitalization, punctuation, and spelling when writing	L2 pp. 192–197
L.3	NA	
L.4	Determine or clarify the meaning of unknown and multiple-meaning words and phrases	L4 pp. 204–209
L.5	Explore word relationships and nuances in word meanings	L5 pp. 210–215
L.6	Use words and phrases acquired through conversations, reading, being read to, and responding to texts	L6 pp. 216–221

Alaska, Grade 1

Alaska Strand/Standard	Focus of Alaska Standard	For More Information
Reading Literature		
RL.1	Ask and answer questions about a text using key details from the text	R1 pp. 6–11
RL.2	Retell stories, including key details, and demonstrate understanding of their message	R2 pp. 12–17
RL.3	Describe characters, settings, and major events in a story, play, or poem	R3 pp. 18–23
RL.4	Identify words or phrases that suggest feelings or appeal to the senses	R4 pp. 24–29
RL.5	Explain major differences between stories and informative texts	R5 pp. 30–35
RL.6	Identify who is telling the story at various points in a text	R6 pp. 36–41
RL.7	Use illustrations and details to describe elements of a story	R7 pp. 42–47
RL.8	NA	
RL.9	Compare and contrast the experiences of characters in stories	R9 pp. 54–59
RL.10	Read texts of appropriate complexity	R10 pp. 60–65
Reading Informational Text		
RI.1	Ask and answer questions about a text using key details from the text	R1 pp. 6–11
RI.2	Identify the main topic or author's purpose and retell key details of a text	R2 pp. 12–17

Shaded bands highlight the overarching strands.

Each standard under the strand is specifically called out.

Each section begins with a restatement of the official anchor standards as they appear in the actual Common Core State Standards document.

College and Career Readiness Anchor Standards for

Reading K–12

The K–2 reading standards outlined on the following pages define what students should understand and be able to do by the end of each grade. Here on this page we present the College and Career Readiness (CCR) anchor standards for K–12 so you can see how students in K–2 work toward the same goals as high school seniors: it's a universal, K–12 vision. The CCR anchor standards and the grade-specific standards correspond to one another by number (1–10). They are necessary complements: the former providing broad standards, the latter providing additional specificity. Together, they define the skills and understandings that all students must eventually demonstrate.

Key Ideas and Details

1. Read closely to determine what the text says explicitly and to make logical inferences from it; cite specific textual evidence when writing or speaking to support conclusions drawn from the text.
2. Determine central ideas or themes of a text and analyze their development; summarize the key supporting details and ideas.
3. Analyze how and why individuals, events, and ideas develop and interact over the course of a text.

Craft and Structure

4. Interpret words and phrases as they are used in a text, including determining technical, connotative, and figurative meanings, and analyze how specific word choices shape meaning or tone.
5. Analyze the structure of texts, including how specific sentences, paragraphs, and larger portions of the text (e.g., a section, chapter, scene, or stanza) relate to each other and the whole.
6. Assess how point of view or purpose shapes the content and style of a text.

Integration of Knowledge and Ideas

7. Integrate and evaluate content presented in diverse media and formats, including visually and quantitatively, as well as in words.*
8. Delineate and evaluate the argument and specific claims in a text, including the validity of the reasoning as well as the relevance and sufficiency of the evidence.
9. Analyze how two or more texts address similar themes or topics in order to build knowledge or to compare the approaches the authors take.

Range of Reading and Level of Text Complexity

10. Read and comprehend complex literary and informational texts independently and proficiently.

*Please consult the full Common Core State Standards document (and all updates and appendices) at http://www.corestandards.org/ELA-Literacy. See "Research to Build Knowledge" in the Writing section and "Comprehension and Collaboration" in the Speaking and Listening section for additional standards relevant to gathering, assessing, and applying information from print and digital sources.

College and Career Readiness Anchor Standards for

Reading

The CCR anchor standards are the same for K–12. The guiding principle here is that the core reading skills should not change as students advance; rather, the level at which students learn and can perform these skills should increase in complexity as they move from one grade to the next. However, for grades K–2, we have to recognize that the standards were back mapped from the secondary level—that is, the authors envisioned what college students need and then wrote standards, working their way down the grades. Thus, as you use this book, remember that children in K–2 can't just "jump over" developmental milestones in an ambitious attempt to achieve an anchor standard. There are certain life and learning experiences they need to have, and certain concepts they need to learn, before they are capable of handling many complex academic skills in a meaningful way. The anchor standards nonetheless are goalposts to work toward. As you read the "gist" of the standards below, remember they represent what our K–2 students will *grow into* during each year and deepen later in elementary, middle, and high school. The journey starts in K–2!

Key Ideas and Details

This first strand of reading standards emphasizes students' ability to identify key ideas and themes in a text, whether literary, informational, primary, or foundational and whether in print, graphic, quantitative, or mixed media formats. The focus of this first set of standards is on reading to understand, during which students focus on what the text says. The premise is that students cannot delve into the deeper meaning of any text if they cannot first grasp the surface meaning of that text. Beyond merely identifying these ideas, readers must learn to see how these ideas and themes, or the story's characters and events, develop and evolve over the course of a text. Such reading demands that students know how to identify, evaluate, assess, and analyze the elements of a text for their importance, function, and meaning within the text.

Craft and Structure

The second set of standards builds on the first, focusing not on what the text says but on how it says it, the emphasis here being on analyzing how texts are made to serve a function or achieve a purpose. These standards ask readers to examine the choices the author makes in words and sentence and paragraph structure and how these choices contribute to the meaning of the text and the author's larger purpose. Inherent in the study of craft and structure is how these elements interact with and influence the ideas and details outlined in the first three standards.

Integration of Knowledge and Ideas

This third strand might be summed up as reading to extend or deepen one's knowledge of a subject by comparing what a range of sources have said about it over time and across different media. In addition, these standards emphasize the importance of being able to read the arguments; that is, they look at how to identify the claims the texts make and evaluate the evidence used to support those claims regardless of the media. Finally, these standards ask students to analyze the author's choices of means and medium and the effects those choices have on ideas and details. Thus, if a writer integrates words, images, and video in a mixed media text, readers should be able to examine how and why the author did that for stylistic and rhetorical purposes.

Range of Reading and Level of Text Complexity

The Common Core State Standards document itself offers the most useful explanation of what this last standard means in a footnote titled "Note on range and content of student reading," which accompanies the reading standards:

To become college and career ready, students must grapple with works of exceptional craft and thought whose range extends across genres, cultures, and centuries. Such works offer profound insights into the human condition and serve as models for students' own thinking and writing. Along with high-quality contemporary works, these texts should be chosen from among seminal U.S. documents, the classics of American literature, and the timeless dramas of Shakespeare. Through wide and deep reading of literature and literary nonfiction of steadily increasing sophistication, students gain a reservoir of literary and cultural knowledge, references, and images; the ability to evaluate intricate arguments; and the capacity to surmount the challenges posed by complex texts. (CCSS 2010, p. 35)

On the facing page, a user-friendly "translation" of each standard gives you a fuller sense of the big picture and big objectives as you consider how it relates to your state's standards.

On this page you'll find accessible translations of the standards at your left so you can better grasp what they mean.

The emphasis now is on what students should do, utilizing the same grade-level structure at your left.

Comprehension questions are included for helping students master thinking moves and skills behind each standard; all can be adapted to a range of class texts and topics or to needs specific to your particular state standards.

Built-in tabs facilitate navigation.

The actual CCSS anchor standard is included for easy reference.

The specific strand situates you within the larger context of the standards.

Grades K–2 Common Core Reading Standard 1 — *Key Ideas and Details*

Standard 1: Read closely to determine what the text says explicitly and to make logical inferences from it; cite specific textual evidence when writing or speaking to support conclusions drawn from the text.

Literature

K With prompting and support, students ask and answer questions about key details in a text.

1 Students ask and answer questions about key details in a text.

2 Students ask and answer such questions as who, what, where, when, why, and how to demonstrate understanding of key details in a text.

Informational Text

K With prompting and support, students ask and answer questions about key details in a text.

1 Students ask and answer questions about key details in a text.

2 Students ask and answer such questions as who, what, where, when, why, and how to demonstrate understanding of key details in a text.

Grades K–2 Common Core Reading Standard 1

What the **Student** Does

Literature

K **Gist:** Students ask and answer questions about key details in a text.

They consider:

- What happens or is said in this text?
- Which words, pictures, and sentences help me know this?

1 **Gist:** Students ask and answer questions about key details in a text.

They consider:

- What happens or is said in this text?
- Which words, pictures, and sentences help me know this?

2 **Gist:** Students ask and answer such questions as who, what, where, when, why, and how to determine the key details in a text.

They consider:

- What happens or is said in this text?
- Which words, pictures, and sentences help me know this?

Informational Text

K **Gist:** Students ask and answer questions about key details in a text.

They consider:

- What happens or is said in this text?
- Which words, illustrations, and sentences help me know this?

1 **Gist:** Students ask and answer questions about key details in a text.

They consider:

- What happens or is said in this text?
- Which words, illustrations, and sentences help me know this?

2 **Gist:** Students ask and answer such questions as who, what, where, when, why, and how to determine the key details in a text.

They consider:

- What happens or is said in this text?
- Which details (words, illustrations, and sentences) support the key ideas?

Note: Although the questions listed above are too difficult for most young students to internalize and apply on their own, we share them to give teachers a detailed sense of what their students should be striving toward as learners. K–2 students may not be able to ask these questions of themselves independently, but teachers can use them as a jumping-off point for lesson content and as prompts and reminders to share with students. Over time, and with instruction, students will be able to pose these questions on their own.

Horizontal and vertical views enable you to consider how the standards change across grade levels.

Standards for each discipline are featured on a single page for easy planning.

The right-hand page utilizes the very same grade-level format to provide two distinct visual paths for understanding the standards.

"Gist" sections provide plain-English synopses of the standards so you can put them to immediate use.

Featured on this spread are specific teaching techniques for realizing each standard. Applicable to all subjects across grades K–2, these strategies focus on what works in the classroom.

What the **Teacher** Does

To teach students how to read closely:

- Before introducing a text, identify the main idea or message for yourself. Go through the book and notice the details that support it and flag them with sticky notes. Then, plan out prompts and questions that you will pose to students. We liken this process to Hansel dropping those pebbles leading homeward; by planning questions ahead of time, you can more easily guide students to spot the main idea. Conversely, when teachers don't plan, lessons can go awry. For example, if the main idea of a passage is that cities create heat (cars, buildings, people) and thereby change the weather, and you don't recognize that this is what students should be reading for, then it becomes difficult to pose a proper "trail" of questions leading students toward the text's significant details.

- During a lesson or while conferring, be sure to give students sufficient time to consider the questions and prompts you pose. Figuring out the author's main idea or message is often hard, subtle work. Don't hesitate to rephrase prompts if students seem stuck. Remind them that they can look for answers in the text, reread, study illustrations, and so forth. Providing time for students to respond can make all the difference in the world.

- Use a text or passage that is brief enough to be read more than once, so that students can begin with an overall understanding before homing in on specifics. As you read, pause occasionally to pose questions about words, actions, and details that require students to look closely at the text or illustrations for answers. (Note: When your goal is to demonstrate where in the text you found something to support your reasoning, make sure that the text is large enough for students to see and interact with. Charts, enlarged texts, and whiteboards help.)

- Model close reading by thinking aloud as you scrutinize a text's words, sentence structures, and other details to understand its meaning. To focus students' attention, write on sticky notes and place them on the text, use chart paper, annotate in the margins, and/or highlight via a tablet or whiteboard.

To help students to determine what the text says explicitly:

- Model how to determine an author's message by saying what happened (literature) and naming the important facts (informational). As you do, point to words, sentences, illustrations, and text features as evidence and record on chart paper or graphic organizers (see online resources at resources.corwin.com/literacycompanionk-2).

- Over weeks of working with different texts, continue to guide students to determine deeper meanings on their own. Use sentence stems and other graphic organizers to support students' explanations of what happened and their recall of important facts; use think-alouds so students hear how you arrive at what texts mean, and point to specific places in the text to support your conclusions.

To help students make logical inferences from a text:

- Select texts to read aloud or share with students that allow them to make logical inferences. Ask questions that lead them to infer (I wonder why he did that? I wonder what she thought? I wonder why the boy in the illustration looks sad?). As students answer these questions, ask them to explain how they arrived at their conclusions using specific words and phrases in the text.

- Routinely ask students to show you the textual evidence that supports their inferences.

To support students in asking and answering questions about key details in a text:

- Model asking questions about a text by writing questions on chart paper or annotating in the margins when using a whiteboard. Try to ask more analytical (how, why) questions than literal (who, what, where, when) questions.

- Elaborate on what led you to ask a question. When reading a book about beavers, you might say, "Whenever I see a picture of a beaver, they're chewing on a tree branch. I wonder why they do this?" This will help students recognize that a question is typically an extension of something we already know.

- Demonstrate how the answers to many of their questions can be found in the text. If the text is on a chart or in a big book, mark the answers to questions with sticky notes or highlighting tape, calling attention to the *exact words* that help answer a question.

To help your English language learners, try this:

- Work with small groups to help students feel more comfortable sharing ideas. Make sure that each student has a copy of the text or that the text is large enough for them all to see comfortably. Allow students time to read a text or a portion of one several times to make sure they have

a basic understanding before focusing on key ideas or making inferences.

- Model asking questions using a short text or poster-size photograph. Elaborate on what leads you to ask questions and point to words and illustrations that provide answers.

Developmental Debrief:

Students, especially those coming to school with low language skills or those who lack the necessary preschool experiences to be academically successful, need to be read to several times throughout the day. This will help them acquire the academic vocabulary and syntax they need to understand complex texts.

In order for students to feel comfortable, it is essential for the teacher to create a risk-free environment where students are encouraged to offer their ideas and opinions openly, without fear that their responses will be judged "right or wrong," "good or bad."

Notes

A dedicated academic vocabulary section offers a quick-reference glossary of key words and phrases for each standard.

A planning template provides prompts to help you develop lesson plans that address and connect standards.

Academic Vocabulary: Key Words and Phrases

Cite specific textual evidence: Readers need to reference the text to support their ideas, rather than simply stating opinions or referring to personal experiences; students should be able to reference illustrations or read words or sentences from the text that prove the points they are trying to make.

Conclusions drawn from the text: Readers take a group of details (different findings, series of events, related examples) and infer from them an insight or understanding about their meaning or importance within the passage or the text as a whole. These insights or conclusions are based on evidence found in the text.

Explicitly: This refers to anything that is clearly and directly stated in precise detail; it may suggest factual information or literal meaning, although this is not necessarily the case.

Informational texts: These include nonfiction texts written for a variety of purposes and audiences, such as expository texts, informational narratives (biography, history, journals and diaries, persuasive texts and essays). Informational texts include written arguments as well as visual images such as charts and diagrams.

Key details: These are parts of a text that support the main idea and enable the reader to draw conclusions/ infer what the text or a portion of a text is about.

Literature: This refers to fiction, poetry, drama, and graphic stories as well as artworks by master painters or distinguished photographers.

Logical inferences (drawn from the text): To infer, readers add what they *learned* from the text to what they already *know* about the subject; however, for an inference to be "logical," it must be based on evidence *from the text*.

Prompting and support: Here the teacher takes the lead role in helping students initiate a particular skill or strategy. She is likely to think aloud and model precisely what she wants students to be able to do on their own later, and to nurture their attempts.

Read closely (close reading): This refers to reading that emphasizes not only surface details but the deeper meaning and larger connections between words, sentences, and the full text; it also requires the reader to attend to the author's craft, including organization, word choice, and style.

Text: In its broadest meaning, a text is whatever one is trying to read: a poem, essay, or article; in its more modern sense, a text can also be an image, an artwork, a speech, or a multimedia format such as a website or film.

Textual evidence: Not all evidence is created equal; students need to choose those pieces of evidence (illustrations, words, or sentences) that provide the best examples of what they are saying or the most compelling references to support their assertions.

Notes

Clearly worded entries decode each word or phrase according to the particular way it is used in a given standard.

Planning Page

Standard: _____

Purpose of Lesson/s:	

Planning the Lesson/s	Questions to Ask

Differentiating Instruction	Thinking Beyond This Standard

The standards guide instruction; they do not dictate it. So as you plan lessons remember you aren't teaching the standards, but instead are teaching students how to read, write, talk, and think through well-crafted lessons that draw from the pedagogy embedded within them. Engaging lessons often have several ELA standards within them and integrate reading, writing, speaking and listening, and language.

Example of a Filled-in Worksheet: First Grade

List the specifics about how you envision the lesson unfolding.

This is a place to write notes about the purpose of your lesson and what you really want your students to take away.

Here, jot down the questions you plan to ask your students to help guide them through your lesson.

Planning Page

Standard: Foundational Skills Standard 4

Purpose of Lesson/s: Working with a small group of readers to give them additional practice reading at a rate and with expression that matches what the text is about. Important to connect how a text is read and what it means.

Planning the Lesson/s	Questions to Ask
Small Group Lesson: (4 students) • The Boy Who Cried Wolf by B.G. Hennessy (picture book); 2 copies of You Read to Me, I'll Read to You: Very Short Fables to Read Together by Mary Ann Hoberman • Read aloud the picture book, stopping at key pages to talk about how the different characters were feeling, e.g., page where the boy wants a bit of excitement; attend to punctuation (question and exclamation marks) • Introduce "two-voices" version of fable; explain that it's the same story only in play format much shorter, and in two voices—townspeople and the boy • Put kids in partners: one to read the orange print (boy) and the other to read the green (townspeople)	Questions to ask that help kids match how they're reading a text with what it's about: • What is this fable about? And what's the moral? • How does it feel when you know someone has played a trick on you? How did the townspeople feel? (Evidence) How might their voices sound when they speak to the boy—when they think there really is a wolf? When they know there isn't one? • How do you think the boy would feel and sound when he knows that no one is coming to help?

Differentiating Instruction	Thinking Beyond This Standard
Independent work: • Let partners practice reading the choral reading version during independent reading • Allow other students who want to try out the two-voice version a chance to do so Whole class: • Partners present to whole class during the reading share and talk about how they're making their voice match what the story is about • Introduce fractured version of The Wolf Who Cried Boy. Demonstrate expressive reading, point to words in bold, exclamation marks, enlarged text etc. This time also attend to speech tags, e.g., whispered, whimpered, signed, moaned	• Point of view, townspeople and the boy (Reading Standard 6) • Additional work attending to punctuation (Language Standard 1) • Attend to tier two vocabulary, e.g. whimpered, peered, shrugged—implicitly and explicitly (Language Standard 4) • Some kids may want to try writing a dramatic version of The Wolf Who Cried Boy in two voices—the Wolf's and Father Wolf • Use punctuation and speech tags in writing to show expression and give meaning (Language Standard 1)

The standards guide instruction, not dictate it. So as you plan lessons remember you aren't teaching the standards, but instead are teaching students how to read, write, talk, and think through well-crafted lessons that draw from the pedagogy embedded within them. Engaging lessons often have several ELA standards within them, and integrate reading, writing, speaking and listening, and language.

Think through how you'll use the lesson to engage all of your learners.

List skills, texts, and ideas for foregrounding or reinforcing other ELA standards.

Planning Page

Standard: Reading Standard 2

Purpose of Lesson/s: Over the course of two or three days, read aloud (and reread) <u>Children Make Terrible Pets</u> to the <u>whole class</u>, and get kids thinking about whether or not it was okay for Lucy to keep Squeaker (the boy) as a pet. Eventually help kids extend and apply the author's message to their own lives by posing a question about whether or not it's okay to keep wild animals in cages and in marine park water tanks.

Planning the Lesson/s	Questions to Ask
Whole class read-aloud: • <u>Children Make Terrible Pets</u> by Peter Brown (Author's message—it's not OK to think that we can <u>own</u> another living thing; to keep wild animals as pets.) • Meeting area where kids can gather and discuss the read-aloud • Easel chart paper, markers to record ideas/questions, etc. • Story map graphic organizer to help students plot out the story events and think through the main idea	Questions to ask that help students get to the author's message: • What is the author trying to teach us? What lesson can we take away to apply to our own lives? • Was it okay for Lucy to own Squeaker (the boy), to keep him as a pet? Why? • How did Lucy feel, what might she be thinking, when she saw Squeaker with his family? What in the text or pictures made you say this? • The whole family, all but the dog, who says "Woof," were making "squeaking" sounds while picnicking in the woods. What is the author trying to tell us?
Differentiating Instruction	**Thinking Beyond This Standard**
Small groups: Break students into groups of three or four to continue discussing what Lucy may have been feeling/thinking when she found Squeaker with his family? Make sure students reference the text. Or have them discuss when Lucy found Squeaker with his family and said, "Something had changed. Squeaker didn't seem like a pet anymore. Lucy knew what she had to do." Independent work: Have students write about the message they can take away from this book to apply to their own lives.	• Can work with point of view, Lucy's and Squeaker's (Reading Standard 6) • Initiate some <u>informational text reading</u> about dolphins (Reading Standard 10) • Kids can <u>write about dolphins</u> independently, or I might introduce an expository writing unit on dolphins (Writing Standards 2 and 4—Informational Text) • Fabulous opportunity to expose kids to <u>dialogue</u>; characters speak in color-coded talking bubbles; a way to help them see how words like "said" and "says"; and quotation marks are used for same purpose (not in standards document but an opportunity not to be missed) • Attend to tier two <u>vocabulary</u>, e.g., scurry, inseparable, implicitly and explicitly (Language Standard 4)

The standards guide instruction, not dictate it. So as you plan lessons remember you aren't teaching the standards, but instead are teaching students how to read, write, talk, and think through well-crafted lessons that draw from the pedagogy embedded within them. Engaging lessons often have several ELA standards within them, and integrate reading, writing, speaking and listening, and language.

Your Literacy Standards Companion, Grades K–2

What They Mean and How to Teach Them

Sharon Taberski

with Jim Burke

resources.corwin.com/literacycompanionk-2

Name: _____

Department: _____

Learning Team: _____

FOR INFORMATION:

Corwin

A SAGE Company

2455 Teller Road

Thousand Oaks, California 91320

(800) 233-9936

www.corwin.com

SAGE Publications Ltd.

1 Oliver's Yard

55 City Road

London EC1Y 1SP

United Kingdom

SAGE Publications India Pvt. Ltd.

B 1/I 1 Mohan Cooperative Industrial Area

Mathura Road, New Delhi 110 044

India

SAGE Publications Asia-Pacific Pte. Ltd.

3 Church Street

#10-04 Samsung Hub

Singapore 049483

Publisher and Senior Program Director: Lisa Luedeke

Senior Acquisitions Editor: Wendy Murray

Editorial Development Manager: Julie Nemer

Editorial Assistant: Nicole Shade

Production Editors: Olivia Weber-Stenis and Melanie Birdsall

Copy Editors: Judy Selhorst and Deanna Noga

Typesetter: C&M Digitals (P) Ltd.

Proofreaders: Scott Oney and Wendy Jo Dymond

Cover Designer: Scott Van Atta

Interior Designer: Auburn Associates, Inc.

Marketing Manager: Rebecca Eaton

Copyright © 2017 by Corwin

National Governors Association Center for Best Practices, Council of Chief State School Officers, Common Core State Standards, English Language Arts Standards. Publisher: National Governors Association Center for Best Practices, Council of Chief State School Officers, Washington, DC. Copyright 2010. For more information, visit http:// www.corestandards.org/ELA-Literacy.

Printed in the United States of America

ISBN 978-1-5063-8682-9

This book is printed on acid-free paper.

21 10 9 8 7 6 5

Contents

Visit the companion website at
resources.corwin.com/literacycompanionk-2
for downloadable versions of the
Indexes Cross-Referencing Your State Standards
and additional resources.

Preface

The standards offer us all a tremendous opportunity to help our students learn what they need to know for success in school and life, but using them requires a lot of something we as teachers have very little of: *time*. Standards demand that we find more time for students to learn in school—more time to think, practice, collaborate, and reflect. And we have to find more time as teachers to plan and teach, to learn the related language and instructional moves implicit in the standards.

With an all too keen sense of my own limited time, I began to create a version of the Common Core State Standards that better met my needs, one I could keep by my side and reference quickly when planning, writing, or participating in meetings related to the Common Core standards. When teachers saw it, they wanted their own copies, and the result was *The Common Core Companion*—one for grades 6–8 and another for 9–12, which were both published in 2013.

What's the big idea behind *Your Literacy Standards Companion*? It's inefficient for us all across the nation to spend time deciphering what our specific state standards say and digesting what they mean for teaching and learning, so I wrote the *Companion* to do that for you. With this book at your side, you can reclaim hours of time to do the most important work: develop your instructional ideas (and the standards themselves) into rich, engaging learning experiences for our students that meet the standards' higher expectations.

Because I often work with literacy coordinators who are responsible for all students in their district, I wanted these *Companion* books to be K–12, districtwide, and school-wide tools. That way teachers and administrators could hit the ground running as they implemented the standards and envisioned professional development that would support all teachers. But I had one problem: I was not an elementary school teacher. For teachers in grades 3–5, I thought of Leslie Blauman, an exemplary teacher and guide to teachers around the country.

When it came to someone in grades K–2, I did not have to think long about whom to ask, for in those grades, all roads lead to Sharon Taberski, whose books *Comprehension From the Ground Up* and *On Solid Ground* did for K–3 instruction what Julia Child did for French cooking. She's that good. And she is also a wise, patient, and generous friend and mentor to any who know her.

More important than her landmark books is the fact that Sharon taught in her own classroom for 28 years and still works in classrooms, now in her role as a coach for teachers. She brings to this K–2 volume what I hoped she would: the ability to carefully balance the high demands of the standards with the developmental needs of young children.

So without further ado, and with deepest gratitude for all she has taught me through the process of writing this book, I introduce you to *Your Literacy Standards Companion*,

Grades K–2. If you're looking for someone to help you understand and, more important, *use* the state standards in your classroom, you have come to the right place, for with Sharon Taberski, you are in good hands. Trust her to help you create exemplary standards-aligned K–2 literacy instruction that will allow you to be the teacher you have been and are capable of becoming.

Jim Burke

Introduction

Turning Standards Into Daily Teaching

*Every time we experience a problem, we have the opportunity to gather
new resources, think about it, frame it, and take action.*

—Renate N. Caine and Geoffrey Caine,
Natural Learning for a Connected World

An excellent education should not be an accident; it should be a right, though nowhere in the United States Constitution or any of our other founding documents do we find that right listed. The Common Core State Standards address that omission and challenge us all—administrators and teachers, parents and children, politicians and the public at large, professors and student teachers—to commit ourselves anew to the success of our children and our country.

This is how Jim Burke opened grades 6–8 and 9–12 of *The Common Core Companion*, the four-volume ELA series he conceived of for Corwin Literacy in 2013. In the 3 years since, these books and the volumes for K–2 and grades 3–5 have been so-called "evergreen" bestsellers, because they help educators everywhere get the important work done of transforming standards into daily learning outcomes. A series for Common Core Mathematics Companion also thrives. Here's the interesting thing: Corwin sales data showed robust book sales even in states that never adopted the Common Core State Standards (CCSS)—educators were purchasing the books to help them refresh or reimagine their own state standards. When Leslie Blauman, the author of the grades 3–5 version, and I heard of these sales, it made great sense: educators are brilliant at adapting resources to suit their needs. Yet maybe more important, it underscored for us that while the politics and assessments tied to the CCSS are fraught—and Leslie and I knew from the get-go of the CCSS adoption that they would be—the standards themselves are timeless and true to what we want our students to be able to do.

It also didn't surprise Leslie, Jim, and me when Corwin Literacy saw this market need and decided to issue this new version, *Your Literacy Standards Companion*, with indexes for each state that opted out of the CCSS, to make it easier for users to go right to the pages most aligned to their state's standards. The following states have indexes in this book:

Alaska	Kansas	Oklahoma
Arizona	Louisiana	Pennsylvania
Arkansas	Maryland	South Carolina
Colorado	Minnesota	Tennessee
Florida	Mississippi	Utah
Georgia	Missouri	Virginia
Indiana	Nebraska	West Virginia
Iowa	New Jersey	

As I write this revised introduction and reflect on how any standards are best put into practice, my advice to you on how to use this resource is twofold: first, overall I would use the "What to Teach" pages as springboards to planning curriculum and deciding upon instructional methods you want each grade level teacher to use. The authors of the CCSS shared the "what," but it's up to us to understand the "why" and provide the "how." Second, I would recommend that you view the standards and this companion from the vantage point of your students' needs and readiness and make adjustments accordingly. For example, there may be times when you should refer to the standards for an earlier grade because your students are more aligned with those skills and behaviors. At other times, you'll feel the need to advance instruction and look at the grade level ahead of the grade you teach. Both decisions are yours to make. The CCSS are guidelines and a wonderful resource for teachers whether or not your state has formally adopted them. It's we educators, assigned with the responsibility of making the day-to-day decisions regarding what to teach, who get to plan the teaching and learning experiences that bring any standard to life.

What the Standards Expect of Us

I cannot emphasize enough that the principles of the Common Core document leave it up to us, the practitioners, to design the teaching and learning that will get students *to* the goals, and so we need to rise to this challenge and not let others define teaching and learning for us. As the document states,

> by emphasizing required achievements, the Standards leave room for teachers, curriculum developers, and states to determine how those goals should be reached and what additional topics should be addressed. Thus, the Standards do not mandate such things as a particular writing process or the full range of metacognitive strategies that students may need to monitor and direct their thinking and learning. Teachers are thus free to provide students with whatever tools and knowledge their professional judgment and experience identify as most helpful for meeting the goals set out in the Standards. (CCSS, 2010, p. 4)

The standards also uphold and advance the strong research base for how learners learn and progress. Students become better readers when they *read*. They become better writers when they *write*. Digging into the CCSS, you find that Reading Standard 10 requires that students read. Writing Standard 10 stipulates that students write for a variety of purposes over an extended time. One of the aspects of the standards I admire most is that they ask us to value authentic texts, purposeful writing, and real conversations around big ideas. Fiction and informational texts written by accomplished writers take center stage.

Five Principles Behind the Teaching Ideas in This Book

Jim Burke, ever wise, cautioned me that the function of *Your Literacy Standards Companion* is to assist educators in the task of accurately knowing the intention of each standard and developing teaching ideas that will enable students to meet each one. Period. Therefore, I have tried to refrain from interpreting the standards, adapting them, or embedding them in too detailed a set of beliefs and practices, because the standards need to succeed in many different kinds of classroom settings, from ones that use basals and other commercial programs to Montessori settings and everything in between. But, that said, I feel compelled to provide the briefest of contexts for the teaching ideas I share, so you will know where I am coming from. The following recommendations are those that I think stand the best chance of developing K–2 students into strategic, engaged learners.

1. **Embrace the reading workshop and writing workshop and its many opportunities to balance and differentiate instruction.** Let's face it, when we teach the whole class we're teaching to the middle and leaving out the students at the top and bottom thirds of the class. The workshop model allows us to give all students what they need.

2. **Let students do more of the heavy lifting. The brain that does the work is the brain that learns.** I don't know who first said, "The brain that does the work is the brain that learns," but it's been a mantra of mine for a few years now. We tend to do too much of the work for our students. We're often inclined to ask leading rather than generative questions, and we frequently provide too little time for students to respond and work things out on their own.

3. **Identify one or two practices that can make all the difference in the world and get really good at them.** Rather than trying to get good at everything, focus on one or two instructional practices that are likely to bring about the greatest progress for students—practices that push students to "own" their learning.

4. **Recognize that your goal is twofold: to help students read, write, think, and converse—and to teach them *how* to learn.** In addition to reading for meaning, writing for real purposes, talking to and learning from one another with ears and eyes wide open, students need to learn *how* to learn.

5. **Hold fast to what you know to be true about teaching and learning, and then follow the trail—instruction that matches your belief.** There, I said it again: lean heavily on the standards and the teachings throughout this book, but at the end of the day, it's *you* and *your* students and what helps them meet the expectations of the standards that matter most. To this end, I include a note at the bottom of each planning page that deserves attention here: "The standards guide instruction; they do not dictate it. So as you plan lessons, remember: you aren't teaching the standards, but instead are teaching students how to read, write, talk, and think through well-crafted lessons that draw from the pedagogy embedded within them. Engaging lessons often have several ELA standards within them and integrate reading, writing, speaking and listening, and language."

A Brief Orientation to *Your Literacy Standards Companion, Grades K–2*

When I was asked to write this book, I was relieved to see I could follow Jim Burke's smart format and design. He envisioned this series as something highly useful to teachers and organized each volume around the following features:

A one-page overview of *all* the anchor standards. Designed for quick reference or self-assessment, this one-page document offers a one-stop place to see all the English Language Arts Common Core Standards. In addition to using this to quickly check the Common Core anchor standards, grade-level teachers or the whole faculty might use the overview to evaluate which standards they know and are addressing effectively and which ones they need to learn and teach.

Side-by-side anchor standards translation. The Common Core State Standards College and Career Readiness anchor standards for each category—reading, foundational skills, writing, speaking and listening, and language—appear in a two-page spread with the original Common Core anchor standards on the left and, on the right, their matching translations in language that is more accessible to those on the run or new to literacy instruction.

A new user-friendly format for each standard. Instead of the two reading standard domains—literature and informational text—spread throughout as they are in the Common Core State Standards document, here you will find the first reading standard for grades K–2 and the two different domains all on one page. This allows you to use *Your Literacy Standards Companion* to see at a glance what Reading Standard 1 looks like in grades K–2 across literature and informational texts. The design makes it easy to see how the standard plays out across grade levels, so you can plan with other teachers just how to increase complexity as students move from grade to grade.

Parallel translation/what students do. Each standard opens to a two-page spread that has the original Common Core standards on the left and a parallel translation of each standard mirrored on the right-hand page in more accessible language (referred to as the "Gist") so you can concentrate on how to *teach* in ways that meet the standards instead of how to understand them. These Gist pages align themselves with the original Common Core, so you can move between the two without turning a page as you think about what the standards mean and how to teach to meet them. Also, beneath each translation of a standard appears a list of *what students consider*. These are brief practical questions that will help students "crack open" the thinking and comprehension skills being asked of them. Ultimately, students pose these questions for themselves—both unconsciously and deliberately—as they engage in the endeavor. But because metacognition is something students grow into, you can use these questions as comprehension questions to pose after you model how to approach them. The goal is to provide ample practice with these questions so that students *internalize* them and own them as readers, writers, and thinkers. So be sure to incorporate them into the fabric of your instruction each and every day, having students talk, listen, and write off them.

Instructional techniques/what the teacher does. In the "What the Teacher Does" pages you will find a great many suggestions. Although I don't always say, "Put your students in groups" or "Put your students in pairs," I can't emphasize enough that the goal is for you to do less whole-class instruction and have students work more often in small groups, in partnerships, or one-on-one with you. Periodically you will see references to online resources, which include graphic organizers, visuals, and other tools that support the teaching of particular standards.

Planning templates. For each standard, a one-page planning template provides prompts to help you develop lesson plans that address and connect standards. As you use these pages, they will become resources for future lessons and records of instruction. They will also be beneficial for collaboration with colleagues.

Academic vocabulary: key words and phrases. Each standard comes with a unique glossary, since terms used in multiple standards have unique meanings from standard to standard. Any word or phrase that could be a source of confusion is defined in detail.

How to Use This Book

Different schools, districts, instructional teams, and individual teachers will pick up *Your Literacy Standards Companion* and have different ideas about how to use it as a tool. And, of course, there is no one right way. Here are some possible ways, which you might adapt, adopt, or ignore as you see fit:

- Provide all teachers on a grade-level team or school with a copy of this K–2 edition to establish a common text to work from throughout standards planning and instructional design work.
- Use this *Companion* in tandem with the grades 3–5 edition by Leslie Blauman to dig into the standards in a whole-school initiative.
- Use this *Companion* along with the grades 3–5, 6–8, and 9–12 volumes for district-level planning and professional development work.
- Bring your *Companion* to all meetings for quick reference or planning with colleagues in your school or on your grade-level team.

- Use the *Companion* to aid in the transition from what you were doing to what you will be doing, treating the planning pages that accompany the standards as places to note what you do or which Common Core State Standard corresponds with one of your district or state standards.
- Use the *Companion* as a resource for revisiting your curriculum plans in Year 2 (or beyond!) of implementing the standards to help you develop, refine, and deepen instruction.
- Begin or end meetings with a brief but carefully planned sample lesson based on a teaching idea in this book. Ask one or more colleagues in the school to present at the next meeting on how the teaching idea might be applied to other grade levels.
- Use the *Companion* in conjunction with your professional learning community to add further cohesion and consistency among all your ideas and plans.

Reference

Caine, R. N., & Caine, G. (2011). *Natural learning for a connected world: Education, technology, and the human brain*. New York, NY: Teachers College Press.

Reading

Key Ideas and Details

1. Read closely to determine what the text says explicitly and to make logical inferences from it; cite specific textual evidence when writing or speaking to support conclusions drawn from the text.

2. Determine central ideas or themes of a text and analyze their development; summarize the key supporting details and ideas.

3. Analyze how and why individuals, events, and ideas develop and interact over the course of a text.

Craft and Structure

4. Interpret words and phrases as they are used in a text, including determining technical, connotative, and figurative meanings, and analyze how specific word choices shape meaning or tone.

5. Analyze the structure of texts, including how specific sentences, paragraphs, and larger portions of the text (e.g., a section, chapter, scene, or stanza) relate to each other and the whole.

6. Assess how point of view or purpose shapes the content and style of a text.

Integration of Knowledge and Ideas

7. Integrate and evaluate content presented in diverse media and formats, including visually and quantitatively, as well as in words.

8. Delineate and evaluate the argument and specific claims in a text, including the validity of the reasoning as well as the relevance and sufficiency of the evidence.

9. Analyze how two or more texts address similar themes or topics in order to build knowledge or to compare the approaches the authors take.

Range of Reading and Level of Text Complexity

10. Read and comprehend complex literary and informational texts independently and proficiently.

Reading: Foundational Skills

Print Concepts

1. Demonstrate understanding of the organization and basic features of print.

Phonological Awareness

2. Demonstrate understanding of spoken words, syllables, and sounds (phonemes).

Phonics and Word Recognition

3. Know and apply grade-level phonics and word analysis skills in decoding words.

Fluency

4. Read with sufficient accuracy and fluency to support comprehension.

Writing

Text Types and Purposes*

1. Write arguments to support claims in an analysis of substantive topics or texts, using valid reasoning and relevant and sufficient evidence.

2. Write informative/explanatory texts to examine and convey complex ideas and information clearly and accurately through the effective selection, organization, and analysis of content.

3. Write narratives to develop real or imagined experiences or events using effective technique, well-chosen details, and well-structured event sequences.

Production and Distribution of Writing

4. Produce clear and coherent writing in which the development, organization, and style are appropriate to task, purpose, and audience.

5. Develop and strengthen writing as needed by planning, revising, editing, rewriting, or trying a new approach.

6. Use technology, including the Internet, to produce and publish writing and to interact and collaborate with others.

Research to Build and Present Knowledge

7. Conduct short as well as more sustained research projects based on focused questions, demonstrating understanding of the subject under investigation.

8. Gather relevant information from multiple print and digital sources, assess the credibility and accuracy of each source, and integrate the information while avoiding plagiarism.

9. Draw evidence from literary or informational texts to support analysis, reflection, and research.

Range of Writing

10. Write routinely over extended time frames (time for research, reflection, and revision) and shorter time frames (a single sitting or a day or two) for a range of tasks, purposes, and audiences.

Speaking and Listening

Comprehension and Collaboration

1. Prepare for and participate effectively in a range of conversations and collaborations with diverse partners, building on others' ideas and expressing their own clearly and persuasively.

2. Integrate and evaluate information presented in diverse media and formats, including visually, quantitatively, and orally.

3. Evaluate a speaker's point of view, reasoning, and use of evidence and rhetoric.

Presentation of Knowledge and Ideas

4. Present information, findings, and supporting evidence such that listeners can follow the line of reasoning and the organization, development, and style are appropriate to task, purpose, and audience.

5. Make strategic use of digital media and visual displays of data to express information and enhance understanding of presentations.

6. Adapt speech to a variety of contexts and communicative tasks, demonstrating command of formal English when indicated or appropriate.

Language

Conventions of Standard English

1. Demonstrate command of the conventions of standard English grammar and usage when writing or speaking.

2. Demonstrate command of the conventions of standard English capitalization, punctuation, and spelling when writing.

Knowledge of Language

3. Apply knowledge of language to understand how language functions in different contexts, to make effective choices for meaning or style, and to comprehend more fully when reading or listening.

Vocabulary Acquisition and Use

4. Determine or clarify the meaning of unknown and multiple-meaning words and phrases by using context clues, analyzing meaningful word parts, and consulting general and specialized reference materials, as appropriate.

5. Demonstrate understanding of figurative language, word relationships, and nuances in word meanings.

6. Acquire and use accurately a range of general academic and domain-specific words and phrases sufficient for reading, writing, speaking, and listening at the college and career readiness level; demonstrate independence in gathering vocabulary knowledge when encountering an unknown term important to comprehension or expression.

*These broad types of writing include many subgenres. See Resource A for definitions of key writing types.

Key Principles and Additional Teaching Strategies for

English Language Learners K–2

Nancy Akhavan

For each standard throughout this book, suggestions for supporting English language learners appear at the ends of the "What the Teacher Does" pages. Here, these instructional ideas are supplemented with additional background, including information on the stages of language acquisition and the implications for differentiated scaffolding.

Focus on Acquisition

The young students in our K–2 classrooms, both native English speakers and English language learners (ELLs), are learning language. In many respects they are remarkably the same in their quests for language acquisition. Both groups of students are rapidly developing their vocabularies, using language to communicate, and learning about academic language and formal English.

However, there is a difference between students who are native English speakers and those who are ELLs. ELLs are acquiring a *second* (or even third) language when they learn English at school; they already have their primary language with which they communicate at home and in the community. Thus, many of these children are fluent in their first language, an important point to remember so that our mind-set as teachers isn't that these young kids are struggling learners overall.

We learn language through two processes. One process is called *acquisition*, and the other is called *language learning*. Language acquisition is "picking up" a language. Language learning is what we experience when we take a class in a foreign language.

In our classrooms we want to focus on the natural process of "picking up" a language. Thus, for both native English speakers and English language learners, this book is filled with strategies and lessons to teach the standards through natural, motivating, and supportive teaching.

Consider the Five Stages

To understand the best ways to help your English language learners, and to differentiate instruction based on their language acquisition needs, it is important to understand that not all students learning English need the same scaffolds, the same types of instruction, or the same performance tasks. What they need depends on which stage of language acquisition they are in. While people don't fit into boxes, and language learning is a fluid process, it truly helps to understand the five stages of language acquisition and assess where your students are so you can tailor instruction based on their language needs. These five stages, as described in the table on the next page, are preproduction, early production, speech emergence, intermediate fluency, and advanced fluency (Haynes & Zacarian, 2010; Krashen, 1982, 2003; Krashen & Terrell, 1983).

It is also important to note that students acquire language in a natural order (Krashen, 1982, 2003; Peregoy & Boyle, 2012). The key idea here is that students learn English not in the order that you teach it but, rather, in the natural way that the brain learns language. In other words, you can't force students to learn a grammar rule by teaching it explicitly, but you can ensure that students acquire English rapidly by providing engaging language—rich, supportive, culturally respectful—and meaningful classroom experiences in English (Akhavan, 2006; Hoover & Patton, 2005).

Offer Collaborative Activities

To support language acquisition, it is important to provide learning activities that encourage English language learners to work together with native English speakers so that they have opportunities to talk, think, read, and write in English. It is also important to take into consideration the prior knowledge of the English language learners and preview, or front-load, information, ideas, and activities with them in small groups before they join the whole group for a lesson in English. This front-loading in small-group discussion gives English language learners the opportunity to develop knowledge about a subject, discuss the topic in a "safe" setting where they can question, and even use their primary language to discuss the lesson so that they have a foundation before receiving the main lesson in English.

Check the Clarity of Your Lessons

Making your lessons understandable to English language learners is the most important thing you can do to help these students be successful in your classroom. Making "input" comprehensible will help your students participate in lessons, help them understand what is going on in the classroom, and encourage them to speak in English as appropriate (Krashen, 2003). You need to provide comprehensible lessons that scaffold the language learner. Scaffolds can include pictures, objects, media from the Internet, and other realia; the important thing is that they powerfully contextualize what you are saying, making it comprehensible and concrete.

Speak Clearly and at an Appropriate Pace

It also helps to slow down your speech rate, and to repeat what you are saying to give students learning English "clues" about what you are teaching and time to process. This is true not only for students new to English but also for students who seem to be proficient because they can speak well in English but may not have yet developed academic language.

Attune Your Teaching and Learning Expectations to the Stages of Language Acquisition

Language-appropriate, culturally relevant instruction and instruction with high expectations for learning can support students as they learn English. The following table explains the five stages of language acquisition and highlights learner characteristics at each stage. You can best support language acquisition by matching your expectations for student production and interaction in English with the stages that your students are in, as evidenced by their oral and written work.

Unfortunately, many students remain in the intermediate and early advanced stages for their entire school careers, never reaching full English proficiency. These students, considered long-term English learners, struggle in content-area classes. This is why it is so important that you know and understand the five stages of language acquisition; this knowledge enables you to differentiate instruction based on student needs.

The Five Stages of Language Acquisition: What to Expect of Students

Stage	Student Characteristics	Time Frame	Appropriate Instructional Activities
Preproduction	Students are silent and do not speak. They may parrot English speakers. They listen a lot and may be able to copy words from the board. They can understand gestures and movements (e.g., they can nod yes or no).	0–6 months	Ask students to point, touch, or use gestures. Provide listening experiences without the expectation to talk in English. Build vocabulary through physical response (i.e., having students act out words and phrases). Pair students with primary language students.
Early Production	Students can speak in one- or two-word chunks and phrases. They may use memorized phrases, but will not always be correct (e.g., May I get a drink of water?). They may produce short sentences with present-tense verbs.	6 months to 1 year	Ask yes or no, either/or, and who and what questions. Provide comprehensible listening activities. Use pictures, language frames, sentence starters, and simplified content through picture books and modified texts. Build vocabulary through pictures and realia.
Speech Emergence	Students can speak in simple sentences. They can understand a lot of what is said. They make grammatical errors in speaking and writing. They may pronounce words incorrectly.	1–3 years	Involve students in short conversations in small groups with other students. Provide short or modified texts. Use graphic organizers and word banks. Provide writing activities through response journals or short writing assignments.

(Continued)

(Continued)

Stage	Student Characteristics	Time Frame	Appropriate Instructional Activities
Speech Emergence (Continued)			Provide contextualized support for content work. Develop vocabulary through matching activities and lessons that develop conceptual understanding.
Intermediate Fluency	Students comprehend basic communication well but may not understand academic and content lessons. They make few grammatical errors when speaking but may still make errors when writing, especially with academic writing. They can use more complex language and can participate in class with teacher support.	3–5 years	Provide longer writing assignments. Engage students in group work, project-based lessons, and relevant instruction. Provide instruction in grammar and language conventions as related to student needs (e.g., assess student needs by examining writing journals and reading records). Provide English language development lessons in vocabulary, content, and grammar tailored to student needs.
Advanced Fluency	Students are near native in their ability to speak and use English in content areas or with academic language. They need continued support with academic language to continue acquiring language and conventions in academic domains.	4–7 years, or longer	Provide rich and engaging instruction based on standards and grade-level content expectations. Continue to contextualize language and content. Provide English language development lessons tailored to student needs.

References

Akhavan, N. (2006). *Help! My kids don't all speak English: How to set up a language workshop in your linguistically diverse classroom.* Portsmouth, NH: Heinemann.

Haynes, J., & Zacarian, D. (2010). *Teaching English language learners: Across the content areas.* Alexandria, VA: ASCD.

Hoover, J., & Patton, J. (2005). Differentiating curriculum and instruction for English-language learners with special needs. *Intervention in School and Clinic, 40*(4), 231–235.

Krashen, S. D. (1982). *Principles and practice in second language acquisition* [Internet edition July 2009]. Retrieved from http://www.sdkrashen.com/content/books/principles_and_practice.pdf

Krashen, S. D. (2003). *Explorations in language acquisition and use: The Taipei lectures.* Portsmouth, NH: Heinemann.

Krashen, S. D., & Terrell, D. (1983). *The natural approach: Language acquisition in the classroom.* Hayward, CA: Alemany Press.

Peregoy, S. F., & Boyle, O. F. (2012). *Reading, writing, and learning in ESL: A resource book for teaching K–12 English learners* (6th ed.). New York, NY: Longman.

Indexes Cross-Referencing Your State Standards

 Available for download at **resources.corwin.com/literacycompanionk-2**

Alaska, Kindergarten

Alaska Strand/Standard	Focus of Alaska Standard	For More Information
Reading Literature		
RL.1	Ask and answer questions about a text using key details	R1 pp. 6–11
RL.2	Retell familiar stories, using key details	R2 pp. 12–17
RL.3	Identify characters, settings, and major events in a story	R3 pp. 18–23
RL.4	Ask and answer questions about unknown words in a text	R4 pp. 24–29
RL.5	Identify common types of text (e.g., storybooks, poems)	R5 pp. 30–35
RL.6	Name the author and illustrator of a story and describe the role of each	R6 pp. 36–41
RL.7	Describe the relationship between the illustrations and the story in which they appear	R7 pp. 42–47
RL.8	NA	
RL.9	Compare and contrast the characters in familiar stories	R9 pp. 54–59
RL.10	Actively engage in reading activities with purpose and understanding	R10 pp. 60–65
Reading Informational Text		
RI.1	Ask and answer questions about information in a text, using key details	R1 pp. 6–11
RI.2	Identify the main topic and retell key details of a text	R2 pp. 12–17
RI.3	Describe the connection between two individuals, events, ideas, or pieces of information in a text	R3 pp. 18–23
RI.4	Ask and answer questions about unknown words in a text	R4 pp. 24–29
RI.5	Identify the front cover, back cover, and title page of a book	R5 pp. 30–35
RI.6	Name the author and illustrator of a text and describe the role of each	R6 pp. 36–41
RI.7	Describe the relationship between visual images and the text in which they appear	R7 pp. 42–47
RI.8	Identify the opinions an author states in a text	R8 pp. 48–53
RI.9	Identify basic similarities and differences between two texts on the same topic	R9 pp. 54–59
RI.10	Actively engage in reading informational text with purpose and understanding	R10 pp. 60–65
Reading Foundational Skills		
RF.1	Print Concepts: Demonstrate understanding of the organization and basic features of print	RF1 pp. 72–77
RF.2	Phonological Awareness: Demonstrate understanding of spoken words, syllables, and sounds (phonemes)	RF2 pp. 78–83
RF.3	Phonics: Know and apply grade-level phonics and word analysis skills in decoding words	RF3 pp. 84–89
RF.4	Fluency: Read level-appropriate texts with purpose and understanding	RF4 pp. 90–95
Writing		
W.1	Use a combination of drawing, dictating, and writing to compose opinion pieces	W1 pp. 100–105
W.2	Use a combination of drawing, dictating, and writing to compose informative/explanatory texts	W2 pp. 106–111
W.3	Use a combination of drawing, dictating, and writing to narrate a single event or several loosely linked events and provide a reaction to what happened	W3 pp. 112–117
W.4	NA	
W.5	Respond to questions and add details to strengthen writing as needed	W5 pp. 118–123

(Continued)

Alaska Strand/Standard	Focus of Alaska Standard	For More Information
Writing		
W.6	Explore a variety of digital tools to produce and publish writing	W6 pp. 124–129
W.7	Participate in shared research and writing projects	W7 pp. 130–135
W.8	Recall information from experiences or gather information from provided sources to answer a question	W8 pp. 136–141
W.9	NA	
W.10	NA	
Speaking and Listening		
SL.1	Participate in collaborative conversations with diverse partners about topics and texts in small and larger groups	SL1 pp. 146–151
SL.2	Ask and answer questions about key details to confirm understanding of a topic	SL2 pp. 152–157
SL.3	Ask and answer questions in order to seek help, get information, or clarify something that is not understood	SL3 pp. 158–163
SL.4	Describe familiar people, places, things, and events	SL4 pp. 164–169
SL.5	Add drawings or other visual displays to descriptions to provide additional detail	SL5 pp. 170–175
SL.6	Speak audibly and express thoughts, ideas, feelings, and ideas clearly in complete sentences when appropriate to task and situation	SL6 pp. 176–181
Language		
L.1	Demonstrate command of the conventions of standard English grammar and usage when writing or speaking	L1 pp. 186–191
L.2	Demonstrate command of the conventions of standard English capitalization, punctuation, and spelling when writing	L2 pp. 192–197
L.3	NA	
L.4	Determine or clarify the meaning of unknown and multiple-meaning words and phrases	L4 pp. 204–209
L.5	Explore word relationships and nuances in word meanings	L5 pp. 210–215
L.6	Use words and phrases acquired through conversations, reading, being read to, and responding to texts	L6 pp. 216–221

Alaska, Grade 1

Alaska Strand/Standard	Focus of Alaska Standard	For More Information
Reading Literature		
RL.1	Ask and answer questions about a text using key details from the text	R1 pp. 6–11
RL.2	Retell stories, including key details, and demonstrate understanding of their message	R2 pp. 12–17
RL.3	Describe characters, settings, and major events in a story, play, or poem	R3 pp. 18–23
RL.4	Identify words or phrases that suggest feelings or appeal to the senses	R4 pp. 24–29
RL.5	Explain major differences between stories and informative texts	R5 pp. 30–35
RL.6	Identify who is telling the story at various points in a text	R6 pp. 36–41
RL.7	Use illustrations and details to describe elements of a story	R7 pp. 42–47
RL.8	NA	
RL.9	Compare and contrast the experiences of characters in stories	R9 pp. 54–59
RL.10	Read texts of appropriate complexity	R10 pp. 60–65
Reading Informational Text		
RI.1	Ask and answer questions about a text using key details from the text	R1 pp. 6–11
RI.2	Identify the main topic or author's purpose and retell key details of a text	R2 pp. 12–17

Alaska Strand/Standard	Focus of Alaska Standard	For More Information
Reading Informational Text		
RI.3	Describe the connection between two individuals, events, ideas, or pieces of information in a text	R3 pp. 18–23
RI.4	Ask and answer questions to clarify the meaning of words in a text	R4 pp. 24–29
RI.5	Use text features to locate information in a text	R5 pp. 30–35
RI.6	Distinguish between information provided by illustrations and information provided by words	R6 pp. 36–41
RI.7	Use illustrations and details to describe key ideas in a text	R7 pp. 42–47
RI.8	Identify the reasons an author gives to support points in a text	R8 pp. 48–53
RI.9	Identify basic similarities and differences between two texts on the same topic	R9 pp. 54–59
RI.10	Actively engage in reading informational text with purpose and understanding	R10 pp. 60–65
Reading Foundational Skills		
RF.1	Print Concepts: Demonstrate understanding of the organization and basic features of print	RF1 pp. 72–77
RF.2	Phonological Awareness: Demonstrate understanding of spoken words, syllables, and sounds (phonemes)	RF2 pp. 78–83
RF.3	Phonics: Know and apply grade-level phonics and word analysis skills in decoding words	RF3 pp. 84–89
RF.4	Fluency: Read level-appropriate texts with accuracy and fluency	RF4 pp. 90–95
Writing		
W.1	Write opinion pieces: introduce the topic, state an opinion, supply reasons, and provide closure	W1 pp. 100–105
W.2	Write informative/explanatory texts: name a topic, supply facts, and provide closure	W2 pp. 106–111
W.3	Write narratives: sequence events, include details, use temporal words, and provide closure	W3 pp. 112–117
W.4	NA	
W.5	Focus on a topic, respond to questions, and add details to strengthen writing as needed	W5 pp. 118–123
W.6	Use a variety of digital tools to produce and publish writing	W6 pp. 124–129
W.7	Participate in shared research and writing projects	W7 pp. 130–135
W.8	Recall information from experiences or gather information from provided sources to answer a question	W8 pp. 136–141
W.9	NA	
W.10	NA	
Speaking and Listening		
SL.1	Participate in collaborative conversations with diverse partners about topics and texts in small and larger groups	SL1 pp. 146–151
SL.2	Ask and answer questions about key details to demonstrate understanding of a topic	SL2 pp. 152–157
SL.3	Ask and answer questions in order to get information or clarify something that is not understood	SL3 pp. 158–163
SL.4	Clearly describe people, places, things, and events	SL4 pp. 164–169
SL.5	Add drawings or other visual displays to descriptions to provide additional detail	SL5 pp. 170–175
SL.6	Produce complete sentences when appropriate to task and situation	SL6 pp. 176–181
Language		
L.1	Demonstrate command of the conventions of standard English grammar and usage when writing or speaking	L1 pp. 186–191
L.2	Demonstrate command of the conventions of standard English capitalization, punctuation, and spelling when writing	L2 pp. 192–197
L.3	NA	
L.4	Determine or clarify the meaning of unknown and multiple-meaning words and phrases	L4 pp. 204–209
L.5	Demonstrate understanding of word relationships and nuances in word meanings	L5 pp. 210–215
L.6	Use words and phrases acquired through conversations, reading, being read to, and responding to texts	L6 pp. 216–221

Alaska, Grade 2

Alaska Strand/Standard	Focus of Alaska Standard	For More Information
Reading Literature		
RL.1	Using key details, ask and answer questions to demonstrate understanding of a text	R1 pp. 6–11
RL.2	Retell stories and determine author's purpose, lesson, or moral	R2 pp. 12–17
RL.3	Describe how characters respond to major events and challenges	R3 pp. 18–23
RL.4	Describe how words or phrases supply rhythm and meaning in a story	R4 pp. 24–29
RL.5	Describe the overall structure of a story, including the beginning, middle, and ending	R5 pp. 30–35
RL.6	Acknowledge differences in characters' points of view	R6 pp. 36–41
RL.7	Use information gathered from illustrations and words to demonstrate understanding of story elements	R7 pp. 42–47
RL.8	NA	
RL.9	Compare and contrast two or more versions of the same story	R9 pp. 54–59
RL.10	Read and comprehend texts of appropriate complexity	R10 pp. 60–65
Reading Informational Text		
RI.1	Ask and answer questions to demonstrate understanding of a text, using key details	R1 pp. 6–11
RI.2	Identify the main topic and retell key details of a text, as well as the focus of specific paragraphs	R2 pp. 12–17
RI.3	Describe the connection between a series of events, ideas, concepts, or steps in a text	R3 pp. 18–23
RI.4	Determine the meaning of words and phrases in a text relevant to a grade-level topic	R4 pp. 24–29
RI.5	Use text features to efficiently locate information in a text	R5 pp. 30–35
RI.6	Identify the main purpose of a text	R6 pp. 36–41
RI.7	Explain how specific images contribute to and clarify a text	R7 pp. 42–47
RI.8	Describe how reasons an author gives support points in a text	R8 pp. 48–53
RI.9	Compare and contrast the most important points in two texts on the same topic	R9 pp. 54–59
RI.10	Read and comprehend informational texts of appropriate complexity	R10 pp. 60–65
Reading Foundational Skills		
RF.1	NA	
RF.2	NA	
RF.3	Phonics: Know and apply grade-level phonics and word analysis skills in decoding words	RF3 pp. 84–89
RF.4	Fluency: Read level-appropriate texts with accuracy and fluency	RF4 pp. 90–95
Writing		
W.1	Write opinion pieces: introduce the topic, state an opinion, supply reasons using linking words, and provide closure	W1 pp. 100–105
W.2	Write informative/explanatory texts: name a topic, use facts to develop points, and provide closure	W2 pp. 106–111
W.3	Write narratives: sequence events; include details to describe actions, thoughts, and feelings; use temporal words; provide closure	W3 pp. 112–117
W.4	NA	
W.5	Focus on a topic and strengthen writing by revising and editing	W5 pp. 118–123
W.6	Use a variety of digital tools to produce and publish writing	W6 pp. 124–129
W.7	Participate in shared research and writing projects	W7 pp. 130–135
W.8	Recall information from experiences or gather information from provided sources to answer a question	W8 pp. 136–141
W.9	NA	
W.10	NA	

Alaska Strand/Standard	Focus of Alaska Standard	For More Information
Speaking and Listening		
SL.1	Participate in collaborative conversations with diverse partners about topics and texts in small and larger groups	SL1 pp. 146–151
SL.2	Retell or describe key ideas or details in information presented orally	SL2 pp. 152–157
SL.3	Ask and answer questions in order to get information, deepen understanding, or clarify comprehension	SL3 pp. 158–163
SL.4	Tell a story or retell and experience with appropriate facts and relevant details	SL4 pp. 164–169
SL.5	Create audio recordings of stories or poems, adding visual displays as appropriate for clarification	SL5 pp. 170–175
SL.6	Produce complete sentences when appropriate to task and situation	SL6 pp. 176–181
Language		
L.1	Demonstrate command of the conventions of standard English grammar and usage when writing or speaking	L1 pp. 186–191
L.2	Demonstrate command of the conventions of standard English capitalization, punctuation, and spelling when writing	L2 pp. 192–197
L.3	Use knowledge of language and its conventions when writing, speaking, reading, or listening	L3 pp. 198–203
L.4	Determine or clarify the meaning of unknown and multiple-meaning words and phrases	L4 pp. 204–209
L.5	Demonstrate understanding of word relationships and nuances in word meanings	L5 pp. 210–215
L.6	Use words and phrases acquired through conversations, reading, being read to, and responding to texts	L6 pp. 216–221

Arizona, Kindergarten

Arizona Strand/Standard	Focus of Arizona Standard	For More Information
Reading Literature		
RL.1	Ask and answer questions about key details in a text	R1 pp. 6–11
RL.2	Retell familiar stories, including key details	R2 pp. 12–17
RL.3	Identify characters, settings, and major events in a story	R3 pp. 18–23
RL.4	Ask and answer questions about unknown words in a text	R4 pp. 24–29
RL.5	Recognize common types of text (e.g., storybooks, poems)	R5 pp. 30–35
RL.6	Name the author and illustrator of a story and define the role of each	R6 pp. 36–41
RL.7	Describe the relationship between the illustrations and the story in which they appear	R7 pp. 42–47
RL.8	NA	
RL.9	Compare and contrast the characters in familiar stories	R9 pp. 54–59
RL.10	Actively engage in reading activities with purpose and understanding	R10 pp. 60–65
Reading Informational Text		
RI.1	Ask and answer questions about key details in a text	R1 pp. 6–11
RI.2	Identify the main topic and retell key details of a text	R2 pp. 12–17
RI.3	Describe the connection between two individuals, events, ideas, or pieces of information in a text	R3 pp. 18–23
RI.4	Ask and answer questions about unknown words in a text	R4 pp. 24–29
RI.5	Identify the front cover, back cover, and title page of a book	R5 pp. 30–35
RI.6	Name the author and illustrator of a text and define the role of each	R6 pp. 36–41
RI.7	Describe the relationship between visual images and the text in which they appear	R7 pp. 42–47
RI.8	Identify the reasons an author gives to support points in a text	R8 pp. 48–53
RI.9	Identify basic similarities and differences between two texts on the same topic	R9 pp. 54–59
RI.10	Actively engage in reading informational text with purpose and understanding	R10 pp. 60–65

(Continued)

Arizona Strand/Standard	Focus of Arizona Standard	For More Information
Reading Foundational Skills		
RF.1	Print Concepts: Demonstrate understanding of the organization and basic features of print	RF1 pp. 72–77
RF.2	Phonological Awareness: Demonstrate understanding of spoken words, syllables, and sounds (phonemes)	RF2 pp. 78–83
RF.3	Phonics: Know and apply grade-level phonics and word analysis skills in decoding words	RF3 pp. 84–89
RF.4	Fluency: Read level-appropriate texts with purpose and understanding	RF4 pp. 90–95
Writing		
W.1	Use a combination of drawing, dictating, and writing to compose opinion pieces	W1 pp. 100–105
W.2	Use a combination of drawing, dictating, and writing to compose informative/explanatory texts	W2 pp. 106–111
W.3	Use a combination of drawing, dictating, and writing to narrate a single event or several loosely linked events and provide a reaction to what happened	W3 pp. 112–117
W.4	NA	
W.5	Respond to questions and add details to strengthen writing as needed	W5 pp. 118–123
W.6	Explore a variety of digital tools to produce some writing	W6 pp. 124–129
W.7	Participate in shared research and writing projects	W7 pp. 130–135
W.8	Recall information from experiences or gather information from provided sources to answer a question	W8 pp. 136–141
W.9	NA	
W.10	NA	
Speaking and Listening		
SL.1	Participate in collaborative conversations with diverse partners about topics and texts in small and larger groups	SL1 pp. 146–151
SL.2	Ask and answer questions about key details to demonstrate understanding of a topic	SL2 pp. 152–157
SL.3	Ask and answer questions in order to seek help, get information, or clarify something that is not understood	SL3 pp. 158–163
SL.4	Describe familiar people, places, things, and events	SL4 pp. 164–169
SL.5	Add drawings or other visual displays to descriptions to provide additional detail	SL5 pp. 170–175
SL.6	Speak audibly and express thoughts, ideas, feelings, and ideas clearly	SL6 pp. 176–181
Language		
L.1	Demonstrate command of the conventions of standard English grammar and usage when writing or speaking	L1 pp. 186–191
L.2	Demonstrate command of the conventions of standard English capitalization, punctuation, and spelling when writing	L2 pp. 192–197
L.3	NA	
L.4	Determine or clarify the meaning of unknown and multiple-meaning words and phrases	L4 pp. 204–209
L.5	Explore word relationships and nuances in word meanings	L5 pp. 210–215
L.6	Use words and phrases acquired through conversations, reading, being read to, and responding to texts	L6 pp. 216–221

Arizona, Grade 1

Arizona Strand/Standard	Focus of Arizona Standard	For More Information
Reading Literature		
RL.1	Ask and answer questions about key details in a text	R1 pp. 6–11
RL.2	Retell stories, including key details	R2 pp. 12–17
RL.3	Describe characters, settings, and major events in a story	R3 pp. 18–23

Arizona Strand/Standard	Focus of Arizona Standard	For More Information
Reading Literature		
RL.4	Identify words or phrases that suggest feelings or appeal to the senses	R4 pp. 24–29
RL.5	Explain major differences between stories and informative texts	R5 pp. 30–35
RL.6	Identify who is telling the story at various points in a text	R6 pp. 36–41
RL.7	Use illustrations to describe elements of a story	R7 pp. 42–47
RL.8	NA	
RL.9	Compare and contrast the experiences of characters in stories	R9 pp. 54–59
RL.10	Read texts of appropriate complexity	R10 pp. 60–65
Reading Informational Text		
RI.1	Ask and answer questions about key details in a text	R1 pp. 6–11
RI.2	Identify the main topic and retell key details of a text	R2 pp. 12–17
RI.3	Describe the connection between two individuals, events, ideas, or pieces of information in a text	R3 pp. 18–23
RI.4	Ask and answer questions to clarify the meaning of words in a text	R4 pp. 24–29
RI.5	Use text features to locate information in a text	R5 pp. 30–35
RI.6	Distinguish between information provided by illustrations and information provided by words	R6 pp. 36–41
RI.7	Use illustrations and details to describe key ideas in a text	R7 pp. 42–47
RI.8	Identify the reasons an author gives to support points in a text	R8 pp. 48–53
RI.9	Identify basic similarities and differences between two texts on the same topic	R9 pp. 54–59
RI.10	Actively engage in reading informational text with purpose and understanding	R10 pp. 60–65
Reading Foundational Skills		
RF.1	Print Concepts: Demonstrate understanding of the organization and basic features of print	RF1 pp. 72–77
RF.2	Phonological Awareness: Demonstrate understanding of spoken words, syllables, and sounds (phonemes)	RF2 pp. 78–83
RF.3	Phonics: Know and apply grade-level phonics and word analysis skills in decoding words	RF3 pp. 84–89
RF.4	Fluency: Read level-appropriate texts with accuracy and fluency	RF4 pp. 90–95
Writing		
W.1	Write opinion pieces: introduce the topic, state an opinion, supply reasons, and provide closure	W1 pp. 100–105
W.2	Write informative/explanatory texts: name a topic, supply facts, and provide closure	W2 pp. 106–111
W.3	Write narratives: sequence events, include details, use temporal words, and provide closure	W3 pp. 112–117
W.4	NA	
W.5	Focus on a topic, respond to questions, and add details to strengthen writing as needed	W5 pp. 118–123
W.6	Use a variety of digital tools to produce and publish writing	W6 pp. 124–129
W.7	Participate in shared research and writing projects	W7 pp. 130–135
W.8	Recall information from experiences or gather information from provided sources to answer a question	W8 pp. 136–141
W.9	NA	
W.10	NA	
Speaking and Listening		
SL.1	Participate in collaborative conversations with diverse partners about topics and texts in small and larger groups	SL1 pp. 146–151
SL.2	Ask and answer questions about key details to demonstrate understanding of a topic	SL2 pp. 152–157
SL.3	Ask and answer questions in order to get information or clarify something that is not understood	SL3 pp. 158–163
SL.4	Clearly describe people, places, things, and events	SL4 pp. 164–169
SL.5	Add drawings or other visual displays to descriptions to provide additional detail	SL5 pp. 170–175
SL.6	Produce complete sentences when appropriate to task and situation	SL6 pp. 176–181

(Continued)

Arizona Strand/Standard	Focus of Arizona Standard	For More Information
Language		
L.1	Demonstrate command of the conventions of standard English grammar and usage when writing or speaking	L1 pp. 186–191
L.2	Demonstrate command of the conventions of standard English capitalization, punctuation, and spelling when writing	L2 pp. 192–197
L.3	NA	
L.4	Determine or clarify the meaning of unknown and multiple-meaning words and phrases	L4 pp. 204–209
L.5	Demonstrate understanding of word relationships and nuances in word meanings	L5 pp. 210–215
L.6	Use words and phrases acquired through conversations, reading, being read to, and responding to texts	L6 pp. 216–221

Arizona, Grade 2

Arizona Strand/Standard	Focus of Arizona Standard	For More Information
Reading Literature		
RL.1	Ask and answer questions about key details in a text	R1 pp. 6–11
RL.2	Recount stories and determine their central message	R2 pp. 12–17
RL.3	Describe how characters respond to major events and challenges	R3 pp. 18–23
RL.4	Describe how words or phrases supply rhythm and meaning	R4 pp. 24–29
RL.5	Describe the overall structure of a story, including the beginning and ending	R5 pp. 30–35
RL.6	Acknowledge differences in characters' points of view	R6 pp. 36–41
RL.7	Use information gathered from illustrations and words to demonstrate understanding of story elements	R7 pp. 42–47
RL.8	NA	
RL.9	Compare and contrast two or more versions of the same story	R9 pp. 54–59
RL.10	Read and comprehend texts of appropriate complexity	R10 pp. 60–65
Reading Informational Text		
RI.1	Ask and answer questions about key details in a text	R1 pp. 6–11
RI.2	Identify the main topic and retell key details of a text, as well as the focus of specific paragraphs	R2 pp. 12–17
RI.3	Describe the connection between a series of events, ideas, concepts, or steps in a text	R3 pp. 18–23
RI.4	Determine the meaning of words and phrases in a text relevant to a grade-level topic	R4 pp. 24–29
RI.5	Use text features to efficiently locate information in a text	R5 pp. 30–35
RI.6	Identify the main purpose of a text	R6 pp. 36–41
RI.7	Explain how specific images contribute to and clarify a text	R7 pp. 42–47
RI.8	Describe how reasons an author gives support points in a text	R8 pp. 48–53
RI.9	Compare and contrast the most important points in two texts on the same topic	R9 pp. 54–59
RI.10	Read and comprehend informational texts of appropriate complexity	R10 pp. 60–65
Reading Foundational Skills		
RF.1	NA	
RF.2	NA	
RF.3	Phonics: Know and apply grade-level phonics and word analysis skills in decoding words	RF3 pp. 84–89
RF.4	Fluency: Read level-appropriate texts with accuracy and fluency	RF4 pp. 90–95

Arizona Strand/Standard	Focus of Arizona Standard	For More Information
Writing		
W.1	Write opinion pieces: introduce the topic, state an opinion, supply reasons using linking words, and provide closure	W1 pp. 100–105
W.2	Write informative/explanatory texts: name a topic, use facts to develop points, and provide closure	W2 pp. 106–111
W.3	Write narratives: sequence events; include details to describe actions, thoughts, and feelings; use temporal words; provide closure	W3 pp. 112–117
W.4	NA	
W.5	Focus on a topic and strengthen writing by revising and editing	W5 pp. 118–123
W.6	Use a variety of digital tools to produce and publish writing	W6 pp. 124–129
W.7	Participate in shared research and writing projects	W7 pp. 130–135
W.8	Recall information from experiences or gather information from provided sources to answer a question	W8 pp. 136–141
W.9	NA	
W.10	NA	
Speaking and Listening		
SL.1	Participate in collaborative conversations with diverse partners about topics and texts in small and larger groups	SL1 pp. 146–151
SL.2	Recount or describe key ideas or details in information presented orally	SL2 pp. 152–157
SL.3	Ask and answer questions in order to get information, deepen understanding, or clarify something that is not understood	SL3 pp. 158–163
SL.4	Recount a story or experience with appropriate facts and relevant details	SL4 pp. 164–169
SL.5	Create audio recordings of stories or poems, adding visual displays as appropriate for clarification	SL5 pp. 170–175
SL.6	Produce complete sentences when appropriate to task and situation	SL6 pp. 176–181
Language		
L.1	Demonstrate command of the conventions of standard English grammar and usage when writing or speaking	L1 pp. 186–191
L.2	Demonstrate command of the conventions of standard English capitalization, punctuation, and spelling when writing	L2 pp. 192–197
L.3	Use knowledge of language and its conventions when writing, speaking, reading, or listening	L3 pp. 198–203
L.4	Determine or clarify the meaning of unknown and multiple-meaning words and phrases	L4 pp. 204–209
L.5	Demonstrate understanding of word relationships and nuances in word meanings	L5 pp. 210–215
L.6	Use words and phrases acquired through conversations, reading, being read to, and responding to texts	L6 pp. 216–221

Arkansas, Kindergarten

Arkansas Strand/Standard	Focus of Arkansas Standard	For More Information
Reading Literature		
RL.K.1	Ask and answer questions about key details in a text	R1 pp. 6–11
RL.K.2	Retell familiar stories, including key details	R2 pp. 12–17
RL.K.3	Identify characters, settings, and major events in a story	R3 pp. 18–23
RL.K.4	Ask and answer questions about unknown words in a text	R4 pp. 24–29
RL.K.5	Recognize common types of text (e.g., storybooks, poems)	R5 pp. 30–35
RL.K.6	Name the author and illustrator of a story and define the role of each	R6 pp. 36–41
RL.K.7	Describe the relationship between the illustrations and the story in which they appear	R7 pp. 42–47
RL.K.8	NA	

(Continued)

Arkansas Strand/Standard	Focus of Arkansas Standard	For More Information
Reading Literature		
RL.K.9	Compare and contrast the characters in familiar stories	R9 pp. 54–59
RL.K.10	Actively engage in teacher-led reading activities with purpose and understanding	R10 pp. 60–65
Reading Informational Text		
RI.K.1	Ask and answer questions about key details in a text	R1 pp. 6–11
RI.K.2	Identify the main topic and retell key details of a text	R2 pp. 12–17
RI.K.3	Describe the connection between two topics (individuals, events, ideas, or scientific concepts)	R3 pp. 18–23
RI.K.4	Ask and answer questions about unknown words in a text	R4 pp. 24–29
RI.K.5	Identify the front cover, back cover, and title page of a book	R5 pp. 30–35
RI.K.6	Name the author and illustrator of a text and define the role of each	R6 pp. 36–41
RI.K.7	Describe the relationship between visual images and the text in which they appear	R7 pp. 42–47
RI.K.8	Identify the details an author gives to support points in a text	R8 pp. 48–53
R.KI.9	Identify basic similarities and differences between two texts on the same topic	R9 pp. 54–59
RI.K.10	Actively engage in teacher-led reading activities with purpose and understanding	R10 pp. 60–65
Reading Foundational Skills		
RF.K.1	Print Concepts: Demonstrate understanding of the organization and basic features of print	RF1 pp. 72–77
RF.K.2	Phonological Awareness: Demonstrate understanding of spoken words, syllables, and sounds (phonemes)	RF2 pp. 78–83
RF.K.3	Phonics: Know and apply grade-level phonics and word analysis skills in decoding words	RF3 pp. 84–89
R.KF.4	Fluency: Read grade-appropriate texts with purpose and understanding	RF4 pp. 90–95
Writing		
W.K.1	Use a combination of drawing, dictating, and writing to compose opinion pieces	W1 pp. 100–105
W.K.2	Use a combination of drawing, dictating, and writing to compose informative/explanatory texts	W2 pp. 106–111
W.K.3	Use a combination of drawing, dictating, and writing to narrate a single event or several loosely linked events and provide a reaction to what happened	W3 pp. 112–117
W.K.4	NA	
W.K.5	Respond to questions and add details to strengthen writing as needed	W5 pp. 118–123
W.K.6	Explore a variety of digital tools to produce some writing	W6 pp. 124–129
W.K.7	Participate in shared research and writing projects	W7 pp. 130–135
W.K.8	Recall information from experiences or gather information from provided sources to answer a question	W8 pp. 136–141
W.K.9	NA	
W.K.10	NA	
Speaking and Listening		
SL.K.1	Participate in collaborative conversations with diverse partners about topics and texts in small and larger groups	SL1 pp. 146–151
SL.K.2	Ask and answer questions about key details to demonstrate understanding of a topic	SL2 pp. 152–157
SL.K.3	Ask and answer questions in order to seek help, get information, or clarify something that is not understood	SL3 pp. 158–163
SL.K.4	Describe familiar people, places, things, and events	SL4 pp. 164–169
SL.K.5	Add drawings or other visual displays to descriptions to provide additional detail	SL5 pp. 170–175
SL.K.6	Speak audibly and express thoughts, ideas, feelings, and ideas clearly	SL6 pp. 176–181
Language		
L.K.1	Demonstrate command of the conventions of standard English grammar and usage when writing or speaking	L1 pp. 186–191
L.K.2	Demonstrate command of the conventions of standard English capitalization, punctuation, and spelling when writing	L2 pp. 192–197
L.K.3	NA	
L.K.4	Determine or clarify the meaning of unknown and multiple-meaning words and phrases	L4 pp. 204–209

Arkansas Strand/Standard	Focus of Arkansas Standard	For More Information
Language		
L.K.5	Explore word relationships and nuances in word meanings	L5 pp. 210–215
L.K.6	Use words and phrases acquired through conversations, reading, being read to, and responding to texts	L6 pp. 216–221

Arkansas, Grade 1

Arkansas Strand/Standard	Focus of Arkansas Standard	For More Information
Reading Literature		
RL.1.1	Ask and answer questions about key details in a text	R1 pp. 6–11
RL.1.2	Retell stories, including key details, and demonstrate understanding of their central message or lesson	R2 pp. 12–17
RL.1.3	Describe characters, settings, and major events in a story	R3 pp. 18–23
RL.1.4	Identify words and phrases in stories or poems that suggest feeling or appeal to the senses	R4 pp. 24–29
RL.1.5	Explain major differences between books that tell stories and books that give information	R5 pp. 30–35
RL.1.6	Identify who is telling the story at various points in a text	R6 pp. 36–41
RL.1.7	Use illustrations and details in a story to describe its characters, setting, or events	R7 pp. 42–47
RL.1.8	NA	
RL.1.9	Compare and contrast the adventures and experiences of characters in stories	R9 pp. 54–59
RL.1.10	Read prose and poetry or appropriate complexity	R10 pp. 60–65
Reading Informational Text		
RI.1.1	Ask and answer questions about key details in a text	R1 pp. 6–11
RI.1.2	Identify the main topic and retell key details of a text	R2 pp. 12–17
RI.1.3	Describe the connection between two individuals, events, ideas, or pieces of information in a text	R3 pp. 18–23
RI.1.4	Ask and answer questions to help determine or clarify the meaning of words and phrases in a text	R4 pp. 24–29
RI.1.5	Know and use various text features to locate key facts or information in a text	R5 pp. 30–35
RI.1.6	Distinguish between information provided by illustrations and information provided by the words in a text	R6 pp. 36–41
RI.1.7	Use the illustrations and details in a text to describe its key ideas	R7 pp. 42–47
RI.1.8	Identify the reasons an author gives to support points in a text	R8 pp. 48–53
RI.1.9	Identify basic similarities and differences between two texts on the same topic	R9 pp. 54–59
RI.1.10	Read appropriately complex informational texts	R10 pp. 60–65
Reading Foundational Skills		
RF.1.1	Print Concepts: Demonstrate understanding of the organization and basic features of print	RF1 pp. 72–77
RF.1.2	Phonological Awareness: Demonstrate understanding of spoken words, syllables, and sounds (phonemes)	RF2 pp. 78–83
RF.1.3	Phonics: Know and apply grade-level phonics and word analysis skills in decoding words	RF3 pp. 84–89
RF.1.4	Fluency: Read grade-level texts with sufficient accuracy and fluency to support comprehension	RF4 pp. 90–95
Writing		
W.1.1.1	Write opinion pieces in which they introduce the topic, state an opinion, supply a reason, and provided some sense of closure	W1 pp. 100–105
W.1.2	Write informative/explanatory texts in which they name a topic, supply some facts, and provide some sense of closure	W2 pp. 106–111
W.1.3	Write narratives in which they recount two or more appropriately sequenced events, include some details, use temporal words to signal order, and provide some sense of closure	W3 pp. 112–117
W.1.4	NA	
W.1.5	Focus on a topic, respond to questions and suggestions, and add details to strengthen writing as needed	W5 pp. 118–123
W.1.6	Use a variety of digital tools to produce and publish some writing	W6 pp. 124–129

(Continued)

Arkansas Strand/Standard	Focus of Arkansas Standard	For More Information
Writing		
W.1.7	Participate in shared research and writing projects	W7 pp. 130–135
W.1.8	Recall information from experiences or gather information from provided sources to answer a question	W8 pp. 136–141
W.1.9	NA	
W.1.10	NA	
Speaking and Listening		
SL.1.1	Participate in collaborative conversations/discussions with diverse partners about topics and texts in small and larger groups	SL1 pp. 146–151
SL.1.2	Ask and answer questions about key details in a text read aloud or information presented orally	SL2 pp. 152–157
SL.1.3	Ask and answer questions in order to gather additional information or clarify something that is not understood	SL3 pp. 158–163
SL.1.4	Describe familiar people, places, things, and events with relevant details	SL4 pp. 164–169
SL.1.5	Add drawings or other visual displays to descriptions to clarify ideas, thoughts, and feelings	SL5 pp. 170–175
SL.1.6	Produce complete sentences when appropriate to task and situation	SL6 pp. 176–181
Language		
L.1.1	Demonstrate command of the conventions of standard English grammar and usage when writing or speaking	L1 pp. 186–191
L.1.2	Demonstrate command of the conventions of standard English capitalization, punctuation, and spelling when writing	L2 pp. 192–197
L.1.3	NA	
L.1.1.4	Determine or clarify the meaning of unknown and multiple-meaning words and phrases	L4 pp. 204–209
L.1.5	Demonstrate understanding of word relationships and nuances in word meanings	L5 pp. 210–215
L.1.6	Use words and phrases acquired through conversations, reading, being read to, and responding to texts	L6 pp. 216–221

Arkansas, Grade 2

Arkansas Strand/Standard	Focus of Arkansas Standard	For More Information
Reading Literature		
RL.2.1	Ask and answer questions such as who, what where, when, why, and how to demonstrate understanding of key details in a text	R1 pp. 6–11
RL.2.2	Recount stories, including fables and folktales from diverse cultures, and determine their central message, lesson, or moral	R2 pp. 12–17
RL.2.3	Describe how characters in a story respond to major events and challenges	R3 pp. 18–23
RL.2.4	Describe how words and phrases supply rhythm and meaning in a story, poem, or song	R4 pp. 24–29
RL.2.5	Describe the overall structure of a story, including how the beginning introduces the story and the ending concludes the action	R5 pp. 30–35
RL.2.6	Acknowledge differences in the perspectives of characters	R6 pp. 36–41
RL.2.7	Use information gained from the illustrations and words in a text to demonstrate understanding of its characters, setting, and plot	R7 pp. 42–47
RL.2.8	NA	
RL.2.9	Compare and contrast two or more versions of the same story by different authors or from different cultures	R9 pp. 54–59
RL.2.10	Read literature of appropriate complexity with proficiency	R10 pp. 60–65
Reading Informational Text		
RI.2.1	Ask and answer such questions as who, what, when, where, why, and how to demonstrate understanding of key details in a text	R1 pp. 6–11
RI.2.2	Identify the main topic as well as the focus of specific paragraphs within a text	R2 pp. 12–17
RI.2.3	Describe the connection between a series of historical events, scientific ideas or concepts, or steps in technical procedures in a text	R3 pp. 18–23

Arkansas Strand/Standard	Focus of Arkansas Standard	For More Information
Reading Informational Text		
RI.2.4	Determine the meaning of words and phrases in a text	R4 pp. 24–29
RI.2.5	Know and use various text features to locate key facts or information in a text efficiently	R5 pp. 30–35
RI.2.6	Identify the main purpose of a text, including what the author wants to answer, explain, or describe	R6 pp. 36–41
RI.2.7	Explain how specific images contribute to and clarify a text	R7 pp. 42–47
RI.2.8	Describe how an author uses reasons to support particular points	R8 pp. 48–53
RI.2.9	Compare and contrast the most important points presented by two texts on the same topic	R9 pp. 54–59
RI.2.10	Read and comprehend appropriately complex informational texts	R10 pp. 60–65
Reading Foundational Skills		
RF.2.1	Print Concepts: Demonstrate understanding of the organization and basic features of print	RF1 pp. 72–77
RF.2.2	Phonological Awareness: Demonstrate understanding of spoken words, syllables, and sounds (phonemes)	RF2 pp. 78–83
RF.2.3	Phonics: Know and apply grade-level phonics and word analysis skills in decoding words	RF3 pp. 84–89
RF.2.4	Fluency: Read grade-level texts with sufficient accuracy and fluency to support comprehension	RF4 pp. 90–95
Writing		
W.2.1	Write opinion pieces in which they introduce the topic, state an opinion, supply reasons, use linking words, and provide a concluding statement	W1 pp. 100–105
W.2.2	Write informative/explanatory texts in which they introduce a topic, use facts to develop points, and provide a concluding statement	W2 pp. 106–111
W.2.3	Write narratives in which they recount a well-elaborated event or sequenced of events; include details to describe actions, thoughts, and feelings; use temporal words to signal order; and provide a sense of closure	W3 pp. 112–117
W.2.4	NA	
W.2.5	Focus on a topic and strengthen writing as needed by revising and editing	W5 pp. 118–123
W.2.6	Use a variety of digital tools to produce and publish some writing	W6 pp. 124–129
W.2.7	Participate in shared research and writing projects	W7 pp. 130–135
W.2.8	Recall information from experiences or gather information from provided sources to answer a question	W8 pp. 136–141
W.2.9	NA	
W.2.10	NA	
Speaking and Listening		
SL.2.1	Participate in collaborative conversations/discussions with diverse partners about topics and texts in small and larger groups	SL1 pp. 146–151
SL.2.2	Recount or describe key details in a text read aloud or information presented orally	SL2 pp. 152–157
SL.2.3	Ask and answer questions in order to clarify comprehension, gather additional information, or deepen understanding	SL3 pp. 158–163
SL.2.4	Tell a story or recount an experience with appropriate facts and relevant details	SL4 pp. 164–169
SL.2.5	Create audio recordings of stories or poems; add drawings or other visual displays to clarify ideas, thoughts, and feelings	SL5 pp. 170–175
SL.2.6	Produce complete sentences when appropriate to task and situation in order to provide requested detail or clarification	SL6 pp. 176–181
Language		
L.2.1	Demonstrate command of the conventions of standard English grammar and usage when writing or speaking	L1 pp. 186–191
L.2.2	Demonstrate command of the conventions of standard English capitalization, punctuation, and spelling when writing	L2 pp. 192–197
L.2.3	NA	
L.2.4	Determine or clarify the meaning of unknown and multiple-meaning words and phrases, choosing flexibly from an array of strategies	L4 pp. 204–209
L.2.5	Demonstrate understanding of word relationships and nuances in word meanings	L5 pp. 210–215
L.2.6	Use words and phrases acquired through conversations, reading, being read to, and responding to texts	L6 pp. 216–221

Colorado, Kindergarten

Colorado Strand/Standard	Focus of Colorado Standard	For More Information
Oral Expression and Listening		
1	Oral communication skills are built within a language-rich environment	SL4 pp. 164–169 SL5 pp. 170–175 SL6 pp. 176–181 L5 pp. 210–215
2	Communication relies on effective verbal and nonverbal skills	SL1 pp. 146–151 SL2 pp. 152–157 SL3 pp. 158–163 L6 pp. 216–221
3	Vocal sounds produce words and meaning to create early knowledge of phonemic awareness	RF2 pp. 78–83
Reading for All Purposes		
1	A concept of print to read and a solid comprehension of literary texts are the building blocks for reading	R1 pp. 6–11 R2 pp. 12–17 R3 pp. 18–23 R4 pp. 24–29 R5 pp. 30–35 R6 pp. 36–41 R7 pp. 42–47 R9 pp. 54–59 R10 pp. 60–65
2	A concept of print to read and a solid comprehension of informational text are the building blocks for reading	R1 pp. 6–11 R2 pp. 12–17 R3 pp. 18–23 R4 pp. 24–29 R5 pp. 30–35 R6 pp. 36–41 R7 pp. 42–47 R8 pp. 48–53 R9 pp. 54–59 R10 pp. 60–65
3	Decoding words in print requires alphabet recognition and knowledge of letter sounds	RF1 pp. 72–77 RF2 pp. 78–83 RF3 pp. 84–89 RF4 pp. 90–95 L4 pp. 204–209
Writing and Composition		
1	Text types and purposes, labels, and familiar words are used to communicate information and ideas	W1 pp. 100–105 W2 pp. 106–111 W3 pp. 112–117 W5 pp. 118–123 W6 pp. 124–129
2	Appropriate mechanics and conventions are used to create simple texts	L1 pp. 186–191 L2 pp. 192–197
Research and Reasoning		
1	A variety of locations must be explored to find information that answers questions of interest	W8 pp. 136–141
2	Identify purpose, information, and question an issue	W7 pp. 130–135 W8 pp. 136–141
3	Quality of thinking depends on the quality of questions	SL3 pp. 158–163

Colorado, Grade 1

Colorado Strand/Standard	Focus of Colorado Standard	For More Information
Oral Expression and Listening		
1	Multiple strategies develop and expand oral vocabulary	SL4 pp. 164–169 SL5 pp. 170–175 SL6 pp. 176–181
2	Verbal and nonverbal language is used to express and receive information	SL1 pp. 146–151 SL2 pp. 152–157 SL3 pp. 158–163
3	Identifying and manipulating phonemes in spoken words allow people to understand the meaning of speech	RF2 pp. 78–83
Reading for All Purposes		
1	Comprehending and fluently reading a variety of literary texts are the beginning traits of readers	R1 pp. 6–11 R2 pp. 12–17 R3 pp. 18–23 R4 pp. 24–29 R5 pp. 30–35 R6 pp. 36–41 R7 pp. 42–47 R9 pp. 54–59 R10 pp. 60–65 RF4 pp. 90–95
2	Comprehending and fluently reading a variety of informational texts are the beginning traits of readers	R1 pp. 6–11 R2 pp. 12–17 R3 pp. 18–23 R4 pp. 24–29 R5 pp. 30–35 R6 pp. 36–41 R7 pp. 42–47 R8 pp. 48–53 R9 pp. 54–59 R10 pp. 60–65 RF4 pp. 90–95
3	Decoding words require the application of alphabetic principles, letter sounds, and letter combinations	RF1 pp. 72–77 RF2 pp. 78–83 RF3 pp. 84–89
4	Understanding word structure, word relationships, and word families needs to be demonstrated to begin to read	L4 pp. 204–209 L5 pp. 210–215 L6 pp. 216–221 RF1 pp. 72–77
Writing and Composition		
1	Exploring the writing process develops ideas for writing texts that carry meaning	W1 pp. 100–105 W2 pp. 106–111 W3 pp. 112–117 W5 pp. 118–123 W6 pp. 124–129
2	Appropriate spelling, conventions, and grammar are applied when writing	L1 pp. 186–191 L2 pp. 192–197
Research and Reasoning		
1	A variety of resources leads to locating information and answering questions of interest	W8 pp. 136–141
2	Purpose, information, and questions about an issue are essential steps in early research	W7 pp. 130–135 W8 pp. 136–141

Colorado, Grade 2

Colorado Strand/Standard	Focus of Colorado Standard	For More Information
Oral Expression and Listening		
1	Discussions contribute and expand on the ideas of self and others	SL4 pp. 164–169 SL5 pp. 170–175 SL6 pp. 176–181
2	New information can be learned and better dialogue created by listening actively	SL1 pp. 146–151 SL2 pp. 152–157 SL3 pp. 158–163
Reading for All Purposes		
1	Fluent reading depends on specific skills and approaches to understanding strategies when reading literary texts	R1 pp. 6–11 R2 pp. 12–17 R3 pp. 18–23 R4 pp. 24–29 R5 pp. 30–35 R6 pp. 36–41 R7 pp. 42–47 R9 pp. 54–59 R10 pp. 60–65 L3 pp. 198–203
2	Fluent reading depends on specific skills and approaches to understanding strategies when reading literary texts	R1 pp. 6–11 R2 pp. 12–17 R3 pp. 18–23 R4 pp. 24–29 R5 pp. 30–35 R6 pp. 36–41 R7 pp. 42–47 R8 pp. 48–53 R9 pp. 54–59 R10 pp. 60–65 L2 pp. 192–197
3	Decoding words with accuracy depends on knowledge of complex spelling patterns and morphology	RF3 pp. 84–89 RF4 pp. 90–95 L4 pp. 204–209 L5 pp. 210–215 L6 pp. 216–221
Writing and Composition		
1	Exploring the writing process helps to plan and draft a variety of literary genres	W1 pp. 100–105 W3 pp. 112–117
2	Exploring the writing process helps to plan and draft a variety of simple informational texts	W2 pp. 106–111
2	Appropriate spelling, capitalization, grammar, and punctuation are used and applied when writing	L1 pp. 186–191 L2 pp. 192–197 W5 pp. 118–123 W6 pp. 124–129
Research and Reasoning		
1	Reference materials help us locate information and answer questions	W8 pp. 136–141
2	Questions are essential to analyze and evaluate the quality of thinking	W7 pp. 130–135

Florida, Kindergarten

Florida Strand/Standard	Focus of Florida Standard	For More Information
Reading Literature		
K.RL.1.1	Ask and answer questions about key details in a text	R1 pp. 6–11
K.RL.1.2	Retell familiar stories, including key details	R2 pp. 12–17
K.RL.1.3	Identify characters, settings, and major events in a story	R3 pp. 18–23
K.RL.2.4	Ask and answer questions about unknown words in a text	R4 pp. 24–29
K.RL.2.5	Recognize common types of text (e.g., storybooks, poems)	R5 pp. 30–35
K.RL.2.6	Name the author and illustrator of a story and define the role of each	R6 pp. 36–41
K.RL.3.7	Describe the relationship between the illustrations and the story in which they appear	R7 pp. 42–47
K.RL.3.8	NA	
K.RL.3.9	Compare and contrast the characters in familiar stories	R9 pp. 54–59
K.RL.4.10	Actively engage in reading activities with purpose and understanding	R10 pp. 60–65
Reading Informational Text		
K.RI.1.1	Ask and answer questions about key details in a text	R1 pp. 6–11
K.RI.1.2	Identify the main topic and retell key details of a text	R2 pp. 12–17
K.RI.1.3	Describe the connection between two individuals, events, ideas, or pieces of information in a text	R3 pp. 18–23
K.RI.2.4	Ask and answer questions about unknown words in a text	R4 pp. 24–29
K.RI.2.5	Identify the front cover, back cover, and title page of a book	R5 pp. 30–35
K.RI.2.6	Name the author and illustrator of a text and define the role of each	R6 pp. 36–41
K.RI.3.7	Describe the relationship between visual images and the text in which they appear	R7 pp. 42–47
K.RI.3.8	Identify the reasons an author gives to support points in a text	R8 pp. 48–53
K.RI.3.9	Identify basic similarities and differences between two texts on the same topic	R9 pp. 54–59
K.RI.4.10	Actively engage in reading informational text with purpose and understanding	R10 pp. 60–65
Reading Foundational Skills		
K.RF.1.1	Print Concepts: Demonstrate understanding of the organization and basic features of print	RF1 pp. 72–77
K.RF.2.2	Phonological Awareness: Demonstrate understanding of spoken words, syllables, and sounds (phonemes)	RF2 pp. 78–83
K.RF.3.3	Phonics: Know and apply grade-level phonics and word analysis skills in decoding words	RF3 pp. 84–89
K.RF.4.4	Fluency: Read level-appropriate texts with purpose and understanding	RF4 pp. 90–95
Writing		
K.W.1.1	Use a combination of drawing, dictating, and writing to compose opinion pieces	W1 pp. 100–105
K.W.1.2	Use a combination of drawing, dictating, and writing to compose informative/explanatory texts	W2 pp. 106–111
K.W.1.3	Use a combination of drawing, dictating, and writing to narrate a single event or several loosely linked events and provide a reaction to what happened	W3 pp. 112–117

(Continued)

Florida Strand/Standard	Focus of Florida Standard	For More Information
Writing		
K.W.2.5	Respond to questions and add details to strengthen writing as needed	W5 pp. 118–123
K.W.2.6	Explore a variety of digital tools to produce and publish writing	W6 pp. 124–129
K.W.3.7	Participate in shared research and writing projects	W7 pp. 130–135
K.W.3.8	Recall information from experiences or gather information from provided sources to answer a question	W8 pp. 136–141
Speaking and Listening		
K.SL.1.1	Participate in collaborative conversations with diverse partners about topics and texts in small and larger groups	SL1 pp. 146–151
K.SL.1.2	Ask and answer questions about key details to demonstrate understanding of a topic	SL2 pp. 152–157
K.SL.1.3	Ask and answer questions in order to seek help, get information, or clarify something that is not understood	SL3 pp. 158–163
K.SL.2.4	Describe familiar people, places, things, and events	SL4 pp. 164–169
K.SL.2.5	Add drawings or other visual displays to descriptions to provide additional detail	SL5 pp. 170–175
K.SL.2.6	Speak audibly and express thoughts, ideas, feelings, and ideas clearly	SL6 pp. 176–181
Language		
K.L.1.1	Demonstrate command of the conventions of standard English grammar and usage when writing or speaking	L1 pp. 186–191
K.L.1.2	Demonstrate command of the conventions of standard English capitalization, punctuation, and spelling when writing	L2 pp. 192–197
K.L.3.4	Determine or clarify the meaning of unknown and multiple-meaning words and phrases	L4 pp. 204–209
K.L.3.5	Explore word relationships and nuances in word meanings	L5 pp. 210–215
K.L.3.6	Use words and phrases acquired through conversations, reading, being read to, and responding to texts	L6 pp. 216–221

Florida, Grade 1

Florida Strand/Standard	Focus of Florida Standard	For More Information
Reading Literature		
1.RL.1.1	Ask and answer questions about key details in a text	R1 pp. 6–11
1.RL.1.2	Retell stories, including key details, and demonstrate understanding of their central message	R2 pp. 12–17
1.RL.1.3	Describe characters, settings, and major events in a story	R3 pp. 18–23
1.RL.2.4	Identify words or phrases that suggest feelings or appeal to the senses	R4 pp. 24–29
1.RL.2.5	Explain major differences between stories and informative texts	R5 pp. 30–35
1.RL.2.6	Identify who is telling the story at various points in a text	R6 pp. 36–41
1.RL.3.7	Use illustrations to describe elements of a story	R7 pp. 42–47

Florida Strand/Standard	Focus of Florida Standard	For More Information
Reading Literature		
1.RL.3.9	Compare and contrast the experiences of characters in stories	R9 pp. 54–59
1.RL.4.10	Read texts of appropriate complexity	R10 pp. 60–65
Reading Informational Text		
1.RI.1.1	Ask and answer questions about key details in a text	R1 pp. 6–11
1.RI..1.2	Identify the main topic and retell key details of a text	R2 pp. 12–17
1.RI.1.3	Describe the connection between two individuals, events, ideas, or pieces of information in a text	R3 pp. 18–23
1.RI.2.4	Ask and answer questions to clarify the meaning of words in a text	R4 pp. 24–29
1.RI.2.5	Use text features to locate information in a text	R5 pp. 30–35
1.RI.2.6	Distinguish between information provided by illustrations and information provided by words	R6 pp. 36–41
1.RI.3.7	Use illustrations and details to describe key ideas in a text	R7 pp. 42–47
1.RI.3.8	Identify the reasons an author gives to support points in a text	R8 pp. 48–53
1.RI.3.9	Identify basic similarities and differences between two texts on the same topic	R9 pp. 54–59
1.RI.4.10	Actively engage in reading informational text of appropriate complexity	R10 pp. 60–65
Reading Foundational Skills		
1.RF.1.1	Print Concepts: Demonstrate understanding of the organization and basic features of print	RF1 pp. 72–77
1.RF.2.2	Phonological Awareness: Demonstrate understanding of spoken words, syllables, and sounds (phonemes)	RF2 pp. 78–83
1.RF.3.3	Phonics: Know and apply grade-level phonics and word analysis skills in decoding words	RF3 pp. 84–89
1.RF.4.4	Fluency: Read level-appropriate texts with accuracy and fluency	RF4 pp. 90–95
Writing		
1.W.1.1	Write opinion pieces: introduce the topic, state an opinion, supply reasons, and provide closure	W1 pp. 100–105
1.W.1.2	Write informative/explanatory texts: name a topic, supply facts, and provide closure	W2 pp. 106–111
1.W.1.3	Write narratives: sequence events, include details, use temporal words, and provide closure	W3 pp. 112–117
1.W.2.5	Focus on a topic, respond to questions, and add details to strengthen writing as needed	W5 pp. 118–123
1.W.2.6	Use a variety of digital tools to produce and publish writing	W6 pp. 124–129
1.W.3.7	Participate in shared research and writing projects	W7 pp. 130–135
1.W.3.8	Recall information from experiences or gather information from provided sources to answer a question	W8 pp. 136–141
Speaking and Listening		
1.SL.1.1	Participate in collaborative conversations with diverse partners about topics and texts in small and larger groups	SL1 pp. 146–151
1.SL.1.2	Ask and answer questions about key details to demonstrate understanding of a topic	SL2 pp. 152–157

(Continued)

Florida Strand/Standard	Focus of Florida Standard	For More Information
Speaking and Listening		
1.SL.1.3	Ask and answer questions in order to get information or clarify something that is not understood	SL3 pp. 158–163
1.SL.2.4	Clearly describe people, places, things, and events with relevant details	SL4 pp. 164–169
1.SL.2.5	Add drawings or other visual displays to descriptions to provide additional detail	SL5 pp. 170–175
1.SL.2.6	Produce complete sentences when appropriate to task and situation	SL6 pp. 176–181
Language		
1.L.1.1	Demonstrate command of the conventions of standard English grammar and usage when writing or speaking	L1 pp. 186–191
1.L.1.2	Demonstrate command of the conventions of standard English capitalization, punctuation, and spelling when writing	L2 pp. 192–197
1.L.3.4	Determine or clarify the meaning of unknown and multiple-meaning words and phrases	L4 pp. 204–209
1.L.3.5	Demonstrate understanding of word relationships and nuances in word meanings	L5 pp. 210–215
1.L.3.6	Use words and phrases acquired through conversations, reading, being read to, and responding to texts	L6 pp. 216–221

Florida, Grade 2

Florida Strand/Standard	Focus of Florida Standard	For More Information
Reading Literature		
2.RL.1.1	Ask and answer questions to demonstrate understanding of key details in a text	R1 pp. 6–11
2.RL.1.2	Recount stories and determine their central message, lesson, or moral	R2 pp. 12–17
2.RL.1.3	Describe how characters respond to major events and challenges	R3 pp. 18–23
2.RL.2.4	Describe how words or phrases supply rhythm and meaning	R4 pp. 24–29
2.RL.2.5	Describe the overall structure of a story, including the beginning and ending	R5 pp. 30–35
2.RL.2.6	Acknowledge differences in characters' points of view	R6 pp. 36–41
2.RL.3.7	Use information gathered from illustrations and words to demonstrate understanding of story elements	R7 pp. 42–47
2.RL.3.9	Compare and contrast two or more versions of the same story	R9 pp. 54–59
2.RL.4.10	Read and comprehend texts of appropriate complexity	R10 pp. 60–65
Reading Informational Text		
2.RI.1.1	Ask and answer questions to demonstrate understanding of key details in a text	R1 pp. 6–11
2.RI.1.2	Identify the main topic as well as the focus of specific paragraphs within a text	R2 pp. 12–17
2.RI.1.3	Describe the connection between a series of events, ideas, concepts, or steps in a text	R3 pp. 18–23
2.RI.2.4	Determine the meaning of words and phrases in a text relevant to a grade-level topic	R4 pp. 24–29
2.RI.2.5	Use text features to efficiently locate information in a text	R5 pp. 30–35

Florida Strand/Standard	Focus of Florida Standard	For More Information
Reading Informational Text		
2.RI.2.6	Identify the main purpose of a text	R6 pp. 36–41
2.RI.3.7	Explain how specific images contribute to and clarify a text	R7 pp. 42–47
2.RI.3.8	Describe how reasons an author gives support points in a text	R8 pp. 48–53
2.RI.3.9	Compare and contrast the most important points in two texts on the same topic	R9 pp. 54–59
2.RI.4.10	Read and comprehend informational texts of appropriate complexity	R10 pp. 60–65
Reading Foundational Skills		
2.RF.3.3	Phonics: Know and apply grade-level phonics and word analysis skills in decoding words	RF3 pp. 84–89
2.RF.4.4	Fluency: Read level-appropriate texts with accuracy and fluency	RF4 pp. 90–95
Writing		
2.W.1.1	Write opinion pieces: introduce the topic, state an opinion, supply reasons using linking words, and provide closure	W1 pp. 100–105
2.W.1.2	Write informative/explanatory texts: introduce a topic, use facts to develop points, and provide closure	W2 pp. 106–111
2.W.1.3	Write narratives: sequence events; include details to describe actions, thoughts, and feelings; use temporal words; provide closure	W3 pp. 112–117
2.W.2.5	Focus on a topic and strengthen writing by revising and editing	W5 pp. 118–123
2.W.2.6	Use a variety of digital tools to produce and publish writing	W6 pp. 124–129
2.W.3.7	Participate in shared research and writing projects	W7 pp. 130–135
2.W.3.8	Recall information from experiences or gather information from provided sources to answer a question	W8 pp. 136–141
2.SL.1.1	Participate in collaborative conversations with diverse partners about topics and texts in small and larger groups	SL1 pp. 146–151
2.SL.1.2	Recount or describe key ideas or details in information presented orally	SL2 pp. 152–157
2.SL.1.3	Ask and answer questions in order to clarify comprehension, get additional information, or deepen understanding	SL3 pp. 158–163
2.SL.2.4	Tell a story or recount an experience with appropriate facts and relevant details	SL4 pp. 164–169
2.SL.2.5	Create audio recordings of stories or poems, adding visual displays as appropriate for clarification	SL5 pp. 170–175
2.SL.2.6	Produce complete sentences when appropriate to task and situation	SL6 pp. 176–181
Language		
2.L.1.1	Demonstrate command of the conventions of standard English grammar and usage when writing or speaking	L1 pp. 186–191
2.L.1.2	Demonstrate command of the conventions of standard English capitalization, punctuation, and spelling when writing	L2 pp. 192–197
2.L.2.3	Use knowledge of language and its conventions when writing, speaking, reading, or listening	L3 pp. 198–203
2.L.3.4	Determine or clarify the meaning of unknown and multiple-meaning words and phrases	L4 pp. 204–209
2.L.3.5	Demonstrate understanding of word relationships and nuances in word meanings	L5 pp. 210–215
2.L.3.6	Use words and phrases acquired through conversations, reading, being read to, and responding to texts	L6 pp. 216–221

Georgia, Kindergarten

Georgia Strand/Standard	Focus of Georgia Standard	For More Information
Reading Literature		
RL.1	Ask and answer questions about key details in a text	R1 pp. 6–11
RL.2	Retell familiar stories, including key details	R2 pp. 12–17
RL.3	Identify characters, settings, and major events in a story	R3 pp. 18–23
RL.4	Ask and answer questions about unknown words in a text	R4 pp. 24–29
RL.5	Recognize common types of text (e.g., storybooks, poems)	R5 pp. 30–35
RL.6	Name the author and illustrator of a story and define the role of each	R6 pp. 36–41
RL.7	Describe the relationship between the illustrations and the story in which they appear	R7 pp. 42–47
RL.8	NA	
RL.9	Compare and contrast the characters in familiar stories	R9 pp. 54–59
RL.10	Actively engage in reading activities with purpose and understanding	R10 pp. 60–65
Reading Informational Text		
RI.1	Ask and answer questions about key details in a text	R1 pp. 6–11
RI.2	Identify the main topic and retell key details of a text	R2 pp. 12–17
RI.3	Describe the connection between two individuals, events, ideas, or pieces of information in a text	R3 pp. 18–23
RI.4	Ask and answer questions about unknown words in a text	R4 pp. 24–29
RI.5	Identify the front cover, back cover, and title page of a book	R5 pp. 30–35
RI.6	Name the author and illustrator of a text and define the role of each	R6 pp. 36–41
RI.7	Describe the relationship between illustrations and the text in which they appear	R7 pp. 42–47
RI.8	Identify the reasons an author gives to support points in a text	R8 pp. 48–53
RI.9	Identify basic similarities and differences between two texts on the same topic	R9 pp. 54–59
RI.10	Actively engage in reading informational text with purpose and understanding	R10 pp. 60–65
Reading Foundational Skills		
RF.1	Print Concepts: Demonstrate understanding of the organization and basic features of print	RF1 pp. 72–77
RF.2	Phonological Awareness: Demonstrate understanding of spoken words, syllables, and sounds (phonemes)	RF2 pp. 78–83
RF.3	Phonics: Know and apply grade-level phonics and word analysis skills in decoding words	RF3 pp. 84–89
RF.4	Fluency: Read common high-frequency words by sight; read level-appropriate texts with purpose and understanding	RF4 pp. 90–95

Georgia Strand/Standard	Focus of Georgia Standard	For More Information
Writing		
W.1	Use a combination of drawing, dictating, and writing to compose opinion pieces	W1 pp. 100–105
W.2	Use a combination of drawing, dictating, and writing to compose informative/explanatory texts	W2 pp. 106–111
W.3	Use a combination of drawing, dictating, and writing to narrate a single event or several loosely linked events and provide a reaction to what happened	W3 pp. 112–117
W.4	NA	
W.5	Respond to questions and add details to strengthen writing as needed	W5 pp. 118–123
W.6	Explore a variety of tools, including digital, to produce and publish writing	W6 pp. 124–129
W.7	Participate in shared research and writing projects	W7 pp. 130–135
W.8	Recall information from experiences or gather information from provided sources to answer a question	W8 pp. 136–141
W.9	NA	
W.10	NA	
Speaking and Listening		
SL.1	Participate in collaborative conversations with diverse partners about topics and texts in small and larger groups	SL1 pp. 146–151
SL.2	Ask and answer questions about key details to demonstrate understanding of information presented orally	SL2 pp. 152–157
SL.3	Ask and answer questions in order to seek help, get information, or clarify something that is not understood	SL3 pp. 158–163
SL.4	Describe familiar people, places, things, and events	SL4 pp. 164–169
SL.5	Add drawings or other visual displays to descriptions to provide additional detail	SL5 pp. 170–175
SL.6	Speak audibly and express thoughts, ideas, feelings, and ideas clearly	SL6 pp. 176–181
Language		
L.1	Demonstrate command of the conventions of standard English grammar and usage when writing or speaking	L1 pp. 186–191
L.2	Demonstrate command of the conventions of standard English capitalization, punctuation, and spelling when writing	L2 pp. 192–197
L.3	NA	
L.4	Determine or clarify the meaning of unknown and multiple-meaning words and phrases	L4 pp. 204–209
L.5	Explore word relationships and nuances in word meanings	L5 pp. 210–215
L.6	Use words and phrases acquired through conversations, reading, being read to, and responding to texts	L6 pp. 216–221

Georgia, Grade 1

Georgia Strand/Standard	Focus of Georgia Standard	For More Information
Reading Literature		
RL.1	Ask and answer questions about key details in a text	R1 pp. 6–11
RL.2	Retell stories, including key details	R2 pp. 12–17
RL.3	Describe characters, settings, and major events in a story	R3 pp. 18–23
RL.4	Identify words or phrases that suggest feelings or appeal to the senses	R4 pp. 24–29
RL.5	Explain major differences between stories and informative texts	R5 pp. 30–35
RL.6	Identify who is telling the story at various points in a text	R6 pp. 36–41
RL.7	Use the illustrations to describe elements of a story	R7 pp. 42–47
RL.8	NA	
RL.9	Compare and contrast the experiences of characters in stories	R9 pp. 54–59
RL.10	Read literary texts of appropriate complexity	R10 pp. 60–65
Reading Informational Text		
RI.1	Ask and answer questions about key details in a text	R1 pp. 6–11
RI.2	Identify the main topic and retell key details of a text	R2 pp. 12–17
RI.3	Describe the connection between two individuals, events, ideas, or pieces of information in a text	R3 pp. 18–23
RI.4	Ask and answer questions to clarify the meaning of words in a text	R4 pp. 24–29
RI.5	Use text features to locate information in a text	R5 pp. 30–35
RI.6	Distinguish between information provided by illustrations and information provided by words	R6 pp. 36–41
RI.7	Use illustrations and details to describe key ideas in a text	R7 pp. 42–47
RI.8	Identify the reasons an author gives to support points in a text	R8 pp. 48–53
RI.9	Identify basic similarities and differences between two texts on the same topic	R9 pp. 54–59
RI.10	Actively engage in reading informational text with purpose and understanding	R10 pp. 60–65
Reading Foundational Skills		
RF.1	Print Concepts: Demonstrate understanding of the organization and basic features of print	RF1 pp. 72–77
RF.2	Phonological Awareness: Demonstrate understanding of spoken words, syllables, and sounds (phonemes)	RF2 pp. 78–83
RF.3	Phonics: Know and apply grade-level phonics and word analysis skills in decoding words	RF3 pp. 84–89
RF.4	Fluency: Read level-appropriate texts with accuracy and fluency	RF4 pp. 90–95

Georgia Strand/Standard	Focus of Georgia Standard	For More Information
Writing		
W.1	Write opinion pieces: introduce the topic, state an opinion, supply reasons, and provide closure	W1 pp. 100–105
W.2	Write informative/explanatory texts: name a topic, supply facts, and provide closure	W2 pp. 106–111
W.3	Write narratives: sequence events, include details, use temporal words, and provide closure	W3 pp. 112–117
W.4	NA	
W.5	Focus on a topic, respond to questions, and add details to strengthen writing as needed	W5 pp. 118–123
W.6	Use a variety of tools, including digital, to produce and publish writing	W6 pp. 124–129
W.7	Participate in shared research and writing projects	W7 pp. 130–135
W.8	Recall information from experiences or gather information from provided sources to answer a question	W8 pp. 136–141
W.9	NA	
W.10	NA	
Speaking and Listening		
SL.1	Participate in collaborative conversations with diverse partners about topics and texts in small and larger groups	SL1 pp. 146–151
SL.2	Ask and answer questions about key details in information presented orally	SL2 pp. 152–157
SL.3	Ask and answer questions in order to get information or clarify something that is not understood	SL3 pp. 158–163
SL.4	Clearly describe people, places, things, and events	SL4 pp. 164–169
SL.5	Add drawings or other visual displays to descriptions to provide additional detail	SL5 pp. 170–175
SL.6	Produce complete sentences when appropriate to task and situation	SL6 pp. 176–181
Language		
L.1	Demonstrate command of the conventions of standard English grammar and usage when writing or speaking	L1 pp. 186–191
L.2	Demonstrate command of the conventions of standard English capitalization, punctuation, and spelling when writing	L2 pp. 192–197
L.3	NA	
L.4	Determine or clarify the meaning of unknown and multiple-meaning words and phrases	L4 pp. 204–209
L.5	Demonstrate understanding of word relationships and nuances in word meanings	L5 pp. 210–215
L.6	Use words and phrases acquired through conversations, reading, being read to, and responding to texts	L6 pp. 216–221

Georgia, Grade 2

Georgia Strand/Standard	Focus of Georgia Standard	For More Information
Reading Literature		
RL.1	Ask and answer questions to demonstrate understanding of key details in a text	R1 pp. 6–11
RL.2	Recount stories and determine their central message	R2 pp. 12–17
RL.3	Describe how characters respond to major events and challenges	R3 pp. 18–23
RL.4	Describe how words or phrases supply rhythm and meaning	R4 pp. 24–29
RL.5	Describe the overall structure of a story, including the beginning, middle, and ending	R5 pp. 30–35
RL.6	Acknowledge differences in characters' points of view	R6 pp. 36–41
RL.7	Use information gathered from illustrations and words to demonstrate understanding of story elements	R7 pp. 42–47
RL.8	NA	
RL.9	Compare and contrast two or more versions of the same story	R9 pp. 54–59
RL.10	Read and comprehend texts of appropriate complexity	R10 pp. 60–65
Reading Informational Text		
RI.1	Ask and answer questions to demonstrate understanding of key details in a text	R1 pp. 6–11
RI.2	Identify the main topic and retell key details of a text, as well as the focus of specific paragraphs	R2 pp. 12–17
RI.3	Describe the connection between a series of events, ideas, concepts, or steps in a text	R3 pp. 18–23
RI.4	Determine the meaning of words and phrases in a text relevant to a grade-level topic	R4 pp. 24–29
RI.5	Use text features to efficiently locate information in a text	R5 pp. 30–35
RI.6	Identify the main purpose of a text	R6 pp. 36–41
RI.7	Explain how specific images contribute to and clarify a text	R7 pp. 42–47
RI.8	Describe how reasons an author gives support points in a text	R8 pp. 48–53
RI.9	Compare and contrast the most important points in two texts on the same topic	R9 pp. 54–59
RI.10	Read and comprehend informational texts of appropriate complexity	R10 pp. 60–65
Reading Foundational Skills		
RF.1	NA	
RF.2	NA	
RF.3	Phonics: Know and apply grade-level phonics and word analysis skills in decoding words	RF3 pp. 84–89
RF.4	Fluency: Read level-appropriate texts with accuracy and fluency	RF4 pp. 90–95

Georgia Strand/Standard	Focus of Georgia Standard	For More Information
Writing		
W.1	Write opinion pieces: introduce the topic, state an opinion, supply reasons using linking words, and provide closure	W1 pp. 100–105
W.2	Write informative/explanatory texts: name a topic, use facts to develop points, and provide closure	W2 pp. 106–111
W.3	Write narratives: sequence events; include details to describe actions, thoughts, and feelings; use temporal words; provide closure	W3 pp. 112–117
W.4	NA	
W.5	Focus on a topic and strengthen writing by revising and editing	W5 pp. 118–123
W.6	Use a variety of tools, including digital, to produce and publish writing	W6 pp. 124–129
W.7	Participate in shared research and writing projects	W7 pp. 130–135
W.8	Recall information from experiences or gather information from provided sources to answer a question	W8 pp. 136–141
W.9	NA	
W.10	NA	
Speaking and Listening		
SL.1	Participate in collaborative conversations with diverse partners about topics and texts in small and larger groups	SL1 pp. 146–151
SL.2	Recount or describe key ideas or details in information presented orally	SL2 pp. 152–157
SL.3	Ask and answer questions in order to get additional information, deepen understanding, or clarify something that is not understood	SL3 pp. 158–163
SL.4	Tell a story or recount an experience with appropriate facts and relevant details	SL4 pp. 164–169
SL.5	Create audio recordings of stories or poems, adding visual displays as appropriate for clarification	SL5 pp. 170–175
SL.6	Produce complete sentences when appropriate to task and situation	SL6 pp. 176–181
Language		
L.1	Demonstrate command of the conventions of standard English grammar and usage when writing or speaking	L1 pp. 186–191
L.2	Demonstrate command of the conventions of standard English capitalization, punctuation, and spelling when writing	L2 pp. 192–197
L.3	Use knowledge of language and its conventions when writing, speaking, reading, or listening	L3 pp. 198–203
L.4	Determine or clarify the meaning of unknown and multiple-meaning words and phrases	L4 pp. 204–209
L.5	Demonstrate understanding of word relationships and nuances in word meanings	L5 pp. 210–215
L.6	Use words and phrases acquired through conversations, reading, being read to, and responding to texts	L6 pp. 216–221

Indiana, Kindergarten

Indiana Strand/Standard	Focus of Indiana Standard	For More Information
Reading Foundational Skills		
RF.2	Print Concepts: Demonstrate understanding of the organization and basic features of print	RF1 pp. 72–77
RF.3	Phonological Awareness: Demonstrate understanding of spoken words, syllables, and sounds (phonemes)	RF2 pp. 78–83
RF.4	Phonics: Know and apply grade-level phonics and word analysis skills in decoding words	RF3 pp. 84–89
RF.5	Fluency: Read level-appropriate texts with purpose and understanding	RF4 pp. 90–95
Reading Literature		
RL.1	Actively engage in reading activities with purpose and understanding	R10 pp. 60–65
RL.2.1	Ask and answer questions about key details in a text	R1 pp. 6–11
RL.2.2	Retell familiar stories, including key details	R2 pp. 12–17
RL.2.3	Identify characters, settings, and major events in a story	R3 pp. 18–23
RL.3.1	Recognize common types of text (e.g., storybooks, poems)	R5 pp. 30–35
RL.3.2	Name the author and illustrator of a story and define the role of each	R6 pp. 36–41
RL.4.1	Describe the relationship between the illustrations and the story in which they appear	R7 pp. 42–47
RL.4.2	Compare and contrast the characters in familiar stories	R9 pp. 54–59
Reading Nonfiction Text		
RN.1	Actively engage in reading informational text with purpose and understanding	R10 pp. 60–65
RN.2.1	Ask and answer questions about key details in a text	R1 pp. 6–11
RN.2.2	Identify the main topic and retell key details of a text	R2 pp. 12–17
RN.2.3	Describe the connection between two individuals, events, ideas, or pieces of information in a text	R3 pp. 18–23
RN.3.1	Identify the features of a nonfiction text	R5 pp. 30–35
RN.3.2	Recognize that nonfiction can be structured to describe a topic	R6 pp. 36–41
RN.4.1	Identify the reasons an author gives to support points in a text	R8 pp. 48–53
RN.4.2	Identify basic similarities and differences between two texts on the same topic	R9 pp. 54–59
Reading Vocabulary		
RV.1	Use words and phrases acquired through conversations, reading, being read to, and responding to texts	L6 pp. 216–221
RV2.2	Identify and sort pictures of objects into categories	L5 pp. 210–215
RV.2.4	Recognize frequently occurring inflections	L4 pp. 204–209
RV.3.1	Ask and answer questions about unknown words in a literary text	R4 pp. 24–29
RV.3.2	Ask and answer questions about unknown words in a nonfiction text	R4 pp. 24–29
Writing		
W.1	Write for specific purposes and audiences	NA
W.2	Demonstrate the ability to write legibly	NA
W.3.1	Use words and pictures to provide logical reasons for suggesting others follow a particular course of action	W1 pp. 100–105
W.3.2	Use words and pictures to develop a main idea and provide some information about a topic	W2 pp. 106–111

Indiana Strand/Standard	Focus of Indiana Standard	For More Information
Writing		
W.3.3	Use words and pictures to narrate a single event or simple story	W3 pp. 112–117
W.4	Revise writing by adding details; review writing for format and conventions; use available technology to produce and publish writing	W5 pp. 118–123 W6 pp. 124–129 L2 pp. 192–197
W.5	Build understanding of a topic using various sources	W8 pp. 136–141
W.6.1	Demonstrate command of the conventions of standard English grammar and usage	L1 pp. 186–191
W.6.2	Demonstrate a command of capitalization, punctuation, and spelling	L2 pp. 192–197
Speaking and Listening		
SL.1	Listen actively and communicate effectively	SL1 pp. 146–151 SL2 pp. 152–157 SL3 pp. 158–163
SL.2.1	Participate in collaborative conversations with diverse partners about topics and texts in small and larger groups	SL1 pp. 146–151
SL.2.3	Listen to others, take turns speaking, add one's own ideas to discussions	SL1 pp. 146–151
SL.2.4	Ask questions in order to seek help, get information, or clarify something that is not understood	SL3 pp. 158–163
SL.2.5	Continue a conversation through multiple exchanges	SL1 pp. 146–151
SL.3.1	Ask and answer questions about key details to demonstrate understanding of a topic	SL2 pp. 152–157
SL.3.2	Ask appropriate questions about what a speaker says	SL2 pp. 152–157
SL.4.1	Speaking audibly; recite poems, rhymes, and songs; and describe familiar people, places, things, and events	SL4 pp. 164–169 SL6 pp. 176–181
SL.4.3	Give, restate, and follow directions	NA

Indiana, Grade 1

Indiana Strand/Standard	Focus of Indiana Standard	For More Information
Reading Foundational Skills		
RF.2	Print Concepts: NA	RF1 pp. 72–77
RF.3	Phonological Awareness: Demonstrate understanding a nd apply knowledge of spoken words, syllables, and sounds	RF2 pp. 78–83
RF.4	Phonics: Know and apply grade-level phonics and word analysis skills in decoding words	RF3 pp. 84–89
RF.5	Fluency: Orally read level-appropriate texts smoothly and accurately and with expression	RF4 pp. 90–95
Reading Literature		
RL.1	Read and comprehend literature that is level appropriate	R10 pp. 60–65
RL.2.1	Ask and answer questions about main idea and key details in a text	R1 pp. 6–11
RL.2.2	Retell stories in sequence, including key details; demonstrate understanding of their central message	R2 pp. 12–17
RL.2.3	Identify and describe the elements of plot, character, and setting	R3 pp. 18–23
RL.3.1	Identify the basic characteristics of familiar narrative text genres	R5 pp. 30–35
RL.3.2	Identify who is telling the story at various points in a text	R6 pp. 36–41

(Continued)

Indiana Strand/Standard	Focus of Indiana Standard	For More Information
Reading Literature		
RL.4.1	Use illustrations and details in a story to describe its characters, setting, or events	R7 pp. 42–47
RL.4.2	Compare and contrast the characters in stories	R9 pp. 54–59
Reading Nonfiction Text		
RN.1	Read and comprehend level-appropriate nonfiction texts	R10 pp. 60–65
RN.2.1	Ask and answer questions about key details in a text to confirm understanding	R1 pp. 6–11
RN.2.2	Retell main ideas and key details of a text	R2 pp. 12–17
RN.2.3	Describe the connection between two individuals, events, or ideas in a text	R3 pp. 18–23
RN.3.1	Use text features to locate and describe key facts or information in a text	R5 pp. 30–35
RN.3.2	Identify how a nonfiction can be structured to explain a cause–effect relationship	R6 pp. 36–41
RN.4.1	Identify the reasons an author gives to support points in a text	R8 pp. 48–53
RN.4.2	Identify similarities and differences between two texts on the same topic	R9 pp. 54–59
Reading Vocabulary		
RV.1	Use words and phrases acquired through conversations, reading, being read to, and responding to texts	L6 pp. 216–221
RV2.1	Understand that context clues and text features can be used to determine the meaning of unknown words	L4 pp. 204–209
RV2.2	Define and sort words into categories	L5 pp. 210–215
RV.2.4	Recognize and use frequently occurring affixes and roots as clues to the meaning of unknown words	L4 pp. 204–209
RV.3.1	Identify words and phrases in texts that suggest feelings or appeal to the senses	R4 pp. 24–29
RV.3.2	Ask and answer questions to help determine or clarify the meaning of words in nonfiction text	R4 pp. 24–29
Writing		
W.1	Write routinely for specific purposes and audiences	NA
W.2	Demonstrate the ability to write legibly	NA
W.3.1	Write a logically connected sentences to make a proposal and give reasons to support it	W1 pp. 100–105
W.3.2	Develop a topic sentence or main idea, provide some facts about the topic, and provide a concluding statement	W2 pp. 106–111
W.3.3	Develop topics for literary texts; use precise words to describe characters and actions and temporal words to signal order; organize ideas into beginning, middle, and ending	W3 pp. 112–117
W.4	Select and organize ideas; revise writing, adding details; edit writing for format and conventions; use available technology to produce and publish writing	W5 pp. 118–123 W6 pp. 124–129 L2 pp. 192–197
W.5	Conduct simple research on a topic; identify sources; gather, organize, and present information	W7 pp. 132–137 W8 pp. 136–141
W.6.1	Demonstrate command of the conventions of standard English grammar and usage	L1 pp. 186–191
W.6.2	Demonstrate a command of capitalization, punctuation, and spelling	L2 pp. 192–197
Speaking and Listening		
SL.1	Listen actively and communicate effectively	SL1 pp. 146–151 SL2 pp. 152–157 SL3 pp. 158–163
SL.2.1	Participate in collaborative conversations with peers and adults about topics and texts in small and larger groups	SL1 pp. 146–151

Indiana Strand/Standard	Focus of Indiana Standard	For More Information
Speaking and Listening		
SL.2.3	Listen to others, take turns speaking about the topics under discussion	SL1 pp. 146–151
SL.2.4	Ask questions to clarify information about topics under discussion	SL3 pp. 158–163
SL.2.5	Build on others' talk in conversations by responding to the comments of others	SL1 pp. 146–151
SL.3.1	Ask and answer questions about key details in a text read aloud or information presented orally	SL2 pp. 152–157
SL.3.2	Ask and answer questions about what a speaker says	SL2 pp. 152–157
SL.4.1	Speaking audibly and using appropriate language, recite texts with careful attention to sensory detail	SL4 pp. 164–169 SL6 pp. 176–181
SL4.2	Add visual displays when sharing information to clarify ideas, thoughts, and feelings	SL5 pp. 170–175
SL.4.3	Give and follow multistep directions	NA

Indiana, Grade 2

Indiana Strand/Standard	Focus of Indiana Standard	For More Information
Reading Foundational Skills		
RF.2	Print Concepts: NA	RF1 pp. 72–77
RF.3	Phonological Awareness: NA	RF2 pp. 78–83
RF.4	Phonics: Know and apply grade-level phonics and word analysis skills in decoding words	RF3 pp. 84–89
RF.5	Fluency: Read level-appropriate texts smoothly and accurately and with expression	RF4 pp. 90–95
Reading Literature		
RL.1	Read and comprehend a variety of literature that is level appropriate	R10 pp. 60–65
RL.2.1	Ask and answer questions to demonstrate understanding of main idea and key details in a text	R1 pp. 6–11
RL.2.2	Recount the beginning, middle, and ending of stories and determine their central message	R2 pp. 12–17
RL.2.3	Describe how characters in a story respond to major events, and how they affect the plot	R3 pp. 18–23
RL.3.1	Describe the overall structure of a story	R5 pp. 30–35
RL.3.2	Acknowledge differences in the points of view of characters	R6 pp. 36–41
RL.4.1	Use information gained from the illustrations and words in a text to demonstrate understanding of its characters, setting, or plot	R7 pp. 42–47
RL.4.2	Compare and contrast different versions of the same stories	R9 pp. 54–59
Reading Nonfiction Text		
RN.1	Read and comprehend a variety of level-appropriate nonfiction texts	R10 pp. 60–65
RN.2.1	Ask and answer questions about main ideas and key details in a text to confirm understanding	R1 pp. 6–11
RN.2.2	Identify the main idea of a multiparagraph text and the topic of each paragraph	R2 pp. 12–17
RN.2.3	Describe the connection between a series of events, ideas, or concepts, and steps in a process	R3 pp. 18–23
RN.3.1	Use text features to locate key facts or information and explain how they contribute to and clarify a text	R5 pp. 30–35

(Continued)

Indiana Strand/Standard	Focus of Indiana Standard	For More Information
Reading Nonfiction Text		
RN.3.2	Identify how a nonfiction can be structured to compare and contrast, describe a procedure, and explain a cause-effect relationship	R6 pp. 36–41
RN.3.3	Identify what the author wants to answer, explain, or describe in the text	R6 pp. 36–41
RN.4.1	Identify how the author uses facts to support specific points in a text	R8 pp. 48–53
RN.4.2	Compare and contrast the most important points presented by two texts on the same topic	R9 pp. 54–59
Reading Vocabulary		
RV.1	Use words and phrases acquired through conversations, reading, being read to, and responding to texts	L6 pp. 216–221
RV2.1	Use context clues to determine the meaning of unknown words	L4 pp. 204–209
RV2.2	Identify relationships among words	L5 pp. 210–215
RV.2.4	Use a known root word as a clue to the meaning of an unknown word with the same root	L4 pp. 204–209
RV.2.5	Consult reference materials to determine the meaning of words and phrases	L4 pp. 204–209
RV.3.1	Recognize that authors use words to provide rhythm and meaning	R4 pp. 24–29
RV.3.2	Determine the meanings of words and phrases in a nonfiction text	R4 pp. 24–29
Writing		
W.1	Write routinely for specific purposes and audiences	NA
W.2	Demonstrate the ability to write legibly	NA
W.3.1	Write a logically connected paragraph or paragraphs that introduce an opinion, with a concluding statement and multiple reasons to support the opinion	W1 pp. 100–105
W.3.2	Write a paragraph or paragraphs on a topic; introduce the topic, provide facts and details, and provide a concluding statement	W2 pp. 106–111
W.3.3	Develop topics for narrative texts that include a beginning, use temporal words to signal event order, provide details, and provide an ending	W3 pp. 112–117
W.4	Generate a draft; revise writing, adding details; edit writing for format and conventions; use available technology to produce and publish writing	W5 pp. 118–123 W6 pp. 124–129 L2 pp. 192–197
W.5	Conduct short research on a topic; identify sources; gather, organize, summarize, and present information	W7 pp. 132–137 W8 pp. 136–141
W.6.1	Demonstrate command of the conventions of standard English grammar and usage	L1 pp. 186–191
W.6.2	Demonstrate a command of capitalization, punctuation, and spelling	L2 pp. 192–197
Speaking and Listening		
SL.1	Listen actively and communicate effectively	SL1 pp. 146–151 SL2 pp. 152–157 SL3 pp. 158–163
SL.2.1	Participate in collaborative conversations with peers and adults about topics and texts in small and larger groups	SL1 pp. 146–151
SL.2.3	Listen to others, take turns speaking about the topics under discussion	SL1 pp. 146–151
SL.2.4	Ask for clarification and further explanation about topics under discussion	SL3 pp. 158–163
SL.2.5	Build on others' talk in conversations by responding to the comments of others	SL1 pp. 146–151
SL.3.1	Paraphrase or describe key ideas or details in information presented orally	SL2 pp. 152–157
SL.3.2	Ask and answer questions about what a speaker says	SL2 pp. 152–157

Indiana Strand/Standard	Focus of Indiana Standard	For More Information
Speaking and Listening		
SL.4.1	Using appropriate language; recite texts or recount an experience with careful attention to sensory detail; speak audibly in coherent sentences	SL4 pp. 164–169 SL6 pp. 176–181
SL4.2	Create simple presentations that maintain a clear focus, using various media when appropriate	SL5 pp. 170–175
SL.4.3	Give and follow multistep directions	NA

Iowa, Kindergarten

Iowa Strand/Standard	Focus of Iowa Standard	For More Information
Reading Literature		
RL.1	Ask and answer questions about key details in a text	R1 pp. 6–11
RL.2	Retell familiar stories, including key details	R2 pp. 12–17
RL.3	Identify characters, settings, and major events in a story	R3 pp. 18–23
RL.4	Ask and answer questions about unknown words in a text	R4 pp. 24–29
RL.5	Recognize common types of text (e.g., storybooks, poems)	R5 pp. 30–35
RL.6	Name the author and illustrator of a story and define the role of each	R6 pp. 36–41
RL.7	Describe the relationship between the illustrations and the story in which they appear	R7 pp. 42–47
RL.8	NA	
RL.9	Compare and contrast the characters in familiar stories	R9 pp. 54–59
RL.10	Actively engage in reading activities with purpose and understanding	R10 pp. 60–65
Reading Informational Text		
RI.1	Ask and answer questions about key details in a text	R1 pp. 6–11
RI.2	Identify the main topic and retell key details of a text	R2 pp. 12–17
RI.3	Describe the connection between two individuals, events, ideas, or pieces of information in a text	R3 pp. 18–23
RI.4	Ask and answer questions about unknown words in a text	R4 pp. 24–29
RI.5	Identify the front cover, back cover, and title page of a book	R5 pp. 30–35
RI.6	Name the author and illustrator of a text and define the role of each	R6 pp. 36–41
RI.7	Describe the relationship between visual images and the text in which they appear	R7 pp. 42–47
RI.8	Identify the reasons an author gives to support points in a text	R8 pp. 48–53
RI.9	Identify basic similarities and differences between two texts on the same topic	R9 pp. 54–59
RI.10	Actively engage in reading informational text with purpose and understanding	R10 pp. 60–65
Reading Foundational Skills		
RF.1	Print Concepts: Demonstrate understanding of the organization and basic features of print	RF1 pp. 72–77
RF.2	Phonological Awareness: Demonstrate understanding of spoken words, syllables, and sounds (phonemes)	RF2 pp. 78–83
RF.3	Phonics: Know and apply grade-level phonics and word analysis skills in decoding words	RF3 pp. 84–89
RF.4	Fluency: Read level-appropriate texts with purpose and understanding	RF4 pp. 90–95

(Continued)

Iowa Strand/Standard	Focus of Iowa Standard	For More Information
Writing		
W.1	Use a combination of drawing, dictating, and writing to compose opinion pieces	W1 pp. 100–105
W.2	Use a combination of drawing, dictating, and writing to compose informative/explanatory texts	W2 pp. 106–111
W.3	Use a combination of drawing, dictating, and writing to narrate a single event or several loosely linked events and provide a reaction to what happened	W3 pp. 112–117
W.4	NA	
W.5	Respond to questions and add details to strengthen writing as needed	W5 pp. 118–123
W.6	Explore a variety of digital tools to produce some writing	W6 pp. 124–129
W.7	Participate in shared research and writing projects	W7 pp. 130–135
W.8	Recall information from experiences or gather information from provided sources to answer a question	W8 pp. 136–141
W.9	NA	
W.10	NA	
Speaking and Listening		
SL.1	Participate in collaborative conversations with diverse partners about topics and texts in small and larger groups	SL1 pp. 146–151
SL.2	Ask and answer questions about key details to demonstrate understanding of a topic	SL2 pp. 152–157
SL.3	Ask and answer questions in order to seek help, get information, or clarify something that is not understood	SL3 pp. 158–163
SL.4	Describe familiar people, places, things, and events	SL4 pp. 164–169
SL.5	Add drawings or other visual displays to descriptions to provide additional detail	SL5 pp. 170–175
SL.6	Speak audibly and express thoughts, ideas, feelings, and ideas clearly	SL6 pp. 176–181
Language		
L.1	Speak audibly and express thoughts, ideas, feelings, and ideas clearly	SL6 pp. 176–181
L.2	Demonstrate command of the conventions of standard English capitalization, punctuation, and spelling when writing	L2 pp. 192–197
L.3	NA	
L.4	Determine or clarify the meaning of unknown and multiple-meaning words and phrases	L4 pp. 204–209
L.5	Explore word relationships and nuances in word meanings	L5 pp. 210–215
L.6	Use words and phrases acquired through conversations, reading, being read to, and responding to texts	L6 pp. 216–221

Iowa, Grade 1

Iowa Strand/Standard	Focus of Iowa Standard	For More Information
Reading Literature		
RL.1	Ask and answer questions about key details in a text	R1 pp. 6–11
RL.2	Retell stories, including key details	R2 pp. 12–17
RL.3	Describe characters, settings, and major events in a story	R3 pp. 18–23

Iowa Strand/Standard	Focus of Iowa Standard	For More Information
Reading Literature		
RL.4	Identify words or phrases that suggest feelings or appeal to the senses	R4 pp. 24–29
RL.5	Explain major differences between stories and informative texts	R5 pp. 30–35
RL.6	Identify who is telling the story at various points in a text	R6 pp. 36–41
RL.7	Use illustrations to describe elements of a story	R7 pp. 42–47
RL.8	NA	
RL.9	Compare and contrast the experiences of characters in stories	R9 pp. 54–59
RL.10	Read texts of appropriate complexity	R10 pp. 60–65
Reading Informational Text		
RI.1	Ask and answer questions about key details in a text	R1 pp. 6–11
RI.2	Identify the main topic and retell key details of a text	R2 pp. 12–17
RI.3	Describe the connection between two individuals, events, ideas, or pieces of information in a text	R3 pp. 18–23
RI.4	Ask and answer questions to clarify the meaning of words in a text	R4 pp. 24–29
RI.5	Use text features to locate information in a text	R5 pp. 30–35
RI.6	Distinguish between information provided by illustrations and information provided by words	R6 pp. 36–41
RI.7	Use illustrations and details to describe key ideas in a text	R7 pp. 42–47
RI.8	Identify the reasons an author gives to support points in a text	R8 pp. 48–53
RI.9	Identify basic similarities and differences between two texts on the same topic	R9 pp. 54–59
RI.10	Actively engage in reading informational text with purpose and understanding	R10 pp. 60–65
Reading Foundational Skills		
RF.1	Print Concepts: Demonstrate understanding of the organization and basic features of print	RF1 pp. 72–77
RF.2	Phonological Awareness: Demonstrate understanding of spoken words, syllables, and sounds (phonemes)	RF2 pp. 78–83
RF.3	Phonics: Know and apply grade-level phonics and word analysis skills in decoding words	RF3 pp. 84–89
RF.4	Fluency: Read level-appropriate texts with accuracy and fluency	RF4 pp. 90–95
Writing		
W.1	Write opinion pieces: introduce the topic, state an opinion, supply reasons, and provide closure	W1 pp. 100–105
W.2	Write informative/explanatory texts: name a topic, supply facts, and provide closure	W2 pp. 106–111
W.3	Write narratives: sequence events, include details, use temporal words, and provide closure	W3 pp. 112–117
W.4	NA	
W.5	Focus on a topic, respond to questions, and add details to strengthen writing as needed	W5 pp. 118–123
W.6	Use a variety of digital tools to produce and publish writing	W6 pp. 124–129
W.7	Participate in shared research and writing projects	W7 pp. 130–135
W.8	Recall information from experiences or gather information from provided sources to answer a question	W8 pp. 136–141
W.9	NA	
W.10	NA	

(Continued)

Iowa Strand/Standard	Focus of Iowa Standard	For More Information
Speaking and Listening		
SL.1	Participate in collaborative conversations with diverse partners about topics and texts in small and larger groups	SL1 pp. 146–151
SL.2	Ask and answer questions about key details to demonstrate understanding of a topic	SL2 pp. 152–157
SL.3	Ask and answer questions in order to get information or clarify something that is not understood	SL3 pp. 158–163
SL.4	Clearly describe people, places, things, and events	SL4 pp. 164–169
SL.5	Add drawings or other visual displays to descriptions to provide additional detail	SL5 pp. 170–175
SL.6	Produce complete sentences when appropriate to task and situation	SL6 pp. 176–181
Language		
L.1	Demonstrate command of the conventions of standard English grammar and usage when writing or speaking	L1 pp. 186–191
L.2	Demonstrate command of the conventions of standard English capitalization, punctuation, and spelling when writing	L2 pp. 192–197
L.3	NA	
L.4	Determine or clarify the meaning of unknown and multiple-meaning words and phrases	L4 pp. 204–209
L.5	Demonstrate understanding of word relationships and nuances in word meanings	L5 pp. 210–215
L.6	Use words and phrases acquired through conversations, reading, being read to, and responding to texts	L6 pp. 216–221

Iowa, Grade 2

Iowa Strand/Standard	Focus of Iowa Standard	For More Information
Reading Literature		
RL.1	Ask and answer questions about key details in a text	R1 pp. 6–11
RL.2	Recount stories and determine their central message	R2 pp. 12–17
RL.3	Describe how characters respond to major events and challenges	R3 pp. 18–23
RL.4	Describe how words or phrases supply rhythm and meaning	R4 pp. 24–29
RL.5	Describe the overall structure of a story, including the beginning and ending	R5 pp. 30–35
RL.6	Acknowledge differences in characters' points of view	R6 pp. 36–41
RL.7	Use information gathered from illustrations and words to demonstrate understanding of story elements	R7 pp. 42–47
RL.8	NA	
RL.9	Compare and contrast two or more versions of the same story	R9 pp. 54–59
RL.10	Read and comprehend texts of appropriate complexity	R10 pp. 60–65
Reading Informational Text		
RI.1	Ask and answer questions about key details in a text	R1 pp. 6–11
RI.2	Identify the main topic and retell key details of a text, as well as the focus of specific paragraphs	R2 pp. 12–17
RI.3	Describe the connection between a series of events, ideas, concepts, or steps in a text	R3 pp. 18–23
RI.4	Determine the meaning of words and phrases in a text relevant to a grade-level topic	R4 pp. 24–29

Iowa Strand/Standard	Focus of Iowa Standard	For More Information
Reading Informational Text		
RI.5	Use text features to efficiently locate information in a text	R5 pp. 30–35
RI.6	Identify the main purpose of a text	R6 pp. 36–41
RI.7	Explain how specific images contribute to and clarify a text	R7 pp. 42–47
RI.8	Describe how reasons an author gives support points in a text	R8 pp. 48–53
RI.9	Compare and contrast the most important points in two texts on the same topic	R9 pp. 54–59
RI.10	Read and comprehend informational texts of appropriate complexity	R10 pp. 60–65
Reading Foundational Skills		
RF.1	NA	
RF.2	NA	
RF.3	Phonics: Know and apply grade-level phonics and word analysis skills in decoding words	RF3 pp. 84–89
RF.4	Fluency: Read level-appropriate texts with accuracy and fluency	RF4 pp. 90–95
Writing		
W.1	Write opinion pieces: introduce the topic, state an opinion, supply reasons using linking words, and provide closure	W1 pp. 100–105
W.2	Write informative/explanatory texts: name a topic, use facts to develop points, and provide closure	W2 pp. 106–111
W.3	Write narratives: sequence events; include details to describe actions, thoughts, and feelings; use temporal words; provide closure	W3 pp. 112–117
W.4	NA	
W.5	Focus on a topic and strengthen writing by revising and editing	W5 pp. 118–123
W.6	Use a variety of digital tools to produce and publish writing	W6 pp. 124–129
W.7	Participate in shared research and writing projects	W7 pp. 130–135
W.8	Recall information from experiences or gather information from provided sources to answer a question	W8 pp. 136–141
W.9	NA	
W.10	NA	
Speaking and Listening		
SL.1	Participate in collaborative conversations with diverse partners about topics and texts in small and larger groups	SL1 pp. 146–151
SL.2	Recount or describe key ideas or details in information presented orally	SL2 pp. 152–157
SL.3	Ask and answer questions in order to get information, deepen understanding, or clarify something that is not understood	SL3 pp. 158–163
SL.4	Recount a story or experience with appropriate facts and relevant details	SL4 pp. 164–169
SL.5	Create audio recordings of stories or poems, adding visual displays as appropriate for clarification	SL5 pp. 170–175
SL.6	Produce complete sentences when appropriate to task and situation	SL6 pp. 176–181
Language		
L.1	Demonstrate command of the conventions of standard English grammar and usage when writing or speaking	L1 pp. 186–191
L.2	Demonstrate command of the conventions of standard English capitalization, punctuation, and spelling when writing	L2 pp. 192–197
L.3	Use knowledge of language and its conventions when writing, speaking, reading, or listening	L3 pp. 198–203
L.4	Determine or clarify the meaning of unknown and multiple-meaning words and phrases	L4 pp. 204–209
L.5	Demonstrate understanding of word relationships and nuances in word meanings	L5 pp. 210–215
L.6	Use words and phrases acquired through conversations, reading, being read to, and responding to texts	L6 pp. 216–221

Kansas, Kindergarten

Kansas Strand/Standard	Focus of Kansas Standard	For More Information
Reading Literature		
RL.K.1	Ask and answer questions about key details in a text	R1 pp. 6–11
RL.K.2	Retell familiar stories, including key details	R2 pp. 12–17
RL.K.3	Identify characters, settings, and major events in a story	R3 pp. 18–23
RL.K.4	Ask and answer questions about unknown words in a text	R4 pp. 24–29
RL.K.5	Recognize common types of text (e.g., storybooks, poems)	R5 pp. 30–35
RL.K.6	Name the author and illustrator of a story and define the role of each	R6 pp. 36–41
RL.K.7	Describe the relationship between the illustrations and the story in which they appear	R7 pp. 42–47
RL.K.8	NA	
RL.K.9	Compare and contrast the characters in familiar stories	R9 pp. 54–59
RL.K.10	Actively engage in reading activities with purpose and understanding	R10 pp. 60–65
Reading Informational Text		
RI.K.1	Ask and answer questions about key details in a text	R1 pp. 6–11
RI.K.2	Identify the main topic and retell key details of a text	R2 pp. 12–17
RI.K.3	Describe the connection between two individuals, events, ideas, or pieces of information in a text	R3 pp. 18–23
RI.K.4	Ask and answer questions about unknown words in a text	R4 pp. 24–29
RI.K.5	Identify the front cover, back cover, and title page of a book	R5 pp. 30–35
RI.K.6	Name the author and illustrator of a text and define the role of each	R6 pp. 36–41
RI.K.7	Describe the relationship between visual images and the text in which they appear	R7 pp. 42–47
RI.K.8	Identify the reasons an author gives to support points in a text	R8 pp. 48–53
R.KI.9	Identify basic similarities and differences between two texts on the same topic	R9 pp. 54–59
RI.K.10	Actively engage in reading informational text with purpose and understanding	R10 pp. 60–65
Reading Foundational Skills		
RF.K.1	Print Concepts: Demonstrate understanding of the organization and basic features of print	RF1 pp. 72–77
RF.K.2	Phonological Awareness: Demonstrate understanding of spoken words, syllables, and sounds (phonemes)	RF2 pp. 78–83
RF.K.3	Phonics: Know and apply grade-level phonics and word analysis skills in decoding words	RF3 pp. 84–89
R.KF.4	Fluency: Read level-appropriate texts with purpose and understanding	RF4 pp. 90–95
Writing		
W.K.1	Use a combination of drawing, dictating, and writing to compose opinion pieces	W1 pp. 100–105
W.K.2	Use a combination of drawing, dictating, and writing to compose informative/explanatory texts	W2 pp. 106–111
W.K.3	Use a combination of drawing, dictating, and writing to narrate a single event or several loosely linked events and provide a reaction to what happened	W3 pp. 112–117
W.K.4	NA	
W.K.5	Respond to questions and add details to strengthen writing as needed	W5 pp. 118–123

Kansas Strand/Standard	Focus of Kansas Standard	For More Information
Writing		
W.K.6	Explore a variety of digital tools to produce some writing	W6 pp. 124–129
W.K.7	Participate in shared research and writing projects	W7 pp. 130–135
W.K.8	Recall information from experiences or gather information from provided sources to answer a question	W8 pp. 136–141
W.K.9	NA	
W.K.10	NA	
Speaking and Listening		
SL.K.1	Participate in collaborative conversations with diverse partners about topics and texts in small and larger groups	SL1 pp. 146–151
SL.K.2	Ask and answer questions about key details to demonstrate understanding of a topic	SL2 pp. 152–157
SL.K.3	Ask and answer questions in order to seek help, get information, or clarify something that is not understood	SL3 pp. 158–163
SL.K.4	Describe familiar people, places, things, and events	SL4 pp. 164–169
SL.K.5	Add drawings or other visual displays to descriptions to provide additional detail	SL5 pp. 170–175
SL.K.6	Speak audibly and express thoughts, ideas, feelings, and ideas clearly	SL6 pp. 176–181
Language		
L.K.1	Demonstrate command of the conventions of standard English grammar and usage when writing or speaking	L1 pp. 186–191
L.K.2	Demonstrate command of the conventions of standard English capitalization, punctuation, and spelling when writing	L2 pp. 192–197
L.K.3	NA	
L.K.4	Determine or clarify the meaning of unknown and multiple-meaning words and phrases	L4 pp. 204–209
L.K.5	Explore word relationships and nuances in word meanings	L5 pp. 210–215
L.K.6	Use words and phrases acquired through conversations, reading, being read to, and responding to texts	L6 pp. 216–221

Kansas, Grade 1

Kansas Strand/Standard	Focus of Kansas Standard	For More Information
Reading Literature		
RL.1.1	Ask and answer questions about key details in a text	R1 pp. 6–11
RL.1.2	Retell stories, including key details	R2 pp. 12–17
RL.1.3	Describe characters, settings, and major events in a story	R3 pp. 18–23
RL.1.4	Identify words or phrases that suggest feelings or appeal to the senses	R4 pp. 24–29
RL.1.5	Explain major differences between stories and informative texts	R5 pp. 30–35
RL.1.6	Identify who is telling the story at various points in a text	R6 pp. 36–41
RL.1.7	Use illustrations to describe elements of a story	R7 pp. 42–47

(Continued)

Kansas Strand/Standard	Focus of Kansas Standard	For More Information
Reading Literature		
RL.1.8	NA	
RL.1.9	Compare and contrast the experiences of characters in stories	R9 pp. 54–59
RL.1.10	Read texts of appropriate complexity	R10 pp. 60–65
Reading Informational Text		
RI.1.1	Ask and answer questions about key details in a text	R1 pp. 6–11
RI.1.2	Identify the main topic and retell key details of a text	R2 pp. 12–17
RI.1.3	Describe the connection between two individuals, events, ideas, or pieces of information in a text	R3 pp. 18–23
RI.1.4	Ask and answer questions to clarify the meaning of words in a text	R4 pp. 24–29
RI.1.5	Use text features to locate information in a text	R5 pp. 30–35
RI.1.6	Distinguish between information provided by illustrations and information provided by words	R6 pp. 36–41
RI.1.7	Use illustrations and details to describe key ideas in a text	R7 pp. 42–47
RI.1.8	Identify the reasons an author gives to support points in a text	R8 pp. 48–53
RI.1.9	Identify basic similarities and differences between two texts on the same topic	R9 pp. 54–59
RI.1.10	Actively engage in reading informational text with purpose and understanding	R10 pp. 60–65
Reading Foundational Skills		
RF.1.1	Print Concepts: Demonstrate understanding of the organization and basic features of print	RF1 pp. 72–77
RF.1.2	Phonological Awareness: Demonstrate understanding of spoken words, syllables, and sounds (phonemes)	RF2 pp. 78–83
RF.1.3	Phonics: Know and apply grade-level phonics and word analysis skills in decoding words	RF3 pp. 84–89
RF.1.4	Fluency: Read level-appropriate texts with accuracy and fluency	RF4 pp. 90–95
Writing		
W.1.1.1	Write opinion pieces: introduce the topic, state an opinion, supply reasons, and provide closure	W1 pp. 100–105
W.1.2	Write informative/explanatory texts: name a topic, supply facts, and provide closure	W2 pp. 106–111
W.1.3	Write narratives: sequence events, include details, use temporal words, and provide closure	W3 pp. 112–117
W.1.4	NA	
W.1.5	Focus on a topic, respond to questions, and add details to strengthen writing as needed	W5 pp. 118–123
W.1.6	Use a variety of digital tools to produce and publish writing	W6 pp. 124–129
W.1.7	Participate in shared research and writing projects	W7 pp. 130–135
W.1.8	Recall information from experiences or gather information from provided sources to answer a question	W8 pp. 136–141
W.1.9	NA	
W.1.10	NA	
Speaking and Listening		
SL.1.1	Participate in collaborative conversations with diverse partners about topics and texts in small and larger groups	SL1 pp. 146–151
SL.1.2	Ask and answer questions about key details to demonstrate understanding of a topic	SL2 pp. 152–157
SL.1.3	Ask and answer questions in order to get information or clarify something that is not understood	SL3 pp. 158–163
SL.1.4	Clearly describe people, places, things, and events	SL4 pp. 164–169

Kansas Strand/Standard	Focus of Kansas Standard	For More Information
Speaking and Listening		
SL.1.5	Add drawings or other visual displays to descriptions to provide additional detail	SL5 pp. 170–175
SL.1.6	Produce complete sentences when appropriate to task and situation	SL6 pp. 176–181
Language		
L.1.1	Demonstrate command of the conventions of standard English grammar and usage when writing or speaking	L1 pp. 186–191
L.1.2	Demonstrate command of the conventions of standard English capitalization, punctuation, and spelling when writing	L2 pp. 192–197
L.1.3	NA	
L.1.1.4	Determine or clarify the meaning of unknown and multiple-meaning words and phrases	L4 pp. 204–209
L.1.5	Demonstrate understanding of word relationships and nuances in word meanings	L5 pp. 210–215
L.1.6	Use words and phrases acquired through conversations, reading, being read to, and responding to texts	L6 pp. 216–221

Kansas, Grade 2

Kansas Strand/Standard	Focus of Kanas Standard	For More Information
Reading Literature		
RL.2.1	Ask and answer questions about key details in a text	R1 pp. 6–11
RL.2.2	Recount stories and determine their central message	R2 pp. 12–17
RL.2.3	Describe how characters respond to major events and challenges	R3 pp. 18–23
RL.2.4	Describe how words or phrases supply rhythm and meaning	R4 pp. 24–29
RL.2.5	Describe the overall structure of a story, including the beginning and ending	R5 pp. 30–35
RL.2.6	Acknowledge differences in characters' points of view	R6 pp. 36–41
RL.2.7	Use information gathered from illustrations and words to demonstrate understanding of story elements	R7 pp. 42–47
RL.2.8	NA	
RL.2.9	Compare and contrast two or more versions of the same story	R9 pp. 54–59
RL.2.10	Read and comprehend texts of appropriate complexity	R10 pp. 60–65
Reading Informational Text		
RI.2.1	Ask and answer questions about key details in a text	R1 pp. 6–11
RI.2.2	Identify the main topic and retell key details of a text, as well as the focus of specific paragraphs	R2 pp. 12–17
RI.2.3	Describe the connection between a series of events, ideas, concepts, or steps in a text	R3 pp. 18–23
RI.2.4	Determine the meaning of words and phrases in a text relevant to a grade-level topic	R4 pp. 24–29
RI.2.5	Use text features to efficiently locate information in a text	R5 pp. 30–35
RI.2.6	Identify the main purpose of a text	R6 pp. 36–41
RI.2.7	Explain how specific images contribute to and clarify a text	R7 pp. 42–47
RI.2.8	Describe how reasons an author gives support points in a text	R8 pp. 48–53

(Continued)

Kansas Strand/Standard	Focus of Kanas Standard	For More Information
Reading Informational Text		
RI.2.9	Compare and contrast the most important points in two texts on the same topic	R9 pp. 54–59
RI.2.10	Read and comprehend informational texts of appropriate complexity	R10 pp. 60–65
Reading Foundational Skills		
RF.2.1	NA	
RF.2.2	NA	
RF.2.3	Phonics: Know and apply grade-level phonics and word analysis skills in decoding words	RF3 pp. 84–89
RF.2.4	Fluency: Read level-appropriate texts with accuracy and fluency	RF4 pp. 90–95
Writing		
W.2.1	Write opinion pieces: introduce the topic, state an opinion, supply reasons using linking words, and provide closure	W1 pp. 100–105
W.2.2	Write informative/explanatory texts: name a topic, use facts to develop points, and provide closure	W2 pp. 106–111
W.2.3	Write narratives: sequence events; include details to describe actions, thoughts, and feelings; use temporal words; provide closure	W3 pp. 112–117
W.2.4	NA	
W.2.5	Focus on a topic and strengthen writing by revising and editing	W5 pp. 118–123
W.2.6	Use a variety of digital tools to produce and publish writing	W6 pp. 124–129
W.2.7	Participate in shared research and writing projects	W7 pp. 130–135
W.2.8	Recall information from experiences or gather information from provided sources to answer a question	W8 pp. 136–141
W.2.9	NA	
W.2.10	NA	
Speaking and Listening		
SL.2.1	Participate in collaborative conversations with diverse partners about topics and texts in small and larger groups	SL1 pp. 146–151
SL.2.2	Recount or describe key ideas or details in information presented orally	SL2 pp. 152–157
SL.2.3	Ask and answer questions in order to get information, deepen understanding, or clarify something that is not understood	SL3 pp. 158–163
SL.2.4	Recount a story or experience with appropriate facts and relevant details	SL4 pp. 164–169
SL.2.5	Create audio recordings of stories or poems, adding visual displays as appropriate for clarification	SL5 pp. 170–175
SL.2.6	Produce complete sentences when appropriate to task and situation	SL6 pp. 176–181
Language		
L.2.1	Demonstrate command of the conventions of standard English grammar and usage when writing or speaking	L1 pp. 186–191
L.2.2	Demonstrate command of the conventions of standard English capitalization, punctuation, and spelling when writing	L2 pp. 192–197
L.2.3	Use knowledge of language and its conventions when writing, speaking, reading, or listening	L3 pp. 198–203
L.2.4	Determine or clarify the meaning of unknown and multiple-meaning words and phrases	L4 pp. 204–209
L.2.5	Demonstrate understanding of word relationships and nuances in word meanings	L5 pp. 210–215
L.2.6	Use words and phrases acquired through conversations, reading, being read to, and responding to texts	L6 pp. 216–221

Louisiana, Kindergarten

Louisiana Strand/Standard	Focus of Louisiana Standard	For More Information
Reading Literature		
RL.1	Ask and answer questions about key details in a text	R1 pp. 6–11
RL.2	Retell familiar stories, including key details	R2 pp. 12–17
RL.3	Identify characters, settings, and major events in a story	R3 pp. 18–23
RL.4	Ask and answer questions about unknown words in a text	R4 pp. 24–29
RL.5	Recognize common types of text (e.g., storybooks, poems)	R5 pp. 30–35
RL.6	Define the role of the author and illustrator in telling a story	R6 pp. 36–41
RL.7	Make connections between the illustrations and the story in which they appear	R7 pp. 42–47
RL.8	NA	
RL.9	Compare and contrast the characters in familiar stories	R9 pp. 54–59
RL.10	Actively engage in reading activities with purpose and understanding	R10 pp. 60–65
Reading Informational Text		
RI.1	Ask and answer questions about key details in a text	R1 pp. 6–11
RI.2	Identify the main topic and retell key details of a text	R2 pp. 12–17
RI.3	Describe the connection between two individuals, events, ideas, or pieces of information in a text	R3 pp. 18–23
RI.4	Ask and answer questions about unknown words in a text	R4 pp. 24–29
RI.5	Identify the front cover, back cover, and title page of a book	R5 pp. 30–35
RI.6	Define the role of the author and illustrator in presenting ideas in a text	R6 pp. 36–41
RI.7	Make connections between visual images and the text in which they appear	R7 pp. 42–47
RI.8	Identify the reasons an author gives to support points in a text	R8 pp. 48–53
RI.9	Identify basic similarities and differences between two texts on the same topic	R9 pp. 54–59
RI.10	Actively engage in reading informational text with purpose and understanding	R10 pp. 60–65
Reading Foundational Skills		
RF.1	Print Concepts: Demonstrate understanding of the organization and basic features of print	RF1 pp. 72–77
RF.2	Phonological Awareness: Demonstrate understanding of spoken words, syllables, and sounds (phonemes)	RF2 pp. 78–83
RF.3	Phonics: Know and apply grade-level phonics and word analysis skills in decoding words	RF3 pp. 84–89
RF.4	Fluency: Read level-appropriate texts with purpose and understanding	RF4 pp. 90–95
Writing		
W.1	Use a combination of drawing, dictating, and writing to compose opinion pieces	W1 pp. 100–105
W.2	Use a combination of drawing, dictating, and writing to compose informative/explanatory texts	W2 pp. 106–111
W.3	Use a combination of drawing, dictating, and writing to narrate a single event or several loosely linked events and provide a reaction to what happened	W3 pp. 112–117
W.4	NA	
W.5	Orally respond to questions and add details to strengthen writing as needed	W5 pp. 118–123

(Continued)

Louisiana Strand/Standard	Focus of Louisiana Standard	For More Information
Writing		
W.6	Explore a variety of digital tools to produce some writing	W6 pp. 124–129
W.7	Participate in shared research and writing projects	W7 pp. 130–135
W.8	Recall information from experiences or gather information from provided sources to answer a question	W8 pp. 136–141
W.9	NA	
W.10	NA	
Speaking and Listening		
SL.1	Participate in collaborative conversations with diverse partners about topics and texts in small and larger groups	SL1 pp. 146–151
SL.2	Ask and answer questions about key details to demonstrate understanding of a topic	SL2 pp. 152–157
SL.3	Ask and answer questions in order to seek help, get information, or clarify something that is not understood	SL3 pp. 158–163
SL.4	Describe familiar people, places, things, and events	SL4 pp. 164–169
SL.5	Add drawings or other visual displays to descriptions to provide additional detail	SL5 pp. 170–175
SL.6	Speak audibly and express thoughts, ideas, feelings, and ideas clearly	SL6 pp. 176–181
Language		
L.1	Demonstrate command of the conventions of standard English grammar and usage when writing or speaking	L1 pp. 186–191
L.2	Demonstrate command of the conventions of standard English capitalization, punctuation, and spelling when writing	L2 pp. 192–197
L.3	NA	
L.4	Determine or clarify the meaning of unknown and multiple-meaning words and phrases	L4 pp. 204–209
L.5	Explore word relationships and nuances in word meanings	L5 pp. 210–215
L.6	Use words and phrases acquired through conversations, reading, being read to, and responding to texts	L6 pp. 216–221

Louisiana, Grade 1

Louisiana Strand/Standard	Focus of Louisiana Standard	For More Information
Reading Literature		
RL.1	Ask and answer questions about key details in a text	R1 pp. 6–11
RL.2	Retell stories, including key details	R2 pp. 12–17
RL.3	Describe characters, settings, and major events in a story	R3 pp. 18–23
RL.4	Identify words or phrases that suggest feelings or appeal to the senses	R4 pp. 24–29
RL.5	Explain major differences between stories and informative texts	R5 pp. 30–35
RL.6	Identify who is telling the story at various points in a text	R6 pp. 36–41
RL.7	Use illustrations and details to describe elements of a story	R7 pp. 42–47

Louisiana Strand/Standard	Focus of Louisiana Standard	For More Information
Reading Literature		
RL.8	NA	
RL.9	Compare and contrast the experiences of characters in stories	R9 pp. 54–59
RL.10	Read literary texts of appropriate complexity	R10 pp. 60–65
Reading Informational Text		
RI.1	Ask and answer questions about key details in a text	R1 pp. 6–11
RI.2	Identify the main topic and retell key details of a text	R2 pp. 12–17
RI.3	Describe the connection between two individuals, events, ideas, or pieces of information in a text	R3 pp. 18–23
RI.4	Ask and answer questions to clarify the meaning of words in a text	R4 pp. 24–29
RI.5	Use text features to locate information in a text	R5 pp. 30–35
RI.6	Distinguish between information provided by illustrations and information provided by words	R6 pp. 36–41
RI.7	Use illustrations and details to describe key ideas in a text	R7 pp. 42–47
RI.8	Identify the reasons an author gives to support points in a text	R8 pp. 48–53
RI.9	Identify basic similarities and differences between two texts on the same topic	R9 pp. 54–59
RI.10	Read level-appropriate informational text with purpose and understanding	R10 pp. 60–65
Reading Foundational Skills		
RF.1	Print Concepts: Demonstrate understanding of the organization and basic features of print	RF1 pp. 72–77
RF.2	Phonological Awareness: Demonstrate understanding of spoken words, syllables, and sounds (phonemes)	RF2 pp. 78–83
RF.3	Phonics: Know and apply grade-level phonics and word analysis skills in decoding words	RF3 pp. 84–89
RF.4	Fluency: Read level-appropriate texts with accuracy and fluency	RF4 pp. 90–95
Writing		
W.1	Write opinion pieces: introduce the topic, state an opinion, supply reasons, and provide closure	W1 pp. 100–105
W.2	Write informative/explanatory texts: name a topic, supply facts, and provide closure	W2 pp. 106–111
W.3	Write narratives: sequence events, include details, use temporal words, and provide closure	W3 pp. 112–117
W.4	NA	
W.5	Focus on a topic, respond to questions, and add details to strengthen writing as needed	W5 pp. 118–123
W.6	Use a variety of digital tools to produce and publish writing	W6 pp. 124–129
W.7	Participate in shared research and writing projects	W7 pp. 130–135
W.8	Recall information from experiences or gather information from provided sources to answer a question	W8 pp. 136–141
W.9	NA	
W.10	NA	
Speaking and Listening		
SL.1	Participate in collaborative conversations with diverse partners about topics and texts in small and larger groups	SL1 pp. 146–151
SL.2	Ask and answer questions about key details in information presented orally	SL2 pp. 152–157

(Continued)

Louisiana Strand/Standard	Focus of Louisiana Standard	For More Information
Speaking and Listening		
SL.3	Ask and answer questions in order to get information or clarify something that is not understood	SL3 pp. 158–163
SL.4	Clearly describe people, places, things, and events	SL4 pp. 164–169
SL.5	Add drawings or other visual displays to descriptions to provide additional detail	SL5 pp. 170–175
SL.6	Produce complete sentences when appropriate to task, audience, and situation	SL6 pp. 176–181
Language		
L.1	Demonstrate command of the conventions of standard English grammar and usage when writing or speaking	L1 pp. 186–191
L.2	Demonstrate command of the conventions of standard English capitalization, punctuation, and spelling when writing	L2 pp. 192–197
L.3	NA	
L.4	Determine or clarify the meaning of unknown and multiple-meaning words and phrases	L4 pp. 204–209
L.5	Demonstrate understanding of word relationships and nuances in word meanings	L5 pp. 210–215
L.6	Use words and phrases acquired through conversations, reading, being read to, and responding to texts	L6 pp. 216–221

Louisiana, Grade 2

Louisiana Strand/Standard	Focus of Louisiana Standard	For More Information
Reading Literature		
RL.1	Ask and answer questions to demonstrate understanding of key details in a text	R1 pp. 6–11
RL.2	Recount stories and determine their central message	R2 pp. 12–17
RL.3	Describe how characters respond to major events and challenges	R3 pp. 18–23
RL.4	Describe how words or phrases supply rhythm and meaning, and determine their meaning as they are used in text	R4 pp. 24–29
RL.5	Describe the overall structure of a story, including the beginning and ending	R5 pp. 30–35
RL.6	Acknowledge differences in characters' points of view	R6 pp. 36–41
RL.7	Use information gathered from illustrations and words to demonstrate understanding of story elements	R7 pp. 42–47
RL.8	NA	
RL.9	Compare and contrast two or more versions of the same story	R9 pp. 54–59
RL.10	Read and comprehend literary texts of appropriate complexity	R10 pp. 60–65
Reading Informational Text		
RI.1	Ask and answer questions to demonstrate understanding of key details in a text	R1 pp. 6–11
RI.2	Identify the main topic and retell key details of a text, as well as the focus of specific paragraphs	R2 pp. 12–17
RI.3	Describe the connection between a series of events, ideas, concepts, or steps in a text	R3 pp. 18–23
RI.4	Determine the meaning of words and phrases in a text relevant to a grade-level topic	R4 pp. 24–29
RI.5	Use text features to efficiently locate information in a text	R5 pp. 30–35
RI.6	Identify the main purpose of a text	R6 pp. 36–41

Louisiana Strand/Standard	Focus of Louisiana Standard	For More Information
Reading Informational Text		
RI.7	Explain how specific images contribute to and clarify a text	R7 pp. 42–47
RI.8	Describe how reasons an author gives support points in a text	R8 pp. 48–53
RI.9	Compare and contrast the most important points in two texts on the same topic	R9 pp. 54–59
RI.10	Read and comprehend informational texts of appropriate complexity	R10 pp. 60–65
Reading Foundational Skills		
RF.1	NA	
RF.2	NA	
RF.3	Phonics: Know and apply grade-level phonics and word analysis skills in decoding words	RF3 pp. 84–89
RF.4	Fluency: Read level-appropriate texts with accuracy and fluency	RF4 pp. 90–95
Writing		
W.1	Write opinion pieces: introduce the topic, state an opinion, supply reasons using linking words, and provide closure	W1 pp. 100–105
W.2	Write informative/explanatory texts: name a topic, use facts to develop points, and provide closure	W2 pp. 106–111
W.3	Write narratives: sequence events; include details to describe actions, thoughts, and feelings; use temporal words; provide closure	W3 pp. 112–117
W.4	NA	
W.5	Focus on a topic and strengthen writing by revising and editing	W5 pp. 118–123
W.6	Use a variety of digital tools to produce and publish writing	W6 pp. 124–129
W.7	Participate in shared research and writing projects	W7 pp. 130–135
W.8	Recall information from experiences or gather information from provided sources to answer a question	W8 pp. 136–141
W.9	NA	
W.10	NA	
Speaking and Listening		
SL.1	Participate in collaborative conversations with diverse partners about topics and texts in small and larger groups	SL1 pp. 146–151
SL.2	Recount or describe key ideas or details in information presented orally	SL2 pp. 152–157
SL.3	Ask and answer questions in order to clarify comprehension, get information, or deepen understanding	SL3 pp. 158–163
SL.4	Tell a story or recount an experience with appropriate facts and relevant details	SL4 pp. 164–169
SL.5	Create audio recordings of stories or poems, adding visual displays as appropriate for clarification	SL5 pp. 170–175
SL.6	Produce complete sentences when appropriate to task and situation	SL6 pp. 176–181
Language		
L.1	Demonstrate command of the conventions of standard English grammar and usage when writing or speaking	L1 pp. 186–191
L.2	Demonstrate command of the conventions of standard English capitalization, punctuation, and spelling when writing	L2 pp. 192–197
L.3	Use knowledge of language and its conventions when writing, speaking, reading, or listening	L3 pp. 198–203
L.4	Determine or clarify the meaning of unknown and multiple-meaning words and phrases	L4 pp. 204–209
L.5	Demonstrate understanding of word relationships and nuances in word meanings	L5 pp. 210–215
L.6	Use words and phrases acquired through conversations, reading, being read to, and responding to texts	L6 pp. 216–221

Maryland, Kindergarten

Maryland Strand/Standard	Focus of Maryland Standard	For More Information
Reading Literature		
RL.1	Ask and answer questions about key details in a text	R1 pp. 6–11
RL.2	Retell familiar stories, including key details	R2 pp. 12–17
RL.3	Identify characters, settings, and major events in a story	R3 pp. 18–23
RL.4	Ask and answer questions about unknown words in a text	R4 pp. 24–29
RL.5	Recognize common types of text (e.g., storybooks, poems)	R5 pp. 30–35
RL.6	Name the author and illustrator of a story and define the role of each	R6 pp. 36–41
RL.7	Describe the relationship between the illustrations and the story in which they appear	R7 pp. 42–47
RL.8	NA	
RL.9	Compare and contrast the characters in familiar stories	R9 pp. 54–59
RL.10	Actively engage in reading activities with purpose and understanding	R10 pp. 60–65
Reading Informational Text		
RI.1	Ask and answer questions about key details in a text	R1 pp. 6–11
RI.2	Identify the main topic and retell key details of a text	R2 pp. 12–17
RI.3	Describe the connection between two individuals, events, ideas, or pieces of information in a text	R3 pp. 18–23
RI.4	Ask and answer questions about unknown words in a text	R4 pp. 24–29
RI.5	Identify the front cover, back cover, and title page of a book	R5 pp. 30–35
RI.6	Name the author and illustrator of a text and define the role of each	R6 pp. 36–41
RI.7	Describe the relationship between visual images and the text in which they appear	R7 pp. 42–47
RI.8	Identify the reasons an author gives to support points in a text	R8 pp. 48–53
RI.9	Identify basic similarities and differences between two texts on the same topic	R9 pp. 54–59
RI.10	Actively engage in reading informational text with purpose and understanding	R10 pp. 60–65
Reading Foundational Skills		
RF.1	Print Concepts: Demonstrate understanding of the organization and basic features of print	RF1 pp. 72–77
RF.2	Phonological Awareness: Demonstrate understanding of spoken words, syllables, and sounds (phonemes)	RF2 pp. 78–83
RF.3	Phonics: Know and apply grade-level phonics and word analysis skills in decoding words	RF3 pp. 84–89
RF.4	Fluency: Read level-appropriate texts with purpose and understanding	RF4 pp. 90–95
Writing		
W.1	Use a combination of drawing, dictating, and writing to compose opinion pieces	W1 pp. 100–105
W.2	Use a combination of drawing, dictating, and writing to compose informative/explanatory texts	W2 pp. 106–111
W.3	Use a combination of drawing, dictating, and writing to narrate a single event or several loosely linked events and provide a reaction to what happened	W3 pp. 112–117
W.4	NA	
W.5	Respond to questions and add details to strengthen writing as needed	W5 pp. 118–123

Maryland Strand/Standard	Focus of Maryland Standard	For More Information
Writing		
W.6	Explore a variety of digital tools to produce some writing	W6 pp. 124–129
W.7	Participate in shared research and writing projects	W7 pp. 130–135
W.8	Recall information from experiences or gather information from provided sources to answer a question	W8 pp. 136–141
W.9	NA	
W.10	NA	
Speaking and Listening		
SL.1	Participate in collaborative conversations with diverse partners about topics and texts in small and larger groups	SL1 pp. 146–151
SL.2	Ask and answer questions about key details to demonstrate understanding of a topic	SL2 pp. 152–157
SL.3	Ask and answer questions in order to seek help, get information, or clarify something that is not understood	SL3 pp. 158–163
SL.4	Describe familiar people, places, things, and events	SL4 pp. 164–169
SL.5	Add drawings or other visual displays to descriptions to provide additional detail	SL5 pp. 170–175
SL.6	Speak audibly and express thoughts, ideas, feelings, and ideas clearly	SL6 pp. 176–181
Language		
L.1	Demonstrate command of the conventions of standard English grammar and usage when writing or speaking	L1 pp. 186–191
L.2	Demonstrate command of the conventions of standard English capitalization, punctuation, and spelling when writing	L2 pp. 192–197
L.3	NA	
L.4	Determine or clarify the meaning of unknown and multiple-meaning words and phrases	L4 pp. 204–209
L.5	Explore word relationships and nuances in word meanings	L5 pp. 210–215
L.6	Use words and phrases acquired through conversations, reading, being read to, and responding to texts	L6 pp. 216–221

Maryland, Grade 1

Maryland Strand/Standard	Focus of Maryland Standard	For More Information
Reading Literature		
RL.1	Ask and answer questions about key details in a text	R1 pp. 6–11
RL.2	Retell stories, including key details	R2 pp. 12–17
RL.3	Describe characters, settings, and major events in a story	R3 pp. 18–23
RL.4	Identify words or phrases that suggest feelings or appeal to the senses	R4 pp. 24–29
RL.5	Explain major differences between stories and informative texts	R5 pp. 30–35
RL.6	Identify who is telling the story at various points in a text	R6 pp. 36–41
RL.7	Use illustrations to describe elements of a story	R7 pp. 42–47

(Continued)

Maryland Strand/Standard	Focus of Maryland Standard	For More Information
Reading Literature		
RL.8	NA	
RL.9	Compare and contrast the experiences of characters in stories	R9 pp. 54–59
RL.10	Read texts of appropriate complexity	R10 pp. 60–65
Reading Informational Text		
RI.1	Ask and answer questions about key details in a text	R1 pp. 6–11
RI.2	Identify the main topic and retell key details of a text	R2 pp. 12–17
RI.3	Describe the connection between two individuals, events, ideas, or pieces of information in a text	R3 pp. 18–23
RI.4	Ask and answer questions to clarify the meaning of words in a text	R4 pp. 24–29
RI.5	Use text features to locate information in a text	R5 pp. 30–35
RI.6	Distinguish between information provided by illustrations and information provided by words	R6 pp. 36–41
RI.7	Use illustrations and details to describe key ideas in a text	R7 pp. 42–47
RI.8	Identify the reasons an author gives to support points in a text	R8 pp. 48–53
RI.9	Identify basic similarities and differences between two texts on the same topic	R9 pp. 54–59
RI.10	Actively engage in reading informational text with purpose and understanding	R10 pp. 60–65
Reading Foundational Skills		
RF.1	Print Concepts: Demonstrate understanding of the organization and basic features of print	RF1 pp. 72–77
RF.2	Phonological Awareness: Demonstrate understanding of spoken words, syllables, and sounds (phonemes)	RF2 pp. 78–83
RF.3	Phonics: Know and apply grade-level phonics and word analysis skills in decoding words	RF3 pp. 84–89
RF.4	Fluency: Read level-appropriate texts with accuracy and fluency	RF4 pp. 90–95
Writing		
W.1	Write opinion pieces: introduce the topic, state an opinion, supply reasons, and provide closure	W1 pp. 100–105
W.2	Write informative/explanatory texts: name a topic, supply facts, and provide closure	W2 pp. 106–111
W.3	Write narratives: sequence events, include details, use temporal words, and provide closure .	W3 pp. 112–117
W.4	NA	
W.5	Focus on a topic, respond to questions, and add details to strengthen writing as needed	W5 pp. 118–123
W.6	Use a variety of digital tools to produce and publish writing	W6 pp. 124–129
W.7	Participate in shared research and writing projects	W7 pp. 130–135
W.8	Recall information from experiences or gather information from provided sources to answer a question	W8 pp. 136–141
W.9	NA	
W.10	NA	
Speaking and Listening		
SL.1	Participate in collaborative conversations with diverse partners about topics and texts in small and larger groups	SL1 pp. 146–151
SL.2	Ask and answer questions about key details to demonstrate understanding of a topic	SL2 pp. 152–157
SL.3	Ask and answer questions in order to get information or clarify something that is not understood	SL3 pp. 158–163

Maryland Strand/Standard	Focus of Maryland Standard	For More Information
Speaking and Listening		
SL.4	Clearly describe people, places, things, and events	SL4 pp. 164–169
SL.5	Add drawings or other visual displays to descriptions to provide additional detail	SL5 pp. 170–175
SL.6	Produce complete sentences when appropriate to task and situation	SL6 pp. 176–181
Language		
L.1	Demonstrate command of the conventions of standard English grammar and usage when writing or speaking	L1 pp. 186–191
L.2	Demonstrate command of the conventions of standard English capitalization, punctuation, and spelling when writing	L2 pp. 192–197
L.3	NA	
L.4	Determine or clarify the meaning of unknown and multiple-meaning words and phrases	L4 pp. 204–209
L.5	Demonstrate understanding of word relationships and nuances in word meanings	L5 pp. 210–215
L.6	Use words and phrases acquired through conversations, reading, being read to, and responding to texts	L6 pp. 216–221

Maryland, Grade 2

Maryland Strand/Standard	Focus of Maryland Standard	For More Information
Reading Literature		
RL.1	Ask and answer questions about key details in a text	R1 pp. 6–11
RL.2	Recount stories and determine their central message	R2 pp. 12–17
RL.3	Describe how characters respond to major events and challenges	R3 pp. 18–23
RL.4	Describe how words or phrases supply rhythm and meaning	R4 pp. 24–29
RL.5	Describe the overall structure of a story, including the beginning and ending	R5 pp. 30–35
RL.6	Acknowledge differences in characters' points of view	R6 pp. 36–41
RL.7	Use information gathered from illustrations and words to demonstrate understanding of story elements	R7 pp. 42–47
RL.8	NA	
RL.9	Compare and contrast two or more versions of the same story	R9 pp. 54–59
RL.10	Read and comprehend texts of appropriate complexity	R10 pp. 60–65
Reading Informational Text		
RI.1	Ask and answer questions about key details in a text	R1 pp. 6–11
RI.2	Identify the main topic and retell key details of a text, as well as the focus of specific paragraphs	R2 pp. 12–17
RI.3	Describe the connection between a series of events, ideas, concepts, or steps in a text	R3 pp. 18–23
RI.4	Determine the meaning of words and phrases in a text relevant to a grade-level topic	R4 pp. 24–29
RI.5	Use text features to efficiently locate information in a text	R5 pp. 30–35
RI.6	Identify the main purpose of a text	R6 pp. 36–41

(Continued)

Maryland Strand/Standard	Focus of Maryland Standard	For More Information
Reading Informational Text		
RI.7	Explain how specific images contribute to and clarify a text	R7 pp. 42–47
RI.8	Describe how reasons an author gives support points in a text	R8 pp. 48–53
RI.9	Compare and contrast the most important points in two texts on the same topic	R9 pp. 54–59
RI.10	Read and comprehend informational texts of appropriate complexity	R10 pp. 60–65
Reading Foundational Skills		
RF.1	NA	
RF.2	NA	
RF.3	Phonics: Know and apply grade-level phonics and word analysis skills in decoding words	RF3 pp. 84–89
RF.4	Fluency: Read level-appropriate texts with accuracy and fluency	RF4 pp. 90–95
Writing		
W.1	Write opinion pieces: introduce the topic, state an opinion, supply reasons using linking words, and provide closure	W1 pp. 100–105
W.2	Write informative/explanatory texts: name a topic, use facts to develop points, and provide closure	W2 pp. 106–111
W.3	Write narratives: sequence events; include details to describe actions, thoughts, and feelings; use temporal words; provide closure	W3 pp. 112–117
W.4	NA	
W.5	Focus on a topic and strengthen writing by revising and editing	W5 pp. 118–123
W.6	Use a variety of digital tools to produce and publish writing	W6 pp. 124–129
W.7	Participate in shared research and writing projects	W7 pp. 130–135
W.8	Recall information from experiences or gather information from provided sources to answer a question	W8 pp. 136–141
W.9	NA	
W.10	NA	
Speaking and Listening		
SL.1	Participate in collaborative conversations with diverse partners about topics and texts in small and larger groups	SL1 pp. 146–151
SL.2	Recount or describe key ideas or details in information presented orally	SL2 pp. 152–157
SL.3	Ask and answer questions in order to get information, deepen understanding, or clarify something that is not understood	SL3 pp. 158–163
SL.4	Recount a story or experience with appropriate facts and relevant details	SL4 pp. 164–169
SL.5	Create audio recordings of stories or poems, adding visual displays as appropriate for clarification	SL5 pp. 170–175
SL.6	Produce complete sentences when appropriate to task and situation	SL6 pp. 176–181
Language		
L.1	Demonstrate command of the conventions of standard English grammar and usage when writing or speaking	L1 pp. 186–191
L.2	Demonstrate command of the conventions of standard English capitalization, punctuation, and spelling when writing	L2 pp. 192–197
L.3	Use knowledge of language and its conventions when writing, speaking, reading, or listening	L3 pp. 198–203
L.4	Determine or clarify the meaning of unknown and multiple-meaning words and phrases	L4 pp. 204–209

Maryland Strand/Standard	Focus of Maryland Standard	For More Information
Language		
L.5	Demonstrate understanding of word relationships and nuances in word meanings	L5 pp. 210–215
L.6	Use words and phrases acquired through conversations, reading, being read to, and responding to texts	L6 pp. 216–221

Minnesota, Kindergarten

Minnesota Strand/Standard	Focus of Minnesota Standard	For More Information
Reading Literature		
1.1.1	Ask and answer questions about key details in a text	R1 pp. 6–11
1.2.2	Retell familiar stories, including key details	R2 pp. 12–17
1.3.3	Identify characters, settings, and major events in a story	R3 pp. 18–23
1.4.4	Ask and answer questions about unknown words in a text	R4 pp. 24–29
1.5.5	Recognize common types of text (e.g., storybooks, poems)	R5 pp. 30–35
1.6.6	Name the author and illustrator of a story and define the role of each	R6 pp. 36–41
1.7.7	Describe the relationship between the illustrations and the story in which they appear	R7 pp. 42–47
1.8.8	NA	
1.9.9	Compare and contrast the characters in familiar stories	R9 pp. 54–59
1.10.10	Actively engage in reading activities with purpose and understanding	R10 pp. 60–65
Reading Informational Text		
2.1.1	Ask and answer questions about key details in a text	R1 pp. 6–11
2.2.2	Identify the main topic and retell key details of a text	R2 pp. 12–17
2.3.3	Describe the connection between two individuals, events, ideas, or pieces of information in a text	R3 pp. 18–23
2.4.4	Ask and answer questions about unknown words in a text	R4 pp. 24–29
2.5.5	Identify the front cover, back cover, and title page of a book	R5 pp. 30–35
2.6.6	Name the author and illustrator of a text and define the role of each	R6 pp. 36–41
2.7.7	Describe the relationship between visual images and the text in which they appear	R7 pp. 42–47
2.8.8	Identify the reasons an author gives to support points in a text	R8 pp. 48–53
2.9.9	Identify basic similarities and differences between two texts on the same topic	R9 pp. 54–59
2.10.10	Actively engage in reading informational text with purpose and understanding	R10 pp. 60–65
Reading Foundational Skills		
3.1.1	Print Concepts: Demonstrate understanding of the organization and basic features of print	RF1 pp. 72–77
3.1.2	Phonological Awareness: Demonstrate understanding of spoken words, syllables, and sounds (phonemes)	RF2 pp. 78–83
3.1.3	Phonics: Know and apply grade-level phonics and word analysis skills in decoding words	RF3 pp. 84–89
3.1.4	Fluency: Read level-appropriate texts with purpose and understanding	RF4 pp. 90–95

(Continued)

Minnesota Strand/Standard	Focus of Minnesota Standard	For More Information
Writing		
6.1.1	Use a combination of drawing, dictating, and writing to compose opinion pieces	W1 pp. 100–105
6.2.2	Use a combination of drawing, dictating, and writing to compose informative/explanatory texts	W2 pp. 106–111
6.3.3	Use a combination of drawing, dictating, and writing to narrate a single event or several loosely linked events and provide a reaction to what happened	W3 pp. 112–117
6.4.4	NA	
6.5.5	Respond to questions and add details to strengthen writing as needed	W5 pp. 118–123
6.6.6	Explore a variety of digital tools to produce some writing	W6 pp. 124–129
6.7.7	Participate in shared research and writing projects	W7 pp. 130–135
6.8.8	Recall information from experiences or gather information from provided sources to answer a question	W8 pp. 136–141
6.9.9	NA	
6.10.10	NA	
Speaking and Listening		
8.1.1	Participate in collaborative conversations with diverse partners about topics and texts in small and larger groups	SL1 pp. 146–151
8.2.2	Ask and answer questions about key details to demonstrate understanding of a topic	SL2 pp. 152–157
8.3.3	Ask and answer questions in order to seek help, get information, or clarify something that is not understood	SL3 pp. 158–163
8.4.4	Describe familiar people, places, things, and events	SL4 pp. 164–169
8.5.5	Add drawings or other visual displays to descriptions to provide additional detail	SL5 pp. 170–175
8.6.6	Speak audibly and express thoughts, ideas, feelings, and ideas clearly	SL6 pp. 176–181
8.7.7	Distinguish among different types of print, digital, and multimodal media	NA
8.8.8	Create and individual or shared multimedia work for a specific purpose	NA
Language		
10.1.1	Demonstrate command of the conventions of standard English grammar and usage when writing or speaking	L1 pp. 186–191
10.2.2	Demonstrate command of the conventions of standard English capitalization, punctuation, and spelling when writing	L2 pp. 192–197
10.3.3	NA	
10.4.4	Determine or clarify the meaning of unknown and multiple-meaning words and phrases	L4 pp. 204–209
10.5.5	Explore word relationships and nuances in word meanings	L5 pp. 210–215
10.6.6	Use words and phrases acquired through conversations, reading, being read to, and responding to texts	L6 pp. 216–221

Minnesota, Grade 1

Minnesota Strand/Standard	Focus of Minnesota Standard	For More Information
Reading Literature		
1.1.1	Ask and answer questions about key details in a text	R1 pp. 6–11
1.2.2	Retell stories, including key details, with understanding	R2 pp. 12–17

Minnesota Strand/Standard	Focus of Minnesota Standard	For More Information
Reading Literature		
1.3.3	Describe characters, settings, and major events in a story	R3 pp. 18–23
1.4.4	Identify words or phrases that suggest feelings or appeal to the senses	R4 pp. 24–29
1.5.5	Explain major differences between stories and informative texts	R5 pp. 30–35
1.6.6	Identify who is telling the story at various points in a text	R6 pp. 36–41
1.7.7	Use illustrations to describe elements of a story	R7 pp. 42–47
1.8.8	NA	
1.9.9	Compare and contrast the experiences of characters in stories	R9 pp. 54–59
1.10.10	Read texts of appropriate complexity	R10 pp. 60–65
Reading Informational Text		
2.1.1	Ask and answer questions about key details in a text	R1 pp. 6–11
2.2.2	Identify the main topic and retell key details of a text	R2 pp. 12–17
2.3.3	Describe the connection between two individuals, events, ideas, or pieces of information in a text	R3 pp. 18–23
2.4.4	Ask and answer questions to clarify the meaning of words in a text	R4 pp. 24–29
2.5.5	Use text features to locate information in a text	R5 pp. 30–35
2.6.6	Distinguish between information provided by illustrations and information provided by words	R6 pp. 36–41
2.7.7	Use illustrations and details to describe key ideas in a text	R7 pp. 42–47
2.8.8	Identify the reasons an author gives to support points in a text	R8 pp. 48–53
2.9.9	Identify basic similarities and differences between two texts on the same topic	R9 pp. 54–59
2.10.10	Actively engage in reading informational text with purpose and understanding	R10 pp. 60–65
Reading Foundational Skills		
3.1.1	Print Concepts: Demonstrate understanding of the organization and basic features of print	RF1 pp. 72–77
3.1.2	Phonological Awareness: Demonstrate understanding of spoken words, syllables, and sounds (phonemes)	RF2 pp. 78–83
3.1.3	Phonics: Know and apply grade-level phonics and word analysis skills in decoding words	RF3 pp. 84–89
3.1.4	Fluency: Read level-appropriate texts with accuracy and fluency	RF4 pp. 90–95
Writing		
6.1.1	Write opinion pieces: introduce the topic, state an opinion, supply reasons, and provide closure	W1 pp. 100–105
6.2.2	Write informative/explanatory texts: name a topic, supply facts, and provide closure	W2 pp. 106–111
6.3.3	Write narratives: sequence events, include details, use temporal words, and provide closure	W3 pp. 112–117
6.4.4	NA	
6.5.5	Focus on a topic, respond to questions, and add details to strengthen writing as needed	W5 pp. 118–123
6.6.6	Use a variety of digital tools to produce and publish writing	W6 pp. 124–129
6.7.7	Participate in shared research and writing projects	W7 pp. 130–135
6.8.8	Recall information from experiences or gather information from provided sources to answer a question	W8 pp. 136–141
6.9.9	NA	
6.10.10	NA	

(Continued)

Minnesota Strand/Standard	Focus of Minnesota Standard	For More Information
Speaking and Listening		
8.1.1	Participate in collaborative conversations with diverse partners about topics and texts in small and larger groups	SL1 pp. 146–151
8.2.2	Ask and answer questions about key details in information presented orally	SL2 pp. 152–157
8.3.3	Ask and answer questions in order to get information or clarify something that is not understood	SL3 pp. 158–163
8.4.4	Clearly describe people, places, things, and events	SL4 pp. 164–169
8.5.5	Add drawings or other visual displays to descriptions to provide additional detail	SL5 pp. 170–175
8.6.6	Produce complete sentences when appropriate to task and situation	SL6 pp. 176–181
8.7.7	Distinguish among and understand purposes of different types of print, digital, and multimodal media	NA
8.8.8	Create and share an individual or shared multimedia work for a specific purpose	NA
Language		
10.1.1	Demonstrate command of the conventions of standard English grammar and usage when writing or speaking	L1 pp. 186–191
10.2.2	Demonstrate command of the conventions of standard English capitalization, punctuation, and spelling when writing	L2 pp. 192–197
10.3.3	NA	
10.4.4	Determine or clarify the meaning of unknown and multiple-meaning words and phrases	L4 pp. 204–209
10.5.5	Demonstrate understanding of word relationships and nuances in word meanings	L5 pp. 210–215
10.6.6	Use words and phrases acquired through conversations, reading, being read to, and responding to texts	L6 pp. 216–221

Minnesota, Grade 2

Minnesota Strand/Standard	Focus of Minnesota Standard	For More Information
Reading Literature		
1.1.1	Ask and answer questions to demonstrate understanding of key details in a text	R1 pp. 6–11
1.2.2	Recount stories and determine their central message	R2 pp. 12–17
1.3.3	Describe how characters respond to major events and challenges	R3 pp. 18–23
1.4.4	Describe how words or phrases supply rhythm and meaning	R4 pp. 24–29
1.5.5	Describe the overall structure of a story, including the beginning and ending	R5 pp. 30–35
1.6.6	Acknowledge differences in characters' points of view	R6 pp. 36–41
1.7.7	Use information gathered from illustrations and words to demonstrate understanding of story elements	R7 pp. 42–47
1.8.8	NA	
1.9.9	Compare and contrast two or more versions of the same story	R9 pp. 54–59
1.10.10	Read and comprehend texts of appropriate complexity	R10 pp. 60–65

Minnesota Strand/Standard	Focus of Minnesota Standard	For More Information
Reading Informational Text		
2.1.1	Ask and answer questions to demonstrate understanding of key details in a text	R1 pp. 6–11
2.2.2	Identify the main topic and retell key details of a text, as well as the focus of specific paragraphs	R2 pp. 12–17
2.3.3	Describe the connection between a series of events, ideas, concepts, or steps in a text	R3 pp. 18–23
2.4.4	Determine the meaning of words and phrases in a text relevant to a grade-level topic	R4 pp. 24–29
2.5.5	Use text features to efficiently locate information in a text	R5 pp. 30–35
2.6.6	Identify the main purpose of a text	R6 pp. 36–41
2.7.7	Explain how specific images contribute to and clarify a text	R7 pp. 42–47
2.8.8	Describe how reasons an author gives support points in a text	R8 pp. 48–53
2.9.9	Compare and contrast the most important points in two texts on the same topic	R9 pp. 54–59
2.10.10	Read and comprehend informational texts of appropriate complexity	R10 pp. 60–65
Reading Foundational Skills		
3.1.1	NA	
3.1.2	NA	
3.1.3	Phonics: Know and apply grade-level phonics and word analysis skills in decoding words	RF3 pp. 84–89
3.1.4	Fluency: Read level-appropriate texts with accuracy and fluency	RF4 pp. 90–95
Writing		
6.1.1	Write opinion pieces: introduce the topic, state an opinion, supply reasons using linking words, and provide closure	W1 pp. 100–105
6.2.2	Write informative/explanatory texts: name a topic, use facts to develop points, and provide closure	W2 pp. 106–111
6.3.3	Write narratives: sequence events; include details to describe actions, thoughts, and feelings; use temporal words; provide closure	W3 pp. 112–117
6.4.4	NA	
6.5.5	Respond to questions and add details to strengthen writing as needed	W5 pp. 118–123
6.6.6	Use a variety of digital tools to produce and publish writing	W6 pp. 124–129
6.7.7	Participate in shared research and writing projects	W7 pp. 130–135
6.8.8	Recall information from experiences or gather information from provided sources to answer a question	W8 pp. 136–141
6.9.9	NA	
6.10.10	NA	
Speaking and Listening		
8.1.1	Participate in collaborative conversations with diverse partners about topics and texts in small and larger groups	SL1 pp. 146–151
8.2.2	Recount or describe key ideas or details in information presented orally	SL2 pp. 152–157
8.3.3	Ask and answer questions in order to get information, deepen understanding, or clarify something that is not understood	SL3 pp. 158–163
8.4.4	Recount a story or experience with appropriate facts and relevant details	SL4 pp. 164–169
8.5.5	Create audio recordings of stories or poems, adding visual displays as appropriate for clarification	SL5 pp. 170–175

(Continued)

Minnesota Strand/Standard	Focus of Minnesota Standard	For More Information
Speaking and Listening		
8.6.6	Produce complete sentences when appropriate to task and situation	SL6 pp. 176–181
8.7.7	Distinguish, understand, and use different types of print, digital, and multimodal media	NA
8.8.8	Create an individual or shared multimedia work for a specific purpose	
Language		
10.1.1	Demonstrate command of the conventions of standard English grammar and usage when writing or speaking	L1 pp. 186–191
10.2.2	Demonstrate command of the conventions of standard English capitalization, punctuation, and spelling when writing	L2 pp. 192–197
10.3.3	Use knowledge of language and its conventions when writing, speaking, reading, or listening	L3 pp. 198–203
10.4.4	Determine or clarify the meaning of unknown and multiple-meaning words and phrases	L4 pp. 204–209
10.5.5	Demonstrate understanding of word relationships and nuances in word meanings	L5 pp. 210–215
10.6.6	Use words and phrases acquired through conversations, reading, being read to, and responding to texts	L6 pp. 216–221

Mississippi, Kindergarten

Mississippi Strand/Standard	Focus of Mississippi Standard	For More Information
Reading Literature		
RL.K.1	Ask and answer questions about key details in a text	R1 pp. 6–11
RL.K.2	Retell familiar stories, including key details	R2 pp. 12–17
RL.K.3	Identify characters, settings, and major events in a story	R3 pp. 18–23
RL.K.4	Ask and answer questions about unknown words in a text	R4 pp. 24–29
RL.K.5	Recognize common types of text (e.g., storybooks, poems)	R5 pp. 30–35
RL.K.6	Name the author and illustrator of a story and define the role of each	R6 pp. 36–41
RL.K.7	Describe the relationship between the illustrations and the story in which they appear	R7 pp. 42–47
RL.K.8	NA	
RL.K.9	Compare and contrast the characters in familiar stories	R9 pp. 54–59
RL.K.10	Actively engage in reading activities with purpose and understanding	R10 pp. 60–65
Reading Informational Text		
RI.K.1	Ask and answer questions about key details in a text	R1 pp. 6–11
RI.K.2	Identify the main topic and retell key details of a text	R2 pp. 12–17
RI.K.3	Describe the connection between two individuals, events, ideas, or pieces of information in a text	R3 pp. 18–23
RI.K.4	Ask and answer questions about unknown words in a text	R4 pp. 24–29
RI.K.5	Identify the front cover, back cover, and title page of a book	R5 pp. 30–35
RI.K.6	Name the author and illustrator of a text and define the role of each	R6 pp. 36–41
RI.K.7	Describe the relationship between visual images and the text in which they appear	R7 pp. 42–47

Mississippi Strand/Standard	Focus of Mississippi Standard	For More Information
Reading Informational Text		
RI.K.8	Identify the reasons an author gives to support points in a text	R8 pp. 48–53
R.KI.9	Identify basic similarities and differences between two texts on the same topic	R9 pp. 54–59
RI.K.10	Actively engage in reading informational text with purpose and understanding	R10 pp. 60–65
Reading Foundational Skills		
RF.K.1	Print Concepts: Demonstrate understanding of the organization and basic features of print	RF1 pp. 72–77
RF.K.2	Phonological Awareness: Demonstrate understanding of spoken words, syllables, and sounds (phonemes)	RF2 pp. 78–83
RF.K.3	Phonics: Know and apply grade-level phonics and word analysis skills in decoding words	RF3 pp. 84–89
R.KF.4	Fluency: Read level-appropriate texts with purpose and understanding	RF4 pp. 90–95
Writing		
W.K.1	Use a combination of drawing, dictating, and writing to compose opinion pieces	W1 pp. 100–105
W.K.2	Use a combination of drawing, dictating, and writing to compose informative/explanatory texts	W2 pp. 106–111
W.K.3	Use a combination of drawing, dictating, and writing to narrate a single event or several loosely linked events and provide a reaction to what happened	W3 pp. 112–117
W.K.4	NA	
W.K.5	Respond to questions and add details to strengthen writing as needed	W5 pp. 118–123
W.K.6	Explore a variety of digital tools to produce some writing	W6 pp. 124–129
W.K.7	Participate in shared research and writing projects	W7 pp. 130–135
W.K.8	Recall information from experiences or gather information from provided sources to answer a question	W8 pp. 136–141
W.K.9	NA	
W.K.10	NA	
Speaking and Listening		
SL.K.1	Participate in collaborative conversations with diverse partners about topics and texts in small and larger groups	SL1 pp. 146–151
SL.K.2	Ask and answer questions about key details to demonstrate understanding of a topic	SL2 pp. 152–157
SL.K.3	Ask and answer questions in order to seek help, get information, or clarify something that is not understood	SL3 pp. 158–163
SL.K.4	Describe familiar people, places, things, and events	SL4 pp. 164–169
SL.K.5	Add drawings or other visual displays to descriptions to provide additional detail	SL5 pp. 170–175
SL.K.6	Speak audibly and express thoughts, ideas, feelings, and ideas clearly	SL6 pp. 176–181
Language		
L.K.1	Demonstrate command of the conventions of standard English grammar and usage when writing or speaking	L1 pp. 186–191
L.K.2	Demonstrate command of the conventions of standard English capitalization, punctuation, and spelling when writing	L2 pp. 192–197
L.K.3	NA	
L.K.4	Determine or clarify the meaning of unknown and multiple-meaning words and phrases	L4 pp. 204–209
L.K.5	Explore word relationships and nuances in word meanings	L5 pp. 210–215
L.K.6	Use words and phrases acquired through conversations, reading, being read to, and responding to texts	L6 pp. 216–221

(Continued)

Mississippi, Grade 1

Mississippi Strand/Standard	Focus of Mississippi Standard	For More Information
Reading Literature		
RL.1.1	Ask and answer questions about key details in a text	R1 pp. 6–11
RL.1.2	Retell stories, including key details	R2 pp. 12–17
RL.1.3	Describe characters, settings, and major events in a story	R3 pp. 18–23
RL.1.4	Identify words or phrases that suggest feelings or appeal to the senses	R4 pp. 24–29
RL.1.5	Explain major differences between stories and informative texts	R5 pp. 30–35
RL.1.6	Identify who is telling the story at various points in a text	R6 pp. 36–41
RL.1.7	Use illustrations to describe elements of a story	R7 pp. 42–47
RL.1.8	NA	
RL.1.9	Compare and contrast the experiences of characters in stories	R9 pp. 54–59
RL.1.10	Read texts of appropriate complexity	R10 pp. 60–65
Reading Informational Text		
RI.1.1	Ask and answer questions about key details in a text	R1 pp. 6–11
RI.1.2	Identify the main topic and retell key details of a text	R2 pp. 12–17
RI.1.3	Describe the connection between two individuals, events, ideas, or pieces of information in a text	R3 pp. 18–23
RI.1.4	Ask and answer questions to clarify the meaning of words in a text	R4 pp. 24–29
RI.1.5	Use text features to locate information in a text	R5 pp. 30–35
RI.1.6	Distinguish between information provided by illustrations and information provided by words	R6 pp. 36–41
RI.1.7	Use illustrations and details to describe key ideas in a text	R7 pp. 42–47
RI.1.8	Identify the reasons an author gives to support points in a text	R8 pp. 48–53
RI.1.9	Identify basic similarities and differences between two texts on the same topic	R9 pp. 54–59
RI.1.10	Actively engage in reading informational text with purpose and understanding	R10 pp. 60–65
Reading Foundational Skills		
RF.1.1	Print Concepts: Demonstrate understanding of the organization and basic features of print	RF1 pp. 72–77
RF.1.2	Phonological Awareness: Demonstrate understanding of spoken words, syllables, and sounds (phonemes)	RF2 pp. 78–83
RF.1.3	Phonics: Know and apply grade-level phonics and word analysis skills in decoding words	RF3 pp. 84–89
RF.1.4	Fluency: Read level-appropriate texts with accuracy and fluency	RF4 pp. 90–95
Writing		
W.1.1.1	Write opinion pieces: introduce the topic, state an opinion, supply reasons, and provide closure	W1 pp. 100–105
W.1.2	Write informative/explanatory texts: name a topic, supply facts, and provide closure	W2 pp. 106–111
W.1.3	Write narratives: sequence events, include details, use temporal words, and provide closure	W3 pp. 112–117
W.1.4	NA	
W.1.5	Focus on a topic, respond to questions, and add details to strengthen writing as needed	W5 pp. 118–123

Mississippi Strand/Standard	Focus of Mississippi Standard	For More Information
Writing		
W.1.6	Use a variety of digital tools to produce and publish writing	W6 pp. 124–129
W.1.7	Participate in shared research and writing projects	W7 pp. 130–135
W.1.8	Recall information from experiences or gather information from provided sources to answer a question	W8 pp. 136–141
W.1.9	NA	
W.1.10	NA	
Speaking and Listening		
SL.1.1	Participate in collaborative conversations with diverse partners about topics and texts in small and larger groups	SL1 pp. 146–151
SL.1.2	Ask and answer questions about key details to demonstrate understanding of a topic	SL2 pp. 152–157
SL.1.3	Ask and answer questions in order to get information or clarify something that is not understood	SL3 pp. 158–163
SL.1.4	Clearly describe people, places, things, and events	SL4 pp. 164–169
SL.1.5	Add drawings or other visual displays to descriptions to provide additional detail	SL5 pp. 170–175
SL.1.6	Produce complete sentences when appropriate to task and situation	SL6 pp. 176–181
Language		
L.1.1	Demonstrate command of the conventions of standard English grammar and usage when writing or speaking	L1 pp. 186–191
L.1.2	Demonstrate command of the conventions of standard English capitalization, punctuation, and spelling when writing	L2 pp. 192–197
L.1.3	NA	
L.1.1.4	Determine or clarify the meaning of unknown and multiple-meaning words and phrases	L4 pp. 204–209
L.1.5	Demonstrate understanding of word relationships and nuances in word meanings	L5 pp. 210–215
L.1.6	Use words and phrases acquired through conversations, reading, being read to, and responding to texts	L6 pp. 216–221

Mississippi, Grade 2

Mississippi Strand/Standard	Focus of Mississippi Standard	For More Information
Reading Literature		
RL.2.1	Ask and answer questions about key details in a text	R1 pp. 6–11
RL.2.2	Recount stories and determine their central message	R2 pp. 12–17
RL.2.3	Describe how characters respond to major events and challenges	R3 pp. 18–23
RL.2.4	Describe how words or phrases supply rhythm and meaning	R4 pp. 24–29
RL.2.5	Describe the overall structure of a story, including the beginning and ending	R5 pp. 30–35
RL.2.6	Acknowledge differences in characters' points of view	R6 pp. 36–41
RL.2.7	Use information gathered from illustrations and words to demonstrate understanding of story elements	R7 pp. 42–47

(Continued)

Mississippi Strand/Standard	Focus of Mississippi Standard	For More Information
Reading Literature		
RL.2.8	NA	
RL.2.9	Compare and contrast two or more versions of the same story	R9 pp. 54–59
RL.2.10	Read and comprehend texts of appropriate complexity	R10 pp. 60–65
Reading Informational Text		
RI.2.1	Ask and answer questions about key details in a text	R1 pp. 6–11
RI.2.2	Identify the main topic and retell key details of a text, as well as the focus of specific paragraphs	R2 pp. 12–17
RI.2.3	Describe the connection between a series of events, ideas, concepts, or steps in a text	R3 pp. 18–23
RI.2.4	Determine the meaning of words and phrases in a text relevant to a grade-level topic	R4 pp. 24–29
RI.2.5	Use text features to efficiently locate information in a text	R5 pp. 30–35
RI.2.6	Identify the main purpose of a text	R6 pp. 36–41
RI.2.7	Explain how specific images contribute to and clarify a text	R7 pp. 42–47
RI.2.8	Describe how reasons an author gives support points in a text	R8 pp. 48–53
RI.2.9	Compare and contrast the most important points in two texts on the same topic	R9 pp. 54–59
RI.2.10	Read and comprehend informational texts of appropriate complexity	R10 pp. 60–65
Reading Foundational Skills		
RF.2.1	NA	
RF.2.2	NA	
RF.2.3	Phonics: Know and apply grade-level phonics and word analysis skills in decoding words	RF3 pp. 84–89
RF.2.4	Fluency: Read level-appropriate texts with accuracy and fluency	RF4 pp. 90–95
Writing		
W.2.1	Write opinion pieces: introduce the topic, state an opinion, supply reasons using linking words, and provide closure	W1 pp. 100–105
W.2.2	Write informative/explanatory texts: name a topic, use facts to develop points, and provide closure	W2 pp. 106–111
W.2.3	Write narratives: sequence events; include details to describe actions, thoughts, and feelings; use temporal words; provide closure	W3 pp. 112–117
W.2.4	NA	
W.2.5	Focus on a topic and strengthen writing by revising and editing	W5 pp. 118–123
W.2.6	Use a variety of digital tools to produce and publish writing	W6 pp. 124–129
W.2.7	Participate in shared research and writing projects	W7 pp. 130–135
W.2.8	Recall information from experiences or gather information from provided sources to answer a question	W8 pp. 136–141
W.2.9	NA	
W.2.10	NA	
Speaking and Listening		
SL.2.1	Participate in collaborative conversations with diverse partners about topics and texts in small and larger groups	SL1 pp. 146–151
SL.2.2	Recount or describe key ideas or details in information presented orally	SL2 pp. 152–157

Mississippi Strand/Standard	Focus of Mississippi Standard	For More Information
Speaking and Listening		
SL.2.3	Ask and answer questions in order to get information, deepen understanding, or clarify something that is not understood	SL3 pp. 158–163
SL.2.4	Recount a story or experience with appropriate facts and relevant details	SL4 pp. 164–169
SL.2.5	Create audio recordings of stories or poems, adding visual displays as appropriate for clarification	SL5 pp. 170–175
SL.2.6	Produce complete sentences when appropriate to task and situation	SL6 pp. 176–181
Language		
L.2.1	Demonstrate command of the conventions of standard English grammar and usage when writing or speaking	L1 pp. 186–191
L.2.2	Demonstrate command of the conventions of standard English capitalization, punctuation, and spelling when writing	L2 pp. 192–197
L.2.3	Use knowledge of language and its conventions when writing, speaking, reading, or listening	L3 pp. 198–203
L.2.4	Determine or clarify the meaning of unknown and multiple-meaning words and phrases	L4 pp. 204–209
L.2.5	Demonstrate understanding of word relationships and nuances in word meanings	L5 pp. 210–215
L.2.6	Use words and phrases acquired through conversations, reading, being read to, and responding to texts	L6 pp. 216–221

Missouri, Kindergarten

Missouri Strand/Standard	Focus of Missouri Standard	For More Information
Reading		
R.1	Develop and apply skills to the reading process	
R.1.A	Comprehension: Develop and demonstrate reading skills in response to read-alouds by making predictions, asking and responding to questions, retelling main ideas, making text-to-self connections, and recognizing beginning, middle, and end	R1 pp. 6–11 R2 pp. 12–17
R.1.B	Vocabulary: Develop an understanding of vocabulary by identifying and sorting pictures into categories, demonstrating understanding of opposites, distinguishing shades of meaning, using a dictionary, and using words and phrases acquired through conversations and reading	L5 pp. 210–215
R.1.C	Making Connections: Make text-to-self and text-to-text connections	R9 pp. 54–59
R.1.D	Independent Text: Read independently for sustained periods by engaging with text as developmentally appropriate.	R10 pp. 60–65
R.2	Develop and apply skills and strategies to comprehend, analyze and evaluate fiction, poetry and drama from a variety of cultures and times	
R.2.A	Fiction: Identify story elements (setting, character, events); retell main events; recognize sensory details; recognize different text types; name and describe the roles of author and illustrator; compare and contrast characters; ask and answer questions about unknown words	R2 pp. 12–17 R4 pp. 24–29 R5 pp. 30–35 R6 pp. 36–41 R9 pp. 54–59
R.2.B	Poetry: Respond to rhythm and rhyme through identifying a regular beat and similarities in word sounds	R4 pp. 24–29
R.2.C	Drama: Identify characters in a puppet play or performance by actors	R3 pp. 18–23

(Continued)

Missouri Strand/Standard	Focus of Missouri Standard	For More Information
Reading		
R.3	Develop and apply skills and strategies to comprehend, analyze and evaluate nonfiction (e.g., narrative, information/explanatory, opinion, persuasive, argumentative) from a variety of cultures and times	
R.3.A	Text Features: Identify topic and details, make predictions, and identify text features	R2 pp. 12–17 R5 pp. 30–35 R6 pp. 36–41
R.3.B	Literary Techniques: Respond to examples of sensory details	L5 pp. 210
R.3.C	Text Structures: Ask and answer questions to clarify meaning; compare and contrast two texts on the same topic; name the main topic and key details of a text; ask and answer questions about unknown words	R1 pp. 6–11 R2 pp. 12–17 R4 pp. 20–25 R9 pp. 54–59
R.4	Comprehend and analyze words, images, graphics, and sounds in various media and digital forms to impact meaning	
R.4.A	Digital and Media Literacy: identify different forms of media and techniques used in media	R7 pp. 42–47
Reading Foundations		
RF.1	Understand how English is written and read	
RF.1.A	Print Awareness: Identify upper and lowercase letters; sequence letters of the alphabet; demonstrate directionality of print and one-to-one correspondence between spoken and written words; know that words are made of letters and sentences are groups of words	RF1 pp. 72–77
RF.2	Understand how English is written and read	
Rf.2.A	Phonemic Awareness: Identify sounds in spoken words; produce and identify rhyming words; recognize alliteration; blend phonemes to form words; isolate phonemes in words; segment words	RF2 pp. 78–83
RF.3	Understand how English is written and read	
RF.3.A	Phonics: Produce and write letter(s) for most consonant and short vowel sounds; read high-frequency words; decode simple words; recognize that that new words can be created when letters are changed, added, or deleted; use letter sound knowledge to write simple messages and words	RF2 pp. 78–83 RF3 pp. 84–89
RF.4	Understand how English is written and read	
RF.4.A	Fluency: Read appropriate texts with purpose and understanding	RF4 pp. 90–95
Writing		
W.1	Apply a writing process to develop a text for audience and purpose	
W.1.A	Prewriting: Generate a writing plan	W5 pp. 118–123
W.1.B	Draft: Develop a draft	W5 pp. 118–123
W.1.C	Revise/Edit: Respond to questions and suggestions, adding details to strengthen writing	W5 pp. 118–123
W.1.D	Produce/Publish and Share Writing: Explore a variety of conventional/digital tools to produce and publish writing	W6 pp. 124–129
W.2	Compose well-developed writing texts for audience and purpose	
W.2.A	Opinion/Argumentative: Use a combination of drawing and/or writing to tell an opinion about a topic or text; give logical reasons for an opinion; use words related to the topic	W1 pp. 100–105
W.2.B	Informative/Explanatory: Use a combination of drawing and/or writing to name and inform about a topic or a text; use words related to the topic	W2 pp. 106–111
W.2.C	Narrative/Literary: Use a combination of drawing and/or writing to narrate a story or experience; tell about a character or event; sequence events; use words related to the topic; provide a reaction to narrated events	W3 pp. 112–117
W.3	Gather, analyze, evaluate and use information from a variety of sources	
W.3.A	Apply research process: Generate a list of open-ended questions about topics; decide what sources or people can answer their questions; gather evidence from sources; use pictures in conjunction with writing to document research	W7 pp. 130–135 W8 pp. 136–141

Missouri Strand/Standard	Focus of Missouri Standard	For More Information
Language		
L.1	Communicate using conventions of English language	
L.1.A	Grammar: Identify nouns and verbs; use plurals in speech; express time and space; use complete sentences; use question words	L1 pp. 186–191
L.1.B	Punctuation, Capitalization, Spelling; Print in upper and lowercase letters; recognize end punctuation; capitalize own name, the first word in a sentence, and the pronoun *I*; use inventive spelling with beginning, final, and medial sounds; write and name letters for consonant and vowel sounds; use correct spelling for own name	L2 pp. 192–197
Speaking/Listening		
SL.1	Listen for a purpose	
SL.1.A	Purpose: Follow classroom listening rules; continue a conversation through multiple exchanges; follow one-step instructions	SL1 pp. 146–151
SL.2	Listen for entertainment	
SL.2.A	Entertainment: Demonstrate active listening	SL1 pp. 146–151
SL.3	Speak effectively in collaborative discussions	
SL.3.A	Collaborative discussions: Take turns speaking, continue conversation through multiple exchanges; confirm comprehension through retelling and asking questions	SL1 pp. 146–151 SL2 pp. 152–157
SL.4	Speak effectively when presenting	
SL.4.A	Presenting: Describe personal experiences using a prop, picture, or other visual aide; speak in complete sentences	SL4 pp. 164–169 SL6 pp. 176–181

Missouri, Grade 1

Missouri Strand/Standard	Focus of Missouri Standard	For More Information
Reading		
R.1	Develop and apply skills to the reading process	
R.1.A	Comprehension: Develop and demonstrate reading skills in response to reading by making predictions; asking and responding to questions; locating facts and details; retelling main ideas; recognizing beginning, middle, and end; and monitoring comprehension	R1 pp. 6–11 R2 pp. 12–17
R.1.B	Vocabulary: Use common affixes to figure out word meaning; identify common root words and their inflectional endings; identify verbs and nouns; recognize compound words; determine word meaning from context clues; sort words into conceptual categories; distinguish shades of meaning; locate words in a dictionary; acquire and utilize new words and phrases	L4 pp. 204–209 L5 pp. 210–215 L6 pp. 216–221
R.1.C	Making Connections: Make text-to-text connections	R9 pp. 54–59
R.1.D	Independent Text: Read independently for sustained periods by engaging with text that is developmentally appropriate; produce evidence of reading	R10 pp. 60–65
R.2	Develop and apply skills and strategies to comprehend, analyze and evaluate fiction, poetry and drama from a variety of cultures and times	
R.2.A	Fiction: Describe story elements (setting, character, problem/solution, events); describe the main idea; describe sensory details; recognize different text types; identify who is telling the story; compare and contrast characters and their experiences	R2 pp. 12–17 R4 pp. 24–29 R5 pp. 30–35 R6 pp. 36–41 R9 pp. 54–59
R.2.B	Poetry: Use rhythm and rhyme through identifying a regular beat and similarities in word sounds	R4 pp. 24–29
R.2.C	Drama: Identify characters in a puppet play or performance by actors; recognize sensory details	R3 pp. 18–23 R4 pp. 24–29

(Continued)

Missouri Strand/Standard	Focus of Missouri Standard	For More Information
Reading		
R.3	Develop and apply skills and strategies to comprehend, analyze and evaluate nonfiction (e.g., narrative, information/explanatory, opinion, persuasive, argumentative) from a variety of cultures and times	
R.3.A	Text Features: Use text features to restate the main idea, explain facts, and locate specific information; follow multistep directions with picture cues	R5 pp. 30–35 R6 pp. 36–41 R7 pp. 44–49
R.3.B	Literary Techniques: Distinguish between fiction and nonfiction; identify examples of sensory details	L5 pp. 210
R.3.C	Text Structures: Ask and answer questions to clarify meaning; identify main ideas and provide supporting details; compare and contrast two texts on the same topic; identify reasons an author gives to support points in a text	R1 pp. 6–11 R2 pp. 12–17 R3 pp. 18–23 R4 pp. 24–29 R9 pp. 54–59
R.4	Comprehend and analyze words, images, graphics, and sounds in various media and digital forms to impact meaning	
R.4.A	Digital and Media Literacy: Distinguish purposes of media and explain techniques	R7 pp. 42–47
Reading Foundations		
RF.1	Understand how English is written and read	
RF.1.A	Print Awareness: Recognize that sentences are groups of words; recognize distinguishing features of a sentence	RF1 pp. 72–77
RF.2	Understand how English is written and read	
Rf.2.A	Phonemic Awareness: Produce and identify sounds and syllables; distinguish between long and short vowel sounds; recognize the change in a spoken word when a specific phoneme is changed; blend phonemes to form 1- or 2-syllable words; segment words of 3–5 phonemes	RF2 pp. 78–83
RF.3	Understand how English is written and read	
RF.3.A	Phonics: Decode words in context; identify letters for spelling short and long vowels; produce consonant blends and digraphs; use common spelling patterns to create and decode words; use syllabication patterns to decode words; read irregularly spelled words, root words with inflectional endings, contractions and compound words, and high-frequency words; demonstrate decoding skills	RF3 pp. 84–89
RF.4	Understand how English is written and read	
RF.4.A	Fluency: Read appropriate texts with fluency and purpose and understanding; use context to confirm or self-correct, rereading as necessary	RF4 pp. 90–95
Writing		
W.1	Apply a writing process to develop a text for audience and purpose	
W.1.A	Prewriting: Brainstorm and record key ideas	W5 pp. 118–123
W.1.B	Draft: Develop a draft by sequencing ideas into sentence, staying on topic; generate opening and closing	W5 pp. 118–123
W.1.C	Revise/Edit: Respond to questions and suggestions, adding details to strengthen writing; edit for language conventions	W5 pp. 118–123
W.1.D	Produce/Publish and Share Writing: Use a variety of conventional/digital tools to produce and publish writing	W6 pp. 124–129
W.2	Compose well-developed writing texts for audience and purpose	
W.2.A	Opinion/Argumentative: Introduce a topic, state an opinion, use topic-specific words, organize writing, and provide a closing	W1 pp. 100–105
W.2.B	Informative/Explanatory: Introduce a topic and supply facts, use topic-specific words, organize writing, and provide a closing	W2 pp. 106–111
W.2.C	Narrative/Literary: Write to narrate a story or experience; use details; sequence events; use linking words to indicate sequence of events; provide a reaction to narrated events	W3 pp. 112–117

Missouri Strand/Standard	Focus of Missouri Standard	For More Information
Writing		
W.3	Gather, analyze, evaluate and use information from a variety of sources	
W.3.A	Research process: Generate a list of open-ended questions about topics, decide what sources can answer the questions, gather evidence from sources, organize information using graphic organizers or other aids, make informal presentations of information, self-evaluate using established criteria	W7 pp. 130–135 W8 pp. 136–141
Language		
L.1	Communicate using conventions of English language	
L.1.A	Grammar: In sentences, use nouns and verbs that designate past, present, and future; adjectives and adverbs; conjunctions; common prepositions; common pronouns; and produce simple and compound sentences	L1 pp. 186–191
L.1.B	Punctuation, Capitalization, Spelling; Print legibly with correct spacing; use ending punctuation; capitalize others' names; use serial commas; spell using regular spelling patterns and phonemic awareness; arrange words alphabetically	L2 pp. 192–197
Speaking/Listening		
SL.1	Listen for a purpose	
SL.1.A	Purpose: Follow classroom listening rules; respond to comments of others in conversations; follow two-step instructions	SL1 pp. 146–151
SL.2	Listen for entertainment	
SL.2.A	Entertainment: Demonstrate active listening	SL1 pp. 146–151
SL.3	Speak effectively in collaborative discussions	
SL.3.A	Collaborative discussions: Take turns speaking; continue conversation through multiple exchanges; confirm comprehension through retelling and asking questions	SL1 pp. 146–151 SL2 pp. 152–157
SL.4	Speak effectively when presenting	
SL.4.A	Presenting: Explain a topic using a prop, picture, or other visual aide; recite poetry in a group or individually; speak in complete sentences, adjusting volume as needed	SL4 pp. 164–169 SL5 pp. 170–175 SL6 pp. 176–181

Missouri, Grade 2

Missouri Strand/Standard	Focus of Missouri Standard	For More Information
Reading		
R.1	Develop and apply skills to the reading process	
R.1.A	Comprehension: Develop and demonstrate reading skills in response to reading by making and confirming predictions; asking and responding to questions; supporting answers with evidence; retelling main ideas; retelling beginning, middle, and end; monitoring comprehension and correcting as necessary	R1 pp. 6–11 R2 pp. 12–17
R.1.B	Vocabulary: Use affixes and root words to determine word meaning; use individual word meaning to determine the meaning of compound words; use context to determine word meaning; use antonyms and synonyms, use a dictionary; distinguish meaning between related verbs and adjectives; recognize literal and nonliteral meanings; use conversational, domain-specific, and academic words and phrases	L4 pp. 204–209 L5 pp. 210–215 L6 pp. 216–221
R.1.C	Making Connections: Make text-to-text and text-to-world connections	R9 pp. 54–59
R.1.D	Independent Text: Read independently for sustained periods by engaging with text that is developmentally appropriate; produce evidence of reading	R10 pp. 60–65

(Continued)

Missouri Strand/Standard	Focus of Missouri Standard	For More Information
Reading		
R.2	Develop and apply skills and strategies to comprehend, analyze and evaluate fiction, poetry and drama from a variety of cultures and times	
R.2.A	Fiction: Describe story elements (setting, character, problem/solution, events), the main idea, and cause-and-effect relationships; explain how the story changes based on who is telling the story; compare and contrast characters and their points of view	R2 pp. 12–17 R4 pp. 24–29 R5 pp. 30–35 R6 pp. 36–41 R9 pp. 54–59
R.2.B	Poetry: Describe how rhyme, rhythm, and repetition create imagery in poetry; use onomatopoeia	R4 pp. 24–29
R.2.C	Drama: Identify characters, setting, acts, and scenes in plays; identify the elements of dialogue and use them in informal plays	R3 pp. 18–23 R4 pp. 24–29
R.3	Develop and apply skills and strategies to comprehend, analyze and evaluate nonfiction (e.g., narrative, information/explanatory, opinion, persuasive, argumentative) from a variety of cultures and times	
R.3.A	Text Features: Use text features to identify the main idea and distinguish it from the topic; locate facts to answer or ask questions, and locate specific information; follow written multistep directions; describe connections between events the sequence of events	R1 pp. 6–11 R3 pp. 18–23 R5 pp. 30–35 R7 pp. 44–49
R.3.B	Literary Techniques: Explain why a text is fiction or nonfiction; ask and answer questions to clarify meaning; explain examples of sensory details	R1 pp. 6–11 R4 pp. 24–29
R.3.C	Text Structures: Explain main ideas and provide supporting details; describe the connections between events; identify authors' purpose; compare and contrast two texts on the same topic	R2 pp. 12–17 R3 pp. 18–23 R4 pp. 24–29 R9 pp. 54–59
R.4	Comprehend and analyze words, images, graphics, and sounds in various media and digital forms to impact meaning	
R.4.A	Digital and Media Literacy: Explain purposes of media and explain techniques	R7 pp. 42–47
Reading Foundations		
RF.1	Understand how English is written and read	
RF.1.A	Print Awareness: Understand that sentences are organized into paragraphs to convey meaning	RF1 pp. 72–77
RF.2	Understand how English is written and read	
Rf.2.A	Phonemic Awareness: No expectations	RF2 pp. 78–83
RF.3	Understand how English is written and read	
RF.3.A	Phonics: Decode multisyllabic words in context by applying common letter–sound correspondences including single letters, consonant blends, consonant and vowel digraphs and vowel diphthongs; distinguish long and short vowels; decode words with vowel diphthongs, vowel digraphs; use common prefixes, suffixes, and contractions; use common syllable patterns; read irregularly spelled high-frequency words	RF3 pp. 84–89
RF.4	Understand how English is written and read	
RF.4.A	Fluency: Read appropriate texts with fluency and purpose and understanding	RF4 pp. 90–95
Writing		
W.1	Apply a writing process to develop a text for audience and purpose	
W.1.A	Prewriting: Brainstorm and record key ideas	W5 pp. 118–123

Missouri Strand/Standard	Focus of Missouri Standard	For More Information
Writing		
W.1.B	Draft: Develop a draft by sequencing ideas into sentences; generate paragraphs with one main idea; create beginning, middle, and end; address appropriate audience	W5 pp. 118–123
W.1.C	Revise/Edit: Respond to questions and suggestions, adding details to strengthen writing; edit for language conventions	W5 pp. 118–123
W.1.D	Produce/Publish and Share Writing: Use a variety of conventional/digital tools to produce and publish writing	W6 pp. 124–129
W.2	Compose well-developed writing texts for audience and purpose	
W.2.A	Opinion/Argumentative: Introduce a topic, state an opinion, and provide reasons; use topic-specific words; organize writing; provide a closing	W1 pp. 100–105
W.2.B	Informative/Explanatory: Use facts to develop points; use topic-specific words; use linking words and phrases; provide a closing	W2 pp. 106–111
W.2.C	Narrative/Literary: Introduce a main character and setting; develop sensory details; follow a logical sequence of events and use linking words to signal order; use topic-related language	W3 pp. 112–117
W.3	Gather, analyze, evaluate and use information from a variety of sources	
W.3.A	Research process: Generate a list of open-ended questions about topics; create an individual question and use it to find information; gather evidence from sources; visually organize information; present and evaluate information	W7 pp. 130–135 W8 pp. 136–141
Language		
L.1	Communicate using conventions of English language	
L.1.A	Grammar: Use nouns, pronouns, collective nouns, irregular nouns, regular verbs, helping verbs, adjectives, and adverbs in sentences; produce declarative, imperative, exclamatory, and interrogative sentences	L1 pp. 186–191
L.1.B	Punctuation, Capitalization, Spelling: Write legibly; use apostrophes and quotation marks appropriately; capitalize weeks, days, months, and titles; arrange words in alphabetical order to the 2nd letter	L2 pp. 192–197
Speaking/Listening		
SL.1	Listen for a purpose	
SL.1.A	Purpose: Follow classroom listening rules; follow three-step instructions	SL1 pp. 146–151
SL.2	Listen for entertainment	
SL.2.A	Entertainment: Demonstrate active listening	SL1 pp. 146–151
SL.3	Speak effectively in collaborative discussions	
SL.3.A	Collaborative discussions: Take turns speaking; confirm comprehension of reading through retelling and asking questions	SL1 pp. 146–151 SL2 pp. 152–157
SL.4	Speak effectively when presenting	
SL.4.A	Presenting: Explain a topic while maintaining eye contact with audience; retell a story with details; use academic language and conventions	SL4 pp. 164–169 SL6 pp. 176–181

Nebraska, Kindergarten

Nebraska Strand/Standard	Focus of Nebraska Standard	For More Information
LA0.1	**Reading:** Students will learn and apply reading skills and strategies to comprehend text.	
LA0.1.1	Concepts of Print: Students will demonstrate knowledge of the concepts of print	RF1 pp. 72–77
LA0.1.2	Phonological Awareness: Students will demonstrate phonological awareness through oral activities	RF2 pp. 78–83
LA0.1.3	Word Analysis: Students will use phonetic analysis to read and write grade-level text	RF3 pp. 84–89
LA0.1.4	Fluency: Students will develop accuracy, phrasing, and expression while reading a variety of grade-level reading experiences to support comprehension	RF4 pp. 90–95
LA0.1.5	Vocabulary: Students will build and use conversational, academic, and content-specific grade-level vocabulary	L4 pp. 204–209 L5 pp. 210–215 L6 pp. 216–221
LA0.1.6	Comprehension: Students will construct meaning by using prior knowledge while reading emergent literary and informational text	R1 pp. 6–11 R2 pp. 12–17 R3 pp. 18–23 R5 pp. 30–35 R6 pp. 36–41 R10 pp. 60–65
LA0.2	**Writing:** Students will learn and apply writing skills and strategies to communicate	
LA0.2.1	Writing Process: Students will apply the writing process to plan, draft, revise, edit, and publish writing using correct spelling, grammar, punctuation, and other conventions of standard English appropriate for grade level	W5 pp. 118–123 W8 pp. 136–141 L1 pp. 186–191 L2 pp. 192–197
LA0.2.2	Writing Modes: Students will write in multiple modes for a variety of purposes and audiences across disciplines	W1 pp. 100–105 W2 pp. 106–111 W3 pp. 112–117 W7 pp. 130–135
LA0.3	**Speaking and Listening:** Students will develop end apply speaking and listening skills and strategies to communicate for a variety of purposes	
LA0.3.1	Speaking: Students will develop, refine, and apply speaking skills and strategies to communicate for a variety of situations	SL4 pp. 164–169 SL5 pp. 170–175 SL6 pp. 176–181
LA0.3.2	Listening: Students will develop and demonstrate active listening skills across a variety of situations	SL2 pp. 152–157 SL3 pp. 158–163
LA0.3.3	Reciprocal Communication: Students will develop, apply, and adapt reciprocal communication skills	SL1 pp. 146–151 SL2 pp. 152–157 SL3 pp. 158–163
LA0.4	**Multiple Literacies:** Students will apply information fluency and practice digital citizenship	
LA0.4.1	Information Fluency: Students will evaluate, create, and communicate information in a variety of media and formats	R7 pp. 42–47 R8 pp. 48–53 W6 pp. 124–129 SL5 pp. 170–175
LA0.4.2	Digital Citizenship: Students will practice the norms of appropriate and responsible technology use	W6 pp. 124–129

Nebraska, Grade 1

Nebraska Strand/Standard	Focus of Nebraska Standard	For More Information
LA1.1	**Reading:** Students will learn and apply reading skills and strategies to comprehend text.	
LA1.1.1	Concepts of Print: Students will demonstrate knowledge of the concepts of print	RF1 pp. 72–77
LA1.1.2	Phonological Awareness: Students will demonstrate phonological awareness through oral activities	RF2 pp. 78–83
LA1.1.3	Word Analysis: Students will use phonetic analysis to read and write grade-level text	RF3 pp. 84–89
LA1.1.4	Fluency: Students will develop accuracy, phrasing, and expression while reading a variety of grade-level text to support comprehension	RF4 pp. 90–95
LA1.1.5	Vocabulary: Students will build and use conversational, academic, and content-specific grade-level vocabulary	L4 pp. 204–209 L5 pp. 210–215 L6 pp. 216–221
LA1.1.6	Comprehension: Students will construct meaning by using prior knowledge and text information while reading grade-level literary and informational text	R1 pp. 6–11 R2 pp. 12–17 R3 pp. 18–23 R5 pp. 30–35 R6 pp. 36–41 R10 pp. 60–65
LA1.2	**Writing:** Students will learn and apply writing skills and strategies to communicate	
LA1.2.1	Writing Process: Students will apply the writing process to plan, draft, revise, edit, and publish writing using correct spelling, grammar, punctuation, and other conventions of standard English appropriate for grade level	W5 pp. 118–123 W8 pp. 136–141 L1 pp. 186–191 L2 pp. 192–197
LA1.2.2	Writing Modes: Students will write in multiple modes for a variety of purposes and audiences across disciplines	W1 pp. 100–105 W2 pp. 106–111 W3 pp. 112–117 W7 pp. 130–135
LA1.3	**Speaking and Listening:** Students will develop end apply speaking and listening skills and strategies to communicate for a variety of purposes	
LA1.3.1	Speaking: Students will develop and apply appropriate speaking skills and strategies to communicate for a variety of purposes	SL4 pp. 164–169 SL5 pp. 170–175 SL6 pp. 176–181
LA1.3.2	Listening: Students will develop and demonstrate active listening skills across a variety of situations	SL2 pp. 152–157 SL3 pp. 158–163
LA1.3.3	Reciprocal Communication: Students will develop, apply, and adapt reciprocal communication skills	SL1 pp. 146–151 SL2 pp. 152–157 SL3 pp. 158–163
LA1.4	**Multiple Literacies:** Students will apply information fluency and practice digital citizenship	
LA1.4.1	Information Fluency: Students will evaluate, create, and communicate information in a variety of media and formats	R7 pp. 42–47 R8 pp. 48–53 W6 pp. 124–129 SL5 pp. 170–175
LA1.4.2	Digital Citizenship: Students will practice the norms of appropriate and responsible technology use	W6 pp. 124–129

Nebraska, Grade 2

Nebraska Strand/Standard	Focus of Nebraska Standard	For More Information
LA2.1	**Reading:** Students will learn and apply reading skills and strategies to comprehend text.	
LA2.1.1	Concepts of Print: Mastered in Grade 1	RF1 pp. 72–77
LA2.1.2	Phonological Awareness: Mastered in Grade 1	RF2 pp. 78–83
LA2.1.3	Word Analysis: Students will use phonetic analysis to read and write grade-level text	RF3 pp. 84–89
LA2.1.4	Fluency: Students will develop accuracy, appropriate pace, phrasing, and expression while reading a variety of grade-level text to support comprehension	RF4 pp. 90–95
LA2.1.5	Vocabulary: Students will build and use conversational, academic, and content-specific grade-level vocabulary	L4 pp. 204–209 L5 pp. 210–215 L6 pp. 216–221
LA2.1.6	Comprehension: Students will construct meaning by using prior knowledge and text information while reading grade-level literary and informational text	R1 pp. 6–11 R2 pp. 12–17 R3 pp. 18–23 R5 pp. 30–35 R6 pp. 36–41 R10 pp. 60–65
LA2.2	**Writing:** Students will learn and apply writing skills and strategies to communicate	
LA2.2.1	Writing Process: Students will apply the writing process to plan, draft, revise, edit, and publish writing using correct spelling, grammar, punctuation, and other conventions of standard English appropriate for grade level	W5 pp. 118–123 W8 pp. 136–141 L1 pp. 186–191 L2 pp. 192–197
LA2.2.2	Writing Modes: Students will write in multiple modes for a variety of purposes and audiences across disciplines	W1 pp. 100–105 W2 pp. 106–111 W3 pp. 112–117 W7 pp. 130–135
LA2.3	**Speaking and Listening:** Students will develop end apply speaking and listening skills and strategies to communicate for a variety of purposes	
LA2.3.1	Speaking: Students will develop, refine, and apply speaking skills and strategies to communicate for a variety of situations	SL4 pp. 164–169 SL5 pp. 170–175 SL6 pp. 176–181
LA2.3.2	Listening: Students will develop and demonstrate active listening skills across a variety of situations	SL2 pp. 152–157 SL3 pp. 158–163
LA2.3.3	Reciprocal Communication: Students will develop, apply, and adapt reciprocal communication skills	SL1 pp. 146–151 SL2 pp. 152–157 SL3 pp. 158–163
LA2.4	**Multiple Literacies:** Students will apply information fluency and practice digital citizenship	
LA2.4.1	Information Fluency: Students will evaluate, create, and communicate information in a variety of media and formats	R7 pp. 42–47 R8 pp. 48–53 W6 pp. 124–129 SL5 pp. 170–175
LA2.4.2	Digital Citizenship: Students will practice the norms of appropriate and responsible technology use	W6 pp. 124–129

New Jersey, Kindergarten

New Jersey Strand/Standard	Focus of New Jersey Standard	For More Information
Reading Literature		
RL.K.1	Ask and answer questions about key details in a text	R1 pp. 6–11
RL.K.2	Retell familiar stories, including key details	R2 pp. 12–17
RL.K.3	Identify characters, settings, and major events in a story	R3 pp. 18–23
RL.K.4	Ask and answer questions about unknown words in a text	R4 pp. 24–29
RL.K.5	Recognize common types of text (e.g., storybooks, poems)	R5 pp. 30–35
RL.K.6	Name the author and illustrator of a story and define the role of each	R6 pp. 36–41
RL.K.7	Describe the relationship between the illustrations and the story in which they appear	R7 pp. 42–47
RL.K.8	NA	
RL.K.9	Compare and contrast the characters in familiar stories	R9 pp. 54–59
RL.K.10	Actively engage in reading activities with purpose and understanding	R10 pp. 60–65
Reading Informational Text		
RI.K.1	Ask and answer questions about key details in a text	R1 pp. 6–11
RI.K.2	Identify the main topic and retell key details of a text	R2 pp. 12–17
RI.K.3	Describe the connection between two individuals, events, ideas, or pieces of information in a text	R3 pp. 18–23
RI.K.4	Ask and answer questions about unknown words in a text	R4 pp. 24–29
RI.K.5	Identify the front cover, back cover, and title page of a book	R5 pp. 30–35
RI.K.6	Name the author and illustrator of a text and define the role of each	R6 pp. 36–41
RI.K.7	Describe the relationship between visual images and the text in which they appear	R7 pp. 42–47
RI.K.8	Identify the reasons an author gives to support points in a text	R8 pp. 48–53
R.KI.9	Identify basic similarities and differences between two texts on the same topic	R9 pp. 54–59
RI.K.10	Actively engage in reading informational text with purpose and understanding	R10 pp. 60–65
Reading Foundational Skills		
RF.K.1	Print Concepts: Demonstrate understanding of the organization and basic features of print	RF1 pp. 72–77
RF.K.2	Phonological Awareness: Demonstrate understanding of spoken words, syllables, and sounds (phonemes)	RF2 pp. 78–83
RF.K.3	Phonics: Know and apply grade-level phonics and word analysis skills in decoding and encoding words	RF3 pp. 84–89
R.KF.4	Fluency: Read level-appropriate texts with purpose and understanding	RF4 pp. 90–95
Writing		
W.K.1	Use a combination of drawing, dictating, and writing to compose opinion pieces	W1 pp. 100–105
W.K.2	Use a combination of drawing, dictating, and writing to compose informative/explanatory texts	W2 pp. 106–111
W.K.3	Use a combination of drawing, dictating, and writing to narrate a single event or several loosely linked events and provide a reaction to what happened	W3 pp. 112–117
W.K.4	NA	

(Continued)

New Jersey Strand/Standard	Focus of New Jersey Standard	For More Information
Writing		
W.K.5	Strengthen writing through response and self-reflection	W5 pp. 118–123
W.K.6	Explore a variety of digital tools to produce some writing	W6 pp. 124–129
W.K.7	Participate in shared research and writing projects	W7 pp. 130–135
W.K.8	Recall information from experiences or gather information from provided sources to answer a question	W8 pp. 136–141
W.K.9	NA	
W.K.10	NA	
Speaking and Listening		
SL.K.1	Participate in collaborative conversations with diverse partners about topics and texts in small and larger groups	SL1 pp. 146–151
SL.K.2	Ask and answer questions about key details to demonstrate understanding of a topic	SL2 pp. 152–157
SL.K.3	Ask and answer questions in order to seek help, get information, or clarify something that is not understood	SL3 pp. 158–163
SL.K.4	Describe familiar people, places, things, and events	SL4 pp. 164–169
SL.K.5	Add drawings or other visual displays to descriptions to provide additional detail	SL5 pp. 170–175
SL.K.6	Speak audibly and express thoughts, ideas, feelings, and ideas clearly	SL6 pp. 176–181
Language		
L.K.1	Demonstrate command of the conventions of standard English grammar and usage when writing or speaking	L1 pp. 186–191
L.K.2	Demonstrate command of the conventions of standard English capitalization, punctuation, and spelling when writing	L2 pp. 192–197
L.K.3	NA	
L.K.4	Determine or clarify the meaning of unknown and multiple-meaning words and phrases	L4 pp. 204–209
L.K.5	Explore word relationships and nuances in word meanings	L5 pp. 210–215
L.K.6	Use words and phrases acquired through conversations, reading, being read to, and responding to texts	L6 pp. 216–221

New Jersey, Grade 1

New Jersey Strand/Standard	Focus of New Jersey Standard	For More Information
Reading Literature		
RL.1.1	Ask and answer questions about key details in a text	R1 pp. 6–11
RL.1.2	Retell stories, including key details	R2 pp. 12–17
RL.1.3	Describe characters, settings, and major events in a story	R3 pp. 18–23
RL.1.4	Identify words or phrases that suggest feelings or appeal to the senses	R4 pp. 24–29
RL.1.5	Explain major differences between stories and informative texts	R5 pp. 30–35
RL.1.6	Identify who is telling the story at various points in a text	R6 pp. 36–41

New Jersey Strand/Standard	Focus of New Jersey Standard	For More Information
Reading Literature		
RL.1.7	Use illustrations to describe elements of a story	R7 pp. 42–47
RL.1.8	NA	
RL.1.9	Compare and contrast the experiences of characters in stories	R9 pp. 54–59
RL.1.10	Read and comprehend texts of appropriate complexity	R10 pp. 60–65
Reading Informational Text		
RI.1.1	Ask and answer questions about key details in a text	R1 pp. 6–11
RI.1.2	Identify the main topic and retell key details of a text	R2 pp. 12–17
RI.1.3	Describe the connection between two individuals, events, ideas, or pieces of information in a text	R3 pp. 18–23
RI.1.4	Ask and answer questions to clarify the meaning of words in a text	R4 pp. 24–29
RI.1.5	Use text features to locate information in a text	R5 pp. 30–35
RI.1.6	Distinguish between information provided by illustrations and information provided by words	R6 pp. 36–41
RI.1.7	Use illustrations and details to describe key ideas in a text	R7 pp. 42–47
RI.1.8	Identify the reasons an author gives to support points in a text and explain the application of this information	R8 pp. 48–53
RI.1.9	Identify basic similarities and differences between two texts on the same topic	R9 pp. 54–59
RI.1.10	Actively engage in reading informational text with purpose and understanding	R10 pp. 60–65
Reading Foundational Skills		
RF.1.1	Print Concepts: Demonstrate mastery of the organization and basic features of print	RF1 pp. 72–77
RF.1.2	Phonological Awareness: Demonstrate mastery of spoken words, syllables, and sounds (phonemes)	RF2 pp. 78–83
RF.1.3	Phonics: Know and apply grade-level phonics and word analysis skills in decoding words	RF3 pp. 84–89
RF.1.4	Fluency: Read level-appropriate texts with accuracy and fluency	RF4 pp. 90–95
Writing		
W.1.1.1	Write opinion pieces: introduce the topic, state an opinion, supply reasons, and provide closure	W1 pp. 100–105
W.1.2	Write informative/explanatory texts: name a topic, supply facts, and provide closure	W2 pp. 106–111
W.1.3	Write narratives: sequence events, include details, use temporal words, and provide closure	W3 pp. 112–117
W.1.4	NA	
W.1.5	Focus on a topic, respond to questions, and add details to strengthen writing and ideas as needed	W5 pp. 118–123
W.1.6	Use a variety of digital tools to produce and publish writing	W6 pp. 124–129
W.1.7	Participate in shared research and writing projects	W7 pp. 130–135
W.1.8	Recall information from experiences or gather information from provided sources to answer a question	W8 pp. 136–141
W.1.9	NA	
W.1.10	NA	
Speaking and Listening		
SL.1.1	Participate in collaborative conversations with diverse partners about topics and texts in small and larger groups	SL1 pp. 146–151
SL.1.2	Ask and answer questions about key details to demonstrate understanding of a topic	SL2 pp. 152–157

(Continued)

New Jersey Strand/Standard	Focus of New Jersey Standard	For More Information
Speaking and Listening		
SL.1.3	Ask and answer questions in order to get information or clarify something that is not understood	SL3 pp. 158–163
SL.1.4	Clearly describe people, places, things, and events	SL4 pp. 164–169
SL.1.5	Add drawings or other visual displays to descriptions to provide additional detail	SL5 pp. 170–175
SL.1.6	Produce complete sentences when appropriate to task and situation	SL6 pp. 176–181
Language		
L.1.1	Demonstrate command of the conventions of standard English grammar and usage when writing or speaking	L1 pp. 186–191
L.1.2	Demonstrate command of the conventions of standard English capitalization, punctuation, and spelling when writing	L2 pp. 192–197
L.1.3	NA	
L.1.1.4	Determine or clarify the meaning of unknown and multiple-meaning words and phrases	L4 pp. 204–209
L.1.5	Demonstrate understanding of word relationships and nuances in word meanings	L5 pp. 210–215
L.1.6	Use words and phrases acquired through conversations, reading, being read to, and responding to texts	L6 pp. 216–221

New Jersey, Grade 2

New Jersey Strand/Standard	Focus of New Jersey Standard	For More Information
Reading Literature		
RL.2.1	Ask and answer questions about key details in a text	R1 pp. 6–11
RL.2.2	Recount stories and determine their central message/theme	R2 pp. 12–17
RL.2.3	Describe how characters respond to major events and challenges using key details	R3 pp. 18–23
RL.2.4	Describe how words or phrases supply rhythm and meaning	R4 pp. 24–29
RL.2.5	Describe the overall structure of a story, including the beginning and ending	R5 pp. 30–35
RL.2.6	Acknowledge differences in characters' points of view	R6 pp. 36–41
RL.2.7	Use information gathered from illustrations and words to demonstrate understanding of story elements	R7 pp. 42–47
RL.2.8	NA	
RL.2.9	Compare and contrast two or more versions of the same story	R9 pp. 54–59
RL.2.10	Read and comprehend literature of appropriate complexity	R10 pp. 60–65
Reading Informational Text		
RI.2.1	Ask and answer questions about key details in a text	R1 pp. 6–11
RI.2.2	Identify the main topic and retell key details of a text, as well as the focus of specific paragraphs	R2 pp. 12–17
RI.2.3	Describe the connection between a series of events, ideas, concepts, or steps in a text	R3 pp. 18–23
RI.2.4	Determine the meaning of words and phrases in a text relevant to a grade-level topic	R4 pp. 24–29
RI.2.5	Use text features to efficiently locate information in a text	R5 pp. 30–35
RI.2.6	Identify the main purpose of a text	R6 pp. 36–41

New Jersey Strand/Standard	Focus of New Jersey Standard	For More Information
Reading Informational Text		
RI.2.7	Explain how specific illustrations and images contribute to and clarify a text	R7 pp. 42–47
RI.2.8	Describe and identify the logical connections of how reasons an author gives support points in a text	R8 pp. 48–53
RI.2.9	Compare and contrast the most important points in two texts on the same topic	R9 pp. 54–59
RI.2.10	Read and comprehend informational texts of appropriate complexity	R10 pp. 60–65
Reading Foundational Skills		
RF.2.1	NA	
RF.2.2	NA	
RF.2.3	Phonics: Know and apply grade-level phonics and word analysis skills in decoding words	RF3 pp. 84–89
RF.2.4	Fluency: Read level-appropriate texts with accuracy and fluency	RF4 pp. 90–95
Writing		
W.2.1	Write opinion pieces: introduce the topic, state an opinion, supply reasons using linking words, and provide closure	W1 pp. 100–105
W.2.2	Write informative/explanatory texts: name a topic, use facts to develop points, and provide closure	W2 pp. 106–111
W.2.3	Write narratives: sequence events; include details to describe actions, thoughts, and feelings; use temporal words; provide closure	W3 pp. 112–117
W.2.4	NA	
W.2.5	Focus on a topic and strengthen writing through self-reflection, revising, and editing	W5 pp. 118–123
W.2.6	Use a variety of digital tools to produce and publish writing	W6 pp. 124–129
W.2.7	Participate in shared research and writing projects	W7 pp. 130–135
W.2.8	Recall information from experiences or gather information from provided sources to answer a question	W8 pp. 136–141
W.2.9	NA	
W.2.10	NA	
Speaking and Listening		
SL.2.1	Participate in collaborative conversations with diverse partners about topics and texts in small and larger groups	SL1 pp. 146–151
SL.2.2	Recount or describe key ideas or details in information presented orally	SL2 pp. 152–157
SL.2.3	Ask and answer questions in order to get information, deepen understanding, or clarify something that is not understood	SL3 pp. 158–163
SL.2.4	Recount a story or experience with appropriate facts and relevant details	SL4 pp. 164–169
SL.2.5	Use multimedia; create recordings of stories or poems, adding visual displays as appropriate for clarification	SL5 pp. 170–175
SL.2.6	Produce complete sentences when appropriate to task and situation	SL6 pp. 176–181
Language		
L.2.1	Demonstrate command of the conventions of standard English grammar and usage when writing or speaking	L1 pp. 186–191
L.2.2	Demonstrate command of the conventions of standard English capitalization, punctuation, and spelling when writing	L2 pp. 192–197
L.2.3	Use knowledge of language and its conventions when writing, speaking, reading, or listening	L3 pp. 198–203
L.2.4	Determine or clarify the meaning of unknown and multiple-meaning words and phrases	L4 pp. 204–209
L.2.5	Demonstrate understanding of word relationships and nuances in word meanings	L5 pp. 210–215
L.2.6	Use words and phrases acquired through conversations, reading, being read to, and responding to texts	L6 pp. 216–221

Oklahoma, Kindergarten

Oklahoma Strand/Standard	Focus of Oklahoma Standard	For More Information
Speaking and Listening		
1.R.1	Listen actively and speak using agreed-upon rules for discussion	SL1 pp. 146–151
1.R.2	Ask and answer questions to seek help, get information, or clarify information	SL3 pp. 158–163
1.R.3	Engage in collaborative discussions	SL1 pp. 146–151
1.R.4	Follow one and two step directions	NA
1.W.1	Orally describe interests or tell stories; speak clearly in complete sentences	SL4 pp. 156–161
1.W.2	Work with others respectfully	SL1 pp. 138–143
Reading Foundations		
2.PA.1–9	Phonological Awareness: Demonstrate understanding of spoken words, syllables, and sounds (phonemes)	RF2 pp. 78–83
2.PC.1	Correctly form letters	L1 pp. 186–191
2.PC.2–8	Print Concepts: Demonstrate understanding of the organization and basic features of print	RF1 pp. 72–77
2.PWS.1–4	Phonics: Know and apply grade-level phonics and word analysis skills in decoding words	RF3 pp. 84–89
2.F.1–2	Read own name in print; read common high-frequency words	RF4 pp. 90–95
Reading and Writing Process		
2.R.1	Retell or reenact major events from a read-aloud	R2 pp. 12–17
2.R.2	Discriminate between fiction and nonfiction	NA
2.R.3	Sequence the events of a story	R2 pp. 12–17 R3 pp. 18–23
2.W.1–3	Develop, sequence, and edit first drafts	W5 pp. 98–103
Critical Reading and Writing		
3.R.1	Name the author and illustrator and explain the roles of each	R6 pp. 36–41
3.R.2	Describe characters and setting in a story	R3 pp. 18–23
3.R.3	Tell what is happening in an illustration	R7 pp. 42–47
3.R.4	Ask and answer questions about texts	R1 pp. 6–11
3.W.1	Use drawing, labeling, dictating, and writing to tell a story, share information, or express an opinion	W1 pp. 100–105 W2 pp. 106–111 W3 pp. 112–117
Vocabulary		
4.R.1	Acquire new academic, domain-specific vocabulary and relate new words to prior knowledge	L6 pp. 216–221
4.R.2	Develop an awareness of context clues	L4 pp. 204–209
4.R.3	Name and sort pictures of objects into categories	L5 pp. 210–215
4.W.1	Use new vocabulary to produce and expand complete sentences	L6 pp. 216–221
4.W.2	Select appropriate language according to purpose	L6 pp. 216–221

Oklahoma Strand/Standard	Focus of Oklahoma Standard	For More Information
Language		
5.R.1–4	Begin to understand the function of grammar; recognize nouns and verbs; determine spatial and time relationships	L1 pp. 186–191
5.W.1–2	Capitalize first name, the pronoun *I*; begin sentences with a capital letter and end with a period or question mark	L2 pp. 192–197
Research		
6.R.1–2	Identify sources of information on a topic of interest; identify graphic features to understand a text	R7 pp. 42–47 W7 pp. 130–135
6.W.1–2	Generate topics of interest; find information from provided sources during group research	W7 pp. 130–135 W8 pp. 136–141
Multimodal Literacies		
7.R.1–2	Recognize formats of print and digital text; explore how topics and ideas are depicted in a variety of media	R9 pp. 54–59
7.W.1–2	Use appropriate technology to communicate with others; use appropriate props or images to support verbal communication	W6 pp. 124–129 SL5 pp. 170–175
Independent Reading and Writing		
8.R	Demonstrate interest and interact independently with books	R10 pp. 60–65
8.W	Express ideas through a combination of drawing and emergent writing	W1 pp. 100–105 W2 pp. 106–111 W3 pp. 112–117

Oklahoma, Grade 1

Oklahoma Strand/Standard	Focus of Oklahoma Standard	For More Information
Speaking and Listening		
1.R.1	Listen actively and speak using agreed-upon rules for discussion	SL1 pp. 146–151
1.R.2	Ask and answer questions to seek help, get information, or clarify information	SL3 pp. 158–163
1.R.3	Engage in collaborative discussions	SL1 pp. 146–151
1.R.4	Restate and follow one- and two-step directions	NA
1.W.1	Orally describe people, places, things, and events with relevant details	SL4 pp. 156–161
1.W.2	Work in groups respectfully	SL1 pp. 138–143
Reading Foundations		
2.PA.1–6	Phonological Awareness: Demonstrate understanding of spoken words, syllables, and sounds (phonemes)	RF2 pp. 78–83
2.PC.1	Correctly form letters	L1 pp. 186–191
2.PC.2	Print Concepts: Recognize the distinguishing features of a sentence	RF1 pp. 72–77
2.PWS.1–3	Phonics: Know and apply grade-level phonics and word analysis skills in decoding words	RF3 pp. 84–89

(Continued)

Oklahoma Strand/Standard	Focus of Oklahoma Standard	For More Information
Reading Foundations		
2.F.1	Read common high-frequency words	RF3 pp. 84–89
2.F.2	Orally read level-appropriate text smoothly and accurately	RF4 pp. 90–95
Reading and Writing Process		
2.R.1	Retell or reenact major events from a read-aloud	R2 pp. 12–17
2.R.2	Discriminate between fiction and nonfiction	NA
2.R.3	Sequence the events of a story	R2 pp. 12–17 R3 pp. 18–23
2.W.1–2	Develop, sequence, and edit first drafts	W5 pp. 98–103
2.W.3–4	Correctly spell level-appropriate decodable and common sight words; use resources to find correct spellings	L2 pp. 192–197
Critical Reading and Writing		
3.R.1	Identify the author's purpose	R6 pp. 36–41
3.R.2	Describe who is telling the story	R6 pp. 36–41
3.R.3	Find examples of literary elements (setting, plot, characters) in a story	R3 pp. 18–23
3.R.4	Ask and answer questions about texts	R1 pp. 6–11
3.R.5	Locate facts stated in a text	R2 pp. 12–17
3.W.1	Begin to write narratives including plot, setting, and characters	W3 pp. 112–117
3.W.2	Begin to write facts about a subject in response to a text read aloud	W2 pp. 106–111
3.W.3	Express an opinion in writing about a topic and provide a supporting reason	W1 pp. 100–105
Vocabulary		
4.R.1	Acquire and apply new academic, domain-specific vocabulary and relate new words to prior knowledge	L6 pp. 216–221
4.R.2	Use word parts to define unfamiliar words	L4 pp. 204–209
4.R.3	Use context clues to determine word meaning	L4 pp. 204–209
4.R.4	Name and sort words into categories	L5 pp. 210–215
4.R.5	Use a dictionary to find words	NA
4.W.1	Use domain-appropriate vocabulary to communicate ideas in writing	L6 pp. 216–221
4.W.2	Select appropriate language according to purpose	L6 pp. 216–221
Language		
5.R.1–4	Recognize nouns, verbs, adjectives, and prepositions; recognize noun–verb agreement	L1 pp. 186–191
5.W.1–2	Capitalize first letter in a sentence, proper names, months and days of the week; compose grammatically correct sentences	L1 pp. 186–191 L2 pp. 192–197
Research		
6.R.1–2	Identify sources of information on a topic of interest; identify graphic features to understand a text; identify the location and purpose of various visual and text reference sources	R7 pp. 42–47 W7 pp. 130–135
6.W.1–2	Generate questions about topics of interest; organize information found during research	W7 pp. 130–135 W8 pp. 136–141
6.W.3	Make informal presentations of information gathered	SL4 pp. 164–169

Oklahoma Strand/Standard	Focus of Oklahoma Standard	For More Information
Multimodal Literacies		
7.R.1–2	Use print and digital resources; explore and compare how ideas and topics are depicted in a variety of media and formats	R6 pp. 36–41 W7 pp. 130–135
7.W.1–2	Use appropriate technology to communicate with others; use visual displays to support and clarify verbal communication	W6 pp. 124–129 SL5 pp. 170–175
Independent Reading and Writing		
8.R	Select and read independently level-appropriate texts for academic and personal purposes	R10 pp. 60–65
8.W	Write independently for extended and shorter periods	NA

Oklahoma, Grade 2

Oklahoma Strand/Standard	Focus of Oklahoma Standard	For More Information
Speaking and Listening		
1.R.1	Listen actively and speak using agreed-upon rules for discussion	SL1 pp. 146–151
1.R.2	Ask and answer questions to seek help, get information, or clarify information	SL3 pp. 158–163
1.R.3	Engage in collaborative discussions	SL1 pp. 146–151
1.R.4	Restate and follow multistep directions	NA
1.W.1	Report on a topic or text, tell a story, or recount an experience with appropriate facts and details	SL4 pp. 156–161
1.W.2	Work in groups respectfully, valuing contributions by group members	SL1 pp. 138–143
Reading Foundations		
2.PC	Correctly form letters	L1 pp. 186–191
2.PWS.1–3	Phonics: Know and apply grade-level phonics and word analysis skills in decoding words	RF3 pp. 84–89
2.F.1	Read common high-frequency words	RF3 pp. 84–89
2.F.2	Orally read level-appropriate text smoothly and accurately	RF4 pp. 90–95
Reading and Writing Process		
2.R.1	Locate the main idea and supporting details of a text	R2 pp. 12–17
2.R.2	Compare and contrast details to discriminate genres	R9 pp. 54–59
2.R.3	Summarize the events of a story	R5 pp. 30–35
2.W.1–2	Develop, sequence, and edit first drafts	W5 pp. 98–103
2.W.3–4	Correctly spell level-appropriate decodable and common sight words; use resources to find correct spellings	L2 pp. 192–197
Critical Reading and Writing		
3.R.1	Determine the author's purpose	R6 pp. 36–41
3.R.2	Infer whether a story is narrated in first or third person	R6 pp. 36–41
3.R.3	Find examples of literary elements (setting, plot, characters) in a story	R3 pp. 18–23
3.R.4	Find examples of literary devices (simile, metaphor)	NA

(Continued)

Oklahoma Strand/Standard	Focus of Oklahoma Standard	For More Information
Critical Reading and Writing		
3.R.5	Locate facts stated in a text	R2 pp. 12–17
3.R.6	Describe the structure of a text	R5 pp. 30–35
3.R.7	Answer inferential questions	R1 pp. 6–11
3.W.1	Write narratives including plot, setting, and characters	W3 pp. 112–117
3.W.2	Write facts about a subject in response to a text read aloud	W2 pp. 106–111
3.W.3	Express an opinion in writing about a topic and provide supporting reasons	W1 pp. 100–105
Vocabulary		
4.R.1	Acquire and apply new academic, domain-specific vocabulary and relate new words to prior knowledge	L6 pp. 216–221
4.R.2	Use word parts to define unfamiliar words	L4 pp. 204–209
4.R.3	Use context clues to determine word meaning	L4 pp. 204–209
4.R.4	Infer relationships among words, including synonyms, antonyms, and multiple-meaning words	L5 pp. 210–215
4.R.5	Use a dictionary to find words	NA
4.W.1	Use domain-appropriate vocabulary to communicate ideas in writing	L6 pp. 216–221
4.W.2	Select appropriate language according to purpose in writing	L6 pp. 216–221
Language		
5.R.1–5	Recognize nouns, pronouns, and irregular plural nouns; recognize different types and tenses of verbs; recognize adjectives and prepositions; recognize subject and predicate of a sentence	L1 pp. 186–191
5.W.1–3	Capitalize and appropriately punctuate; use simple contractions; compose grammatically correct sentences	L2 pp. 192–197
Research		
6.R.1–3	Create questions to find information on a topic of interest; use graphic features to understand a text; consult visual and text reference sources	R7 pp. 42–47 W7 pp. 130–135
6.W.1–2	Generate questions about topics of interest; organize information found during research	W7 pp. 130–135 W8 pp. 136–141
6.W.3	Make written or oral presentations of information	SL4 pp. 164–169
Multimodal Literacies		
7.R.1–2	Use print and digital resources; explain how ideas and topics are depicted in a variety of media and formats	R6 pp. 36–41 W7 pp. 130–135
7.W.1–2	Select and use appropriate technology to communicate with others; create an audio, visual, and/or multimedia presentation	W6 pp. 124–129 SL5 pp. 170–175
Independent Reading and Writing		
8.R	Select and read independently level-appropriate texts for academic and personal purposes	R10 pp. 60–65
8.W	Write independently for extended and shorter periods	NA

Pennsylvania, Kindergarten

Pennsylvania Strand/Standard	Focus of Pennsylvania Standard	For More Information
Foundational Skills		
CC.1.1.B	Print Concepts: Demonstrate understanding of the organization and basic features of print	RF1 pp. 72–77
CC.1.1.C	Phonological Awareness: Demonstrate understanding of spoken words, syllables, and sounds (phonemes)	RF2 pp. 78–83
CC.1.1.D	Phonics: Know and apply grade-level phonics and word analysis skills in decoding words	RF3 pp. 84–89
CC.1.1.E	Fluency: Read level-appropriate texts with purpose and understanding	RF4 pp. 90–95
Reading Informational Text		
CC.1.2.A	Identify the main topic and retell key details of a text	R2 pp. 12–17
CC.1.2.B	Ask and answer questions about key details in a text	R1 pp. 6–11
CC.1.2.C	Describe the connection between two individuals, events, ideas, or pieces of information in a text	R3 pp. 18–23
CC1.2.E	Identify parts of a book (title, author) and parts of a text (beginning, middle, end)	R5 pp. 30–35 R6 pp. 36–41
CC1.2.F	Ask and answer questions about unknown words in a text	R4 pp. 24–29
CC1.2.G	Describe the relationship between visual images and the text in which they appear	R7 pp. 42–47
CC1.2.H	Identify the reasons an author gives to support points in a text	R8 pp. 48–53
CC1.2.I	Identify basic similarities and differences between two texts on the same topic	R9 pp. 54–59
CC1.2.J	Use words and phrases acquired through conversations, reading, being read to, and responding to texts	L6 pp. 216–221
CC1.2.K	Determine or clarify the meaning of unknown and multiple-meaning words and phrases	L4 pp. 204–209
CC1.2.I	Actively engage in group reading activities with purpose and understanding	R10 pp. 60–65
Reading Literature		
CC1.3.A	Retell familiar stories, including key details	R2 pp. 12–17
CC1.3.B	Ask and answer questions about key details in a text	R1 pp. 6–11
CC1.3.C	Identify characters, settings, and major events in a story	R3 pp. 18–23
CC1.3.D	Name the author and illustrator of a story and define the role of each	R6 pp. 36–41
CC1.3.E	Recognize common types of text (e.g., storybooks, poems)	R5 pp. 30–35
CC1.3.F	Ask and answer questions about unknown words in a text	R4 pp. 24–29
CC1.3.G	Describe the relationship between the illustrations and the story in which they appear	R7 pp. 42–47
CC1.3.H	Compare and contrast the characters in familiar stories	R9 pp. 54–59
CC1.3.I	Determine or clarify the meaning of unknown and multiple-meaning words and phrases	L4 pp. 204–209
CC1.3.J	Use words and phrases acquired through conversations, reading, being read to, and responding to texts	L6 pp. 216–221
CC1.3.K	Actively engage in group reading activities with purpose and understanding	R10 pp. 60–65

(Continued)

Pennsylvania Strand/Standard	Focus of Pennsylvania Standard	For More Information
Writing		
CC1.4.A-F	Use a combination of drawing, dictating, and writing to compose informative/explanatory texts; demonstrate command of the conventions of standard English capitalization, punctuation, and spelling when writing	W2 pp. 106–111 L2 pp. 192–197
CC1.4.G-L	Use a combination of drawing, dictating, and writing to compose opinion pieces; demonstrate command of the conventions of standard English capitalization, punctuation, and spelling when writing	W1 pp. 100–105 L2 pp. 192–197
CC1.4.M-R	Use a combination of drawing, dictating, and writing to compose narratives that describe real or imagined events; demonstrate command of the conventions of standard English capitalization, punctuation, and spelling when writing	W3 pp. 112–117 L2 pp. 192–197
CC1.4.T	Respond to questions and add details to strengthen writing as needed	W5 pp. 118–123
CC1.4.U	Explore a variety of digital tools to produce and publish writing	W6 pp. 124–129
CC1.4.V	Participate in shared research and writing projects	W7 pp. 130–135
CC1.4.W	Recall information from experiences or gather information from provided sources to answer a question	W8 pp. 136–141
CC1.4.X	Write routinely over short time frames	NA
Speaking and Listening		
CC1.5.A	Participate in collaborative conversations with peers and adults about topics and texts in small and larger groups	SL1 pp. 146–151
CC1.5.B	Ask and answer questions about key details to demonstrate understanding of a topic	SL2 pp. 152–157
CC1.5.C	Ask and answer questions in order to seek help, get information, or clarify something that is not understood	SL3 pp. 158–163
CC1.5.D	Share stories, familiar experiences, and interests, speaking clearly and with appropriate volume	SL4 pp. 164–169
CC1.5.E	Speak audibly and express thoughts, ideas, feelings, and ideas clearly	SL6 pp. 176–181
CC1.5.F	NA	SL5 pp. 162–167
CC1.5.G	Demonstrate command of the conventions of standard English grammar and usage when writing or speaking	L1 pp. 186–191

Pennsylvania, Grade 1

Pennsylvania Strand/Standard	Focus of Pennsylvania Standard	For More Information
Foundational Skills		
CC.1.1.B	Print Concepts: Demonstrate understanding of the organization and basic features of print	RF1 pp. 72–77
CC.1.1.C	Phonological Awareness: Demonstrate understanding of spoken words, syllables, and sounds (phonemes)	RF2 pp. 78–83
CC.1.1.D	Phonics: Know and apply grade-level phonics and word analysis skills in decoding words	RF3 pp. 84–89
CC.1.1.E	Fluency: Read level-appropriate texts with purpose and understanding	RF4 pp. 90–95
Reading Informational Text		
CC.1.2.A	Identify the main topic and retell key details of a text	R2 pp. 12–17
CC.1.2.B	Ask and answer questions about key details in a text	R1 pp. 6–11

Pennsylvania Strand/Standard	Focus of Pennsylvania Standard	For More Information
Reading Informational Text		
CC.1.2.C	Describe the connection between two individuals, events, ideas, or pieces of information in a text	R3 pp. 18–23
CC1.2.E	Use text features to locate information in a text	R5 pp. 30–35
CC1.2.F	Ask and answer questions to clarify the meaning of words in a text	R4 pp. 24–29
CC1.2.G	Use illustrations and details to describe key ideas in a text	R7 pp. 42–47
CC1.2.H	Identify the reasons an author gives to support points in a text	R8 pp. 48–53
CC1.2.I	Identify basic similarities and differences between two texts on the same topic	R9 pp. 54–59
CC1.2.J	Use words and phrases acquired through conversations, reading, being read to, and responding to texts	L6 pp. 216–221
CC1.2.K	Determine or clarify the meaning of unknown and multiple-meaning words and phrases	L4 pp. 204–209
CC1.2.I	Read and comprehend level-appropriate informational text	R10 pp. 60–65
Reading Literature		
CC1.3.A	Retell stories, including key details	R2 pp. 12–17
CC1.3.B	Ask and answer questions about key details in a text	R1 pp. 6–11
CC1.3.C	Describe characters, settings, and major events in a story	R3 pp. 18–23
CC1.3.D	Identify who is telling the story at various points in a text	R6 pp. 36–41
CC1.3.E	Explain major differences between stories and informative texts	R5 pp. 30–35
CC1.3.F	Identify words or phrases that suggest feelings or appeal to the senses	R4 pp. 24–29
CC1.3.G	Use illustrations to describe elements of a story	R7 pp. 42–47
CC1.3.H	Compare and contrast the experiences of characters in stories	R9 pp. 54–59
CC1.3.I	Determine or clarify the meaning of unknown and multiple-meaning words and phrases	L4 pp. 204–209
CC1.3.J	Use words and phrases acquired through conversations, reading, being read to, and responding to texts	L6 pp. 216–221
CC1.3.K	Read and comprehend level-appropriate literature	R10 pp. 60–65
Writing		
CC1.4.A-F	Write informative/explanatory texts: name a topic, supply facts, and provide closure; demonstrate command of the conventions of standard English capitalization, punctuation, and spelling when writing	W2 pp. 106–111 L2 pp. 192–197
CC1.4.G-L	Write opinion pieces: introduce the topic, state an opinion, supply reasons, and provide closure; demonstrate command of the conventions of standard English capitalization, punctuation, and spelling when writing	W1 pp. 100–105 L2 pp. 192–197
CC1.4.M-R	Write narratives: sequence events, include details, use temporal words, and provide closure; demonstrate command of the conventions of standard English capitalization, punctuation, and spelling when writing	W3 pp. 112–117 L2 pp. 192–197
CC1.4.T	Focus on a topic, respond to questions and add details to strengthen writing as needed	W5 pp. 118–123
CC1.4.U	Use a variety of digital tools to produce and publish writing	W6 pp. 124–129
CC1.4.V	Participate in individual or shared research and writing projects	W7 pp. 130–135
CC1.4.W	Recall information from experiences or gather information from provided sources to answer a question	W8 pp. 136–141
CC1.4.X	Write routinely over extended time frames	NA

(Continued)

Pennsylvania Strand/Standard	Focus of Pennsylvania Standard	For More Information
Speaking and Listening		
CC1.5.A	Participate in collaborative conversations with peers and adults about topics and texts in small and larger groups	SL1 pp. 146–151
CC1.5.B	Ask and answer questions about key details to demonstrate understanding of a topic, requesting clarification if something is not understood	SL2 pp. 152–157
CC1.5.C	Ask and answer questions about what the speaker says in order to seek help, get information, or clarify something that is not understood	SL3 pp. 158–163
CC1.5.D	Clearly describe people, places, things, and events	SL4 pp. 164–169
CC1.5.E	Produce complete sentences when appropriate to task and situation	SL6 pp. 176–181
CC1.5.F	Add drawings or other visual displays to descriptions to clarify thoughts, ideas, or feelings	SL5 pp. 162–167
CC1.5.G	Demonstrate command of the conventions of standard English grammar and usage when writing or speaking	L1 pp. 186–191

Pennsylvania, Grade 2

Pennsylvania Strand/Standard	Focus of Pennsylvania Standard	For More Information
Foundational Skills		
CC.1.1.B	Print Concepts: NA	RF1 pp. 72–77
CC.1.1.C	Phonological Awareness: NA	RF2 pp. 78–83
CC.1.1.D	Phonics: Know and apply grade-level phonics and word analysis skills in decoding words	RF3 pp. 84–89
CC.1.1.E	Fluency: Read level-appropriate texts with purpose and understanding	RF4 pp. 90–95
Reading Informational Text		
CC.1.2.A	Identify the main topic and retell key details of a text, as well as the focus of specific paragraphs	R2 pp. 12–17
CC.1.2.B	Ask and answer questions about key details in a text	R1 pp. 6–11
CC.1.2.C	Describe the connection between a series of events, ideas, concepts, or steps in a text	R3 pp. 18–23
CC1.2.E	Use text features to efficiently locate information in a text	R5 pp. 30–35
CC1.2.F	Determine the meaning of words and phrases in a text relevant to a grade-level topic	R4 pp. 24–29
CC1.2.G	Explain how specific images contribute to and clarify a text	R7 pp. 42–47
CC1.2.H	Describe how reasons an author gives support points in a text	R8 pp. 48–53
CC1.2.I	Compare and contrast the most important points in two texts on the same topic	R9 pp. 54–59
CC1.2.J	Use words and phrases acquired through conversations, reading, being read to, and responding to texts	L6 pp. 216–221
CC1.2.K	Determine or clarify the meaning of unknown and multiple-meaning words and phrases	L4 pp. 204–209
CC1.2.I	Read and comprehend level-appropriate informational text	R10 pp. 60–65
Reading Literature		
CC1.3.A	Recount stories and determine their central message	R2 pp. 12–17
CC1.3.B	Ask and answer questions about key details in a text	R1 pp. 6–11

Pennsylvania Strand/Standard	Focus of Pennsylvania Standard	For More Information
Reading Literature		
CC1.3.C	Describe how characters respond to major events and challenges	R3 pp. 18–23
CC1.3.D	Acknowledge differences in characters' points of view	R6 pp. 36–41
CC1.3.E	Describe the overall structure of a story, including the beginning and ending	R5 pp. 30–35
CC1.3.F	Describe how words or phrases supply rhythm and meaning	R4 pp. 24–29
CC1.3.G	Use information gathered from illustrations and words to demonstrate understanding of story elements	R7 pp. 42–47
CC1.3.H	Compare and contrast two or more versions of the same story	R9 pp. 54–59
CC1.3.I	Determine or clarify the meaning of unknown and multiple-meaning words and phrases	L4 pp. 204–209
CC1.3.J	Use words and phrases acquired through conversations, reading, being read to, and responding to texts	L6 pp. 216–221
CC1.3.K	Read and comprehend level-appropriate literature	R10 pp. 60–65
Writing		
CC1.4.A-F	Write informative/explanatory texts: name a topic, use facts to develop points, provide closure; demonstrate command of the conventions of standard English capitalization, punctuation, and spelling when writing	W2 pp. 106–111 L2 pp. 192–197
CC1.4.G-L	Write opinion pieces: introduce the topic, state an opinion, supply reasons using linking words, provide closure; demonstrate command of the conventions of standard English capitalization, punctuation, and spelling when writing	W1 pp. 100–105 L2 pp. 192–197
CC1.4.M-R	Write narratives: sequence events, include details to describe actions, thoughts and feelings, use temporal words, and provide closure; demonstrate command of the conventions of standard English capitalization, punctuation, and spelling when writing	W3 pp. 112–117 L2 pp. 192–197
CC1.4.T	Focus on a topic and strengthen writing by revising and editing	W5 pp. 118–123
CC1.4.U	Use a variety of digital tools to produce and publish writing	W6 pp. 124–129
CC1.4.V	Participate in individual or shared research and writing projects	W7 pp. 130–135
CC1.4.W	Recall information from experiences or gather information from provided sources to answer a question	W8 pp. 136–141
CC1.4.X	Write routinely over extended time frames	NA
Speaking and Listening		
CC1.5.A	Participate in collaborative conversations with peers and adults about topics and texts in small and larger groups	SL1 pp. 146–151
CC1.5.B	Recount or describe key ideas or details in information presented orally	SL2 pp. 152–157
CC1.5.C	Ask and answer questions in order to get information, deepen understanding, or clarify something that is not understood	SL3 pp. 158–163
CC1.5.D	Recount a story or experience with appropriate facts and relevant details	SL4 pp. 164–169
CC1.5.E	Produce complete sentences when appropriate to task and situation	SL6 pp. 176–181
CC1.5.F	Add drawings or other visual displays to descriptions to clarify thoughts, ideas, or feelings	SL5 pp. 162–167
CC1.5.G	Demonstrate command of the conventions of standard English grammar and usage when writing or speaking	L1 pp. 186–191

South Carolina, Kindergarten

South Carolina Strand/Standard	Focus of South Carolina Standard	For More Information
Reading Literary Text		
	Principles of Reading	
1	Demonstrate understanding of the organization and basic features of print	RF1 pp. 72–77
2	Demonstrate understanding of spoken words, syllables, and sounds (phonemes)	RF2 pp. 78–83
3	Know and apply grade-level phonics and word analysis skills in decoding words	RF3 pp. 84–89
4	Read level-appropriate texts with purpose and understanding	RF4 pp. 90–95
	Meaning and Context	
5	Ask and answer questions about a text, referring to key details	R1 pp. 6–11
6	Describe the relationship between illustrations and the text	R7 pp. 42–47
7	Retell a familiar text; compare familiar texts	R2 pp. 12–17 R9 pp. 54–59
8	Identify characters, settings, problem and solution, and major events in a story	R3 pp. 18–23
	Language, Craft, and Structure	
9	Identify literary devices and when an author uses them; identify how word choices and illustrations contribute to meaning	R4 pp. 24–29
10	Ask and answer questions about unknown words in a text	R4 pp. 24–29
11	Name the author and illustrator of a story and define the role of each	R6 pp. 36–41
12	Recognize and sort types of literary texts	R5 pp. 30–35
	Range and Complexity	
13	Engage in whole- and small-group reading; read independently for sustained periods	R10 pp. 60–65
Reading Informational Text		
	Principles of Reading	
1	Demonstrate understanding of the organization and basic features of print	RF1 pp. 72–77
2	Demonstrate understanding of spoken words, syllables, and sounds (phonemes)	RF2 pp. 78–83
3	Know and apply grade-level phonics and word analysis skills in decoding words	RF3 pp. 84–89
4	Read level-appropriate texts with purpose and understanding	RF4 pp. 90–95
	Meaning and Context	
5	Ask and answer questions about a text, referring to key details	R1 pp. 6–11
6	Retell the central idea and identify key details to summarize a text	R2 pp. 12–17
7	Compare topics or ideas between texts	R9 pp. 54–59
	Language, Craft, and Structure	
8	Identify words, phrases, and illustrations used to provide information; use text features to locate information	R5 pp. 30–35 R7 pp. 42–47
9	Ask and answer questions about unknown words in a text; use words and phrases acquired through talk and text	R4 pp. 24–29 L6 pp. 216–221
10	Identify the author and illustrator and define the role of each	R6 pp. 36–41
11	Identify the reasons an author gives to support a position	R8 pp. 48–53
	Range and Complexity	
12	Engage in whole- and small-group reading; read independently for sustained periods	R10 pp. 60–65

South Carolina Strand/Standard	Focus of South Carolina Standard	For More Information
Writing		
	Meaning, Context, and Craft	
1	Use a combination of drawing, dictating, and writing to compose opinion pieces; plan, revise, and edit strengthen writing	W1 pp. 100–105 W5 pp. 118–123
2	Use a combination of drawing, dictating, and writing to compose informative/explanatory texts; plan revise and edit to strengthen writing	W2 pp. 106–111 W5 pp 118–123
3	Use a combination of drawing, dictating, and writing to narrate a single event or several loosely linked events and provide a reaction to what happened; plan, revise, and edit to strengthen writing	W3 pp. 112–117 W5 pp. 118–123
	Language	
4	Demonstrate command of the conventions of standard English grammar and usage when writing or speaking	L1 pp. 186–191
5	Demonstrate command of the conventions of standard English capitalization, punctuation, and spelling when writing	L2 pp. 192–197
Communication		
	Meaning and Context	
1	Participate in conversations with diverse partners about topics and texts in small and large groups; explain personal ideas and build on the ideas of others	SL1 pp. 146–151 SL6 pp. 176–181
2	Recall information from experiences or gather information from sources to ask and answer questions; participate in shared research	SL3 pp. 158–163 SL4 pp. 164–169 W7 pp. 130–135
3	Explore a variety of media; use appropriate props, images, or illustrations to support communication	SL5 pp. 170–175 W6 pp. 124–129
4	Identify speaker's purpose and key elements of the presentation	SL2 pp. 152–157
5	Employ speaking techniques to engage and impact the audience	SL6 pp. 176–181

South Carolina, Grade 1

South Carolina Strand/Standard	Focus of South Carolina Standard	For More Information
Reading Literary Text		
	Principles of Reading	
1	Demonstrate understanding of the organization and basic features of print	RF1 pp. 72–77
2	Demonstrate understanding of spoken words, syllables, and sounds (phonemes)	RF2 pp. 78–83
3	Know and apply grade-level phonics and word analysis skills in decoding words	RF3 pp. 84–89
4	Read level-appropriate texts with purpose and understanding	RF4 pp. 90–95
	Meaning and Context	
5	Ask and answer questions to show understanding of a text; use key details to make inferences and draw conclusions	R1 pp. 6–11
6	Describe the relationship between illustrations and the characters, setting, or events	R7 pp. 42–47
7	Retell text including beginning, middle, and end; compare and contrast familiar texts	R2 pp. 12–17 R9 pp. 54–59
8	Describe characters, settings, plot, and cause-and-effect relationships in a story	R3 pp. 18–23

(Continued)

South Carolina Strand/Standard	Focus of South Carolina Standard	For More Information
Reading Literary Text		
	Language, Craft, and Structure	
9	Identify literary devices and how an author uses them; identify how word choices and illustrations contribute to meaning	R4 pp. 24–29
10	Ask and answer questions about unknown words in a text	R4 pp. 24–29
11	Identify who is telling the story at various points in a text	R6 pp. 36–41
12	Classify literary texts according to characteristics of genre	R5 pp. 30–35
	Range and Complexity	
13	Engage in whole- and small-group reading; read independently for sustained periods	R10 pp. 60–65
Reading Informational Text		
	Principles of Reading	
1	Demonstrate understanding of the organization and basic features of print	RF1 pp. 72–77
2	Demonstrate understanding of spoken words, syllables, and sounds (phonemes)	RF2 pp. 78–83
3	Know and apply grade-level phonics and word analysis skills in decoding words	RF3 pp. 84–89
4	Read level-appropriate texts with purpose and understanding	RF4 pp. 90–95
	Meaning and Context	
5	Ask and answer questions to demonstrate understanding of a text; use key details to make inferences and draw conclusions	R1 pp. 6–11
6	Retell the central idea and identify key details to summarize a text	R2 pp. 12–17
7	Compare and contrast topics or ideas between texts	R9 pp. 54–59
	Language, Craft, and Structure	
8	Identify words, phrases, and illustrations used to provide information; use text features to locate information	R5 pp. 30–35 R7 pp. 42–47
9	Ask and answer questions about unknown words in a text; use words and phrases acquired through talk and text	R4 pp. 24–29 L6 pp. 216–221
10	Identify the author's purpose	NA
11	Identify the reasons an author gives to support a position	R8 pp. 48–53
	Range and Complexity	
12	Engage in whole- and small-group reading; read independently for sustained periods	R10 pp. 60–65
Writing		
	Meaning, Context, and Craft	
1	Explore print and multimedia sources to compose opinion pieces; plan, revise, and edit strengthen writing	W1 pp. 100–105 W5 pp. 118–123
2	Explore print and multimedia sources to compose informative/explanatory texts; plan revise and edit to strengthen writing	W2 pp. 106–111 W5 pp. 118–123
3	Explore print and multimedia sources to narrate two or more sequenced events; plan, revise, and edit to strengthen writing	W3 pp. 112–117 W5 pp. 118–123
	Language	
4	Demonstrate command of the conventions of standard English grammar and usage when writing or speaking	L1 pp. 186–191
5	Demonstrate command of the conventions of standard English capitalization, punctuation, and spelling when writing	L2 pp. 192–197

South Carolina Strand/Standard	Focus of South Carolina Standard	For More Information
Communication		
	Meaning and Context	
1	Participate in conversations with diverse partners about topics and texts in small and large groups; explain personal ideas and build on the ideas of others	SL1 pp. 146–151 SL6 pp. 176–181
2	Clearly express ideas gathered from various resources; participate in shared research	SL3 pp. 158–163 SL4 pp. 164–169 W7 pp. 130–135
3	Explore how ideas are depicted in a variety of media; use visual displays to support communication	SL5 pp. 170–175 W6 pp. 124–129
4	Identify speaker's purpose and key elements of the presentation	SL2 pp. 152–157
5	Employ speaking techniques to engage and impact the audience	SL6 pp. 176–181

South Carolina, Grade 2

South Carolina Strand/Standard	Focus of South Carolina Standard	For More Information
Reading Literary Text		
	Principles of Reading	
1	NA	
2	Demonstrate understanding of spoken words, syllables, and sounds (phonemes)	RF2 pp. 78–83
3	Know and apply grade-level phonics and word analysis skills in decoding words	RF3 pp. 84–89
4	Read level-appropriate texts with purpose and understanding	RF4 pp. 90–95
	Meaning and Context	
5	Ask and answer literal and inferential questions to show understanding of a text; use specific details to make inferences and draw conclusions	R1 pp. 6–11
6	Use information gained from illustrations and words to demonstrate understanding of a text's characters, setting, or plot	R7 pp. 42–47
7	Retell the sequence of events using key details; compare and contrast multiple versions of the same story	R2 pp. 12–17 R9 pp. 54–59
8	Compare and contrast characters' actions, feelings, and responses to challenges	R3 pp. 18–23
	Language, Craft, and Structure	
9	Identify literary devices and how an author uses them; identify how word choices and illustrations contribute to meaning	R4 pp. 24–29
10	Ask and answer questions about unknown words in a text	R4 pp. 24–29
11	Recognize differences between the points of view and perspective of the narrator and various characters	R6 pp. 36–41
12	Describe the overall structure of a narrative, including how the beginning introduces and the ending concludes the action	R5 pp. 30–35
	Range and Complexity	
13	Engage in whole- and small-group reading; read independently for sustained periods	R10 pp. 60–65
Reading Informational Text		
	Principles of Reading	
1	NA	

(Continued)

South Carolina Strand/Standard	Focus of South Carolina Standard	For More Information
Reading Informational Text		
2	Demonstrate understanding of spoken words, syllables, and sounds (phonemes)	RF2 pp. 78–83
3	Know and apply grade-level phonics and word analysis skills in decoding words	RF3 pp. 84–89
4	Read level-appropriate texts with purpose and understanding	RF4 pp. 90–95
	Meaning and Context	
5	Ask and answer literal and inferential questions to show understanding of a text; use specific details to make inferences and draw conclusions	R1 pp. 6–11
6	Retell the central idea and key details from multiparagraph texts; summarize text by stating the topic of each paragraph	R2 pp. 12–17
7	Compare and contrast topics or ideas across texts	R9 pp. 54–59
Reading Informational Text		
	Language, Craft, and Structure	
8	Identify how the author uses words, phrases, and images to inform, explain, or describe; use text features to locate information	R5 pp. 30–35 R7 pp. 42–47
9	Determine the meaning of unknown words in a text; use words and phrases acquired through talk and text	R4 pp. 24–29 L6 pp. 216–221
10	Identify and analyze the author's purpose	R6 pp. 36–41
11	Identify how an author supports specific points	R8 pp. 48–53
	Range and Complexity	
12	Engage in whole- and small-group reading; read independently for sustained periods	R10 pp. 60–65
Writing		
	Meaning, Context, and Craft	
1	Explore print and multimedia sources to compose opinion pieces; plan, revise, and edit strengthen writing	W1 pp. 100–105 W5 pp. 118–123
2	Explore print and multimedia sources to compose informative/explanatory texts; plan revise and edit to strengthen writing	W2 pp. 106–111 W5 pp. 118–123
3	Explore print and multimedia sources to narrate one well-elaborated event or a short sequence of events; plan, revise, and edit to strengthen writing	W3 pp. 112–117 W5 pp. 118–123
	Language	
4	Demonstrate command of the conventions of standard English grammar and usage when writing or speaking	L1 pp. 186–191
5	Demonstrate command of the conventions of standard English capitalization, punctuation, and spelling when writing	L2 pp. 192–197
Communication		
	Meaning and Context	
1	Participate in conversations with diverse partners about topics and texts in small and large groups; explain personal ideas and build on the ideas of others	SL1 pp. 146–151 SL6 pp. 176–181
2	Articulate ideas and information gathered from various resources; participate in shared research	SL3 pp. 158–163 SL4 pp. 164–169 W7 pp. 130–135
3	Explain how ideas are depicted in a variety of media; create a presentation using audio, visual, and/or multimedia tools to support communication	SL5 pp. 170–175 W6 pp. 124–129
4	Identify speaker's purpose and details that keep the listener engaged	SL2 pp. 152–157
5	Employ speaking techniques to engage and impact the audience	SL6 pp. 176–181

Tennessee, Kindergarten

Tennessee Strand/Standard	Focus of Tennessee Standard	For More Information
Reading Literature		
RL.K.1	Ask and answer questions about key details in a text	R1 pp. 6–11
RL.K.2	Retell familiar stories, including key details	R2 pp. 12–17
RL.K.3	Identify characters, settings, and major events in a story	R3 pp. 18–23
RL.K.4	Ask and answer questions about unknown words in a text	R4 pp. 24–29
RL.K.5	Recognize common types of text (e.g., storybooks, poems)	R5 pp. 30–35
RL.K.6	Name the author and illustrator of a story and define the role of each	R6 pp. 36–41
RL.K.7	Describe the relationship between the illustrations and the story in which they appear	R7 pp. 42–47
RL.K.8	NA	
RL.K.9	Compare and contrast the characters in familiar stories	R9 pp. 54–59
RL.K.10	Actively engage in reading activities with purpose and understanding	R10 pp. 60–65
Reading Informational Text		
RI.K.1	Ask and answer questions about key details in a text	R1 pp. 6–11
RI.K.2	Identify the main topic and retell key details of a text	R2 pp. 12–17
RI.K.3	Describe the connection between two individuals, events, ideas, or pieces of information in a text	R3 pp. 18–23
RI.K.4	Ask and answer questions about unknown words in a text	R4 pp. 24–29
RI.K.5	Identify the front cover, back cover, and title page of a book	R5 pp. 30–35
RI.K.6	Name the author and illustrator of a text and define the role of each	R6 pp. 36–41
RI.K.7	Describe the relationship between visual images and the text in which they appear	R7 pp. 42–47
RI.K.8	Identify the reasons an author gives to support points in a text	R8 pp. 48–53
R.KI.9	Identify basic similarities and differences between two texts on the same topic	R9 pp. 54–59
RI.K.10	Actively engage in reading informational text with purpose and understanding	R10 pp. 60–65
Reading Foundational Skills		
RF.K.1	Print Concepts: Demonstrate understanding of the organization and basic features of print	RF1 pp. 72–77
RF.K.2	Phonological Awareness: Demonstrate understanding of spoken words, syllables, and sounds (phonemes)	RF2 pp. 78–83
RF.K.3	Phonics: Know and apply grade-level phonics and word analysis skills in decoding words	RF3 pp. 84–89
R.KF.4	Fluency: Read level-appropriate texts with purpose and understanding	RF4 pp. 90–95
Writing		
W.K.1	Use a combination of drawing, dictating, and writing to compose opinion pieces	W1 pp. 100–105
W.K.2	Use a combination of drawing, dictating, and writing to compose informative/explanatory texts	W2 pp. 106–111
W.K.3	Use a combination of drawing, dictating, and writing to narrate a single event or several loosely linked events and provide a reaction to what happened	W3 pp. 112–117
W.K.4	NA	
W.K.5	Respond to questions and add details to strengthen writing as needed	W5 pp. 118–123
W.K.6	Explore a variety of digital tools to produce some writing	W6 pp. 124–129
W.K.7	Participate in shared research and writing projects	W7 pp. 130–135

(Continued)

Tennessee Strand/Standard	Focus of Tennessee Standard	For More Information
Writing		
W.K.8	Recall information from experiences or gather information from provided sources to answer a question	W8 pp. 136–141
W.K.9	NA	
W.K.10	NA	
Speaking and Listening		
SL.K.1	Participate in collaborative conversations with diverse partners about topics and texts in small and larger groups	SL1 pp. 146–151
SL.K.2	Ask and answer questions about key details to demonstrate understanding of a topic	SL2 pp. 152–157
SL.K.3	Ask and answer questions in order to seek help, get information, or clarify something that is not understood	SL3 pp. 158–163
SL.K.4	Describe familiar people, places, things, and events	SL4 pp. 164–169
SL.K.5	Add drawings or other visual displays to descriptions to provide additional detail	SL5 pp. 170–175
SL.K.6	Speak audibly and express thoughts, ideas, feelings, and ideas clearly	SL6 pp. 176–181
Language		
L.K.1	Demonstrate command of the conventions of standard English grammar and usage when writing or speaking	L1 pp. 186–191
L.K.2	Demonstrate command of the conventions of standard English capitalization, punctuation, and spelling when writing	L2 pp. 192–197
L.K.3	NA	
L.K.4	Determine or clarify the meaning of unknown and multiple-meaning words and phrases	L4 pp. 204–209
L.K.5	Explore word relationships and nuances in word meanings	L5 pp. 210–215
L.K.6	Use words and phrases acquired through conversations, reading, being read to, and responding to texts	L6 pp. 216–221

Tennessee, Grade 1

Tennessee Strand/Standard	Focus of Tennessee Standard	For More Information
Reading Literature		
RL.1.1	Ask and answer questions about key details in a text	R1 pp. 6–11
RL.1.2	Retell stories, including key details	R2 pp. 12–17
RL.1.3	Describe characters, settings, and major events in a story	R3 pp. 18–23
RL.1.4	Identify words or phrases that suggest feelings or appeal to the senses	R4 pp. 24–29
RL.1.5	Explain major differences between stories and informative texts	R5 pp. 30–35
RL.1.6	Identify who is telling the story at various points in a text	R6 pp. 36–41
RL.1.7	Use illustrations to describe elements of a story	R7 pp. 42–47
RL.1.8	NA	
RL.1.9	Compare and contrast the experiences of characters in stories	R9 pp. 54–59
RL.1.10	Read texts of appropriate complexity	R10 pp. 60–65

Tennessee Strand/Standard	Focus of Tennessee Standard	For More Information
Reading Informational Text		
RI.1.1	Ask and answer questions about key details in a text	R1 pp. 6–11
RI.1.2	Identify the main topic and retell key details of a text	R2 pp. 12–17
RI.1.3	Describe the connection between two individuals, events, ideas, or pieces of information in a text	R3 pp. 18–23
RI.1.4	Ask and answer questions to clarify the meaning of words in a text	R4 pp. 24–29
RI.1.5	Use text features to locate information in a text	R5 pp. 30–35
RI.1.6	Distinguish between information provided by illustrations and information provided by words	R6 pp. 36–41
RI.1.7	Use illustrations and details to describe key ideas in a text	R7 pp. 42–47
RI.1.8	Identify the reasons an author gives to support points in a text	R8 pp. 48–53
RI.1.9	Identify basic similarities and differences between two texts on the same topic	R9 pp. 54–59
RI.1.10	Actively engage in reading informational text with purpose and understanding	R10 pp. 60–65
Reading Foundational Skills		
RF.1.1	Print Concepts: Demonstrate understanding of the organization and basic features of print	RF1 pp. 72–77
RF.1.2	Phonological Awareness: Demonstrate understanding of spoken words, syllables, and sounds (phonemes)	RF2 pp. 78–83
RF.1.3	Phonics: Know and apply grade-level phonics and word analysis skills in decoding words	RF3 pp. 84–89
RF.1.4	Fluency: Read level-appropriate texts with accuracy and fluency	RF4 pp. 90–95
Writing		
W.1.1.1	Write opinion pieces: introduce the topic, state an opinion, supply reasons, and provide closure	W1 pp. 100–105
W.1.2	Write informative/explanatory texts: name a topic, supply facts, and provide closure	W2 pp. 106–111
W.1.3	Write narratives: sequence events, include details, use temporal words, and provide closure	W3 pp. 112–117
W.1.4	NA	
W.1.5	Focus on a topic, respond to questions, and add details to strengthen writing as needed	W5 pp. 118–123
W.1.6	Use a variety of digital tools to produce and publish writing	W6 pp. 124–129
W.1.7	Participate in shared research and writing projects	W7 pp. 130–135
W.1.8	Recall information from experiences or gather information from provided sources to answer a question	W8 pp. 136–141
W.1.9	NA	
W.1.10	NA	
Speaking and Listening		
SL.1.1	Participate in collaborative conversations with diverse partners about topics and texts in small and larger groups	SL1 pp. 146–151
SL.1.2	Ask and answer questions about key details to demonstrate understanding of a topic	SL2 pp. 152–157
SL.1.3	Ask and answer questions in order to get information or clarify something that is not understood	SL3 pp. 158–163
SL.1.4	Clearly describe people, places, things, and events	SL4 pp. 164–169
SL.1.5	Add drawings or other visual displays to descriptions to provide additional detail	SL5 pp. 170–175
SL.1.6	Produce complete sentences when appropriate to task and situation	SL6 pp. 176–181

(Continued)

Tennessee Strand/Standard	Focus of Tennessee Standard	For More Information
Language		
L.1.1	Demonstrate command of the conventions of standard English grammar and usage when writing or speaking	L1 pp. 186–191
L.1.2	Demonstrate command of the conventions of standard English capitalization, punctuation, and spelling when writing	L2 pp. 192–197
L.1.3	NA	
L.1.1.4	Determine or clarify the meaning of unknown and multiple-meaning words and phrases	L4 pp. 204–209
L.1.5	Demonstrate understanding of word relationships and nuances in word meanings	L5 pp. 210–215
L.1.6	Use words and phrases acquired through conversations, reading, being read to, and responding to texts	L6 pp. 216–221

Tennessee, Grade 2

Tennessee Strand/Standard	Focus of Tennessee Standard	For More Information
Reading Literature		
RL.2.1	Ask and answer questions about key details in a text	R1 pp. 6–11
RL.2.2	Recount stories and determine their central message	R2 pp. 12–17
RL.2.3	Describe how characters respond to major events and challenges	R3 pp. 18–23
RL.2.4	Describe how words or phrases supply rhythm and meaning	R4 pp. 24–29
RL.2.5	Describe the overall structure of a story, including the beginning and ending	R5 pp. 30–35
RL.2.6	Acknowledge differences in characters' points of view	R6 pp. 36–41
RL.2.7	Use information gathered from illustrations and words to demonstrate understanding of story elements	R7 pp. 42–47
RL.2.8	NA	
RL.2.9	Compare and contrast two or more versions of the same story	R9 pp. 54–59
RL.2.10	Read and comprehend texts of appropriate complexity	R10 pp. 60–65
Reading Informational Text		
RI.2.1	Ask and answer questions about key details in a text	R1 pp. 6–11
RI.2.2	Identify the main topic and retell key details of a text, as well as the focus of specific paragraphs	R2 pp. 12–17
RI.2.3	Describe the connection between a series of events, ideas, concepts, or steps in a text	R3 pp. 18–23
RI.2.4	Determine the meaning of words and phrases in a text relevant to a grade-level topic	R4 pp. 24–29
RI.2.5	Use text features to efficiently locate information in a text	R5 pp. 30–35
RI.2.6	Identify the main purpose of a text	R6 pp. 36–41
RI.2.7	Explain how specific images contribute to and clarify a text	R7 pp. 42–47
RI.2.8	Describe how reasons an author gives support points in a text	R8 pp. 48–53
RI.2.9	Compare and contrast the most important points in two texts on the same topic	R9 pp. 54–59
RI.2.10	Read and comprehend informational texts of appropriate complexity	R10 pp. 60–65

Tennessee Strand/Standard	Focus of Tennessee Standard	For More Information
Reading Foundational Skills		
RF.2.1	NA	
RF.2.2	NA	
RF.2.3	Phonics: Know and apply grade-level phonics and word analysis skills in decoding words	RF3 pp. 84–89
RF.2.4	Fluency: Read level-appropriate texts with accuracy and fluency	RF4 pp. 90–95
Writing		
W.2.1	Write opinion pieces: introduce the topic, state an opinion, supply reasons using linking words, and provide closure	W1 pp. 100–105
W.2.2	Write informative/explanatory texts: name a topic, use facts to develop points, and provide closure	W2 pp. 106–111
W.2.3	Write narratives: sequence events; include details to describe actions, thoughts, and feelings; use temporal words; provide closure	W3 pp. 112–117
W.2.4	NA	
W.2.5	Focus on a topic and strengthen writing by revising and editing	W5 pp. 118–123
W.2.6	Use a variety of digital tools to produce and publish writing	W6 pp. 124–129
W.2.7	Participate in shared research and writing projects	W7 pp. 130–135
W.2.8	Recall information from experiences or gather information from provided sources to answer a question	W8 pp. 136–141
W.2.9	NA	
W.2.10	NA	
Speaking and Listening		
SL.2.1	Participate in collaborative conversations with diverse partners about topics and texts in small and larger groups	SL1 pp. 146–151
SL.2.2	Recount or describe key ideas or details in information presented orally	SL2 pp. 152–157
SL.2.3	Ask and answer questions in order to get information, deepen understanding, or clarify something that is not understood	SL3 pp. 158–163
SL.2.4	Recount a story or experience with appropriate facts and relevant details	SL4 pp. 164–169
SL.2.5	Create audio recordings of stories or poems, adding visual displays as appropriate for clarification	SL5 pp. 170–175
SL.2.6	Produce complete sentences when appropriate to task and situation	SL6 pp. 176–181
Language		
L.2.1	Demonstrate command of the conventions of standard English grammar and usage when writing or speaking	L1 pp. 186–191
L.2.2	Demonstrate command of the conventions of standard English capitalization, punctuation, and spelling when writing	L2 pp. 192–197
L.2.3	Use knowledge of language and its conventions when writing, speaking, reading, or listening	L3 pp. 198–203
L.2.4	Determine or clarify the meaning of unknown and multiple-meaning words and phrases	L4 pp. 204–209
L.2.5	Demonstrate understanding of word relationships and nuances in word meanings	L5 pp. 210–215
L.2.6	Use words and phrases acquired through conversations, reading, being read to, and responding to texts	L6 pp. 216–221

Utah, Kindergarten

Utah Strand/Standard	Focus of Utah Standard	For More Information
Reading Literature		
RL.1	Ask and answer questions about key details in a text	R1 pp. 6–11
RL.2	Retell familiar stories, including key details	R2 pp. 12–17
RL.3	Identify characters, settings, and major events in a story	R3 pp. 18–23
RL.4	Ask and answer questions about unknown words in a text	R4 pp. 24–29
RL.5	Recognize common types of text (e.g., storybooks, poems)	R5 pp. 30–35
RL.6	Name the author and illustrator of a story and define the role of each	R6 pp. 36–41
RL.7	Describe the relationship between the illustrations and the story in which they appear	R7 pp. 42–47
RL.8	NA	
RL.9	Compare and contrast the characters in familiar stories	R9 pp. 54–59
RL.10	Actively engage in reading activities with purpose and understanding	R10 pp. 60–65
Reading Informational Text		
RI.1	Ask and answer questions about key details in a text	R1 pp. 6–11
RI.2	Identify the main topic and retell key details of a text	R2 pp. 12–17
RI.3	Describe the connection between two individuals, events, ideas, or pieces of information in a text	R3 pp. 18–23
RI.4	Ask and answer questions about unknown words in a text	R4 pp. 24–29
RI.5	Identify the front cover, back cover, and title page of a book	R5 pp. 30–35
RI.6	Name the author and illustrator of a text and define the role of each	R6 pp. 36–41
RI.7	Describe the relationship between visual images and the text in which they appear	R7 pp. 42–47
RI.8	Identify the reasons an author gives to support points in a text	R8 pp. 48–53
RI.9	Identify basic similarities and differences between two texts on the same topic	R9 pp. 54–59
RI.10	Actively engage in reading informational text with purpose and understanding	R10 pp. 60–65
Reading Foundational Skills		
RF.1	Print Concepts: Demonstrate understanding of the organization and basic features of print	RF1 pp. 72–77
RF.2	Phonological Awareness: Demonstrate understanding of spoken words, syllables, and sounds (phonemes)	RF2 pp. 78–83
RF.3	Phonics: Know and apply grade-level phonics and word analysis skills in decoding words	RF3 pp. 84–89
RF.4	Fluency: Read level-appropriate texts with purpose and understanding	RF4 pp. 90–95
Writing		
W.1	Use a combination of drawing, dictating, and writing to compose opinion pieces	W1 pp. 100–105
W.2	Use a combination of drawing, dictating, and writing to compose informative/explanatory texts	W2 pp. 106–111
W.3	Use a combination of drawing, dictating, and writing to narrate a single event or several loosely linked events and provide a reaction to what happened	W3 pp. 112–117
W.4	NA	
W.5	Respond to questions and add details to strengthen writing as needed	W5 pp. 118–123
W.6	Explore a variety of digital tools to produce some writing	W6 pp. 124–129
W.7	Participate in shared research and writing projects	W7 pp. 130–135

Utah Strand/Standard	Focus of Utah Standard	For More Information
Writing		
W.8	Recall information from experiences or gather information from provided sources to answer a question	W8 pp. 136–141
W.9	NA	
W.10	NA	
Speaking and Listening		
SL.1	Participate in collaborative conversations with diverse partners about topics and texts in small and larger groups	SL1 pp. 146–151
SL.2	Ask and answer questions about key details to demonstrate understanding of a topic	SL2 pp. 152–157
SL.3	Ask and answer questions in order to seek help, get information, or clarify something that is not understood	SL3 pp. 158–163
SL.4	Describe familiar people, places, things, and events	SL4 pp. 164–169
SL.5	Add drawings or other visual displays to descriptions to provide additional detail	SL5 pp. 170–175
SL.6	Speak audibly and express thoughts, ideas, feelings, and ideas clearly	SL6 pp. 176–181
Language		
L.1	Demonstrate command of the conventions of standard English grammar and usage when writing or speaking	L1 pp. 186–191
L.2	Demonstrate command of the conventions of standard English capitalization, punctuation, and spelling when writing	L2 pp. 192–197
L.3	NA	
L.4	Determine or clarify the meaning of unknown and multiple-meaning words and phrases	L4 pp. 204–209
L.5	Explore word relationships and nuances in word meanings	L5 pp. 210–215
L.6	Use words and phrases acquired through conversations, reading, being read to, and responding to texts	L6 pp. 216–221

Utah, Grade 1

Utah Strand/Standard	Focus of Utah Standard	For More Information
Reading Literature		
RL.1	Ask and answer questions about key details in a text	R1 pp. 6–11
RL.2	Retell stories, including key details	R2 pp. 12–17
RL.3	Describe characters, settings, and major events in a story	R3 pp. 18–23
RL.4	Identify words or phrases that suggest feelings or appeal to the senses	R4 pp. 24–29
RL.5	Explain major differences between stories and informative texts	R5 pp. 30–35
RL.6	Identify who is telling the story at various points in a text	R6 pp. 36–41
RL.7	Use illustrations to describe elements of a story	R7 pp. 42–47
RL.8	NA	
RL.9	Compare and contrast the experiences of characters in stories	R9 pp. 54–59
RL.10	Read texts of appropriate complexity	R10 pp. 60–65

(Continued)

Utah Strand/Standard	Focus of Utah Standard	For More Information
Reading Informational Text		
RI.1	Ask and answer questions about key details in a text	R1 pp. 6–11
RI.2	Identify the main topic and retell key details of a text	R2 pp. 12–17
RI.3	Describe the connection between two individuals, events, ideas, or pieces of information in a text	R3 pp. 18–23
RI.4	Ask and answer questions to clarify the meaning of words in a text	R4 pp. 24–29
RI.5	Use text features to locate information in a text	R5 pp. 30–35
RI.6	Distinguish between information provided by illustrations and information provided by words	R6 pp. 36–41
RI.7	Use illustrations and details to describe key ideas in a text	R7 pp. 42–47
RI.8	Identify the reasons an author gives to support points in a text	R8 pp. 48–53
RI.9	Identify basic similarities and differences between two texts on the same topic	R9 pp. 54–59
RI.10	Actively engage in reading informational text with purpose and understanding	R10 pp. 60–65
Reading Foundational Skills		
RF.1	Print Concepts: Demonstrate understanding of the organization and basic features of print	RF1 pp. 72–77
RF.2	Phonological Awareness: Demonstrate understanding of spoken words, syllables, and sounds (phonemes)	RF2 pp. 78–83
RF.3	Phonics: Know and apply grade-level phonics and word analysis skills in decoding words	RF3 pp. 84–89
RF.4	Fluency: Read level-appropriate texts with accuracy and fluency	RF4 pp. 90–95
Writing		
W.1	Write opinion pieces: introduce the topic, state an opinion, supply reasons, and provide closure	W1 pp. 100–105
W.2	Write informative/explanatory texts: name a topic, supply facts, and provide closure	W2 pp. 106–111
W.3	Write narratives: sequence events, include details, use temporal words, and provide closure	W3 pp. 112–117
W.4	NA	
W.5	Focus on a topic, respond to questions, and add details to strengthen writing as needed	W5 pp. 118–123
W.6	Use a variety of digital tools to produce and publish writing	W6 pp. 124–129
W.7	Participate in shared research and writing projects	W7 pp. 130–135
W.8	Recall information from experiences or gather information from provided sources to answer a question	W8 pp. 136–141
W.9	NA	
W.10	NA	
Speaking and Listening		
SL.1	Participate in collaborative conversations with diverse partners about topics and texts in small and larger groups	SL1 pp. 146–151
SL.2	Ask and answer questions about key details to demonstrate understanding of a topic	SL2 pp. 152–157
SL.3	Ask and answer questions in order to get information or clarify something that is not understood	SL3 pp. 158–163
SL.4	Clearly describe people, places, things, and events	SL4 pp. 164–169
SL.5	Add drawings or other visual displays to descriptions to provide additional detail	SL5 pp. 170–175
SL.6	Produce complete sentences when appropriate to task and situation	SL6 pp. 176–181

Utah Strand/Standard	Focus of Utah Standard	For More Information
Language		
L.1	Demonstrate command of the conventions of standard English grammar and usage when writing or speaking	L1 pp. 186–191
L.2	Demonstrate command of the conventions of standard English capitalization, punctuation, and spelling when writing	L2 pp. 192–197
L.3	NA	
L.4	Determine or clarify the meaning of unknown and multiple-meaning words and phrases	L4 pp. 204–209
L.5	Demonstrate understanding of word relationships and nuances in word meanings	L5 pp. 210–215
L.6	Use words and phrases acquired through conversations, reading, being read to, and responding to texts	L6 pp. 216–221

Utah, Grade 2

Utah Strand/Standard	Focus of Utah Standard	For More Information
Reading Literature		
RL.1	Ask and answer questions about key details in a text	R1 pp. 6–11
RL.2	Recount stories and determine their central message	R2 pp. 12–17
RL.3	Describe how characters respond to major events and challenges	R3 pp. 18–23
RL.4	Describe how words or phrases supply rhythm and meaning	R4 pp. 24–29
RL.5	Describe the overall structure of a story, including the beginning and ending	R5 pp. 30–35
RL.6	Acknowledge differences in characters' points of view	R6 pp. 36–41
RL.7	Use information gathered from illustrations and words to demonstrate understanding of story elements	R7 pp. 42–47
RL.8	NA	
RL.9	Compare and contrast two or more versions of the same story	R9 pp. 54–59
RL.10	Read and comprehend texts of appropriate complexity	R10 pp. 60–65
Reading Informational Text		
RI.1	Ask and answer questions about key details in a text	R1 pp. 6–11
RI.2	Identify the main topic and retell key details of a text, as well as the focus of specific paragraphs	R2 pp. 12–17
RI.3	Describe the connection between a series of events, ideas, concepts, or steps in a text	R3 pp. 18–23
RI.4	Determine the meaning of words and phrases in a text relevant to a grade-level topic	R4 pp. 24–29
RI.5	Use text features to efficiently locate information in a text	R5 pp. 30–35
RI.6	Identify the main purpose of a text	R6 pp. 36–41
RI.7	Explain how specific images contribute to and clarify a text	R7 pp. 42–47
RI.8	Describe how reasons an author gives support points in a text	R8 pp. 48–53
RI.9	Compare and contrast the most important points in two texts on the same topic	R9 pp. 54–59
RI.10	Read and comprehend informational texts of appropriate complexity	R10 pp. 60–65

(Continued)

Utah Strand/Standard	Focus of Utah Standard	For More Information
Reading Foundational Skills		
RF.1	NA	
RF.2	NA	
RF.3	Phonics: Know and apply grade-level phonics and word analysis skills in decoding words	RF3 pp. 84–89
RF.4	Fluency: Read level-appropriate texts with accuracy and fluency	RF4 pp. 90–95
Writing		
W.1	Write opinion pieces: introduce the topic, state an opinion, supply reasons using linking words, and provide closure	W1 pp. 100–105
W.2	Write informative/explanatory texts: name a topic, use facts to develop points, and provide closure	W2 pp. 106–111
W.3	Write narratives: sequence events; include details to describe actions, thoughts, and feelings; use temporal words; provide closure	W3 pp. 112–117
W.4	NA	
W.5	Focus on a topic and strengthen writing by revising and editing	W5 pp. 118–123
W.6	Use a variety of digital tools to produce and publish writing	W6 pp. 124–129
W.7	Participate in shared research and writing projects	W7 pp. 130–135
W.8	Recall information from experiences or gather information from provided sources to answer a question	W8 pp. 136–141
W.9	NA	
W.10	NA	
Speaking and Listening		
SL.1	Participate in collaborative conversations with diverse partners about topics and texts in small and larger groups	SL1 pp. 146–151
SL.2	Recount or describe key ideas or details in information presented orally	SL2 pp. 152–157
SL.3	Ask and answer questions in order to get information, deepen understanding, or clarify something that is not understood	SL3 pp. 158–163
SL.4	Recount a story or experience with appropriate facts and relevant details	SL4 pp. 164–169
SL.5	Create audio recordings of stories or poems, adding visual displays as appropriate for clarification	SL5 pp. 170–175
SL.6	Produce complete sentences when appropriate to task and situation	SL6 pp. 176–181
Language		
L.1	Demonstrate command of the conventions of standard English grammar and usage when writing or speaking	L1 pp. 186–191
L.2	Demonstrate command of the conventions of standard English capitalization, punctuation, and spelling when writing	L2 pp. 192–197
L.3	Use knowledge of language and its conventions when writing, speaking, reading, or listening	L3 pp. 198–203
L.4	Determine or clarify the meaning of unknown and multiple-meaning words and phrases	L4 pp. 204–209
L.5	Demonstrate understanding of word relationships and nuances in word meanings	L5 pp. 210–215
L.6	Use words and phrases acquired through conversations, reading, being read to, and responding to texts	L6 pp. 216–221

Virginia, Kindergarten

Virginia Strand/Standard	Focus of Virginia Standard	For More Information
Oral Language		
K.1	Demonstrate growth in the use of oral language	SL2 pp. 152–157 SL4 pp. 164–169 SL6 pp. 176–181
K.2	Expand understanding and use of word meanings	SL3 pp. 158–163 L1 pp. 186–191 L6 pp. 216–221
K.3	Build oral communication skills	SL1 pp. 146–151 SL2 pp. 152–157
K.4	Identify, say, segment, and blend various units of speech sounds	RF2 pp. 78–83
Reading		
K.5	Understand how print is organized and read	RF1 pp. 72–77 R6 pp. 36–41 R7 pp. 42–47
K.6	Demonstrate an understanding that print conveys meaning	RF1 pp. 72–77
K.7	Develop an understanding of basic phonetic principles	RF1 pp. 72–77 RF3 pp. 84–89
K.8	Expand vocabulary	R4 pp. 24–29 L6 pp. 216–221
K.9	Demonstrate comprehension of fictional texts	
	• Identify the roles of the author and illustrator	R6 pp. 36–41
	• Use pictures to make predictions	R7 pp. 42–47
	• Ask and answer questions about what is read	R1 pp. 6–11
	• Retell familiar stories, using beginning, middle, and end	R2 pp. 12–17
	• Discuss characters, setting, and events	R3 pp. 18–23
K.10	Demonstrate comprehension of nonfiction texts	
	• Use pictures to identify topic and make predictions	R7 pp. 42–47
	• Identify text features such as titles, headings, and pictures	R5 pp. 30–35
Writing		
K.11	Print in manuscript	L1 pp. 186–191
K.12	Write to communicate ideas for a variety of purposes	W1 pp. 100–105 W2 pp. 106–111 W3 pp. 112–117 L2 pp. 192–197
K.13	Use available technology for reading and writing	W6 pp. 124–129

Virginia, Grade 1

Virginia Strand/Standard	Focus of Virginia Standard	For More Information
Oral Language		
1.1	Demonstrate growth in the use of oral language	SL2 pp. 152–157 SL4 pp. 164–169 SL6 pp. 176–181
1.2	Expand understanding and use of word meanings	SL3 pp. 158–163 L1 pp. 186–191 L6 pp. 216–221
1.3	Adapt or change oral language to fit the situation	SL1 pp. 146–151 SL2 pp. 152–157
1.4	Identify, produce, and manipulate various units of speech sounds within words	RF2 pp. 78–83
Reading		
1.5	Apply knowledge of how print is organized and read	RF1 pp. 72–77
1.6	Apply phonetic principles to read and spell	RF3 pp. 84–89 L2 pp. 192–197
1.7	Use semantic clues and syntax to expand vocabulary when reading	L4 pp. 204–209
1.8	Expand vocabulary	R4 pp. 24–29 L6 pp. 216–221
1.9	Read and demonstrate comprehension of a variety of fictional texts	R6 pp. 36–41
	• Ask and answer questions about what is read	R1 pp. 6–11
	• Identify characters, setting, and important events	R3 pp. 18–23
	• Retell stories, using beginning, middle, and end	R2 pp. 12–17
	• Identify the main idea or theme	R2 pp. 12–17
	• Read with fluency, accuracy, and meaningful expression	RF4 pp. 90–95
1.10	Read and demonstrate comprehension of a variety of nonfiction texts	
	• Identify text features such as titles, headings, and pictures	R5 pp. 30–35
	• Ask and answer questions about what is read	R1 pp. 6–11
	• Identify the main idea	R2 pp. 12–17
	• Read with fluency, accuracy, and meaningful expression	RF4 pp. 90–95
1.11	Use simple reference materials	NA
Writing		
1.12	Print legibly	L1 pp. 186–191
1.13	Write to communicate ideas for a variety of purposes	W1 pp. 100–105 W2 pp. 106–111 W3 pp. 112–117 L2 pp. 192–197
1.14	Use available technology for reading and writing	W6 pp. 124–129

Virginia, Grade 2

Virginia Strand/Standard	Focus of Virginia Standard	For More Information
Oral Language		
2.1	Demonstrate an understanding of oral language structure	SL4 pp. 164–169 SL6 pp. 176–181 L1 pp. 186–191
2.2	Expand understanding and use of word meanings	SL3 pp. 158–163 L1 pp. 186–191 L6 pp. 216–221
2.3	Use oral communication skills	SL1 pp. 146–151 SL4 pp. 164–169
2.4	Identify, produce, and manipulate various units of speech sounds within words	RF2 pp. 78–83
Reading		
2.5	Use phonetic strategies when reading and spelling	RF3 pp. 84–89 L2 pp. 192–197
2.6	Use semantic clues and syntax to expand vocabulary when reading	L4 pp. 204–209 R4 pp. 24–29
2.7	Expand vocabulary when reading	R4 pp. 24–29 L4 pp. 204–209 L6 pp. 216–221
2.8	Read and demonstrate comprehension of fictional texts	
	• Ask and answer questions about what is read	R1 pp. 6–11
	• Locate information to answer questions	R1 pp. 6–11
	• Describe characters, setting, and important events	R3 pp. 18–23
	• Identify the main idea	R2 pp. 12–17
	• Summarize stories and events with beginning, middle, and end in the correct sequence	R3 pp. 18–23
	• Read with fluency, accuracy, and meaningful expression	RF4 pp 90–95
2.9	Read and demonstrate comprehension of nonfiction texts	
	• Preview the selection using text features	R5 pp. 30–35
	• Ask and answer questions about what is read	R1 pp. 6–11
	• Identify the main idea	R2 pp. 12–17
	• Read with fluency, accuracy, and meaningful expression	RF4 pp. 90–95
2.10	Demonstrate comprehension of information in reference materials	R5 pp. 30–35
Writing		
2.11	Maintain legible printing and begin transition to cursive	NA
2.12	Write stories, letters, and simple explanations	W2 pp. 106–111 W3 pp. 112–117 W5 pp. 118–123
2.13	Edit writing for correct grammar, capitalization, punctuation, and spelling	L1 pp. 186–191 L2 pp. 192–197
2.14	Use available technology for reading and writing	W6 pp. 124–129

West Virginia, Kindergarten

West Virginia Strand/Standard	Focus of West Virginia Standard	For More Information
Reading Literature		
R.C1.1	Ask and answer questions about key details in a text	R1 pp. 6–11
R.C1.2	Retell familiar stories, including key details	R2 pp. 12–17
R.C1.3	Identify characters, settings, and major events in a story	R3 pp. 18–23
R.C2.1	Ask and answer questions about unknown words in a text	R4 pp. 24–29
R.C2.2	Recognize common types of text (e.g., storybooks, poems)	R5 pp. 30–35
R.C2.3	Name the author and illustrator of a story and define the role of each	R6 pp. 36–41
R.C3.1	Describe the relationship between the illustrations and the story in which they appear	R7 pp. 42–47
R.C3.2	Compare and contrast the characters in familiar stories	R9 pp. 54–59
R.C4.1	Actively engage in reading activities with purpose and understanding	R10 pp. 60–65
Reading Informational Text		
R.C1.4	Ask and answer questions about key details in a text	R1 pp. 6–11
R.C1.5	Identify the main topic and retell key details of a text	R2 pp. 12–17
R.C1.6	Describe the connection between two individuals, events, ideas, or pieces of information in a text	R3 pp. 18–23
R.C2.4	Ask and answer questions about unknown words in a text	R4 pp. 24–29
R.C2.5	Identify the front cover, back cover, and title page of a book	R5 pp. 30–35
R.C2.6	Name the author and illustrator of a text and define the role of each	R6 pp. 36–41
R.C3.3	Describe the relationship between visual images and the text in which they appear	R7 pp. 42–47
R.C3.4	Identify the reasons an author gives to support points in a text	R8 pp. 48–53
R.C3.5	Identify basic similarities and differences between two texts on the same topic	R9 pp. 54–59
R.C4.2	Actively engage in reading informational text with purpose and understanding	R10 pp. 60–65
Reading Foundational Skills		
R.C5.1	Print Concepts: Demonstrate understanding of the organization and basic features of print	RF1 pp. 72–77
R.C6.1	Phonological Awareness: Demonstrate understanding of spoken words, syllables, and sounds (phonemes)	RF2 pp. 78–83
R.C7.1	Phonics: Know and apply grade-level phonics and word analysis skills in decoding words	RF3 pp. 84–89
R.C8.1	Fluency: Read level-appropriate texts with purpose and understanding	RF4 pp. 90–95
Writing		
W.C9.1	Use a combination of drawing, dictating, and writing to compose opinion pieces	W1 pp. 100–105
W.C9.2	Use a combination of drawing, dictating, and writing to compose informative/explanatory texts	W2 pp. 106–111
W.C9.3	Use a combination of drawing, dictating, and writing to narrate a single event or several loosely linked events and provide a reaction to what happened	W3 pp. 112–117
W.C10.1	NA	
W.C10.2	Respond to questions and add details to strengthen writing as needed	W5 pp. 118–123
W.C10.3	Explore a variety of digital tools to produce some writing	W6 pp. 124–129

West Virginia Strand/Standard	Focus of West Virginia Standard	For More Information
Writing		
W.C11.1	Participate in shared research and writing projects	W7 pp. 130–135
W.C11.2	Recall information from experiences or gather information from provided sources to answer a question	W8 pp. 136–141
W.9	NA	
W.10	NA	
Speaking and Listening		
SL.C13.1	Participate in collaborative conversations with diverse partners about topics and texts in small and larger groups	SL1 pp. 146–151
SL.C13.2	Ask and answer questions about key details to demonstrate understanding of a topic	SL2 pp. 152–157
SL.C13.3	Ask and answer questions in order to seek help, get information, or clarify something that is not understood	SL3 pp. 158–163
SL.C14.1	Describe familiar people, places, things, and events	SL4 pp. 164–169
SL.C14.2	Add drawings or other visual displays to descriptions to provide additional detail	SL5 pp. 170–175
SL.C14.3	Speak audibly and express thoughts, ideas, feelings, and ideas clearly	SL6 pp. 176–181
Language		
L.C15.1	Demonstrate command of the conventions of standard English grammar and usage when writing or speaking	L1 pp. 186–191
L.C15.2	Demonstrate command of the conventions of standard English capitalization, punctuation, and spelling when writing	L2 pp. 192–197
L.C16.1	NA	
L.C17.1	Determine or clarify the meaning of unknown and multiple-meaning words and phrases	L4 pp. 204–209
L.C17.2	Explore word relationships and nuances in word meanings	L5 pp. 210–215
L.C17.3	Use words and phrases acquired through conversations, reading, being read to, and responding to texts	L6 pp. 216–221

West Virginia, Grade 1

West Virginia Strand/Standard	Focus of West Virginia Standard	For More Information
Reading Literature		
R.C1.1	Ask and answer questions about key details in a text	R1 pp. 6–11
R.C1.2	Retell stories, including key details	R2 pp. 12–17
R.C1.3	Describe characters, settings, and major events in a story	R3 pp. 18–23
R.C2.1	Identify words or phrases that suggest feelings or appeal to the senses	R4 pp. 24–29
R.C2.2	Explain major differences between stories and informative texts	R5 pp. 30–35
R.C2.3	Identify who is telling the story at various points in a text	R6 pp. 36–41
R.C3.1	Use illustrations to describe elements of a story	R7 pp. 42–47
R.C3.2	Compare and contrast the experiences of characters in stories	R9 pp. 54–59
R.C4.1	Read texts of appropriate complexity	R10 pp. 60–65

(Continued)

West Virginia Strand/Standard	Focus of West Virginia Standard	For More Information
Reading Informational Text		
R.C1.4	Ask and answer questions about key details in a text	R1 pp. 6–11
R.C1.5	Identify the main topic and retell key details of a text	R2 pp. 12–17
R.C1.6	Describe the connection between two individuals, events, ideas, or pieces of information in a text	R3 pp. 18–23
R.C2.4	Ask and answer questions to clarify the meaning of words in a text	R4 pp. 24–29
R.C2.5	Use text features to locate information in a text	R5 pp. 30–35
R.C2.6	Distinguish between information provided by illustrations and information provided by words	R6 pp. 36–41
R.C3.3	Use illustrations and details to describe key ideas in a text	R7 pp. 42–47
R.C3.4	Identify the reasons an author gives to support points in a text	R8 pp. 48–53
R.C3.5	Identify basic similarities and differences between two texts on the same topic	R9 pp. 54–59
R.C4.2	Actively engage in reading informational text with purpose and understanding	R10 pp. 60–65
Reading Foundational Skills		
R.C5.1	Print Concepts: Demonstrate understanding of the organization and basic features of print	RF1 pp. 72–77
R.C6.1	Phonological Awareness: Demonstrate understanding of spoken words, syllables, and sounds (phonemes)	RF2 pp. 78–83
R.C7.1	Phonics: Know and apply grade-level phonics and word analysis skills in decoding words	RF3 pp. 84–89
R.C8.1	Fluency: Read level-appropriate texts with accuracy and fluency	RF4 pp. 90–95
Writing		
W.C9.1	Write opinion pieces: introduce the topic, state an opinion, supply reasons, and provide closure	W1 pp. 100–105
W.C9.2	Write informative/explanatory texts: name a topic, supply facts, and provide closure	W2 pp. 106–111
W.C9.3	Write narratives: sequence events, include details, use temporal words, and provide closure	W3 pp. 112–117
W.C10.1	NA	
W.C10.2	Focus on a topic, respond to questions, and add details to strengthen writing as needed	W5 pp. 118–123
W.C10.3	Use a variety of digital tools to produce and publish writing	W6 pp. 124–129
W.C11.1	Participate in shared research and writing projects	W7 pp. 130–135
W.C11.2	Recall information from experiences or gather information from provided sources to answer a question	W8 pp. 136–141
W.9	NA	
W.10	NA	
Speaking and Listening		
SL.C13.1	Participate in collaborative conversations with diverse partners about topics and texts in small and larger groups	SL1 pp. 146–151
SL.C13.2	Ask and answer questions about key details to demonstrate understanding of a topic	SL2 pp. 152–157
SL.C13.3	Ask and answer questions in order to get information or clarify something that is not understood	SL3 pp. 158–163
SL.C14.1	Clearly describe people, places, things, and events	SL4 pp. 164–169
SL.C14.2	Add drawings or other visual displays to descriptions to provide additional detail	SL5 pp. 170–175
SL.C14.3	Produce complete sentences when appropriate to task and situation	SL6 pp. 176–181

West Virginia Strand/Standard	Focus of West Virginia Standard	For More Information
Language		
L.C15.1	Demonstrate command of the conventions of standard English grammar and usage when writing or speaking	L1 pp. 186–191
L.C15.2	Demonstrate command of the conventions of standard English capitalization, punctuation, and spelling when writing	L2 pp. 192–197
L.C16.1	NA	
L.C17.1	Determine or clarify the meaning of unknown and multiple-meaning words and phrases	L4 pp. 204–209
L.C17.2	Demonstrate understanding of word relationships and nuances in word meanings	L5 pp. 210–215
L.C17.3	Use words and phrases acquired through conversations, reading, being read to, and responding to texts	L6 pp. 216–221

West Virginia, Grade 2

West Virginia Strand/Standard	Focus of West Virginia Standard	For More Information
Reading Literature		
R.C1.1	Ask and answer questions about key details in a text	R1 pp. 6–11
R.C1.2	Recount stories and determine their central message	R2 pp. 12–17
R.C1.3	Describe how characters respond to major events and challenges	R3 pp. 18–23
R.C2.1	Describe how words or phrases supply rhythm and meaning	R4 pp. 24–29
R.C2.2	Describe the overall structure of a story, including the beginning and ending	R5 pp. 30–35
R.C2.3	Acknowledge differences in characters' points of view	R6 pp. 36–41
R.C3.1	Use information gathered from illustrations and words to demonstrate understanding of story elements	R7 pp. 42–47
R.C3.2	Compare and contrast two or more versions of the same story	R9 pp. 54–59
R.C4.1	Read and comprehend texts of appropriate complexity	R10 pp. 60–65
RL.10	Read and comprehend texts of appropriate complexity	R10 pp. 60–65
Reading Informational Text		
R.C1.4	Ask and answer questions about key details in a text	R1 pp. 6–11
R.C1.5	Identify the main topic and retell key details of a text, as well as the focus of specific paragraphs	R2 pp. 12–17
R.C1.6	Describe the connection between a series of events, ideas, concepts, or steps in a text	R3 pp. 18–23
R.C2.4	Determine the meaning of words and phrases in a text relevant to a grade-level topic	R4 pp. 24–29
R.C2.5	Use text features to efficiently locate information in a text	R5 pp. 30–35
R.C2.6	Identify the main purpose of a text	R6 pp. 36–41
R.C3.3	Explain how specific images contribute to and clarify a text	R7 pp. 42–47
R.C3.4	Describe how reasons an author gives support points in a text	R8 pp. 48–53
R.C3.5	Compare and contrast the most important points in two texts on the same topic	R9 pp. 54–59
R.C4.2	Read and comprehend informational texts of appropriate complexity	R10 pp. 60–65

(Continued)

West Virginia Strand/Standard	Focus of West Virginia Standard	For More Information
Reading Foundational Skills		
R.C5.1	NA	
R.C6.1	NA	
R.C7.1	Phonics: Know and apply grade-level phonics and word analysis skills in decoding words	RF3 pp. 84–89
R.C8.1	Fluency: Read level-appropriate texts with accuracy and fluency	RF4 pp. 90–95
Writing		
W.C9.1	Write opinion pieces: introduce the topic, state an opinion, supply reasons using linking words, and provide closure	W1 pp. 100–105
W.C9.2	Write informative/explanatory texts: name a topic, use facts to develop points, and provide closure	W2 pp. 106–111
W.C9.3	Write narratives: sequence events; include details to describe actions, thoughts, and feelings; use temporal words; provide closure	W3 pp. 112–117
W.C10.1	NA	
W.C10.2	Focus on a topic and strengthen writing by revising and editing	W5 pp. 118–123
W.C10.3	Use a variety of digital tools to produce and publish writing	W6 pp. 124–129
W.C11.1	Participate in shared research and writing projects	W7 pp. 130–135
W.C11.2	Recall information from experiences or gather information from provided sources to answer a question	W8 pp. 136–141
W.9	NA	
W.10	NA	
Speaking and Listening		
SL.C13.1	Participate in collaborative conversations with diverse partners about topics and texts in small and larger groups	SL1 pp. 146–151
SL.C13.2	Recount or describe key ideas or details in information presented orally	SL2 pp. 152–157
SL.C13.3	Ask and answer questions in order to get information, deepen understanding, or clarify something that is not understood	SL3 pp. 158–163
SL.C14.1	Recount a story or experience with appropriate facts and relevant details	SL4 pp. 164–169
SL.C14.2	Create audio recordings of stories or poems, adding visual displays as appropriate for clarification	SL5 pp. 170–175
SL.C14.3	Produce complete sentences when appropriate to task and situation	SL6 pp. 176–181
Language		
L.C15.1	Demonstrate command of the conventions of standard English grammar and usage when writing or speaking	L1 pp. 186–191
L.C15.2	Demonstrate command of the conventions of standard English capitalization, punctuation, and spelling when writing	L2 pp. 192–197
L.C16.1	Use knowledge of language and its conventions when writing, speaking, reading, or listening	L3 pp. 198–203
L.C17.1	Determine or clarify the meaning of unknown and multiple-meaning words and phrases	L4 pp. 204–209
L.C17.2	Demonstrate understanding of word relationships and nuances in word meanings	L5 pp. 210–215
L.C17.3	Use words and phrases acquired through conversations, reading, being read to, and responding to texts	L6 pp. 216–221

The Complete Common Core State Standards: Decoded

The Common Core State Standards

Reading

College and Career Readiness Anchor Standards for
Reading K–12

Source: Common Core State Standards

The K–2 reading standards outlined on the following pages define what students should understand and be able to do by the end of each grade. Here on this page we present the College and Career Readiness (CCR) anchor standards for K–12 so you can see how students in K–2 work toward the same goals as high school seniors: it's a universal, K–12 vision. The CCR anchor standards and the grade-specific standards correspond to one another by number (1–10). They are necessary complements: the former providing broad standards, the latter providing additional specificity. Together, they define the skills and understandings that all students must eventually demonstrate.

Key Ideas and Details

1. Read closely to determine what the text says explicitly and to make logical inferences from it; cite specific textual evidence when writing or speaking to support conclusions drawn from the text.
2. Determine central ideas or themes of a text and analyze their development; summarize the key supporting details and ideas.
3. Analyze how and why individuals, events, and ideas develop and interact over the course of a text.

Craft and Structure

4. Interpret words and phrases as they are used in a text, including determining technical, connotative, and figurative meanings, and analyze how specific word choices shape meaning or tone.
5. Analyze the structure of texts, including how specific sentences, paragraphs, and larger portions of the text (e.g., a section, chapter, scene, or stanza) relate to each other and the whole.
6. Assess how point of view or purpose shapes the content and style of a text.

Integration of Knowledge and Ideas

7. Integrate and evaluate content presented in diverse media and formats, including visually and quantitatively, as well as in words.*
8. Delineate and evaluate the argument and specific claims in a text, including the validity of the reasoning as well as the relevance and sufficiency of the evidence.
9. Analyze how two or more texts address similar themes or topics in order to build knowledge or to compare the approaches the authors take.

Range of Reading and Level of Text Complexity

10. Read and comprehend complex literary and informational texts independently and proficiently.

*Please consult the full Common Core State Standards document (and all updates and appendices) at http://www.corestandards.org/ELA-Literacy. See "Research to Build Knowledge" in the Writing section and "Comprehension and Collaboration" in the Speaking and Listening section for additional standards relevant to gathering, assessing, and applying information from print and digital sources.

College and Career Readiness Anchor Standards for

Reading

The CCR anchor standards are the same for K–12. The guiding principle here is that the core reading skills should not change as students advance; rather, the level at which students learn and can perform these skills should increase in complexity as they move from one grade to the next. However, for grades K–2, we have to recognize that the standards were back mapped from the secondary level—that is, the authors envisioned what college students need and then wrote standards, working their way down the grades. Thus, as you use this book, remember that children in K–2 can't just "jump over" developmental milestones in an ambitious attempt to achieve an anchor standard. There are certain life and learning experiences they need to have, and certain concepts they need to learn, before they are capable of handling many complex academic skills in a meaningful way. The anchor standards nonetheless are goalposts to work toward. As you read the "gist" of the standards below, remember they represent what our K–2 students will *grow into* during each year and deepen later in elementary, middle, and high school. The journey starts in K–2!

Key Ideas and Details

This first strand of reading standards emphasizes students' ability to identify key ideas and themes in a text, whether literary, informational, primary, or foundational and whether in print, graphic, quantitative, or mixed media formats. The focus of this first set of standards is on reading to understand, during which students focus on what the text says. The premise is that students cannot delve into the deeper meaning of any text if they cannot first grasp the surface meaning of that text. Beyond merely identifying these ideas, readers must learn to see how these ideas and themes, or the story's characters and events, develop and evolve over the course of a text. Such reading demands that students know how to identify, evaluate, assess, and analyze the elements of a text for their importance, function, and meaning within the text.

Craft and Structure

The second set of standards builds on the first, focusing not on what the text says but on how it says it, the emphasis here being on analyzing how texts are made to serve a function or achieve a purpose. These standards ask readers to examine the choices the author makes in words and sentence and paragraph structure and how these choices contribute to the meaning of the text and the author's larger purpose. Inherent in the study of craft and structure is how these elements interact with and influence the ideas and details outlined in the first three standards.

Integration of Knowledge and Ideas

This third strand might be summed up as reading to extend or deepen one's knowledge of a subject by comparing what a range of sources have said about it over time and across different media. In addition, these standards emphasize the importance of being able to read the arguments; that is, they look at how to identify the claims the texts make and evaluate the evidence used to support those claims regardless of the media. Finally, these standards ask students to analyze the author's choices of means and medium and the effects those choices have on ideas and details. Thus, if a writer integrates words, images, and video in a mixed media text, readers should be able to examine how and why the author did that for stylistic and rhetorical purposes.

Range of Reading and Level of Text Complexity

The Common Core State Standards document itself offers the most useful explanation of what this last standard means in a footnote titled "Note on range and content of student reading," which accompanies the reading standards:

> To become college and career ready, students must grapple with works of exceptional craft and thought whose range extends across genres, cultures, and centuries. Such works offer profound insights into the human condition and serve as models for students' own thinking and writing. Along with high-quality contemporary works, these texts should be chosen from among seminal U.S. documents, the classics of American literature, and the timeless dramas of Shakespeare. Through wide and deep reading of literature and literary nonfiction of steadily increasing sophistication, students gain a reservoir of literary and cultural knowledge, references, and images; the ability to evaluate intricate arguments; and the capacity to surmount the challenges posed by complex texts. (CCSS 2010, p. 35)

Source: Adapted from Jim Burke, *The Common Core Companion: The Standards Decoded, Grades 6–8* (Thousand Oaks, CA: Corwin, 2013).

Standard 1: Read closely to determine what the text says explicitly and to make logical inferences from it; cite specific textual evidence when writing or speaking to support conclusions drawn from the text.

Literature

K With prompting and support, students ask and answer questions about key details in a text.

1 Students ask and answer questions about key details in a text.

2 Students ask and answer such questions as *who, what, where, when, why*, and *how* to demonstrate understanding of key details in a text.

Informational Text

K With prompting and support, students ask and answer questions about key details in a text.

1 Students ask and answer questions about key details in a text.

2 Students ask and answer such questions as *who, what, where, when, why*, and *how* to demonstrate understanding of key details in a text.

What the **Student** Does

Literature	Informational Text

[K] Gist: Students ask and answer questions about key details in a text.

They consider:

- What happens or is said in this text?
- Which words, pictures, and sentences help me know this?

[1] Gist: Students ask and answer questions about key details in a text.

They consider:

- What happens or is said in this text?
- Which words, pictures, and sentences help me know this?

[2] Gist: Students ask and answer such questions as *who, what, where, when, why,* and *how* to determine the key details in a text.

They consider:

- What happens or is said in this text?
- Which words, pictures, and sentences help me know this?

[K] Gist: Students ask and answer questions about key details in a text.

They consider:

- What happens or is said in this text?
- Which words, illustrations, and sentences help me know this?

[1] Gist: Students ask and answer questions about key details in a text.

They consider:

- What happens or is said in this text?
- Which words, illustrations, and sentences help me know this?

[2] Gist: Students ask and answer such questions as *who, what, where, when, why,* and *how* to determine the key details in a text.

They consider:

- What happens or is said in this text?
- Which details (words, illustrations, and sentences) support the key ideas?

Note: Although the questions listed above are too difficult for most young students to internalize and apply on their own, we share them to give teachers a detailed sense of what their students should be striving toward as learners. K–2 students may not be able to ask these questions of themselves independently, but teachers can use them as a jumping-off point for lesson content and as prompts and reminders to share with students. Over time and with instruction, students will be able to pose these questions on their own.

What the **Teacher** Does

To teach students how to read closely:

- Before introducing a text, identify the main idea or message for yourself. Go through the book and notice the details that support it and flag them with sticky notes. Then, plan out prompts and questions that you will pose to students. We liken this process to Hansel dropping those pebbles leading homeward; by planning questions ahead of time, you can more easily guide students to spot the main idea. Conversely, when teachers don't plan, lessons can go awry. For example, if the main idea of a passage is that cities create heat (cars, buildings, people) and thereby change the weather, and you don't recognize that this is what students should be reading for, then it becomes difficult to pose a proper "trail" of questions leading students toward the text's significant details.

- During a lesson or while conferring, be sure to give students sufficient time to consider the questions and prompts you pose. Figuring out the author's main idea or message is often hard, subtle work. Don't hesitate to rephrase prompts if students seem stuck. Remind them that they can look for answers in the text, reread, study illustrations, and so forth. Providing time for students to respond can make all the difference in the world.

- Use a text or passage that is brief enough to be read more than once, so that students can begin with an overall understanding before homing in on specifics. As you read, pause occasionally to pose questions about words, actions, and details that require students to look closely at the text or illustrations for answers. (Note: When your goal is to demonstrate where in the text you found something to support your reasoning, make sure that the text is large enough for students to see and interact with. Charts, enlarged texts, and whiteboards help.)

- Model close reading by thinking aloud as you scrutinize a text's words, sentence structures, and other details to understand its meaning. To focus students' attention, write on sticky notes and place them on the text, use chart paper, annotate in the margins, and/or highlight via a tablet or whiteboard.

To help students to determine what the text says explicitly:

- Model how to determine an author's message by saying what happened (literature) and naming the important facts (informational). As you do, point to words, sentences, illustrations, and text features as evidence and record on chart paper or graphic organizers (see online resources at resources.corwin.com/literacycompanionk-2).

- Over weeks of working with different texts, continue to guide students to determine deeper meanings on their own. Use sentence stems and other graphic organizers to support students' explanations of what happened and their recall of important facts; use think-alouds so students hear how you arrive at what texts mean, and point to specific places in the text to support your conclusions.

To help students make logical inferences from a text:

- Select texts to read aloud or share with students that allow them to make logical inferences. Ask questions that lead them to infer (I wonder why he did that? I wonder what she thought? I wonder why the boy in the illustration looks sad?). As students answer these questions, ask them to explain how they arrived at their conclusions using specific words and phrases in the text.

- Routinely ask students to show you the textual evidence that supports their inferences.

To support students in asking and answering questions about key details in a text:

- Model asking questions about a text by writing questions on chart paper or annotating in the margins when using a whiteboard. Try to ask more analytical (how, why) questions than literal (who, what, where, when) questions.

- Elaborate on what led you to ask a question. When reading a book about beavers, you might say, "Whenever I see a picture of a beaver, they're chewing on a tree branch. I wonder why they do this?" This will help students recognize that a question is typically an extension of something we already know.

- Demonstrate how the answers to many of their questions can be found in the text. If the text is on a chart or in a big book, mark the answers to questions with sticky notes or highlighting tape, calling attention to the *exact words* that help answer a question.

To help your English language learners, try this:

- Work with small groups to help students feel more comfortable sharing ideas. Make sure that each student has a copy of the text or that the text is large enough for them all to see comfortably. Allow students time to read a text or a portion of one several times to make sure they have a basic understanding before focusing on key ideas or making inferences.

- Model asking questions using a short text or poster-size photograph. Elaborate on what leads you to ask questions and point to words and illustrations that provide answers.

Developmental Debrief:

Students, especially those coming to school with low language skills or those who lack the necessary preschool experiences to be academically successful, need to be read to several times throughout the day. This will help them acquire the academic vocabulary and syntax they need to understand complex texts.

In order for students to feel comfortable, it is essential for the teacher to create a risk-free environment where students are encouraged to offer their ideas and opinions openly, without fear that their responses will be judged "right or wrong," "good or bad."

Notes

Academic Vocabulary: Key Words and Phrases

Cite specific textual evidence: Readers need to reference the text to support their ideas, rather than simply stating opinions or referring to personal experiences; students should be able to reference illustrations or read words or sentences from the text that prove the points they are trying to make.

Conclusions drawn from the text: Readers take a group of details (different findings, series of events, related examples) and infer from them an insight or understanding about their meaning or importance within the passage or the text as a whole. These insights or conclusions are based on evidence found in the text.

Explicitly: This refers to anything that is clearly and directly stated in precise detail; it may suggest factual information or literal meaning, although this is not necessarily the case.

Informational texts: These include nonfiction texts written for a variety of purposes and audiences, such as expository texts, informational narratives (biography, history, journals and diaries, persuasive texts and essays). Informational texts include written arguments as well as visual images such as charts and diagrams.

Key details: These are parts of a text that support the main idea and enable the reader to draw conclusions/infer what the text or a portion of a text is about.

Literature: This refers to fiction, poetry, drama, and graphic stories as well as artworks by master painters or distinguished photographers.

Logical inferences (drawn from the text): To infer, readers add what they *learned* from the text to what they already *know* about the subject; however, for an inference to be "logical," it must be based on evidence *from the text*.

Prompting and support: Here the teacher takes the lead role in helping students initiate a particular skill or strategy. She is likely to think aloud and model precisely what she wants students to be able to do on their own later, and to nurture their attempts.

Read closely (close reading): This refers to reading that emphasizes not only surface details but the deeper meaning and larger connections between words, sentences, and the full text; it also requires the reader to attend to the author's craft, including organization, word choice, and style.

Text: In its broadest meaning, a text is whatever one is trying to read: a poem, essay, or article; in its more modern sense, a text can also be an image, an artwork, a speech, or a multimedia format such as a website or film.

Textual evidence: Not all evidence is created equal; students need to choose those pieces of evidence (illustrations, words, or sentences) that provide the best examples of what they are saying or the most compelling references to support their assertions.

Notes

Planning Page

Standard: _____

Purpose of Lesson/s:

Planning the Lesson/s	Questions to Ask

Differentiating Instruction	Thinking Beyond This Standard

The standards guide instruction; they do not dictate it. *So as you plan lessons remember you aren't teaching the standards, but instead are teaching students how to read, write, talk, and think through well-crafted lessons that draw from the pedagogy embedded within them. Engaging lessons often have several ELA standards within them and integrate reading, writing, speaking and listening, and language.*

Standard 2: Determine central ideas or themes of a text and analyze their development; summarize the key supporting details and ideas.

Literature

K With prompting and support, students retell familiar stories, including key details.

1 Students retell stories, including key details, and demonstrate understanding of their central message or lesson.

2 Students recount stories, including fables and folktales from diverse cultures, and determine their central message, lesson, or moral.

Informational Text

K With prompting and support, students identify the main topic and retell key details of a text.

1 Students identify the main topic and retell key details of a text.

2 Students identify the main topic of a multiparagraph text as well as the focus of specific paragraphs within the text.

What the **Student** Does

Literature

K Gist: Students identify the central message or lesson of a familiar story, then report on the key ideas, details, and events that help convey this message or lesson.

They consider:

- Who is the story mostly about?
- What problem is this character facing?
- How does the character resolve it?
- How is this character different at the end of the story than at the beginning?

1 Gist: Students identify the central message or lesson of a story, then report on the key ideas, details, and events, including just the important information, not every single detail.

They consider:

- What problem/need is the main character experiencing?
- What gets in the character's way?
- How is the problem resolved?
- What events lead to a resolution of the character's problem?
- How is the main character different at the end of the story than at the beginning?

2 Gist: Students identify the central message, lesson, or moral of a story, including fables and folktales, then chronologically recount the main events, including just the most important information, not every single detail.

They consider:

- What message, lesson, or moral does the author want me to take away from reading this text?
- What details led me to determine this?
- What details from the beginning, middle, and end would I include when retelling or recounting this story?

Informational Text

K Gist: Students identify the main topic of an informational text, then report on the key ideas, details, and events that help convey the main topic.

They consider:

- What is the main topic of this text?
- What is the most important information about the main topic that the author wants me to know?

1 Gist: Students identify the main topic of a text, then report on the key ideas, details, and events, including just the important information, not every single detail.

They consider:

- What is the main topic of this text or section?
- What is the most important information about the main topic that the author wants me to know?

2 Gist: Students identify the main topic of a multiparagraph text, then recount the key ideas, details, and events in each paragraph that help explain the main topic, including just the important information, not every single detail.

They consider:

- What is the main topic of this text?
- What key ideas, details, and events in each paragraph helped me determine this?
- What details would I include when recounting what this text is about?

Note: Although the questions listed above are too difficult for most young students to internalize and apply on their own, we share them to give teachers a detailed sense of what their students should be striving toward as learners. K–2 students may not be able to ask these questions of themselves independently, but teachers can use them as a jumping-off point for lesson content and as prompts and reminders to share with students. Over time and with instruction, students will be able to pose these questions on their own.

What the **Teacher** Does

To have students determine the central ideas, message, or main topic of the text:

- Make talking about the central or main message (literature) and main topic (informational) a routine part of what you do when you read aloud to students or confer with them.

- Think aloud about how you determine the author's central message and main topic, and point out the details—words, sentences, and illustrations—that helped you reason and infer.

- Share big books or enlarged texts with students and have them participate in figuring out the author's central message or main topic by attending to specific words, phrases, and images in the text.

- Plan lessons that demonstrate how the illustrations in both literature and informational text help readers figure out and elaborate on the central message or main topic. Repeat similar lessons throughout the year in which students study illustrations to glean information.

- Guide students to consider how the title, headings, pictures/captions, and bold words in an informational text help readers figure out the main topic, pointing out to students when the author plainly states the main idea in a paragraph's first sentence and other places.

To have students analyze the development of the central message:

- Help students to recognize that focusing on the elements of story grammar (i.e., character, setting, problem, main events, and resolution) is one of the most effective ways to determine how a story is developing. Use a story grammar graphic organizer to illustrate this point (resources.corwin.com/literacycompanionk-2).

- Give students regular practice in thinking and talking about the main character in a story they're reading on their own. For example, they might think about the problem that character has, how other characters support the main character or stand in his or her way, and how the main character eventually solves the problem or resolves the conflict.

To have students retell or recount stories, including fables and folktales:

- As you read aloud, introduce students to different types of stories, such as realistic stories, adventure stories, graphic novels, folktales, and fantasy stories. Give students opportunities to discuss them and then compare and chart the attributes of the different types.

- After a story has been read a couple of times, demonstrate how to retell/recount it. First, explain that a retell/recount involves an opening statement, followed by key events listed in sequential or chronological order, and a conclusion. Have students practice retelling/recounting stories orally by working with partners and then sharing with the class.

- Engage students in an activity called "Story Bookends," in which a story is read aloud and then students decide on the problem the main character is experiencing (the left bookend) and the resolution (the right bookend). Two students then illustrate the bookends on separate pieces of chart paper. Next, engage the entire class in a discussion of the "events" that should go in the middle, and ask for volunteers to represent or stand in for each "event." Line up the students representing the two "bookends" and the "events" in the front of the classroom in chronological order and have them describe how the problem is resolved.

To have students identify the main topic of an informational text and recall key supporting details:

- Help students understand that by attending to the title and the front and back cover illustrations, readers can get a general sense of what a text is about.

- Direct students to pay close attention to section titles, words in bold, and illustrations before, during, and after they read.

- Help students identify words that are repeated frequently, since these often refer to the key details the author wants readers to know.

To have students identify the focus of a specific paragraph within a multiparagraph text:

- Teach students what a topic sentence is and how it most often comes at the beginning or end of a paragraph.

- Think aloud your process for noticing special vocabulary or repeated/related words that provide clues to the main topic, such as *eat*, *meal*, *plants*, *diet*, and *feeding* in a paragraph whose main topic is "what deer eat."

- Give students practice in locating topic sentences and identifying the details that support them. Project a paragraph on a whiteboard, think through with students' help what the topic sentence might be, and then underline or annotate the key details.

To help your English language learners, try this:

- Bring in actual bookends (realia) to help make the "Story Bookends" activity more concrete.

- Make certain that students understand the academic vocabulary you're using, such as the terms *main character*, *problem*, and *resolution*.

- Have students work in small groups to practice retelling stories orally. Use pictures as props to help students' retellings. Encourage students to act out the stories.

- Have students work in small groups to practice sharing main ideas and details orally from nonfiction text. Use pictures as props to help them describe the main topics and supporting details, pointing to the text as appropriate to show where in the text the information is presented.

Developmental Debrief:

Since teaching students to *summarize* officially begins in third grade, we do not address this skill per se in this K–2 volume. However, retellings/recounts are on the developmental continuum leading toward students eventually learning to summarize in later grades.

In K–2 classrooms, it is advisable for students to talk about the central message in a piece of literature rather than try to determine its "theme," a concept that's more appropriate for students in grade 3.

Notes

Academic Vocabulary: Key Words and Phrases

Analyze their development: This refers to the careful and close examination of the parts or elements from which something is made and how those parts affect or function within the whole to create meaning.

Central ideas: Some ideas are more important to a work than others; these are the ideas you could not cut out without fundamentally changing the meaning or quality of the text. Think of the "central" ideas of a text as you would the beams in a building: They are the main elements that make up the text and that all the supporting details help to develop.

Central message, lesson, or moral: This relates to what the author thinks is right or the proper way to behave. In upper elementary grades, this is often referred to as the theme. Generally, in fiction, the message/lesson/moral addresses the author's point of view about relationships between people.

Fables: These are legendary stories of supernatural happenings or narratives that attempt to impart truths (often through morals)—especially in stories where animals speak and have human characteristics.

Folktales (and fairy tales): Folktales are short stories that were first passed down from generation to generation by word of mouth. These tales typically have to do with everyday life, with a character of poor and humble origins triumphing over a wealthier, more powerful superior. Fairy tales are a subgenre of folktales that include magical elements or creatures, such as dragons, goblins, and elves. The entire folktale genre generally reflects or validates certain aspects of the culture or group.

Key supporting details and ideas: Key details and ideas support the larger ideas the text develops over time and are used to advance the author's claim(s). Since not all details and ideas are equally important, students must learn to identify those that matter the most in the context of the text.

Main topic: This refers to what an informational text is all about (e.g., how animals prepare for winter). The main topic is the most important or central idea of a paragraph or of a larger part of a text. It's what the author wants you to remember most.

Retelling or recounting stories, including key details: Retelling/recounting involves giving an oral account of the key details of a story. This typically includes an opening statement, a chronological listing of key events, and a concluding statement. (Even though *retell* and *recount* have slightly different meanings, we use them interchangeably throughout this volume.)

Summarize: When readers summarize, they identify and report on the key ideas, details, or events in the text, giving just the important information, not every single detail.

Themes: These are what the text is actually about, and there can be more than one. A theme can be the central message, the lesson, or what the author wants you to come away with. Common themes include survival, good versus evil, showing respect for others, adventure, love, and friendship.

Notes

Standard: _____

Purpose of Lesson/s:	
Planning the Lesson/s	**Questions to Ask**
Differentiating Instruction	**Thinking Beyond This Standard**

The standards guide instruction; they do not dictate it. *So as you plan lessons remember you aren't teaching the standards, but instead are teaching students how to read, write, talk, and think through well-crafted lessons that draw from the pedagogy embedded within them. Engaging lessons often have several ELA standards within them and integrate reading, writing, speaking and listening, and language.*

Standard 3: Analyze how and why individuals, events, and ideas develop and interact over the course of a text.

Literature

K With prompting and support, students identify characters, settings, and major events in a story.

1 Students describe characters, settings, and major events in a story, using key details.

2 Students describe how characters in a story respond to major events and challenges.

Informational Text

K With prompting and support, students describe the connection between two individuals, events, ideas, or pieces of information in a text.

1 Students describe the connection between two individuals, events, ideas, or pieces of information in a text.

2 Students describe the connection between a series of historical events, scientific ideas or concepts, or steps in technical procedures in a text.

What the **Student** Does

Literature

K **Gist:** Students identify the characters, setting, and major events in a story.

They consider:

- Who is the main character and what is he or she like?
- Who are the other characters and how does the main character get along with them?
- How does the main character react to major events that occur?
- Would the story have been the same if it had taken place at a different location?

1 **Gist:** Students describe the characters, setting, and major events in a story, using key details.

They consider:

- How does the main character behave at the beginning of the story? Why? What problem is causing him or her to act that way?
- How do other characters make things better or worse for the main character?
- What, if anything, has the main character learned by the end of the story? Or has what was once a problem been resolved? What events caused this to happen?
- Would the story be the same if it had taken place at a different location or at a different time?

2 **Gist:** Students describe how characters respond to major events and challenges.

They consider:

- How does the main character behave at the beginning, middle, and end of the story?
- Why does the main character's behavior change from the beginning of the story to the end?
- What event is the turning point of the story, when the main character does something or understands something that helps solve the problem?

Informational Text

K **Gist:** Students describe how two individuals, events, ideas, or pieces of information relate to one another.

They consider:

- How does the title help me understand what the text is about?
- Which pieces of information explain the title?
- How is the text organized? Do the sections or chapters follow in a helpful order?
- How do the illustrations and the words *work together* to help me understand the main topic?

1 **Gist:** Students describe how two individuals, events, ideas, or pieces of information relate to one another.

They consider:

- What does the title tell me about the topic? How about the headings?
- How is the text organized? Do the sections or chapters follow in a logical order?
- How does the information in each section relate to the section title and the main topic as a whole?
- How do the illustrations, the text features, and the words *work together* to help me understand the main topic?

2 **Gist:** Students describe the connection between historical events, scientific ideas or concepts, or steps in technical procedures.

They consider:

- Is the author's purpose to describe people, events, and concepts; to give steps in a process; or to describe how to do something?
- How do the illustrations, the text features, and the words *work together* to help me understand the main topic?
- When I "add up" the section headings, what do I learn? How do they build on one another to give information about the main topic?

Note: Although the questions listed above are too difficult for most young students to internalize and apply on their own, we share them to give teachers a detailed sense of what their students should be striving toward as learners. K–2 students may not be able to ask these questions of themselves independently, but teachers can use them as a jumping-off point for lesson content and as prompts and reminders to share with students. Over time and with instruction, students will be able to pose these questions on their own.

What the **Teacher** Does

To help students identify the characters, setting, and major events in a story:

- Read aloud and share texts whose story elements and/or organization are straightforward and a good fit with the story elements you're highlighting. Look for traditionally organized stories, such as "The Three Billy Goats Gruff" and Rosemary Wells's *Timothy Goes to School*, and use story map graphic organizers to chart the stories' development (resources.corwin.com/literacycompanionk-2).

- Make a list of all the characters in a story and determine which is the main character and which ones play more of a supporting role. Elicit from students *why* they categorize the characters as they do, and direct them back to the text for evidence.

- Create character webs to help students identify what the main and supporting characters are like, how they feel, and what motivates them to behave in certain ways. As students read the text, help them draw connections between the characters, for example, between the hardworking Little Red Hen and the lazy Dog, Duck, and Pig. Help students identify how the Little Red Hen's request for help and Dog's, Duck's, and Pig's refusal to help lead her to act as she does at the end.

- Help students understand that *setting* refers to both where (city, country, in school, at home, and so on) and when (time of day or season) a story takes place. This also includes the geographic and/or historical location of the story. Help students keep track of any changes in the setting of the story and help them identify the words the author uses to alert them to such changes.

To help students describe and explain how characters respond to major events and challenges:

- Have students identify the wants or needs of key characters and parts of the story where their various wants and needs conflict. Examine what those conflicts reveal about the characters.

- On a second reading, build a major events (plot) map with students to record the most important happenings. Illustrate how a plot builds. Have students identify the turning point in the story. Lead them in a discussion of what came before and after (resources.corwin.com/literacycompanionk-2).

- As you read a picture book a second time, invite students to hold up yellow sticky notes to signal major moments in the story. Pause to have them examine the illustration that depicts the scene and describe how the character is behaving, and why. Continue this activity until the story's end. Help them notice whether or not characters typically act in certain ways.

- Create a three-column chart with students that you can add to over the year, listing the main character's name, a personality trait, and whether or not the character changes by the end of story. Doing so helps children see that in some stories the main character does change, while in others the author has the character stay the same on purpose (e.g., Curious George, Amelia Bedelia, Judy Moody, Clifford, Spinky in *Spinky Sulks*).

To help students describe how individuals, events, ideas, and pieces of information relate to one another:

- Select a portion of a text and model how you absorb each sentence, noticing when two things connect in a particularly striking, important way. (For example, in a book about rain forest animals, you might note the connection between a parrot's brightly colored feathers, camouflage, and the concept of predator/prey. In a biography of Jackie Robinson, Robinson and the owner of the Brooklyn Dodgers, Branch Rickey, have a significant connection because Rickey dared to break the Major League Baseball color barrier by allowing Robinson to play.)

- Help students identify language that lets them know two pieces of information, ideas, concepts, or events are being compared (*but, however, in contrast, versus*). Likewise, help them identify words that signal the information is organized in a sequence (*first, next, and then*).

To help students describe the connection between historical events, scientific ideas or concepts, or steps in technical procedures:

- Help students determine *why* something happened as it did. This will help them begin to identify cause/effect relationships between concepts, people, and events.

- Gather a few texts that offer different and clear examples of signal words. Read the texts and chart the signal words, posting them on the wall for student reference. For example, some authors use timelines, dates, numbered steps, and words like *first, second, next, last, most important*, and *years ago*.

To help your English language learners, try this:

- Guide a small group of students through a basic story in which the story elements are obvious and unambiguous. If students don't each have their own copy of the story, use an enlarged text. Wordless books offer students the opportunity to focus on the story elements shown in the illustrations.

- Provide students with a story structure graphic organizer and have them discuss the story elements and fill them in as you or they read. For nonfiction text, use a graphic organizer that matches the text structure and fill in the organizer as you read or discuss the text.

- Make certain students understand the academic vocabulary you're using, such as *main character*, *problem*, and *resolution*, and for nonfiction text, *main idea* and *details*.

Developmental Debrief:

Nascent readers typically focus more on the plot than on the characters. The teacher, therefore, is instrumental in helping students make the move from focusing on the plot to attending to how and why the characters behave as they do. Select read-aloud and shared-reading texts with multidimensional characters and guide students to recognize how the characters' personality traits and ways of thinking or acting ultimately affect how the story turns out.

Notes

Academic Vocabulary: Key Words and Phrases

Analyze: This means to look closely at something for the key parts and how they work together.

Characters: Characters can be simple (flat, static) or complex (round, dynamic); only characters that change, that have rich inner lives and interact with people and their environments, can be considered "complex."

Cause/effect relationship: This is the relationship between the reason (or "why") something happens and the consequences of that action. The *cause* is why something happens. The *effect* is what happens as a result of the cause.

Compare/contrast: This requires students to identify and analyze what is similar (compare) and what is different (contrast) about two things.

Connections: This refers to how one idea, event, piece of information, or character interacts with or relates to another idea, event, piece of information, or character. When connecting one idea to another idea or one event to another event, students often have to consider cause and effect, or why things turned out as they did. When connecting characters, they might need to consider how the changes in characters from the beginning of a story to the end relate to how the main character interacts with or relates to other characters or events in the story.

Develop and interact: As stories unfold, events and characters change; these changes are the consequences of interactions that take place between people, events, and ideas within a story or an actual social event. In addition, as individuals, events, and ideas change or develop, they often grow more complex or evolve into something altogether different.

Key details: In the context of literature, key details relate to story grammar elements—that is, character, setting, problem, major events, and resolution—and how they interact. In the context of informational text, key details refer to the facts and ideas the author selects to support the text's main idea.

Major events: These are the most important events in a story, typically related to how the main character resolves a problem or handles a challenge.

Sequence of events: This is the order in which the events in a story or text occur, or the order in which specific tasks are performed.

Setting: This is the place and time in which a story, novel, or drama takes place. To determine the setting, students describe *where* it takes place (there may be more than one setting in a text) and *when* it takes place, which may refer to a specific time period or can be the *past*, *present*, or *future*.

Steps in technical procedures: Whether in social studies or science, the idea here is that in any series of steps or stages, some steps or stages are more crucial than others. Students must be able to discern this so they can understand why the steps or stages are so important and how they affect other people or events.

Notes

Standard: _____

Purpose of Lesson/s:

Planning the Lesson/s	Questions to Ask

Differentiating Instruction	Thinking Beyond This Standard

The standards guide instruction; they do not dictate it. So as you plan lessons remember you aren't teaching the standards, but instead are teaching students how to read, write, talk, and think through well-crafted lessons that draw from the pedagogy embedded within them. Engaging lessons often have several ELA standards within them and integrate reading, writing, speaking and listening, and language.

Standard 4: Interpret words and phrases as they are used in a text, including determining technical, connotative, and figurative meanings, and analyze how specific word choices shape meaning or tone.

Literature

K Students ask and answer questions about unknown words in a text.

1 Students identify words and phrases in stories or poems that suggest feelings or appeal to the senses.

2 Students describe how words and phrases (e.g., regular beats, alliteration, rhymes, repeated lines) supply rhythm and meaning in a story, poem, or song.

Informational Text

K With prompting and support, students ask and answer questions about unknown words in a text.

1 Students ask and answer questions to help determine or clarify the meaning of words and phrases in a text.

2 Students determine the meaning of words and phrases in a text relevant to a grade 2 topic or subject area.

What the **Student** Does

Literature	Informational Text

Literature

K **Gist:** Students ask and answer questions about unknown words in a text.

They consider:

- What words do I not understand?
- Are there words or phrases I do know that can help me figure out those I don't know?
- Do the illustrations help me figure out the meaning of a word?

1 **Gist:** Students identify words and phrases in stories or poems that suggest feelings or appeal to the senses.

They consider:

- Which words or phrases help me experience the text with my senses (sight, smell, taste, touch)?
- Which words or phrases seem surprising or funny and may have a fancy (figurative) rather than normal (literal) meaning?
- Are there words or phrases that help me picture what's happening?

2 **Gist:** Students determine the meaning of words and phrases in a story, poem, or song, and how they supply rhythm and meaning.

They consider:

- Which words tell me the most about the characters or actions?
- Which words or phrases seem surprising or funny and so may have a fancy (figurative) rather than a normal (literal) meaning?
- Which fancy words or phrases help me experience or understand the text in a deeper, more powerful way?
- Are there words in a poem or song that repeat or rhyme? How does this add to my understanding and enjoyment?

Informational Text

K **Gist:** Students ask and answer questions about unknown words in a text.

They consider:

- What words or phrases are hard for me?
- What do I think they mean?
- Do the illustrations give clues about the meaning of a word?
- Are some words written in bold (to signal that they're important)? Is there an illustration on the page that helps me understand the word in bold?

1 **Gist:** Students ask and answer questions to determine or clarify the meaning of unfamiliar words.

They consider:

- Do the illustrations or text features (titles, headings, captions) help me figure out the meaning of a word?
- Are there words the author uses repeatedly? (These often indicate the main topic, key ideas, or key details.)
- Are there words written in bold?
- Can I substitute another word in place of the unknown word that would make sense?
- Can I use the words and sentences around the unknown word to figure out what it means?

2 **Gist:** Students determine the meaning of words or phrases in a text that are relevant to a content-area topic.

They consider:

- Do the illustrations or text features (titles, headings, captions) help me figure out the meaning of a word?
- Are there words the author uses repeatedly?
- Are there words the author has written in bold? Is there a picture/caption or glossary that refers to the word in bold?
- Can I substitute another word in place of the unknown word that would make sense?
- Can I use the context to figure out special, important words (domain-specific words)?

Note: Although the questions listed above are too difficult for most young students to internalize and apply on their own, we share them to give teachers a detailed sense of what their students should be striving toward as learners. K–2 students may not be able to ask these questions of themselves independently, but teachers can use them as a jumping-off point for lesson content and as prompts and reminders to share with students. Over time and with instruction, students will be able to pose these questions on their own.

What the **Teacher** Does

To have students ask and answer questions about unfamiliar words and phrases in a text:

- Explain to students that understanding what individual words mean has everything to do with how well they understand a text. It's the reader's job to be on the lookout for words he or she understands or doesn't understand.

- When working with students in whole-class and small-group settings, and when conferring one-on-one, encourage students to acknowledge when they don't know what a word or phrase means. Explain that the best readers readily pause when they don't know a word, admit to themselves they're confused, and work to figure it out. Share words that you yourself find confusing; it's also fine occasionally to pretend you don't know the meaning of a word or phrase to demonstrate this process.

- Using both fiction and nonfiction, think aloud as you *decode* a word, puzzling through how to read it, and contrast it with thinking aloud about your process for understanding what words *mean*. Chart various strategies for each of these processes and refer to them frequently to demonstrate the difference between decoding and comprehension (resources.corwin.com/literacycompanionk-2).

- Instead of simply telling students the meaning of an unfamiliar word when reading aloud or sharing a text, mark the text with a sticky note and return to it later and help students figure it out. Provide students with sticky notes to mark their own texts when reading in small groups or independently.

- Show students how to use the words and sentences surrounding an unknown word to figure it out. Also, be sure to explain and show examples of instances when using context clues is not helpful. For example, the sentence "These sod houses were very cozy" would not help a reader figure out the meaning of *cozy*.

To have students interpret the meanings of words and phrases as they are used in a text:

- Work with students regularly to help them figure out the meanings of unknown words and phrases instead of telling them what the words or phrases mean.

- Direct students to use the pictures that accompany stories, poems, and songs, and the illustrations, photos/captions, and diagrams in informational texts to determine the meanings of words or phrases.

- Select words to teach explicitly that are most important to understanding an author's message. For example,

when reading *Hurty Feelings* by Helen Lester, we would teach the word *fragile* because the main character's name is Fragility and she (a hippo) is most definitely sensitive and "breakable"—at least on the inside.

- Show students how authors often include the meaning of a word in the sentence itself or in one that follows. Two examples are "Woodchucks dig *burrows*, or holes, in the ground, where they hibernate for the winter" and "*Canine* teeth are for biting and tearing your food."

- Guide students to identify root words and affixes to help them understand what a word means. Take apart compound words and work with homophones, synonyms, and antonyms as well.

- Devote a large section of your wall space to the posting of vocabulary charts, word webs, and so on that you've generated with students so that you have easy access to them when you want to review or add to the lists.

To have students identify and determine the figurative meanings of words and phrases:

- Keep a basket of books that contain rich vocabulary and figurative language to read aloud and for students to read on their own. Helen Lester's and Margie Palatini's picture books are among those you'll want to include.

- Provide each student with a copy of a poem or song containing figurative language or project the text on a whiteboard. Read the text several times and allow students time to discuss what it means. Help students identify figurative words and phrases and help them recognize how they help create a picture in a reader's mind. Note that any attention given to figurative language (similes, metaphors, alliteration, idioms, and onomatopoeia) in grades K–2 should be done with a light and playful touch.

- Give students opportunities to illustrate idiomatic figures of speech, such as "butterflies in my stomach" and "a fish out of water." The resulting illustrations might be compiled into a book.

To have students describe how words and phrases supply rhythm and meaning in a story, poem, or song:

- Have students look back through a text that has been read aloud or shared to identify words and phrases they find interesting or pleasurable, and ask them to explain why. They might say that they like the way a word sounds or that they've never heard it before. We want students to learn to love words and enjoy distinguishing shades of meaning.

- Post a running list of *onomatopoeic words* (words like *whoosh, clang, click, burp*) since onomatopoeia shows up frequently in children's books. These kinds of words are fun, and children can easily incorporate them into their own writing to give it voice.

- Help students recognize that when we want to highly exaggerate or emphasize something, we often use hyperbole. For example, the phrase "I've told you a million times not to do that" means I've told you repeatedly.

- Select alliterative poems and rhymes, such as "Peter Piper picked a peck of pickled peppers" to read with students. Help them see how repeating the same sounds at the beginnings of words is similar to rhyming words at the ends of lines of poetry.

To help your English language learners, try this:

- Meet with a small group of students for interactive read-aloud or shared reading to allow them to talk about words whose meanings they don't know and for you to help them in an intimate setting.

- Facilitate conversation about words students love or find interesting. Create a chart on which to record these words.

Developmental Debrief:

The best way to help students recognize the important role that word meanings play in reading and comprehension is to read aloud to them *at least* once a day. Reading a text aloud multiple times provides *implicit* vocabulary instruction. By hearing words used in the context of a story, informational text, poem, or song, children will often be able to determine their meaning. At the very least it might be their first exposure to a word, upon which they can build. In addition, when reading aloud be sure to use facial and vocal expression and body language, and give brief explanations of what some of the unfamiliar words mean. It's equally important to provide *explicit* vocabulary instruction, in which you decide beforehand which words you will teach directly through planned and purposeful experiences before, during, and after reading a text.

Notes

Academic Vocabulary: Key Words and Phrases

Alliteration: Repetition of the initial consonant sound in words that are close to one another (e.g., "wonderful wacky words").

Figurative meanings: Figures of speech (or figurative language) are often-colorful ways of saying something that help create a picture in the mind of the reader. For K–2 students the most common figures of speech are metaphor, simile, and personification. A *metaphor* compares two things that are not typically associated with each other (e.g., "That room is an oven"). A *simile* typically uses the word *like* or *as* when making a comparison (e.g., "A blue whale's skin is as slippery as a bar of soap"). Personification involves attributing human characteristics to something that is nonhuman (e.g., "The wind howled").

Interpret: This is best understood as a way of explaining what an author wrote using more accessible, familiar language for those who lack experience with or knowledge of the subject or type of text.

Technical meaning: In general this term relates to words with specialized meanings that are specific to a topic or subject being investigated. For K–2 students we can narrow this down to mean domain-specific words that typically occur in texts related to a specific content area, such as rocks and minerals (*igneous*) or weather (*cumulus*).

Tone: When thinking of tone, think about tone *of voice*. The formal tone of the U.S. Constitution matches the work's importance and subject; the informal tone of a literary text signals the relationship between the individuals and reveals the character of the speaker.

Notes

Planning Page

Standard: _____

Purpose of Lesson/s:	

Planning the Lesson/s	**Questions to Ask**

Differentiating Instruction	**Thinking Beyond This Standard**

The standards guide instruction; they do not dictate it. So as you plan lessons remember you aren't teaching the standards, but instead are teaching students how to read, write, talk, and think through well-crafted lessons that draw from the pedagogy embedded within them. Engaging lessons often have several ELA standards within them and integrate reading, writing, speaking and listening, and language.

Standard 5: Analyze the structure of texts, including how specific sentences, paragraphs, and larger portions of the text (e.g., a section, chapter, scene, or stanza) relate to each other and the whole.

Literature

K Students recognize common types of texts (e.g., storybooks, poems).

1 Students explain major differences between books that tell stories and books that give information, drawing on a wide reading of a range of text types.

2 Students describe the overall structure of a story, including describing how the beginning introduces the story and the ending concludes the action.

Informational Text

K Students identify the front cover, back cover, and title page of a book.

1 Students know and use various text features (e.g., headings, tables of contents, glossaries, electronic menus, icons) to locate key facts or information in a text.

2 Students know and use various text features (e.g., captions, bold print, subheadings, glossaries, indexes, electronic menus, icons) to locate key facts or information in a text efficiently.

What the **Student** Does

Literature	Informational Text

K **Gist:** Students name the type of text they are reading or discussing (e.g., story, poem).

They consider:

- Am I reading a story, poem, or drama?
- How do I know?

1 **Gist:** Students explain the difference between a story and informational text.

They consider:

- What are books that tell stories like?
- What are informational texts like?
- Why do authors write stories?
- Why do they write informational texts?
- What are some differences between the two?

2 **Gist:** When describing how stories are organized, students include how the beginning introduces the story and the ending concludes it.

They consider:

- What happens at the beginning of a story? (Characters are introduced and described, the setting is made clear, and the problem the main character will face is alluded to.)
- What happens in the middle of the story? (Most of the story occurs here. The main character faces a problem or dilemma, and either the character takes action or events occur to resolve the problem.)
- What happens at the end of the story? (The problem is resolved or the main character learns a lesson, and the story draws to a close.)

K **Gist:** Students refer to the front and back covers and the title page when reading or speaking about a text.

They consider:

- What information do the front and back covers contain?
- What's on the title page?

1 **Gist:** Students use informational text features to locate key facts and information.

They consider:

- How do headings help me get information?
- What does a table of contents do?
- What is a glossary used for?
- How do I use electronic menus and icons to get information?

2 **Gist:** Students use informational text features to locate key facts and information.

They consider:

- What are captions? How do they help me understand the pictures and words on this page?
- How do words in bold (which highlight key ideas and concepts) relate to the illustrations, the text, and the glossary?
- How does reading all the headings help me understand this text?
- What is a glossary used for?
- How do indexes help me get information?
- How do I use electronic menus and icons to get information?

Note: Although the questions listed above are too difficult for most young students to internalize and apply on their own, we share them to give teachers a detailed sense of what their students should be striving toward as learners. K–2 students may not be able to ask these questions of themselves independently, but teachers can use them as a jumping-off point for lesson content and as prompts and reminders to share with students. Over time and with instruction, students will be able to pose these questions on their own.

What the **Teacher** Does

To have students recognize common types of literary texts:

- Read aloud a variety of literary texts, making sure to include various subgenres, such as folktales, realistic fiction, poetry, and drama. As you read and compare texts from two subgenres (e.g., folktales and realistic fiction), chart the subgenres' distinguishing features so that students can refer to the chart as they read and write.

- Set up book boxes labeled "New Stories," "New Poetry," and "New Dramas." As you bring books into the classroom, read them aloud and have students help decide in which box each belongs.

- Provide spaces on students' daily reading logs for them to indicate, often by color coding, whether their books are fiction, informational, or poetry. Note that we include three of the four primary genre categories, since these represent the range of texts students are likely to read throughout the week. We do not include drama because most students' independent reading does not include that category. When grade 2 students are engaged in a specific genre study (e.g., informational texts), their logs may reflect whether the book they read on a particular day is an expository, biographical, procedural, or other subgenre of informational text (see samples of student logs in the online resources at resources.corwin.com/literacycompanionk-2).

To have students recognize the difference between stories and books that give information:

- Compare a literary (fiction) text and an informational (nonfiction) text that on the surface appear to be about the same topic. At first glance, for example, both may seem to be about wolves, but upon closer examination the nonfiction (expository) text describes what wolves are like, the nature of their packs, how they are related to dogs, and so on. The literary text, on the other hand, is actually about a wolf named Willy who runs away from his pack because he doesn't feel appreciated.

- Make two charts and title them "What Authors of Stories Do" and "What Authors of Informational Texts Do" when they write. Add to each list as you read aloud and share texts with students. You might list on the story chart that authors "make up the story" and "often include magic." On the informational text chart you might write that authors "give true information" and "sometimes include a glossary."

- When conferring with students, have them select a literary text and an informational text from their book bag or basket. Ask them to explain the differences between the two. (Make sure that students have a healthy balance of literary and informational texts in their independent book bag or basket.)

- Give a committee of students the opportunity to determine whether new books you receive for your classroom library are literary or informational. Ask them to explain and discuss their decisions with the rest of the class.

- Help students recognize that there is a category of picture books—blended books—that combine elements of literary and informational texts. While the overall structure of a blended book may follow a typical story line, the author also includes a significant amount of content knowledge about the topic. Gather examples of blended books in a separate basket and label it "Blended Picture Books."

To help students describe the overall structure of stories:

- When reading stories, use a variety of story structure graphic organizers to help students understand how stories are organized (see examples at resources.corwin.com/literacycompanionk-2). To achieve this goal, it's also helpful to show students how other genres are organized in contrast—procedural and expository texts, for example.

- Make copies of graphic organizers for students to use occasionally and as needed when reading in small groups and independently. However, be very careful not to overdo their use.

To help students use various informational text features:

- As students read and write, call attention to informational text features (e.g., tables of contents, headings, pictures/captions, and scale drawings) and the purpose each serves. Encourage students to use such features as they write nonfiction. Photocopy pages of student writing in which students have used text features and have students paste their examples into a large blank book, which can be either handmade or purchased online.

Title the book "Our Nonfiction Text Feature Book" and add to it throughout the year.

- Invite students to sort informational text features into two categories according to the jobs they do—those that help readers "access information" and those that "extend information." For example, tables of contents, headings, and indexes help readers access or find information; captions, illustrations, glossaries, scale drawings, and charts help to elaborate and extend information that is presented in the text (words).

- Help students recognize that the use of bold print means something different in literature than it means in informational texts. In informational texts, bold print indicates that the word (concept, idea) is important and directs readers to pay close attention to its meaning as described in the text, the graphics, and the glossary. In literature, bold is used to indicate the intensity with which something is experienced or for emphasis.

To help your English language learners, try this:

- Work with students in a small group before or after a whole-class lesson or demonstration. Meeting with them prior to the lesson will give them an edge on understanding what you're demonstrating; meeting after the lesson will give them time to discuss and process more thoroughly.

- Working with small groups of students, select texts whose structure is simple and unambiguous. Provide a graphic organizer on large chart paper to help students discuss and record information as they read. Also, focus on text features such as bold words, pictures, and graphs that can clue the students in to how the text is organized.

Developmental Debrief:

Regardless of the standard with which you're working, regularly assess your students to determine what they actually need additional help with. In this instance, *assess* means to "sit alongside" learners to determine what they know and need to learn, and most often involves observing them as they read and write. Therefore, even though Reading Standard 5 for grade 2 implies that students will have already learned what's recommended under the kindergarten and grade 1 standards, you will need to determine whether or not this is the case. Likewise, students in grade 1 may already demonstrate an understanding of a particular grade 1 standard, so you needn't teach it. Always do what is most appropriate for your students.

Notes

Academic Vocabulary: Key Words and Phrases

Analyze the structure of a specific paragraph or group of sentences: This involves considering how information in general and sentences in particular are arranged within a paragraph, particularly as the structure relates to the author's purpose. Also crucial is the sequence or arrangement of the sentences within a paragraph, especially as they express cause and effect or otherwise serve to develop an idea.

Analyze the structure of texts: This refers to how authors organize their ideas and their texts as a whole. Through structural patterns—at the sentence, paragraph, and whole-text level—authors emphasize certain ideas and create such effects as tension, mystery, and humor.

Electronic menu and icons: These are the dropdown menus on computer applications and programs or icons on digital devices that users activate to get information.

Range of text types: The Common Core State Standards divide texts into literature and informational texts. The subcategories under literature are stories, drama, and poetry. Stories include children's adventure stories, folktales, legends, fables, fantasy, realistic fiction, and myth. Drama includes staged dialogue and brief familiar scenes. Poetry includes nursery rhymes and the subgenres of the narrative poem, limerick, and free verse poem. Subcategories under informational texts are literary nonfiction and historical, scientific, and technical texts. These include biographies and autobiographies; books about history, social studies, science, and the arts; technical texts, including directions, forms, and information displayed in graphs, charts, and maps; and digital sources on a range of topics.

Relate to each other and the whole: Throughout this standard, students are asked to consider the part in its relation to the whole; this then refers to how the sentence relates to the paragraph of which it is a part, or the paragraph in relation to the whole, the scene in relation to the act—or the whole play.

Structure of texts: This refers to how authors organize their ideas and the text as a whole. Through structural patterns such as problem/resolution and cause/effect, authors emphasize certain ideas, events, concepts, or information.

Text features: These are features of an informational text that help the reader get information. Readers need to understand that they can use text features such as tables of contents, headings, and indexes to access information. They can also gain information about a topic that is not expressly stated in the text (words) itself from maps, illustrations, scale drawings, charts, and graphs.

Notes

Standard: _____

Purpose of Lesson/s:

Planning the Lesson/s	Questions to Ask

Differentiating Instruction	Thinking Beyond This Standard

The standards guide instruction; they do not dictate it. So as you plan lessons remember you aren't teaching the standards, but instead are teaching students how to read, write, talk, and think through well-crafted lessons that draw from the pedagogy embedded within them. Engaging lessons often have several ELA standards within them and integrate reading, writing, speaking and listening, and language.

Standard 6: Assess how point of view or purpose shapes the content and style of a text.

Literature

K With prompting and support, students name the author and illustrator of a story and define the role of each in telling the story.

1 Students identify who is telling the story at various points in a text.

2 Students acknowledge differences in the points of view of characters, including by speaking in a different voice for each character when reading dialogue aloud.

Informational Text

K Students name the author and illustrator of a text and define the role of each in presenting the ideas or information in a text.

1 Students distinguish between information provided by pictures or other illustrations and information provided by the words in a text.

2 Students identify the main purpose of a text, including what the author wants to answer, explain, or describe.

What the **Student** Does

Literature	Informational Text

Literature

K Gist: Students explain the roles of both the author and the illustrator in telling a story.

They consider:

- What does the author do to make the story enjoyable?
- How does the illustrator help tell the story?

1 Gist: Students identify who is telling the story at various points in a text.

They consider:

- How do I know when a character is talking?
- Is the main character telling the story?
- How do I know when someone else (the narrator) is explaining or describing what's happening?

2 Gist: Students determine the differences in the ways characters think and act in each scene of the story.

They consider:

- What are the characters thinking or feeling at different parts of the story?
- Do the characters show what they are feeling or do they hide it?
- How do the characters' actions show what they are thinking or feeling inside?

Informational Text

K Gist: Students explain the roles of both the author and the illustrator in presenting ideas and information.

They consider:

- What does the author do to make the text interesting?
- How does the illustrator help me understand the text better?

1 Gist: Students distinguish between information presented through pictures and other illustrations and information provided by the words in a text.

They consider:

- What information do I get from reading the words?
- What information do I get from looking at the pictures and other illustrations?

2 Gist: Students determine the author's purpose in writing the text.

They consider:

- Why did the author write this text?
- Did the author want me to know everything about this topic? Or just some things?
- Does this text teach me the steps of how to do something?
- Does the author want to share information about a topic that matters to him or her?

Note: Although the questions listed above are too difficult for most young students to internalize and apply on their own, we share them to give teachers a detailed sense of what their students should be striving toward as learners. K–2 students may not be able to ask these questions of themselves independently, but teachers can use them as a jumping-off point for lesson content and as prompts and reminders to share with students. Over time and with instruction, students will be able to pose these questions on their own.

What the **Teacher** Does

To have students determine the roles of the author and the illustrator in telling a story and presenting ideas and information:

- State the names of the author and illustrator when reading aloud to students and indicate when they are one and the same. Be sure to "thank" the author and illustrator for a job well done. Be specific about what you like about their writing and illustration styles, and invite students to offer their compliments as well.

- Visit the websites of favorite children's authors and illustrators to deepen students' understanding and appreciation of the work authors and illustrators do and what motivates them to publish their work for others to read. (Check out the Meet the Author series published by Richard C. Owen Publishers, which includes autobiographies of 32 of the most popular children's authors.)

- Have students write and illustrate their own stories and informational pieces. Gather students to discuss the decisions they made as writers and as illustrators, and chart what they did.

- Have students work in partnerships in which each student writes a story or an expository piece and then exchanges papers with another student to illustrate. Provide opportunities for students to discuss what this experience was like. Did their partners/illustrators get it right? Did their partners select key parts of their stories or nonfiction pieces to illustrate?

To have students identify who is telling a story at various points (i.e., differentiate between narration and dialogue):

- Explain that most stories unfold with the help of both the characters and a narrator. (See "point of view" in the academic vocabulary section for the different types of narration.)

- Show students examples of narration and dialogue and help them differentiate between the two by working with an enlarged text or putting a text up on a whiteboard. Use different colors of highlighting tape to indicate what the narrator and each of the key characters say, or annotate in the margins. *Children Make Terrible Pets* by Peter Brown is a favorite go-to book for this activity because the narration is printed in green rectangles and the characters speak in color-coded talking bubbles.

- As you read stories aloud or during shared reading, help students identify how the characters are thinking and feeling, both inside and out, and consider how students might express those thoughts or feelings when reading the story aloud. For example, what "voice" (loud, quiet, afraid, excited) might best fit each character? Invite students to read a portion of the text (either an enlarged text or one on a whiteboard) with you and assume the voice of the character.

- Engage students in Readers Theater, a drama experience in which, as they read a script, they use their voices to express the thoughts or emotions the characters are experiencing, thus making the script come alive for their audience (typically students in their class).

To have students differentiate between information provided by the pictures (and other illustrations) and information provided by the words:

- Read aloud a short passage or section of a literary or informational text and have students create images in their minds from just the words alone. Then read the passage again, this time showing the picture that accompanies it. Have students compare the two experiences.

- Show a poster-size photo or a chart/graph that relates to a content-area topic. Have students discuss what they see and are learning from just this one graphic. Explain that the pictures and other illustrations in informational texts often provide as much information as an author can effectively communicate through words alone, if not more. Chart some of the information students can learn from graphics.

To have students determine the points of view of the characters:

- Read aloud stories in which the point of view is obvious, such as Doreen Cronin's *Diary of a Spider* and Brenda Parkes and Judith Smith's *The Little Red Hen*. Discuss with students how each story is told from the main character's point of view, even though in *Diary of a Spider* the spider is telling his story and in *The Little Red Hen* it's the narrator who tells the reader what happened (but from Hen's perspective).

- Guide students to pay close attention to the characters—what they're like, how they feel, what they're thinking, how they behave, and how they relate to other characters. In addition, have students attend to the illustrations, especially the characters' facial expressions showing their reactions to what's happening.

- Start by making a main character web as you read a story, and record what you're learning on spokes around the hub. Then move on to comparing the points of view of different characters using charts and graphic organizers to record information (see examples of graphic organizers in the online resources at resources.corwin.com/literacycompanionk-2).

- Read aloud and compare fairy tales told from the perspectives of different characters. For example, the traditional tale of "Jack and the Beanstalk" might be read alongside and compared with Eric Braun's *Trust Me, Jack's Beanstalk Stinks! The Story of Jack and the Beanstalk as Told by the Giant.*

- When students write stories, ask them to describe what their characters are like at the beginning, middle, and end of the story. Use the same terminology with students during your writing time of day as you do during reading. For example, ask: What is this character like? How does she feel? How might this affect how your story turns out?

To have students identify the main purpose of an informational text:

- Call students' attention to the title and subtitle, headings, and table of contents for an overview of how the text is organized and what the author wants the reader to know.

- Have students read the "author notes" (if there are any) at the beginning or end of the book. Authors often directly share their purpose and point of view with readers.

- Point out that authors of informational texts write primarily to share *information* they hope the reader will find interesting or helpful, and sometimes also to express or to state *opinions* (often with the intention of convincing the reader to agree with them). As students become more familiar with informational texts, they will recognize that within a given text an author will both give information and try to convince readers to feel or act a certain way. For example, in *Oil Spill*, author Melvin Berger wants to teach readers about oil spills and the harm they do to our environment; he also wants readers to take action.

To help your English language learners, try this:

- Work with students in small groups and call attention to the illustrations, especially the characters' facial expressions, for help in determining their points of view.

- Working with informational text, discuss with students why they think the author wrote the text (purpose) and what the author wanted the reader to learn. Discuss whether the author had a motive (point of view). It might help to use texts that are simple and ones to which students can relate, such as a short text an author wrote about dogs because the author seems to love dogs.

Developmental Debrief:

Identifying point of view can be difficult for young students, so make sure that you work with texts in which the point of view is obvious. When explaining point of view, it's helpful to have students think of personal experiences in which their point of view is clearly opposed to another's — for example, perhaps when a student and a sibling are both convinced they are right about something.

Deciding on the main purpose of a text is also a skill that usually clicks into place later in the primary grades, so it's okay if students are better at naming a main topic than they are at stating a main purpose.

Notes

Academic Vocabulary: Key Words and Phrases

Assess: In this instance, *assess*, rather than meaning to evaluate text, means to determine what a character's point of view is and how it shapes the story.

Content and style of a text: The perspective from which a story is told limits the content that can be included and the style used to write it. Point of view determines what the narrator sees, knows, hears, and can say—and how he or she can say it.

Main purpose of the text: Once readers identify the author's main purpose (i.e., to persuade, inform, express, or entertain), they have an easier time understanding the text and determining precisely what the author does to achieve that purpose.

Point of view: This is the perspective through which a story is told or an event is related. Stories and informational texts for K–2 students are typically told in either the first or third person. When the point of view is expressed in the first person, one character, usually the

main character, expresses his or her thoughts, ideas, and feelings. When the story is told in the third person, there's a narrator who usually identifies with the main character's point of view. Occasionally, there is an omniscient narrator—an outside observer—who knows what all the characters think and feel.

Points of view of characters: To fully understand a story and how it develops, readers must pay close attention to the characters—what they're like, how they act, and how they relate to the problem or situation that's unfolding. By identifying with the characters, especially the main character, readers gain a deeper understanding and appreciation of the story and its theme.

Purpose: People want to accomplish one of four purposes when they write or speak: to persuade, inform, express, or entertain. One could add others—to explain or inspire, for example—but these four account for most situations.

Notes

Planning Page

Standard: _____

Purpose of Lesson/s:

Planning the Lesson/s	Questions to Ask

Differentiating Instruction	Thinking Beyond This Standard

The standards guide instruction; they do not dictate it. So as you plan lessons remember you aren't teaching the standards, but instead are teaching students how to read, write, talk, and think through well-crafted lessons that draw from the pedagogy embedded within them. Engaging lessons often have several ELA standards within them and integrate reading, writing, speaking and listening, and language.

Standard 7: Integrate and evaluate content presented in diverse media and formats, including visually and quantitatively, as well as in words.

Literature

K With prompting and support, students describe the relationship between illustrations and the story in which they appear (e.g., what moment in a story an illustration depicts).

1 Students use illustrations and details in a story to describe its characters, setting, or events.

2 Students use information gained from the illustrations and words in a print or digital text to demonstrate understanding of its characters, setting, or plot.

Informational Text

K With prompting and support, students describe the relationship between illustrations and the text in which they appear (e.g., what person, place, thing, or idea in the text an illustration depicts).

1 Students use the illustrations and details in a text to describe its key ideas.

2 Students explain how specific images (e.g., a diagram showing how a machine works) contribute to and clarify a text.

What the **Student** Does

Literature	Informational Text

Literature

K **Gist:** Students describe how the words and illustrations work together to tell a story.

They consider:

- Is it possible to understand the story without the illustrations? Why?
- Is it possible to understand the story with only pictures and no words? Why?
- What details about important moments in the story do the illustrations show me?

1 **Gist:** Students describe how both the details in a story and the illustrations describe the characters, setting, and events.

They consider:

- What role do the words play in describing the characters?
- How do the details in the story help me understand the setting and what happens (events)?
- How do the illustrations help me picture the characters, setting, and events?
- What types of details can the illustrator show better with pictures than the author can with words?

2 **Gist:** Students explain how the illustrations and the words in a print or digital text describe the characters, setting, and plot.

They consider:

- What role do the words play in describing the characters, setting, and plot?
- What role do the illustrations play in describing the characters, setting, and plot?
- What do the illustrations in this picture book give me that the words don't?

Informational Text

K **Gist:** Students describe how the words and illustrations work together to provide information.

They consider:

- What information do the words tell me?
- What information do the pictures provide?
- Do I learn more when I combine the words and pictures?

1 **Gist:** Students describe how both the words and the illustrations in a text describe the key details.

They consider:

- What role do the words play in describing the key details on this page?
- What role do the illustrations play in describing the key details on this page?
- What key details do the illustrations provide that the words don't?

2 **Gist:** Students explain how specific images contribute to or clarify a text.

They consider:

- How do this picture and caption add to what the text says?
- How does this diagram or chart help me understand the information in this section or the whole text?
- How do the words in bold relate to the illustration on this page? When I read them together, what do I understand better?

Note: Although the questions listed above are too difficult for most young students to internalize and apply on their own, we share them to give teachers a detailed sense of what their students should be striving toward as learners. K–2 students may not be able to ask these questions of themselves independently, but teachers can use them as a jumping-off point for lesson content and as prompts and reminders to share with students. Over time and with instruction, students will be able to pose these questions on their own.

What the **Teacher** Does

To have students describe how the words and the illustrations together help tell a story or give information:

- Share a wordless book with students, and with each page, have them tell the unfolding story orally, citing exactly what is happening in the pictures to make them think that way. One example is Sylvia van Ommen's *The Surprise*, in which Sheep sets out to make a special gift for her friend. On a second "read," you might have students retell/recount the story as you record what they say on a chart. Then revisit the book (pictures) and ask them to find evidence for what they have written. Think of asking students to find evidence *in the pictures* as a precursor to asking them to find evidence in texts that include both words and pictures.

- Share a poster-size picture with students (for example, a photograph of a busy city street or two children catching tadpoles in a pond). Give them time to talk about what they see. Scribe their words once they've agreed on them. Make sure students explain exactly what in the picture is helping them formulate a text. Allow time for them to process the experience and discuss how both the picture and the words are important.

- Have children illustrate a favorite or important part of a story or informational text and write what's happening (e.g., "This is the part when . . ." or "The spider is making a web"). Encourage them to write as much as they can about their pictures. Give them an opportunity to share with you, a small group of peers, or the entire class precisely how their pictures and words *together* give a more complete rendition of what occurred. It's enough for kindergarten students to simply draw a picture and write one or two words until they're capable of writing more.

To have students explain how the words and the illustrations convey key details about the story or informational topic:

- Help students identify key words on a page or in a short section of text. Mark these words with highlighting tape or annotate when using a whiteboard. Then examine the picture or illustration that accompanies the words to determine how the picture expresses or expands on the same ideas and information.

- Assign each reader a partner and provide each partnership with a short picture book or informational text. Have them read it, select one illustration that helps

them to better understand the text, and put a sticky note on the exact place in the illustration that matches the text. Students may annotate their sticky notes to explain their reasoning or draw arrows on them to indicate more specifically the places in the text to which they are referring.

To have students discuss and evaluate content from multiple media sources:

- Have students compare a book and a video clip on the same topic, such as *Martha Washington* by Sally Lee and "Meet Martha Washington" (at http://kids.usa.gov). After experiencing both, let students discuss these questions: What are some things a book can do that a video clip can't? And what are some things a video clip can do that a book can't?

- Print out two easy-to-read articles from online on the same high-interest topic with which students may be familiar. Be sure the articles include photographs and/or other images. Divide the class in half. Give half of the students copies of one article and the other half copies of the second article. Distribute sticky notes and instruct students to flag facts and details that strike them as interesting as you read each article aloud. Then have students take turns sharing their favorite facts and posting their sticky notes on a chart that refers to and is labeled with the titles of the two articles. Doing so provides a concrete way for young children to see that nonfiction authors who write about the same topics often select different important details to share with readers.

To help your English language learners, try this:

- Make it a point to discuss the artwork in any text you read aloud to students or with students in small groups so that they can better comprehend what they're reading.

- If artwork is not included with the text, find pictures, clip art, or realia whenever you are reading a story or informational text. For example, when reading the folktale "The Magic Fish," we use clip art of a hut to drive home the point that the fisherman and his wife are of meager means at the start—and unfortunately also at the end.

Developmental Debrief:

Pictures and illustrations play an especially important part in helping K–2 students understand what they read, and every effort should be made to supplement children's learning with photos, pictures, and illustrations.

Teachers can make informational texts that, word-wise, are too difficult for students to read on their own more accessible by showing students how to read the pictures. Once this is demonstrated repeatedly, students can include "look books" in their independent reading book bags or boxes and expect to learn from the information the pictures provide.

Notes

Academic Vocabulary: Key Words and Phrases

Digital text: This is any document of any sort created or reformatted to be read, viewed, or experienced on a computer, tablet, smartphone, or other digital technology.

Diverse formats: This refers to presentation of the same information through numbers, narrative, and images. Graphic, written, mixed media, and spoken formats allow readers to consider a subject from multiple perspectives but also to know and see why and how others communicate the same information differently through various formats.

Diverse media: These include print, pictures and illustrations, and electronic and new media (e.g., Internet).

Integrate: Readers must combine different perspectives from various media into a coherent understanding or position about the subject.

Plot: This is the story line or sequence of actions built around a conflict or problem the main character in a fictional text is experiencing. Even an expository text has a "plot" of sorts. The plot is like a road map that gets the reader, in a logically organized way, from point A (which in an informational text is typically an introduction) to point B (the conclusion). For example, it would make little sense to begin a book about raptors by explaining how they build their nests. That type of information would come later in the text.

Visually and quantitatively: The emphasis here is on how the same ideas can be expressed in different ways through images or graphic representations of amounts. For example, maps are images that can show topography often more effectively than words; pie charts and bar graphs are effective ways of showing how much there is of something.

Notes

Planning Page

Standard: _____

Purpose of Lesson/s:

Planning the Lesson/s	Questions to Ask

Differentiating Instruction	Thinking Beyond This Standard

The standards guide instruction; they do not dictate it. *So as you plan lessons remember you aren't teaching the standards, but instead are teaching students how to read, write, talk, and think through well-crafted lessons that draw from the pedagogy embedded within them. Engaging lessons often have several ELA standards within them and integrate reading, writing, speaking and listening, and language.*

Standard 8: Delineate and evaluate the argument and specific claims in a text, including the validity of the reasoning as well as the relevance and sufficiency of the evidence.

Literature

K (Not applicable to literature)

1 (Not applicable to literature)

2 (Not applicable to literature)

Informational Text

K With prompting and support, students identify the reasons an author gives to support points in a text.

1 Students identify the reasons an author gives to support points in a text.

2 Students describe how reasons support specific points the author makes in a text.

What the **Student** Does

Literature	Informational Text

K **Gist:** (Not applicable to literature)

1 **Gist:** (Not applicable to literature)

2 **Gist:** (Not applicable to literature)

K **Gist:** Students identify key points in a text and the reasons the author gives to support those points.

They consider:

- What are some things the author wants us to know most of all about this topic?
- How does the author make his or her key points clear?
- What reasons does the author give to support these points? Are there illustrations that help support the points?

1 **Gist:** Students identify key points in a text and the reasons the author gives to support those points.

They consider:

- What are some key points the author wants us to know about this topic?
- How does the author make his or her points clear?
- What reasons does the author give to support these points? Are there illustrations that help support the points?

2 **Gist:** Students identify key points in a text and the reasons the author gives to support those points; students then describe how the author's reasons support the key points.

They consider:

- What are some key points the author wants us to know about this topic?
- How does the author make his or her points clear? Are there illustrations that help support the points?
- What reasons does the author give to support these points?
- Does the author effectively describe or explain his or her reasons in support of the key points?

Note: Although the questions listed above are too difficult for most young students to internalize and apply on their own, we share them to give teachers a detailed sense of what their students should be striving toward as learners. K–2 students may not be able to ask these questions of themselves independently, but teachers can use them as a jumping-off point for lesson content and as prompts and reminders to share with students. Over time and with instruction, students will be able to pose these questions on their own.

What the **Teacher** Does

To have students identify the key points in a text and the reasons the author gives to support them:

- To help students understand what you mean by *key points* and *reasons*, explain these terms using examples that are close to their life experiences. For example, you might make the statement (key point) "Julia is a top-notch soccer player." To support that point, you might say, (1) "She was the highest-scoring player last season"; (2) "She was selected to be part of a traveling team"; (3) "She practices every night after school and on weekends." Have students provide statements of their own and reasons to back them up. (Note that when working with actual texts, students will have to differentiate between reasons that are more personal and less reliable and others that are more verifiable.)

- When reading informational texts in any setting, emphasize that these texts provide information about topics—and that there is an author behind each text, who in a sense is like a puppeteer making a puppet move. The author moves facts into a pleasing order to make a "bigger" point or to share a main *idea* about something. For example, Jim Arnosky has written many books about animals, including manatees. In *All About Manatees*, his *topic* may be manatees, or how manatees grow and live, but one *key point* he wants to make is that manatees are precious creatures and humans must do what we can to protect their habitats.

- In a shared text, have students highlight a key point the author is making. (This is often written as the topic sentence.) Then guide students to reread the text to look for evidence in the text that backs up the author's key point. Mark the evidence with highlighting tape or sticky notes, or annotate in the margins.

- Have students examine the illustrations and text features (e.g., pictures and captions, scale drawings, and diagrams) in a shared text for evidence that supports a key point.

- As you read aloud or share a text, identify one key point for students to examine. Make a "statement/evidence chart" on which you write out the full statement at the top of the chart and then list below that the evidence you found to support the statement, with page numbers (when applicable) and/or a description of the text feature that provided the evidence. It's helpful to divide the entire chart into horizontal boxes before you start so that you have discrete places in which to record the reasons

(see resources.corwin.com/literacycompanionk-2). For example:

A bird's body is made for flying.
1. Birds have hollow bones and light feathers to make it easier for them to fly. (words on page 4)
2. Their bodies are streamlined to help them move through the air. (picture and caption, page 3)
3. They have air sacs to help them take in more oxygen that they'll need for flying. (chart and words on page 3)

- When working with second-grade students, make a "T" chart and label it "Statement" and "Evidence." As you and the students engage in a science or social studies unit and over the course of several weeks, identify and list key points the author makes and then in a few words jot down the reasons/evidence the author gives in support.

- After you finish reading a nonfiction text, ask: What is the big or main idea here? What is the author trying to say about this topic? What's the author's angle? This gets students accustomed to the fact that authors can put forth several key points about a topic, and that they add up to a main idea.

- As students write informational texts of their own, help them transfer what they're learning about key ideas and reasons/evidence by attempting to do this with their own texts. They should decide on a key idea they want to communicate and then back it up with supporting arguments, ideas, and information.

To have students describe or explain how the author's reasons support the key points:

- After gathering the reasons and evidence in support of a main idea or key point, have students evaluate and explain if the author has provided adequate reasons and evidence to support the point. For example, in *Big Blue Whale* by Nicola Davies, a key point is that the whale is the biggest creature that has ever lived on Earth. Read aloud the sentences after that statement, and have students look at the pictures too. Go sentence by sentence, asking students, "Does this sentence help prove that point about the whale's size? What about the pictures?"

To help your English language learners, try this:

- Work with them to make sure they understand the concept of main idea (or key point). Discuss what they think the author wants them to learn from a text that they're reading. Then have them point to a reason in the text that shows this is true.

Developmental Debrief:

In kindergarten (and even in first grade) students need ample support and scaffolding to be able to identify the key points an author is making and the reasons he or she is giving in support. Likewise, determining whether or not an author has provided adequate support for a key point is challenging for students throughout the primary grades, and this is especially true for ELLs and students who struggle in reading. What is essential is that K–2 students begin to recognize the key points and the reasons offered in their support, and over time and through multiple experiences they will develop the skill to do this on their own.

Encouraging students to "say more" or give an example when speaking or writing helps them recognize how this process works and makes them better prepared to understand an author's statements and evidence as they read.

Even though the standards mention only the author's key points, informational texts that are illustrated often have illustrators dedicated to revealing evidence that supports the author's points through images and graphics. Thus, we encourage you to allow students to look at illustrations when finding evidence for the key points.

Notes

Academic Vocabulary: Key Words and Phrases

Argument: This is the reason or set of reasons a writer or speaker uses to persuade others to think or feel differently about an issue or to change the way they act. The writer or speaker is successful only when the claim he or she is making is supported by reasons and evidence.

Claims: A claim is what an author wants a reader to accept as true. The author must, therefore, provide the reader with evidence so he or she can decide whether the claim is valid, logical, and verifiable.

Delineate: The reader must be able to describe or represent in precise detail the author's argument as well as his or her claims, reasoning, and evidence.

Evidence (relevance and sufficiency of): It is the reader's job to determine whether or not an author has provided the right kind of evidence, and enough of it, to adequately support the claim/point he or she is attempting to prove. Most of the evidence an author provides should be based on observable and objective facts and observations.

Validity of the reasoning: This refers to the quality of one's thinking—whether it is logically or factually sound or cogent.

Notes

Standard: _____

Purpose of Lesson/s:

Planning the Lesson/s	Questions to Ask

Differentiating Instruction	Thinking Beyond This Standard

The standards guide instruction; they do not dictate it. *So as you plan lessons remember you aren't teaching the standards, but instead are teaching students how to read, write, talk, and think through well-crafted lessons that draw from the pedagogy embedded within them. Engaging lessons often have several ELA standards within them and integrate reading, writing, speaking and listening, and language.*

Standard 9: Analyze how two or more texts address similar themes or topics in order to build knowledge or to compare the approaches the authors take.

Literature

K With prompting and support, students compare and contrast the adventures and experiences of characters in familiar stories.

1 Students compare and contrast the adventures and experiences of characters in stories.

2 Students compare and contrast two or more versions of the same story (e.g., Cinderella stories) by different authors or from different cultures.

Informational Text

K With prompting and support, students identify basic similarities in and differences between two texts on the same topic (e.g., in illustrations, descriptions, or procedures).

1 Students identify basic similarities in and differences between two texts on the same topic (e.g., in illustrations, descriptions, or procedures).

2 Students compare and contrast the most important points presented by two texts on the same topic.

What the **Student** Does

Literature	Informational Text

Literature

K **Gist:** Students identify how the adventures and experiences of characters in two distinct but similar familiar stories are alike and different.

They consider:

- Who is the main character in each story? What is he or she like? Kind? Shy? Courageous?
- Where does each story take place?
- What kinds of experiences does each character have, and how are their experiences alike or different?
- What does each main character do to resolve his or her problem or conflict?

1 **Gist:** Students describe how the adventures and experiences of characters in stories are alike or different.

They consider:

- Who is the main character in each story? What is he or she like? Kind? Shy? Courageous?
- Where does each story take place?
- What kinds of experiences does each character have, and how are their experiences alike or different?
- What does each main character do to resolve his or her problem or conflict?

2 **Gist:** Students compare and contrast two versions of the same story by different authors or from different cultures.

They consider:

- Who is the main character in each version?
- Where do the stories take place? Do the authors set their stories in different periods of history?
- How are the adventures and experiences of *all* the characters alike? How are they different?
- What can I tell from the pictures about how the versions are alike or different?
- Is one version funnier, happier, scarier, or sadder than the other?

Informational Text

K **Gist:** Students identify how two texts on the same topic are alike or different.

They consider:

- What is the topic of both texts? What is the title of each text?
- What information did I find in both texts?
- Is there information in one text that is not in the other?
- Are the pictures the same or different?

1 **Gist:** Students identify how two texts on the same topic are alike or different.

They consider:

- What is the topic of both texts? What is the title of each text?
- What information is in both texts?
- Is there information in one text that is not in the other?
- Are the illustrations and text features in the two texts the same or different?

2 **Gist:** Students compare and contrast two texts on the same topic, focusing on the most important points.

They consider:

- What are the important points in each text?
- Where can I look to confirm my ideas about what's important (e.g., headings, first sentences of paragraphs, tables of contents)?
- How are the important points in the two texts similar?
- How are the important points in the two texts different?

Note: Although the questions listed above are too difficult for most young students to internalize and apply on their own, we share them to give teachers a detailed sense of what their students should be striving toward as learners. K–2 students may not be able to ask these questions of themselves independently, but teachers can use them as a jumping-off point for lesson content and as prompts and reminders to share with students. Over time and with instruction, students will be able to pose these questions on their own.

What the **Teacher** Does

To have students identify how the characters' adventures and experiences in two stories (familiar or otherwise) are alike or different:

- Make sure that when you begin, you select stories to compare that follow basic and simple story lines, and that the characters are archetypical: good or evil, beautiful or ugly—nothing in between. You can later move to comparing more complicated characters and divergent stories once students have more experience with basic ones.

- Highlight how most of the main character's experiences and adventures occur in the "middle" of the story. Read each story aloud and focus on the events that occur in each or the steps each main character takes to get from "the problem" (the beginning) to "the resolution" (the ending). On separate pieces of chart paper, list the two stories' main events and have students compare the similarities and differences.

- Over weeks and months, keep deepening the discussion of how all stories, even those written for children, and perhaps especially fairy tales, depict struggles for power. You might chart what students notice about the quests depicted in the two stories you're comparing. From the Wicked Queen, driven by vanity, wanting the beautiful Snow White dead to Kevin Henkes's memorable character Lilly, who wants to be noticed and loved for her beautiful new purple plastic purse, all stories describe experiences of negotiating a world of competing needs.

To have students compare and contrast two or more versions of the same story:

- With students working in partnerships and over the course of several days, read aloud each version of the story. On a large sheet of paper, have several students collaborate on drawing a picture of the main character and labeling it with a brief caption; in this instance, a sentence naming the character would suffice. Then do the same for the setting, the problem, and the resolution of each story. Post the matching charts (i.e., the two character charts, the two setting charts, and so on) alongside each other. Have students note how they are the same and different.

- Read aloud a traditional folktale/fairy tale, such as *Cinderella* by Marcia Brown, and a fractured version of the same tale, such as Frances Minters's *Cinder-Elly*, a modern, urban, rap-based tale. Have students compare the two. How are they the alike and different, in terms of the basic story elements? Language? Illustrations?

After working with several of such traditional/fractured pairs, have students team up with partners to write their own versions of a traditional folktale or fairy tale.

To have students identify how two texts on the same topic are alike or different:

- Assemble a collection of books on the same topic in a bag or basket and label it. The topic might relate to a content-area subject you and your students are currently studying or soon will be, or it may simply be one that students find interesting. It's important to do both. Select titles to read aloud from this collection.

- Share via read-aloud two informational books on the same topic. Guide students to examine the covers and the titles for similarities and differences. Provide time for them to talk about what they've observed. On a second and third day, gather students to examine the tables of contents in both texts and discuss how these can help them determine what each author thinks is important. Provide students time to talk about why the authors may have made the decisions they did. Follow the same procedure in regard to the text features in each book.

- Select two books on one topic that vary in text difficulty, illustrations, and organization. Read the books aloud and allow students to identify the similarities and differences. Engage students in a discussion, asking questions such as the following: Which book might they want to read if they knew little about the topic, and why? Which book most clearly outlines what's coming in a section, chapter, or throughout the text, and how? Which book would be most helpful if they needed ideas for how to illustrate and organize their own writing, and why?

To have students compare and contrast two texts on the same topic, focusing on the most important points:

- Chart the similarities and differences between the information students glean from two texts on the same topic. Lead students to note instances of where the texts include the same information and where they don't, and annotate these on the chart.

- Find two books on the same topic that have significantly different opening sentences/paragraphs, and perhaps strikingly different final sentences. Use these books to lead a discussion about how authors can choose to research and write on the same topic but still decide to focus on different aspects of the topic.

- Refer to the tables of contents in two books on the same topic to identify the topics each addresses. Guide students to notice the similarities and differences, and discuss what may have led each author to include or leave out certain information.

- Read texts that are short, or focus on only one chapter in each book, so that students can reread the text and refer back to it to verify their reasoning. Have students identify the most important points in each and how the graphics in each help illustrate these points.

To help your English language learners, try this:

- Make sure students understand the meanings of the academic terms you use, such as *compare*, *contrast*, and *text features*.

- Allow English language learners to work with native English speakers in partnerships when comparing and contrasting texts. Be sure to select native English speakers who are patient and supportive. Also, if possible, have students work with native language partners so they can work through the compare/contrast activities in their primary language, then have the pairs share in English how they organized information and ideas.

- Have students draw pictures of the main characters in two texts and talk about how they are alike and different. Do the same with "setting" and "problem."

Developmental Debrief:

Make collecting and working with high-quality short texts a top priority. This gives students the opportunity to read a text multiple times and refer back to it to verify their thinking. More and more publishers recognize this need and are providing an assortment of excellent short texts for use with students. Another wonderful source of short texts is children's magazines, such as *Ranger Rick*, *National Geographic Kids*, and *Time for Kids*.

Notes

Academic Vocabulary: Key Words and Phrases

Approaches: This refers to the ways different authors approach their subject matter—that is, through voice, imagery, and format. For example, while one author might write in straightforward prose, another might choose to be more lyrical. *Approach* can also refer to point of view or genre.

Approaches to similar themes and topics: As it applies to several of the standards here, this phrase refers to the act of comparing and contrasting the approaches to the same topic used by different authors, different texts, and different types of texts. That is, a topic such as sea animals may be addressed in an alphabet book, in mini-chapters (e.g., as a sequence of 10 fascinating facts), in a nonfiction narrative, and so on.

Build knowledge: This refers to the author's efforts to increase the reader's knowledge about the subject of the text. Not only do different authors often provide distinct facts that help children accrue knowledge about a topic, but also authors' different styles and those of illustrators provide a range of tones that appeal to students with different learning styles and reading levels.

Compare and contrast the approaches authors take: This refers to looking at the similarities (compare) and differences (contrast) when examining how the authors of two texts present their subject (e.g., an event, a person, or an action).

Theme: For the purpose of several standards here, the theme is the central meaning, message, or idea in a literary text that the author wants to communicate. Themes are not stated explicitly; they must be inferred by the reader from the evidence in the text. (One exception is the fable, where the theme is typically clearly stated either at the very beginning or at the end of the tale.)

Topic: In the case of informational texts, the topic is the main subject or content at hand—migration, animal habitats, machines, farm life, outer space, and so on.

Notes

Planning Page

Standard: _____

Purpose of Lesson/s:

Planning the Lesson/s	Questions to Ask

Differentiating Instruction	Thinking Beyond This Standard

The standards guide instruction; they do not dictate it. *So as you plan lessons remember you aren't teaching the standards, but instead are teaching students how to read, write, talk, and think through well-crafted lessons that draw from the pedagogy embedded within them. Engaging lessons often have several ELA standards within them and integrate reading, writing, speaking and listening, and language.*

Range of Reading and Level of Text Complexity

Standard 10: Read and comprehend complex literary and informational texts independently and proficiently.

Literature

K Students actively engage in group reading activities with purpose and understanding.

1 With prompting and support, students read prose and poetry of appropriate complexity for grade 1.

2 By the end of the year, students read and comprehend literature, including stories and poetry, in the grades 2–3 text complexity band proficiently, with scaffolding as needed at the high end of the range.

Informational Text

K Students actively engage in group reading activities with purpose and understanding.

1 With prompting and support, students read informational texts appropriately complex for grade 1.

2 By the end of year, students read and comprehend informational texts, including history/ social studies, science, and technical texts, in the grades 2–3 text complexity band proficiently, with scaffolding as needed at the high end of the range.

What the **Student** Does

Literature	Informational Text

K **Gist:** Students actively engage in group reading activities with purpose and understanding.

Students use what they learned from standards 1–9 to read prose and poetry in group settings.

K **Gist:** Students actively engage in group reading activities with purpose and understanding.

Students use what they learned from standards 1–9 to read informational texts in group settings.

1 **Gist:** With prompting and support, students read prose and poetry of appropriate complexity for grade 1.

Students use what they have learned from standards 1–9 to read grade-level prose and poetry.

1 **Gist:** With prompting and support, students read a range of informational texts that are appropriately complex for grade 1.

Students use what they have learned from standards 1–9 to read a range of informational texts.

2 **Gist:** Students read a range of literary texts in the grades 2–3 text complexity band, receiving help only when needed at the high end of the band.

They consider:

- How easy or difficult is this text?
- Will I need help reading it?
- What, if any, kind of help will I need?

2 **Gist:** Students read a range of informational texts in the grades 2–3 text complexity band, receiving help only when needed at the high end of the band.

They consider:

- How easy or difficult is this text?
- Will I need help reading it?
- What, if any, kind of help will I need?

Note: Although the questions listed above are too difficult for most young students to internalize and apply on their own, we share them to give teachers a detailed sense of what their students should be striving toward as learners. K–2 students may not be able to ask these questions of themselves independently, but teachers can use them as a jumping-off point for lesson content and as prompts and reminders to share with students. Over time and with instruction, students will be able to pose these questions on their own.

What the **Teacher** Does

To help kindergarten students actively engage in group reading activities involving prose, poetry, and informational texts:

- Select high-quality read-aloud texts and big books to share with students. Read the text more than once and get students to talk about the author's message or what they're learning. Children comprehend narrative and informational texts more easily when we consistently talk about the author's role in creating them. Somewhat abstract concepts like character motivation, theme, and ideas become concrete when students understand that they are the results of decisions made by a real-life author (and illustrator).

- Share nursery rhymes and chants with students. Put the words on chart paper or on a whiteboard and have students read along with you. Later in the school year, when kindergarten and first-grade students know more of the words, look for opportunities for them to lead the reading aloud. This oral language experience is instrumental in developing children's phonemic awareness and concepts of words.

- Ask generative questions that will get students thinking about the text. Generative questions are typically analytical and often involve asking "Why?" and "How?" Some examples of generative questions are "What made you say [or ask] that?" and "How does this story relate to me?"

- Encourage students to elaborate. Do not accept one-word or one-sentence responses. Ask students to say more, give an example, or be specific.

- Provide opportunities for students to respond to texts that are read aloud and shared by having them discuss and write about texts and engage in dramatic, musical, and artistic experiences.

- Set up and manage a simple independent reading program so that students have opportunities to put into practice the skills and strategies you've demonstrated through whole-group read-aloud and shared reading. In addition, send two or three books home with each student every week in zip-top bags so students can practice reading at home with their families.

To help grade 1 students read grade-level texts of appropriate complexity and to help grade 2 students read texts in the grades 2–3 text complexity band:

- Engage students in interactive read-aloud and shared reading of high-quality texts that would be too difficult for them to read on their own. While the goal is to challenge students, the challenge mustn't be so high that it dampens their spirit.

- Understand that your goal, in addition to challenging students to work harder and figure things out on their own, is to scaffold and support their efforts. Continually monitor the experience for evidence that the task is too hard or that students are at their frustration level. Students who act out or who can't attend to the task at hand for even a minimal amount of time are often sending signals that what we're asking of them is too difficult. To be helpful in the long run and to instill a love of reading, make sure the tasks you assign are not only challenging but also doable. Only then can they inspire students to want to read more.

- Select texts to read aloud and to share that are shorter, rather than longer, so that students can read them multiple times and discuss the authors' messages and information.

- Provide opportunities for students to write in response to reading to help them determine the author's message and integrate it into what they already know. However, do not assign reading responses every time students read.

- Work with students in small reading groups to differentiate the instruction you provide. Most often the groups will involve guiding students through a text that would be too difficult for them to read on their own. However, you might also gather students for interactive read-alouds or shared reading, oral language intervention, skill and strategy groups, and literature circles.

- Confer with students one-on-one to learn what they do well and need to learn. During these conferences you can also address any skills or strategies you have observed they need help with.

- Match students with texts they can read independently. That means they can read the words accurately and fluently, and they demonstrate a basic understanding of the text.

- Give students plenty of time and opportunities to practice reading and to process and incorporate new skills and strategies into their repertoire. This processing time involves talking and writing in response to texts as well as voluminous amounts of time each day spent actually reading—just reading.

- Remind students to monitor their reading for meaning. They need to understand that reading involves more than calling words, and if they don't understand what they read, they're not really reading.

To help your English language learners, try this:

- Whenever possible, use the preview-view-review strategy. Meet with English language learners before and after a whole-group session to prepare them for what they'll be doing or to process what happened.

- Use pictures and realia (artifacts) to make concepts students are exposed to through texts more concrete and accessible.

Developmental Debrief:

First and foremost, teachers of K–2 students must realistically assess students' strengths and needs and teach them what they need to know. Do not deceive yourself into thinking students can achieve more if they only try harder. It does little good to ignore a student's actual reading level and try to teach him or her at a level beyond what the student can handle. We need to provide developmentally appropriate experiences, instruction, and supports so that students not only learn to read but also choose to read when they don't have to.

For K–1 teachers: While there are ways to scaffold young students' understanding of complex text as you read aloud or share a big book, the main focus of this standard is to prepare students to read and understand complex text on their own. Therefore, in preparation you should devote much of your attention to the foundational skills students will need to know and own, such as understanding concepts of print and knowing and applying grade-level phonics to texts they read independently. This—more than insisting they read texts for which they aren't ready—will provide more bang for the buck in the long run.

If students can't decode the texts you and they are reading together or they are reading on their own, they won't be able to absorb any other aspect about the text structure or content, so worry less about "complex" texts and focus on developing accurate, fluent reading of appropriate texts. Remember, the *discussions* you have about rich and engaging texts can bring about "complexity" of ideas and develop students' higher-level thinking about texts.

Notes

Academic Vocabulary: Key Words and Phrases

Appropriate complexity: Students in kindergarten and grade 1 are exempt from having to read complex text independently and proficiently. It is acknowledged that much of students' attention in these early grades should be naturally directed to mastering the foundational skills so that they can later read complex text with deep understanding.

Complex literary and informational texts: *Complex* is not the same as *difficult*; literary and informational texts are complex for different reasons. Why? Because they are written for different reasons and for mostly different purposes. Texts can be complex due to sentence structure, syntax, and other structural factors. But they can also be complex in content and ideas, despite short, simple sentences. In the context of K–2, it's most fruitful to look for high-quality engaging fiction and informational texts written by well-respected writers for your grade level; usually doing that alone will bring sufficient complexity into your classroom.

Group reading activities: These are activities that students do as a whole class, such as read-aloud and shared reading, or when working in small groups, such as guided reading.

High end of the range: For second grade, this means the high end of the grades 2–3 text complexity band; students reading at this level at the end of a year should be able to read independently, with little, less, or no teacher guidance.

Independently: This refers to a student's ability to read whatever texts are assigned without the aid of a teacher or, when challenged by the teacher to read or work with a complex text, to do the work as assigned without the aid of scaffolding or guided instruction.

Proficiently: This describes the way and level at which the individual student is able to read complex texts; proficiency is equated with skill, although not mastery.

Scaffolding: This is support from teachers, aides, or other students that helps a student read text or complete a task; examples include providing background knowledge, reading aloud, and any other strategy designed to help students become independent readers or writers.

Text complexity band: The individual text complexity bands correspond with associated grade levels, such as grades 2–3. The levels themselves are determined by the three-part model of text complexity discussed in Appendix A of the complete CCSS document. The three factors in text complexity are *qualitative dimensions* (levels of meaning, language complexity as determined by an attentive reader), *quantitative dimensions* (word length and frequency, sentence length, and cohesion), and *reader and task considerations* (factors related to a specific reader, such as motivation, background knowledge, or persistence; others associated with the task itself, such as purpose or demands of the task).

Notes

Planning Page

Standard: _____

Purpose of Lesson/s:

Planning the Lesson/s	Questions to Ask

Differentiating Instruction	Thinking Beyond This Standard

The standards guide instruction; they do not dictate it. So as you plan lessons remember you aren't teaching the standards, but instead are teaching students how to read, write, talk, and think through well-crafted lessons that draw from the pedagogy embedded within them. Engaging lessons often have several ELA standards within them and integrate reading, writing, speaking and listening, and language.

The Common Core State Standards

Reading: Foundational Skills

College and Career Readiness Anchor Standards for
Reading Standards: Foundational Skills K–5

Source: Common Core State Standards

The foundational skills standards are directed toward fostering students' understanding and working knowledge of concepts of print, the alphabetic principle, and other basic conventions of the English writing system. These foundational skills are not an end in and of themselves; rather, they are necessary and important components of an effective, comprehensive reading program designed to develop proficient readers with the capacity to comprehend texts across a range of types and disciplines. Instruction should be differentiated: good readers will need much less practice with these concepts than struggling readers will. The point is to teach students what they need to learn and not what they already know—to discern when particular children or activities warrant more or less attention.

Print Concepts (Applies to K–1 Only)

1. Demonstrate understanding of the organization and basic features of print.

Phonological Awareness (Applies to K–1 Only)

2. Demonstrate understanding of spoken words, syllables, and sounds (phonemes).

Phonics and Word Recognition

3. Know and apply grade-level phonics and word analysis skills in decoding words.

Fluency

Kindergarten:

4. Read emergent-reader texts with purpose and understanding.

Grades 1–5:

5. Read with sufficient accuracy and fluency to support comprehension.

College and Career Readiness Anchor Standards for

Reading Standards: Foundational Skills K–5

The reading foundational standards are exclusive to the elementary grades. These are the print, phonological awareness, word recognition, and fluency pieces that aid in comprehension, which is the ultimate goal of reading instruction. As with the other reading standards, students should be working in grade-level texts of increasing complexity as the year progresses. The first two standards, print concepts and phonological awareness, are directed to students in kindergarten and grade 1; however, students in grades 3–5 may benefit from practice in these skills, depending on their needs.

Print Concepts (Grades K–1)

This first strand pertains primarily to our youngest learners, who are new to understanding the organization and basic features of print. The focus of instruction is on the following five skills:

- Follow words from left to right, top to bottom, and page by page.
- Recognize that spoken words are represented in written language by specific sequences of letters.
- Understand that words are separated by spaces in print.
- Recognize and name all upper- and lowercase letters of the alphabet.
- Recognize the distinguishing features of a sentence (e.g., first word, capitalization, ending punctuation) (grade 1 only)

Phonological Awareness (Grades K–1)

This second set of skills develops simultaneously with the first and focuses on students' ability to demonstrate understanding of spoken words, syllables, and sounds (phonemes) and also recognize and produce rhyming words. The standards address the aspects of phonological awareness that children are expected to master.

Kindergarten:

- Recognize and produce rhyming words.
- Count, pronounce, blend, and segment syllables in spoken words.
- Blend and segment onsets and rimes of single-syllable spoken words.
- Isolate and pronounce the initial, medial vowel, and final sounds (phonemes) in three-phoneme (consonant-vowel-consonant, or CVC) words.* (This does not include CVCs ending with /l/, /r/, or /x/.)
- Add or substitute individual sounds (phonemes) in simple, one-syllable words to make new words.

Grade 1:

- Distinguish long from short vowel sounds in spoken single-syllable words.
- Orally produce single-syllable words by blending sounds (phonemes), including consonant blends.
- Isolate and pronounce initial, medial vowel, and final sounds (phonemes) in spoken single-syllable words.
- Segment spoken single-syllable words into their complete sequence of individual sounds (phonemes).

*Words, syllables, or phonemes written in /slashes/ refer to their pronunciation or phonology. Thus, /CVC/ is a word with three phonemes regardless of the number of letters in the spelling of the word.

Phonics and Word Recognition (K–5)

This third strand of foundational skills focuses on students' ability to recognize and identify written words. Phonics is included in this standard, as well as decoding multisyllabic words and knowing syllabication patterns. Another aspect of this standard is morphology, which is the study of how words are formed in language. When students recognize meaningful *morphological units* in unfamiliar words—specifically, prefixes, root words, and suffixes—they can identify unfamiliar words. Teaching the meanings of common prefixes, suffixes, and root words is an integral part of this standard. In addition, students learn to read and understand unfamiliar words using the context of the text. The standards' grade-level distinctions take into account students' developing abilities with language.

Kindergarten:

- Demonstrate basic knowledge of one-to-one letter-sound correspondences by producing the primary sound or many of the most frequent sounds for each consonant.
- Associate the long and short sounds with common spellings (graphemes) for the five major vowels.
- Read common high-frequency words by sight (e.g., *the, of, to, you, she, my, is, are, do, does*).
- Distinguish between similarly spelled words by identifying the sounds of the letters that differ.

Grade 1:

- Know the spelling-sound correspondences for common consonant digraphs.
- Decode regularly spelled one-syllable words.
- Know final -e and common vowel team conventions for representing long vowel sounds.
- Use knowledge that every syllable must have a vowel sound to determine the number of syllables in a printed word.
- Decode two-syllable words following basic patterns by breaking the words into syllables.
- Read words with inflectional endings.
- Recognize and read grade-appropriate irregularly spelled words.

Grade 2:

- Distinguish long and short vowels when reading regularly spelled one-syllable words.
- Know spelling-sound correspondences for additional common vowel teams.
- Decode regularly spelled two-syllable words with long vowels.
- Decode words with common prefixes and suffixes.
- Identify words with inconsistent but common spelling-sound correspondences.
- Recognize and read grade-appropriate irregularly spelled words.

Grade 3:

- Identify and know the meaning of the most common prefixes and derivational suffixes.
- Decode words with common Latin suffixes.
- Decode multisyllable words.
- Read grade-appropriate irregularly spelled words

Grade 4:

- Use combined knowledge of all letter-sound correspondences, syllabication patterns, and morphology (e.g., roots and affixes) to read accurately unfamiliar multisyllabic words in context and out of context.

Grade 5:

- Use combined knowledge of all letter-sound correspondences, syllabication patterns, and morphology (e.g., roots and affixes) to read accurately unfamiliar multisyllabic words in context and out of context.

Fluency

The key words in this standard are *purpose* and *understanding*. Students read grade-level texts silently or orally with purpose and understanding as they learn to decode text. In addition, students become accurate and fluent readers. Students read poetry and prose orally, practicing by rereading and increasing their fluency, accuracy, and expression. The skills are quite consistent for grades K–5:

- Read grade-level text with purpose and understanding.
- Read grade-level text orally with accuracy, appropriate rate, and expression on successive readings.
- Use context to confirm or self-correct word recognition and understanding, rereading as necessary.

Standard 1: Demonstrate understanding of the organization and basic features of print.

K Students demonstrate understanding of the organization and basic features of print.

  a. Follow words from left to right, top to bottom, and page by page.
  b. Recognize that spoken words are represented in written language by specific sequences of letters.
  c. Understand that words are separated by spaces in print.
  d. Recognize and name all upper- and lowercase letters of the alphabet.

1 Students demonstrate understanding of the organization and basic features of print.

  a. Recognize the distinguishing features of a sentence (e.g., first word, capitalization, ending punctuation).

* These broad types of writing include many subgenres. See Appendix A in the Common Core State Standards for definitions of key writing types.

What the **Student** Does

K **Gist:** Students demonstrate understanding of the organization and basic features of print.

They consider:

- Do I recognize that words I speak can be written with specific letters and letter sequences?
- Can I point to the beginning of the word? The middle? The end?
- Do I recognize that the print, and not the pictures, carries most of the meaning?
- Do I recognize that words are separated by spaces? (Do I leave spaces between words when I write?)
- Do I read words from left to right? (Do I write words from left to right?)
- Do I read lines of text from left to right and from the top line to the bottom line? (Do I write my words like this?)
- Do I know that when I get to the end of a line I should return to the first word on the next line?
- Do I know to read the left page before the right page?
- Do I recognize that pages in stories cannot be skipped? Do I read every page in order?
- Can I recognize and name all upper- and lowercase letters of the alphabet? (Do I use upper- and lowercase letters correctly when I write?)

1 **Gist:** Students demonstrate understanding of the organization and basic features of print.

They consider:

- Can I point to the first word in a sentence? Can I point to the last word in a sentence?
- Do I know that the first word in a sentence begins with a capital letter? (Do I capitalize the first word of sentences I write?)
- Do I know that sentences end with a period, a question mark, or an exclamation point? (Do I end the sentences I write with a period, a question mark, or an exclamation point?)
- Do I know that my voice should go down when I come to a period and up when I come to a question mark or exclamation point?
- Do I know what a period, question mark, and exclamation point mean as a reader? (As a writer?)

Note: Although the questions listed above are too difficult for most young students to internalize and apply on their own, we share them to give teachers a detailed sense of what their students should be striving toward as learners. K–2 students may not be able to ask these questions of themselves independently, but teachers can use them as a jumping-off point for lesson content and as prompts and reminders to share with students. Over time and with instruction, students will be able to pose these questions on their own.

What the **Teacher** Does

To help students understand the organization and basic features of print during reading:

- Each day, expose students to big books and enlarged texts so that they can easily see the print. Narrate how you begin and move through a book to give students a helpful "audio track" of how text works. For example, "Now let me see, where should I start? I'll go to the top [pointing to the top] and to the left margin [pointing to the left margin] and start there."

- Designate a carpeted meeting area that is comfortable and inviting to enhance the message that reading is a pleasurable pursuit—and worth the hard thinking and work that goes into learning how to do it. Have students sit up close, near the text and you. Of course, you can also display text on a whiteboard, but we fear that words and pictures become more abstract and formidable when projected on a big screen. Conversely, there's something concrete about sitting alongside a hard copy of a text while the teacher points directly under the words as she reads. Consider both options, but we strongly suggest that you lean more in favor of using authentic, hard copies of texts with students.

- During shared reading, point under individual words as you read the text. Call students up to the big book or enlarged text to point out or frame words. Gradually, as students acquire basic print concepts, you will sweep your finger or pointer along the bottom of phrases to indicate how readers naturally chunk words together so that their reading sounds more fluent, but for now (at the emergent stage) it's wise to point word by word.

- Reference *print* as you read aloud to students. While we typically do this when using big books and enlarged texts during lessons, this is often not the case when reading aloud; we tend to favor the pictures. By calling students' attention to print—for example, "*Giraffe* is a long word; it has a lot of letters" and "There are words written on the sign in front of this shop; what do you think they say?"—we quicken the pace by which children understand how texts work. For more information on print referencing, use an online search engine to search "print referencing during read-alouds" and look for the *Reading Teacher* article "Print Referencing During Read-Alouds: A Technique for Increasing Emergent Readers' Print Knowledge," by Tricia A. Zucker, Allison E. Ward, and Laura M. Justice.

- Confer with students regularly so you can observe firsthand how they handle print. Having them read to you one-on-one reveals a great deal about their understanding of how print works. Be sure to be specific with students about what they're doing well (e.g., "I love the way you knew to come back to the left side of the page when you finished a line").

- Encourage emergent readers to point to words as they read. Emphasizing the one-to-one correspondence between spoken and written words helps to consolidate their awareness of concepts of print. As students progress in reading, they should pull their fingers back and track print with their eyes. Be aware, however, that a child's finger naturally points to an unfamiliar word when she's stuck and puzzling over the sequence of letters in the word. When students have difficulty figuring out a word, we might ask them to frame words so they can attend more closely to the letters. Refrain from having students cover up yet-to-be-read lines of text with a note card, since good readers typically look ahead and scan the page for clues as to what they're reading.

To help students understand the organization and basic features of print by connecting reading to writing:

- Capitalize on the reciprocity between reading (decoding) and writing (encoding). There's a close relationship between these two processes—especially when it comes to concepts of print—and children intuitively know that learning one helps them learn the other. A child fresh off a read-aloud of Laura Numeroff's *If You Give a Mouse a Cookie* has myriad concepts of print dancing in his head as he puts pen to paper and tries his own version of this patterned story, from capitalizing the *I* in *If* to the concept of a sentence.

- Engage students in interactive writing—an instructional practice in which students are given a sentence or short passage to write (one student writes on chart paper while the others write on individual wipe-off boards) and the teacher either guides them through the process or provides feedback when they're done. This is yet another opportunity for students to see the thinking that goes on in a writer's head as she puts ideas on paper.

- Write language experience charts with students so that they see print *as it is being composed* and written down. The beauty of class-generated charts is that they can be posted around the room and referred back to as needed.

- Engage students in a daily writing workshop. If you are unfamiliar with this approach to developing students' writing, we recommend Ann Marie Corgill's *Of Primary Importance: What's Essential in Teaching Young Writers* and Katie Wood Ray's *About the Authors: Writing Workshop With Our Youngest Writers,* but there are many others. No other approach is as effective as workshop in helping students understand both the purpose for writing and the process.

- Confer with students as they read and write. It's quite simple to point to words in a text and see if students can do the same, or to observe whether or not students can track print by pointing to each word as it is read. Likewise, as students write you can see how they put spaces between words, end sentences with periods, and so on. When it comes to concepts of print, there's nothing like sitting alongside students and showing them how.

- Have students write throughout the day for real purposes. Write notes to other classes, birthday greetings, and invitations; provide a message board for students to post notes to one another; and make individual and class books.

To help students understand features of a sentence:

- Write several sentences on a chart or whiteboard, leaving off ending punctuation. Read each sentence out loud, with your voice noticeably lower when a period is needed and rising when a question mark or exclamation point is called for. Ask students to decide which ending punctuation mark to use and explain how they knew this. In addition to noting your voice going up or down, students will also explain that you can tell that some sentences are questions because they begin with a "question" word (*who*, *what*, and so on).

- Using sentence strips, write sentences from a story or poem with which the students are familiar. These could be several sentences from a shared text or a read-aloud. Cut the sentences apart word by word and place the words on a sentence strip holder in jumbled order. Have students remake each sentence, and ask them how they knew which was the first word in the sentence and which was the last.

- Find poems to read with students that have an extra heavy dose of question marks and exclamation points, such as "The Two Mice" in Mary Ann Hoberman's *You Read to Me, I'll Read to You: Very Short Stories to Read Together.* The first couple of lines go like this: "I see a mouse." "I see one, too!" "We see two mice. What shall we do?" We can imagine students having oodles of fun reading this with partners, practicing the ups and downs in their voices to match the ending punctuation, and then presenting their readings to the class.

To help your English language learners, try this:

- Be aware that concepts of print prove challenging for students whose native language works according to principles different from those of English. For example, some languages convey sounds through characters instead of combinations of letters; in some languages print goes from bottom to top instead of top to bottom and from right to left instead of left to right. Meet with students to help them understand and sort through the differences between their language and English.

Developmental Debrief:

Students acquire concepts of print as they work with texts, both those they read and those they write. So the more exposures students have to written text throughout the day, the more easily and quickly they'll learn the ins and outs of how print works.

Notes

Academic Vocabulary: Key Words and Phrases

Organization and basic features of print: These are the rules that dictate how print is written and read. As this standard explicitly states, these rules include the left to right, top to bottom progression of print and text; the sequencing of letters to represent words; the understanding that words are separated by spaces; recognition of upper- and lowercase letters; and recognition of the distinguishing features of a sentence. It should be noted that readers continue to develop their concepts of print throughout their lifetimes (for example, understanding graphic concepts of print) and that the concepts presented here are the ones students need to acquire to gain basic access to the messages that print holds.

Distinguishing features of a sentence: This refers to "what makes a sentence a sentence?" As this standard explicitly states, a sentence begins with a capital letter and ends with a period, a question mark, or an exclamation point. Without knowing where declarative statements, exclamations, and questions begin and end, students will have a hard time distinguishing one from another.

Notes

Planning Page

Standard: _____

Purpose of Lesson/s:

Planning the Lesson/s	Questions to Ask

Differentiating Instruction	Thinking Beyond This Standard

The standards guide instruction; they do not dictate it. So as you *plan lessons remember you aren't teaching the standards, but instead are teaching students how to read, write, talk, and think through well-crafted lessons that draw from the pedagogy embedded within them. Engaging lessons often have several ELA standards within them and integrate reading, writing, speaking and listening, and language.*

Standard 2: Demonstrate understanding of spoken words, syllables, and sounds (phonemes).

K Students demonstrate understanding of spoken words, syllables, and sounds (phonemes).

    a. Recognize and produce rhyming words.

    b. Count, pronounce, blend, and segment syllables in spoken words.

    c. Blend and segment onsets and rimes of single-syllable spoken words.

    d. Isolate and pronounce the initial, medial vowel, and the final sounds (phonemes) in three-phoneme (consonant-vowel-consonant, or CVC) words. (This does not include CVCs ending with /l/, /r/, or /x/.)

    e. Add or substitute individual sounds (phonemes) in simple, one-syllable words to make new words.

1 Students demonstrate understanding of spoken words, syllables, and sounds (phonemes).

    a. Distinguish long from short vowel sounds in spoken single-syllable words.

    b. Orally produce single-syllable words by blending sounds (phonemes), including consonant blends.

    c. Isolate and pronounce initial, medial vowel, and final sounds (phonemes) in spoken single-syllable words.

    d. Segment spoken single-syllable words into their complete sequence of individual sounds (phonemes).

What the **Student** Does

K **Gist:** Students demonstrate understanding of spoken words, syllables, and sounds (phonemes).

They consider:

- Do I recognize and can I produce rhyming words?
- Can I count, produce, blend, and segment syllables in spoken single-syllable words?
- Can I blend and segment onsets and rimes of spoken single-syllable words?
- Do I hear and can I pronounce the beginning, middle, and ending sounds in CVC words?
- Can I make new words by changing one individual sound in simple, one-syllable words?

1 **Gist:** Students demonstrate understanding of spoken words, syllables, and sounds (phonemes).

They consider:

- Can I tell the difference between long and short vowel sounds in spoken single-syllable words?
- Can I blend sounds together to make single-syllable spoken words, including consonant blends?
- Do I hear and can I pronounce the beginning, middle, and ending sounds in spoken single-syllable words?
- Can I break apart single-syllable words into their complete sequence of individual sounds?

Note: Although the questions listed above are too difficult for most young students to internalize and apply on their own, we share them to give teachers a detailed sense of what their students should be striving toward as learners. K–2 students may not be able to ask these questions of themselves independently, but teachers can use them as a jumping-off point for lesson content and as prompts and reminders to share with students. Over time and with instruction, students will be able to pose these questions on their own.

What the **Teacher** Does

To help students recognize and produce rhyming words:

- Sing songs and recite chants, rhyming poems, and nursery rhymes together as a class. Be aware of the cultural diversity of students and try to select songs, rhymes, and so on that reflect these differences. It's okay to have the words written on a chart while students are learning the songs, chants, and rhymes, but once you turn your attention to oral rhyming, remove the text so that students pay closer attention to the words you are saying and asking them to notice and rhyme. The challenge with phonemic awareness is that all the activities need to be oral—once you include written letters or words, you've moved into phonics.

- Invite students to coin the name of your poetry time (e.g., Pop-Up Poetry, Rhyme Time) and devote a few moments each day to reading poetry aloud together. Poets that are especially great with rhyme include Marilyn Singer, Rebecca Kai Dotlich, Jack Prelutsky, and Mary Ann Hoberman. But do find your way to your own favorites. Make use of online resources such as the Poetry Foundation website (www.poetryfoundation.org).

To help students count, pronounce, blend, and segment syllables in single-syllable spoken words:

- Play "I'll Be the Tortoise. You Be the Hare." Read the fable "The Tortoise and the Hare," calling attention to how Tortoise moves slowly and probably even speaks slowly, while Hare does everything fast. Explain that you'll say a word slowly and carefully, like the Tortoise (e.g., *b-a-t*), and they'll repeat the word quickly, like the Hare (e.g., *bat*). Then play this game in reverse, starting with how Hare would say a word (e.g., *goat*, *made*) and letting students translate it into Tortoise's "turtle-talk."

- Say a single-syllable word with a one- or two-second pause between phonemes. Then ask students what word the sounds make. For example, /r/ /oa/ /d/ makes *road*. Or conversely, say the word (*road*) and ask students to segment it into sounds (/r/ /oa/ /d/).

- Use Elkonin boxes to help small groups of students segment words into phonemes (sounds):

  1. Decide whether you will work with words having two or three phonemes.

  2. Gather pictures of words having that number of sounds. (Old phonics workbooks can be of use

in this regard.) For example, if you are working with words that have three phonemes, you might collect a picture of a "cake," a "box," a "pool," and so on.

3. Give each student the appropriate two- or three-section Elkonin box template and as many chips (bingo chips, pennies) as there are sounds in the words you'll ask them to segment. (See the online resources at resources.corwin.com/literacycompanionk-2 for the templates; laminate them for endurance.)

4. Lay one picture on the table at a time, saying its name. Then ask students to repeat the word slowly and slip a chip into a box (following the left-to-right arrow) for each sound they hear.

To help students blend and segment onsets and rimes in single-syllable spoken words:

- Check out the list of Wylie and Durrell's 37 dependable rimes in the online resources (at resources.corwin.com/literacycompanionk-2). This list will be helpful when you are working with phonemic awareness (this standard) and phonics (Foundational Skills Standard 3) activities.

- Teach students the Humpty Dumpty nursery rhyme. Ask them to be the "king's men (and ladies)" and try to put Humpty Dumpty (the onsets and rimes) together again. This is similar to the "Tortoise and Hare" activity described above, but this time, use onsets and rimes instead of individual phonemes. And instead of having students sound out each phoneme (e.g., /b/ /a/ /t/), emphasize and differentiate instead the sound of onset (/b/) from the entire rime (/at/).

- Sitting at the meeting area, divide the class into two groups—one responsible for providing the onset and the other the rime. Say a word, such as *pop*. Have the onset group say, "The onset of *pop* is /p/." Then have the rime group say, "The rime of *pop* is /op/." Repeat this with several other words.

- Read lists of three words, two of which rhyme, such as *deer*, *stick*, and *near*. Ask students to identify the words that rhyme and the one that doesn't. Then ask them to provide additional words that rhyme with the two rhyming words and words that rhyme with the one that had no rhyme. Remember that this needs to be done orally, not in writing.

To help students isolate, pronounce, and manipulate the beginning, middle, and ending sounds in CVC words:

- Play word games with students. For example, "Say *mat* without the /m/," or "Say *stay* without the /st/." You can play word games like this while lining up, while walking in the hall, or during any downtime. You can do this with beginning and ending sounds as well. Students might take turns leading the game.

- Use a whisper phone to direct a student's voice back to his ear as he reads or says a word. A whisper phone, which looks like a telephone, helps the student hear his own voice and focus on the sounds in the words he is saying. Whisper phones can be purchased online from school supply stores.

To help your English language learners, try this:

- One of the best ways to teach phonemic awareness to English language learners is through songs, rhymes, chants, and poems. Be patient with students' efforts to identify phonemes, since the phonemes in their native language may differ from those that make up the English language.

- In small groups made up of only English language learners, play rhyming games and phoneme segmentation games and activities to give the students extra time and a supportive, "risk-free" group time to play with the English language and its sounds.

Developmental Debrief:

Recognize the important role that phonemic awareness plays in students' learning to read. Also recognize that most students learn phonemic awareness quite naturally and, dare we say, effortlessly through singing songs, chanting, and repeating nursery rhymes. It would be foolhardy to skip over the rhymes, songs, and chants, which engage K–2 students' whole being, and jump to the more isolated skill and drill activities. Granted, some students will require more intensive instruction, but this should never occur at the expense of their being deprived of abundant and rich opportunities to hear the sounds and pleasing patterns of our language through song, rhyme, and chant.

Notes

Academic Vocabulary: Key Words and Phrases

Add or substitute individual sounds: This refers to the fact that we can manipulate phonemes in one-syllable spoken words by adding or substituting new sounds at the beginnings, middles, or endings of words. For example, we can change *man* to *tan* by changing the beginning phoneme /m/ to /t/; we can change *soap* to *sip* by changing the /oa/ to /i/; and we can change *cat* to *can* by changing the /t/ to /n/.

Blend and segment (syllables, onsets and rimes): To blend syllables and onsets and rimes, we put the individual sounds we hear in syllables and onsets and rimes *together* to make them into words that are natural sounding and recognizable. To segment syllables and onsets and rimes, we start with the word and break it into its individual sounds.

Onsets and rimes (of single-syllable spoken words): First, a definition of onsets and rimes: in a single-syllable word, the onset is the initial consonant or consonant blend before the vowel, and the rime is the vowel and any consonants that follow. For example, in the word *stop*, /st/ is the onset and /op/ is the rime. In this standard, the focus is on spoken, not written, single-syllable words.

Phonemes: These are the smallest units of speech sounds; they make words when combined with other phonemes. Students need to be able to hear and manipulate phonemes to make new spoken words. For example, when the phoneme /e/ in *red* is changed to /i/, a new word (*rid*) with a new meaning is made.

Phonemic awareness: This is the ability to hear, identify, and manipulate individual phonemes in words.

Rhyming words: These are words that end with the same sound, such as *slam* and *jam*, and *kite* and *night*. Note that in the first example the rime is spelled the same, and in the second example the rime is spelled differently.

Sequence of individual sounds: Each word has its own sound sequence, and in order to produce a word correctly, a student must speak the sounds in their proper sequence.

Spoken single-syllable words: The fact that words are spoken, and not written, lies at the heart and soul of this phonemic awareness standard. Single-syllable words have, by definition, only one syllable.

Syllables (in spoken words): This refers to units of spoken words, and where words are naturally divided when spoken. After phonemes, syllables are the next-largest unit of speech; each syllable has to include at least one vowel.

Three-phoneme (CVC) words: These are consonant-vowel-consonant words in which the initial sound comes from a consonant or consonant blend; the middle sound comes from a vowel or combination of vowels that make only one sound, such as in *feed*; and the ending sound comes from a consonant or consonant blend, such as in *desk*. As relates to this standard, these CVC words should be spoken, not written, for the purposes of phonemic awareness activities.

Notes

Planning Page

Standard: _____

Purpose of Lesson/s:

Planning the Lesson/s	Questions to Ask

Differentiating Instruction	Thinking Beyond This Standard

The standards guide instruction; they do not dictate it. So as you plan lessons remember you aren't teaching the standards, but instead are teaching students how to read, write, talk, and think through well-crafted lessons that draw from the pedagogy embedded within them. Engaging lessons often have several ELA standards within them and integrate reading, writing, speaking and listening, and language.

Standard 3: Know and apply grade-level phonics and word analysis skills in decoding words.

K Students know and apply grade-level phonics and word analysis skills in decoding words.

    a. Demonstrate basic knowledge of one-to-one letter-sound correspondences by producing the primary sound or many of the most frequent sounds for each consonant.

    b. Associate the long and short sounds with common spellings (graphemes) for the five major vowels.

    c. Read common high-frequency words by sight (e.g., *the, of, to, you, she, my, is, are, do, does*).

    d. Distinguish between similarly spelled words by identifying the sounds of the letters that differ.

1 Students know and apply grade-level phonics and word analysis skills in decoding words.

    a. Know the spelling-sound correspondences for common consonant digraphs.

    b. Decode regularly spelled one-syllable words.

    c. Know final -e and common vowel team conventions for representing long vowel sounds.

    d. Use knowledge that every syllable must have a vowel sound to determine the number of syllables in a printed word.

    e. Decode two-syllable words following basic patterns by breaking the words into syllables.

    f. Read words with inflectional endings.

    g. Recognize and read grade-appropriate irregularly spelled words.

2 Students know and apply grade-level phonics and word analysis skills in decoding words.

    a. Distinguish long and short vowels when reading regularly spelled one-syllable words.

    b. Know spelling-sound correspondences for additional common vowel teams.

    c. Decode regularly spelled two-syllable words with long vowels.

    d. Decode words with common prefixes and suffixes.

    e. Identify words with inconsistent but common spelling-sound correspondences.

    f. Recognize and read grade-appropriate irregularly spelled words.

What the **Student** Does

K **Gist:** Students know and apply grade-level phonics and word analysis skills in decoding words.

They consider:

- Do I know the basic consonants? And many of the most frequent sounds for each consonant?
- Do I know the five major vowels and their sounds? Do I know the common spellings of the short vowel sounds? Do I know the common spellings of the long vowel sounds?
- Can I read common high-frequency words accurately and quickly without sounding them out?
- Can I identify the sounds of the letters that are different in words that are similarly spelled? Can I identify the differences between words that look almost alike? Can I read them?
- Do I use what I know about letter-sound relationships when I read on my own?
- Do I use phonics together with what makes sense and sounds right?
- Do I look all the way through words to the end to make sure that more than just the beginning sounds and letters match?

1 **Gist:** Students know and apply grade-level phonics and word analysis skills in decoding words.

They consider:

- Do I know the letter-sound relationships for common consonant digraphs?
- Can I decode regularly spelled one-syllable words?
- Do I know final -e and common vowel team conventions for representing long vowel sounds?
- Do I know that every syllable must have a vowel and use that to help me count the number of syllables in a printed word?
- Can I figure out two-syllable words by breaking the words into syllables?
- Can I read words with inflectional endings?
- Can I read irregularly spelled words that are at my grade level?
- Do I use what I know about letter-sound relationships when I read on my own?
- Do I use phonics together with what makes sense and sounds right?
- Do I look all the way through words to the end to make sure that more than just the beginning sounds and letters match?

2 **Gist:** Students know and apply grade-level phonics and word analysis skills in decoding words.

They consider:

- Do I know the difference between long and short vowels when reading regularly spelled one-syllable words?
- Do I know letter-sound correspondences of common vowel teams?
- Can I read regularly spelled two-syllable words with long vowels?
- Can I decode words with common prefixes and suffixes?
- Can I identify words with inconsistent but common letter-sound correspondences?
- Can I read irregularly spelled words at my grade level?
- Do I use what I know about letter-sound relationships when I read on my own?
- Do I use phonics together with what makes sense and sounds right?
- Do I look all the way through words to the end to make sure that more than just the beginning sounds and letters match?

Note: Although the questions listed above are too difficult for most young students to internalize and apply on their own, we share them to give teachers a detailed sense of what their students should be striving toward as learners. K–2 students may not be able to ask these questions of themselves independently, but teachers can use them as a jumping-off point for lesson content and as prompts and reminders to share with students. Over time and with instruction, students will be able to pose these questions on their own.

What the **Teacher** Does

Considering the expansive nature of this standard—that is, it addresses all of the phonetic elements students need to know in K–2 classrooms—we provide some broad instructional principles and practices that apply to all of these phonetic elements, rather than addressing each element individually.

To help students know and apply grade-level phonics and word analysis skills in decoding words:

- Provide systematic, explicit phonics instruction from a research-based resource (consider works by Wiley Blevins and Marilyn Jager Adams). Along with the resource, which should provide a scope and sequence for learning the letters and the sounds they make, give students voluminous opportunities to practice their developing skills with fiction and nonfiction books, rhymes, songs, and so on. One approach without the other is insufficient and simply does not work; the meaningful, engaging texts motivate students to do the hard work of cracking the code of the English language and, more to the point, give them the forum for applying their knowledge to texts.

- Make the point to students that understanding phonics will help them read all their favorite books on their own. See it through this comprehension lens too, so that you gear your phonics instruction toward an emphasis on automatic word recognition. Why? Brain research has proven that we have a limited amount of capacity in our working memory, and so if we use it for one thing, it's not available for another. When students can't read words automatically and have to spend loads of time working on identifying words, they're using their brain capacity on letter sounds and don't have it available to make sense of the author's message. This is why it's critical that, early on, students learn a large bank of sight words—that is, words they can recognize automatically. (Sight words are discussed in more depth in Foundational Skills Standard 4, fluency.)

- When using authentic texts to introduce a particular phonics element, teach from the whole to the parts. That is, begin a phonics lesson by appreciating the whole book and then move to the sentence, then from the sentence to the word, and then from the word to letter combinations and letters. Doing so is far more effective than introducing and practicing skills with workbooks or worksheets. Just as it's easier to fill in puzzle pieces after you've seen the entire picture on the cover of the box, it's easier for students to work with letters when they know their place in the meaningful whole.

- To teach letter-sound relationships, conduct lots of letter and sound searches. Young children love the gamelike quality of such activities, and they are "whole to part." That is, students begin with a whole text and then identify the specific letters or sounds on which to focus. (For help with how to do letter-sound searches, see the online resources at resources.corwin.com/literacycompanionk-2.) Teaching with this approach does not preclude teaching phonics systematically; it's just a great way to augment such teaching.

- Recognize the power of knowing the 37 dependable rimes in helping students read accurately and automatically. (In a single-syllable word, the onset is the initial consonant or consonant blend before the vowel, and the rime is the vowel and any consonants that follow. For example, in the word *flop*, /fl/ is the onset and /op/ is the rime.) (For this list of 37 rimes, see the online resources at resources.corwin.com/literacycompanionk-2.) Helping students become familiar with spelling patterns in words enables them to move beyond seeing isolated words to seeing chunks of letters that make specific sounds.

- Show students how to use phonics together with semantics (meaning) and syntax (grammar) to figure out words they don't know. Relying on just one cueing system, such as letter-sound relationships, deprives students of the natural clues they would get by considering the message the text is conveying or how the unknown word is used in the sentence. However, it's equally problematic to rely too heavily on semantics and have students guess at a word using only its initial sound. All three cueing systems—letter-sound relationships, semantics, and syntax—are important.

- Make the cloze procedure a standard practice in your classroom. (For information on how to do the cloze procedure, see the online resources at resources.corwin.com/literacycompanionk-2.)

- Leverage phonics skills with writing. One of the most powerful ways to teach and have students practice connecting sounds to letters and letter combinations is through writing. When students write, they're using and consolidating the very same sound and letter combinations you're teaching in reading. A writing center stocked with paper and colored markers can be the hub of short, student-generated books; as a class, write fun phonics-laced books (e.g., "That cat sleeps in the sun"; "That cat isn't thin but he sure isn't fat").

- In addition to your standardized method of assessing students' knowledge of letter sounds, examine students' writing for what they know and need to learn.

- Trust that students can, in fact, read unfamiliar words without knowing all the letters. The trick, of course, is that the word is embedded in a meaningful context. When it is, students can use the meaning of the sentence or text as a whole and their knowledge of English syntax to figure out the word. When they have daily opportunities to read just-right texts, they eventually learn the sounds that correspond with different letters and spelling patterns.

- Analyze words for their roots and affixes. This not only helps students figure out the meanings of words; it also helps them identify words. Use an online search engine to search "word roots and affixes games for kids" to find helpful lists and fun games to play with students.

To help your English language learners, try this:

- Children learning English need explicit instruction in letters and the sounds they make when combined; thus, these students benefit from a comprehensive phonics resource. However, they also need exposure to many books with large numbers of sight words to put the phonics in context. Have them illustrate and write a simple story that uses the letter/sound combinations you are working on.

- In small groups made up of only English language learners, provide "play" time with letter cards, word cards, and pocket charts. Students can create words and work in pairs or teams to sound them out together. You can use onset and rime lists, root words and common prefixes, and suffixes and words from patterned texts that students are familiar with. Working in this way with groups composed exclusively of English language learners gives students supportive "risk-free" group time to play with the language and sounds.

Developmental Debrief:

Young readers and writers need to see how what they're learning fits into the larger picture. For K–2 students, this makes it particularly important that you work from the whole to the part. Shared reading, in which students read along with and understand a text, is the perfect setting for emphasizing the individual letter sounds you want students to learn.

Notes

Academic Vocabulary: Key Words and Phrases

Apply grade-level phonics and word analysis skills in decoding words: It's not enough for students simply to be exposed to phonetic skills and strategies in whole-class lessons; they also need to have daily opportunities to read and write on their own so they can try out these skills and strategies.

Common prefixes and suffixes: Prefixes are meaningful units of letters that come before a root word, and suffixes are meaningful units that come after a root word. The most common prefixes are *dis-*, *re-*, *un-*, and *in-* (*im-*, *il-*, *ir-*), all of which mean "not." The most common suffixes, which include inflectional endings, are *-s* and *-es*, *-ed*, *-ing*, and *-ly*. (Others that come up a lot are *-less*, *-able*, and *-sion/tion*.) Common prefixes and suffixes show up frequently in elementary-age texts.

Consonant digraphs: These are two or more consonants representing a single sound, such as *kn* and *ck*. They are different from consonant blends because in blends all of the two or three consonant sounds are heard (e.g., *dr* and *str*). Both consonant digraphs and blends can come at the beginnings or ends of words.

Decoding: This refers to applying knowledge of letter-sound relationships to a set of letters, thus making it into a meaningful word. Decoding is the opposite of encoding, which involves changing spoken words into print.

Final -e convention: This refers to how the vowel in CVCe (consonant-vowel-consonant-silent *e*) words is given a long sound by the silent *e*. For example, the word *rob* is changed to *robe* and *tap* to *tape*. This is often referred to as a split digraph, where two vowels that make one sound are split by a consonant, such as *a-e* in *take* and *i-e* in *bite*.

Grade-level phonics: This refers to phonics instruction that is appropriate for students at a particular age and grade level, and from which they are likely to benefit. For example, it would be unwise and inappropriate to try to teach diphthongs to kindergarten students. (Consonant and vowel sounds would be more appropriate.) Likewise, in second grade it makes little sense to spend instructional time on consonant sounds, since most students have advanced far beyond that point.

Graphemes: These are letters (or a single letter) that represent or spell a sound in a word. The concept of graphemes applies to written language, whereas the concept of phonemes (the smallest meaningful units of sound) applies to spoken language. The two together are sometimes referred to as the grapheme-phoneme relationship (or letter-sound) relationship.

High-frequency words: These are often referred to as sight words because many do not sound like what their spelling suggests (e.g., *does* and *our*), and therefore readers must recognize them accurately and automatically on sight. It is crucial for students to recognize an ever-growing bank of sight words instantaneously, since such words make up a high percentage (as much as 50%) of the words school-age students read in and out of school. Instant recall of these words allows students to attend to the messages, as well as other more challenging words, in the texts they read. Two lists of high-frequency words to which we often refer are the Dolch list of 220 words and the Fry list of 600. As students progress through the grades, they will need to commit thousands more words to sight.

Inflectional endings: These are added to the end of a root word to change its meaning (i.e., *-s*, *-es*, *-ed*, *-ing*).

Irregularly spelled words: These are words that do not follow regular spelling patterns, such as *been* and *come*, and as such cannot be easily sounded out.

Phonics: This method of teaching reading relies on matching the sounds that letters and letter combinations make with words in print.

Regularly spelled words: These are words that follow regular spelling patterns, such as *team* and *bake*.

Vowel team conventions for representing long vowel sounds: This occurs when two vowels together make the same long vowel sound almost all of the time, such as *-oa*, *-ai*, *-ee*, and *-ea*. The ditty "When two vowels go walking, the first one does the talking" is one that students learn early on and can be relied on much of the time. That said, frustration can set in when students happen upon words that don't follow the convention, like *ready*, *said*, and *chief*.

Word analysis skills: These skills involve breaking a word down into its smaller parts—its root, prefixes, and suffixes—so it can be read and understood. This is different from phonics, which relies on matching sounds to letters and letter combinations.

Planning Page

Standard: _____

<table>
<tr><td colspan="2">Purpose of Lesson/s:

</td></tr>
<tr><td>Planning the Lesson/s</td><td>Questions to Ask</td></tr>
<tr><td>

</td><td></td></tr>
<tr><td>Differentiating Instruction</td><td>Thinking Beyond This Standard</td></tr>
<tr><td>

</td><td></td></tr>
</table>

The standards guide instruction; they do not dictate it. So as you plan lessons remember you aren't teaching the standards, but instead are teaching students how to read, write, talk, and think through well-crafted lessons that draw from the pedagogy embedded within them. Engaging lessons often have several ELA standards within them and integrate reading, writing, speaking and listening, and language.

Standard 4: Read with sufficient accuracy and fluency to support comprehension.

K Students read emergent-reader texts with purpose and understanding.

1 Students read with sufficient accuracy and fluency to support comprehension.
   a. Read grade-level text with purpose and understanding.
   b. Read grade-level text orally with accuracy, appropriate rate, and expression on successive readings.
   c. Use context to confirm or self-correct word recognition and understanding, rereading as necessary.

2 Students read with sufficient accuracy and fluency to support comprehension.
   a. Read grade-level text with purpose and understanding.
   b. Read grade-level text orally with accuracy, appropriate rate, and expression on successive readings.
   c. Use context to confirm or self-correct word recognition and understanding, rereading as necessary.

What the **Student** Does

K **Gist:** Students read emergent-reader texts with purpose and understanding.

They consider:

- Is this a good (appropriate) text for me?
- Are there any words I don't know?
- How can I figure out any words I don't know?
- Do I understand what I'm reading?
- How is the pace of my reading? If I were reading out loud, would my audience be able to understand?
- Do I need to reread any parts of the text?

1 **Gist:** Students read with sufficient accuracy and fluency to support comprehension.

They consider:

- Is this a good (appropriate) text for me?
- Are there any words I don't know?
- How can I figure out any words I don't know?
- Do I understand what I'm reading?
- Do I read with good expression?
- How is the pace of my reading? If I were reading out loud, would my audience be able to understand?
- Do I need to reread any parts of the text?

2 **Gist:** Students read with sufficient accuracy and fluency to support comprehension.

They consider:

- Is this a good (appropriate) text for me?
- Are there any words I don't know?
- How can I figure out any words I don't know?
- Do I understand what I'm reading?
- Do I read with good expression?
- How is the pace of my reading? If I were reading out loud, would my audience be able to understand?
- Do I need to reread any parts of the text?

Note: Although the questions listed above are too difficult for most young students to internalize and apply on their own, we share them to give teachers a detailed sense of what their students should be striving toward as learners. K–2 students may not be able to ask these questions of themselves independently, but teachers can use them as a jumping-off point for lesson content and as prompts and reminders to share with students. Over time and with instruction, students will be able to pose these questions on their own.

What the **Teacher** Does

To teach students to read with sufficient accuracy and fluency to support comprehension:

- Invest in developing students' bank of sight words (also known as high-frequency words, i.e., words that they recognize automatically, or on sight, while reading). Why is this important? It frees up the students' minds to grapple with more difficult words and the text's concepts. Lists of sight words for various grade levels are readily available online.

- Give students daily opportunities to read and write—doing so builds vocabulary more swiftly and surely than decontextualized memorization of word lists. In addition, highlight sight words when you come across them in shared-reading texts; play games with sight words; give students a book of sight words to use as they write, or engage them in making their own; and provide wipe-off and magnetic boards for students to practice making these common words.

- Make fluency a vivid concept by pouring water from one glass to another a few times. Ask, "What do you notice?" and draw out ideas about liquid flowing smoothly. Write the word *fluid* on the board and connect its meaning to the idea that fluent reading is reading that flows smoothly, as the reader recognizes words and moves past them fluently, like water rolling over rocks in a stream. Read aloud and choral read with students to model swift, cadenced reading of an accessible text.

- Demonstrate fluent reading during read-aloud and shared reading. Convey that fluent reading sounds like the way we regularly talk to one another. Call students' attention to how chunking words into phrases makes reading sound more natural. When reading aloud, breathe life into your interpretation of the text by attending to how the characters are feeling and acting. Do the same during shared reading while you move your pointer under phrases so students can see how good readers naturally chunk words into phrases.

- Liken the connection between fluency and comprehension to a bridge over which students move back and forth: the more students understand the text, the better they're able to read fluently, and the more fluently they read, the more deeply they're able to understand what the text says.

- Attend to text cues such as exclamation points, question marks, quotation marks, words in bold, and words printed larger or smaller than the others. These all signal how a text should be read and help readers to better comprehend the text. Notice features of print that indicate how to read a word: bold print, italics, small print, large print. Deliberately read a section of text aloud without fluency, using a monotone voice, bulldozing past text cues, and so on, to show how this makes it harder to understand the meaning.

- Provide audiobooks for students to listen to and follow along with.

- Develop a class chart (e.g., "Top Five Ways to Read With Expression") and have students illustrate it so that they have a handy wall reference.

To have students read grade-level text with purpose and understanding:

- Have a wide variety of grade-level texts available for students to read. Without an abundance of these texts, students will be unable to try out the strategies you're showing them. We recommend a minimum of 1,500 books in every classroom library so that all students can find within the library an ample number of grade-level texts to try reading.

- Teach explicitly what *reading with purpose* means—such as to read for enjoyment, to read for a specific task, or to read to gain new information or understanding. For example, you might model how you read aloud a poem by Shel Silverstein in a jaunty beat for enjoyment. To demonstrate reading to gain new information from a text, you might model taking time to carefully preview the pictures and read the captions to see what information they provide, information that's likely to be elaborated on once you start reading.

- Work with students in small groups and, as you do, set a purpose for reading and check for understanding as they read and discuss the text.

To have students read grade-level text orally with accuracy, appropriate rate, and expression on successive readings:

- Regularly engage students in choral reading and Readers Theater to give them opportunities to practice the fluent reading strategies you've been demonstrating. The beauty here is that they can practice repeatedly for authentic reasons (i.e., to present to an audience) rather than simply rereading a fluency card passage multiple times. There's nothing like choral reading and

Readers Theater for motivating students to read and practice their reading until they're reading effortlessly, with appropriate accuracy, rate, and expression.

- Record yourself as you read aloud a shared-reading passage or poem with expression. Allow students to listen to the recording several times as they follow the text. Guide them to notice what you've done to read fluently and what they should be trying to do. Then give students opportunities to read the passage or poem out loud themselves.

- Read aloud books like Shelly Lyons's *If You Were a Question Mark* and *If You Were an Exclamation Point* (Word Fun series) to help students grasp that punctuation leads readers to the author's intended meaning of the text. Then provide them with texts, such as Mary Ann Hoberman's *You Read to Me, I'll Read to You: Very Short Fables to Read Together*, which are chock-full of question marks and exclamation points, and have students practice differentiating between the two as they read out loud with a partner.

To have students use context to confirm or self-correct word recognition and understanding, rereading as necessary:

- Direct students to monitor their reading, listening for "clicks" and "clunks" as they read. When things are going smoothly and making sense, they hear a friendly click-click-clicking sound, indicating all's well. However, when meaning has broken down, a warning "clunk" signals them to stop and fix what's wrong. Students should ask themselves, "Does this word look right, sound right, and make sense within the context of this sentence or passage?"

- Ensure that students have time to read independently. This allows them to practice the confirming and self-correcting strategies you've been demonstrating. Without the time to practice and transfer what you're showing them, students will not benefit fully from your demonstrations and hard work.

To help your English language learners, try this:

- Make every effort to engage students in Readers Theater (even if this means giving them disproportionate opportunities to do so). Students who are learning English benefit greatly from working with groups of readers in which many of the participants read at a higher level and more fluently than they do. By hearing others read and having opportunities to read and revise their own presentation, they can greatly improve their fluency skills.

- Make audio recordings of yourself reading some of the students' favorite books or easy-to-read books, texts, and poems. Have students listen to the recordings while reading the books/texts/poems to follow along with your voice.

Developmental Debrief: Remember, it's unlikely that nascent readers will be able to read a text fluently on their first try. They will first need to work through some of the words they're unfamiliar with, and then, on subsequent readings, they'll be increasingly able to attend to reading rate and expression.

Notes

Academic Vocabulary: Key Words and Phrases

Accuracy: This refers to reading words correctly or precisely. Readers need to read accurately to get an author's intended meaning.

Appropriate rate: This refers to the speed, in number of words per minute (WPM), at which a student can effortlessly read a text orally with comprehension. Fountas and Pinnell set the expected rate of oral reading for grade 1 students reading J–K level books at 75–100 WPM, and the rate for grade 2–3 students reading level L–M–N books at 90–120 WPM.

Confirm or self-correct word recognition and understanding: This refers to readers checking back to make sure that they've read particular words correctly. They either *confirm* that they've read the words correctly or they *self-correct* when they find that what they've read doesn't match the words in print. Readers do the same for comprehension: they confirm that they understand or they intervene with a strategy to make sense of what they're reading.

Context: This is the information and graphics that surround the unknown word. Readers use this information to help figure out words that are unknown to them.

Emergent-reader texts: These are texts (F & P levels A–C or DRA levels A–3) that match the skills and abilities of emergent readers, such as using pictures to predict meaning; tracking print; learning sight words; learning the names of letters and their sounds; using visual, syntactic, and semantic cues together; and developing fluency with familiar texts. Emergent-reader texts are designed to scaffold and extend the efforts of beginning readers.

Expression: This refers to conveying emotion or feeling when reading orally. This may include inflections, pacing, and noticing different speakers in dialogue.

Fluency: This is the ability to read a text accurately, easily, and smoothly with proper rate and expression. Students who read fluently pronounce words correctly, use punctuation cues, and read with expression.

Read grade-level text with purpose and understanding: A grade-level text is one that is appropriate, in terms of difficulty and content, for students in a particular grade. Reading with purpose and understanding is reading for a reason (to be entertained, to learn, to get information, and so on) and with comprehension of what is being read. Writers generally have one of four purposes when they write: to persuade, to inform, to express, or to entertain. Readers choose specific texts for reasons that match their purposes.

Rereading as necessary: This refers to the fact that, most often, K–2 readers' first attempt at reading a text will involve them taking the time to figure out words they don't know. This will affect their accuracy, rate, and expression. As they read the same text again (and again), their accuracy, rate, and expression will improve.

Sufficient accuracy and fluency to support comprehension: Accuracy and fluency are directly related to comprehension. Students must be able to read accurately and fluently (with the proper rate and expression) in order to understand the texts they're reading.

Notes

Planning Page

Standard: _____

Purpose of Lesson/s:

Planning the Lesson/s	Questions to Ask

Differentiating Instruction	Thinking Beyond This Standard

The standards guide instruction; they do not dictate it. So as you plan lessons remember you aren't teaching the standards, but instead are teaching students how to read, write, talk, and think through well-crafted lessons that draw from the pedagogy embedded within them. Engaging lessons often have several ELA standards within them and integrate reading, writing, speaking and listening, and language.

The Common Core State Standards

Writing

College and Career Readiness Anchor Standards for
Writing K–12

**Source:
Common Core
State Standards**

The K–2 writing standards outlined on the following pages define what students should understand and be able to do by the end of each grade. Here on this page we present the College and Career Readiness (CCR) anchor standards for K–12 so you can see how students in K–2 work toward the same goals as high school seniors: it's a universal, K–12 vision. The CCR anchor standards and the grade-specific standards correspond to one another by number (1–10). They are necessary complements: the former providing broad standards, the latter providing additional specificity. Together, they define the skills and understandings that all students must eventually demonstrate.

Text Types and Purposes*

1. Write arguments to support claims in an analysis of substantive topics or texts, using valid reasoning and relevant and sufficient evidence.
2. Write informative/explanatory texts to examine and convey complex ideas and information clearly and accurately through the effective selection, organization, and analysis of content.
3. Write narratives to develop real or imagined experiences or events using effective technique, well-chosen details, and well-structured event sequences.

Production and Distribution of Writing

4. Produce clear and coherent writing in which the development, organization, and style are appropriate to task, purpose, and audience. (begins in grade 3)
5. Develop and strengthen writing as needed by planning, revising, editing, rewriting, or trying a new approach.
6. Use technology, including the Internet, to produce and publish writing and to interact and collaborate with others.

Research to Build and Present Knowledge

7. Conduct short as well as more sustained research projects based on focused questions, demonstrating understanding of the subject under investigation.
8. Gather relevant information from multiple print and digital sources, assess the credibility and accuracy of each source, and integrate the information while avoiding plagiarism.
9. Draw evidence from literary or informational texts to support analysis, reflection, and research. (begins in grade 3)

Range of Writing

10. Write routinely over extended time frames (time for research, reflection, and revision) and shorter time frames (a single sitting or a day or two) for a range of tasks, purposes, and audiences. (begins in grade 3)

Note on Range and Content of Student Writing

To build a foundation for college and career readiness, students need to learn to use writing as a way of offering and supporting opinions, demonstrating understanding of the subjects they are studying, and conveying real and imagined experiences and events. They learn to appreciate that a key purpose of writing is to communicate clearly to an external, sometimes unfamiliar audience, and they begin to adapt the form and content of their writing to accomplish a particular task and purpose. They develop the capacity to build knowledge on a subject through research projects and to respond analytically to literary and informational sources. To meet these goals, students must devote significant time and effort to writing, producing numerous pieces over short and extended time frames throughout the year.

*These broad types of writing include many subgenres. See Appendix A for definitions of key writing types.

College and Career Readiness Anchor Standards for

Writing

The CCR anchor standards are the same for K–12. The guiding principle here is that the core writing skills should not change as students advance; rather, the level at which students learn and can perform these skills should increase in complexity as they move from one grade to the next. However, for grades K–2, we have to recognize that the standards were back mapped from the secondary level—that is, the authors envisioned what college students need and then wrote standards, working their way down the grades. Thus, as you use this book remember that children in K–2 can't just "jump over" developmental milestones in an ambitious attempt to achieve an anchor standard. There are certain life and learning experiences they need to have, and certain concepts they need to learn, before they are capable of handling many complex academic skills in a meaningful way. The anchor standards nonetheless are goalposts to work toward. As you read the "gist" of the standards below, remember they represent what our K–2 students will *grow into* during each year and deepen later in elementary, middle, and high school. The journey starts in K–2!

Text Types and Purposes*

Argument appears first as it is essential to success in college and develops the critical faculties needed in the adult world. Crafting arguments requires students to analyze texts or topics and determine which evidence best supports their arguments. Informational/explanatory writing conveys ideas, events, and findings by choosing and explaining the behavior, meaning, or importance of key details. Students draw from a range of sources, including primary and secondary sources. Narrative writing includes not just stories but also accounts of historical events and lab procedures. Students write to change minds, hearts, and actions (argument); to extend readers' knowledge or acceptance of ideas and procedures (informational/ explanatory); and to inform, inspire, persuade, or entertain (narrative).

Production and Distribution of Writing

This set of anchor standards involves the stages of the writing process. These standards also highlight the importance of knowing who the audience is and the style and format the writer should use to achieve a purpose. Students also learn the skills needed throughout the writing process: generating ideas and trying other styles, structures, perspectives, or processes as they bring their ideas into focus and some final form. Finally, these standards call for writers to use technology not only to publish but also to collaborate throughout the writing process with others.

Research to Build and Present Knowledge

These standards focus on inquiry processes of varying lengths, all of which should develop students' knowledge of the subject they are investigating and the skills needed to conduct that investigation. Students acquire and refine the ability to find, evaluate, and use a range of sources during these research projects, which can take as long as a period to as much as a month. Such inquiries demand that students correctly cite the sources of all information to ensure they learn what plagiarism is and how to avoid it.

Range of Writing

This standard emphasizes not only what students write but also how often and for what purposes they write over the course of the school year. Writing, as this standard makes clear, is something students should be doing constantly and for substantial lengths of time. Also, they should write for an array of reasons and audiences and in response to a mix of topics and tasks.

Source: Adapted from Jim Burke, *The Common Core Companion: The Standards Decoded, Grades 6–8* (Thousand Oaks, CA: Corwin, 2013).

*These broad types of writing include many subgenres. See Appendix A for definitions of key writing types.

Standard 1: Write arguments to support claims in an analysis of substantive topics or texts, using valid reasoning and relevant and sufficient evidence.

K Students use a combination of drawing, dictating, and writing to compose opinion pieces in which they tell a reader the topic or the name of the book they are writing about and state an opinion or preference about the topic or book (e.g., *My favorite book is . . .*).

1 Students write opinion pieces in which they introduce the topic or name the book they are writing about, state an opinion, supply a reason for the opinion, and provide some sense of closure.

2 Students write opinion pieces in which they introduce the topic or book they are writing about, state an opinion, supply reasons that support the opinion, use linking words (e.g., *because, and, also*) to connect opinion and reasons, and provide a concluding statement or section.

What the **Student** Does

K **Gist:** Students write opinion pieces about a topic or a book, using a combination of drawing, dictating, and writing.

They consider:

- What is the topic? Or, what is the name of the book?
- What do I think about the topic? Or, what do I think about the book?
- Why do I think this?
- What picture can I draw to show my opinion?

1 **Gist:** Students write an opinion piece about a topic or a book.

They consider:

- What is the topic? Or, what is the name of the book?
- What do I think about the topic? Or, what do I think about the book?
- What is one reason I think this way about the topic? The book?
- What words and pictures work best to tell what I think?
- How can I write an ending to show I'm finished?

2 **Gist:** Students write an opinion piece about a topic or a book.

They consider:

- What is the topic? Or, what book am I writing about?
- What is my opinion on the topic? Or, what is my opinion of the book?
- What are two or three reasons I can write to show what I think?
- Have I used linking words such as *because* and *next* to connect my opinion to my reasons?
- How can I write an ending sentence or two that restates my opinion?

Note: Although the questions listed above are too difficult for most young students to internalize and apply on their own, we share them to give teachers a detailed sense of what their students should be striving toward as learners. K–2 students may not be able to ask these questions of themselves independently, but teachers can use them as a jumping-off point for lesson content and as prompts and reminders to share with students. Over time and with instruction, students will be able to pose these questions on their own.

What the **Teacher** Does

To give students practice in stating their opinions and backing them up with reasons:

- Start by teaching students what it means to have an opinion. Make a statement such as "I love rainy days," and invite them to agree or disagree, give a reason, and explain why. For example, a student might say, "I don't like rainy days *because* I have to stay inside." Or "I like rainy days *because* I get to jump over puddles." Provide students with regular opportunities to state what they like or don't like about their everyday experiences and give reasons. Be sure to applaud students' use of the word *because* and vary the like/don't like constructions and other sentence structures, such as "The best ___ is ___ because . . ."

- Regularly invite students to state their opinion on a content-area topic they're studying or on a book you're reading aloud. Be sure to have them back up their opinions with reasons, and encourage them to include the word *because* (or something to that effect) when stating the reasons for their opinions. Be careful to neither refute students' less valid reasons (e.g., Grizzly bears are more dangerous than black bears because they are taller) nor applaud reasons that are objectively stronger (e.g., Grizzly bears are more dangerous than black bears because they can't climb trees to get away from danger as well as black bears can, so they've learned to fight). The goal is for students to feel comfortable expressing their opinions and trying their best to back them up with sound reasoning.

- Brainstorm a class "Wish List" of all the things students would love to change. For example, "I wish we could get new equipment for our school playground," or "I wish there were no zoos so that animals could live free." Have students work in pairs and select one idea from the "Wish List" to discuss. Encourage them to come up with several reasons for their opinions, and give them opportunities to share with the class. Post the "Wish List" prominently in the classroom so that you and your students can add to it regularly and discuss selected items (see a sample list in the online resources at resources.corwin.com/literacycompanionk-2).

- Make a bar graph to represent students' responses to a question that relates to a science or social studies topic (such as "Which community helper do you most want to learn about?") from a list of three or four choices. Once students' responses have been graphed, give each student a note card. On one side have them write, "I

want to learn about ___ (e.g., firefighters, chefs, pilots) because ___." Then on the other side of the note card have them write one reason or several, depending on the students' grade. Sort the cards into categories and, one category at a time, have students read what they wrote.

To teach students to write an opinion piece about a topic:

- Collect examples of opinion pieces and persuasive letters written by students from prior years or from online sources to give your students exemplars of opinion pieces written by students their age.

- Model writing an opinion piece with the entire class. Be sure to include the following: a one- or two-sentence introduction in which students state their opinion; at least two reasons for their opinion (see the "Developmental Debrief" section below); words like *also*, *because*, and *and* to connect the opinion and reasons; and a concluding statement. Post this model opinion piece so that students can later draw on this collective experience when writing their own.

- Introduce persuasive letter writing (which contains the same basic elements as an opinion piece) and explain that a persuasive letter, like an opinion piece, is written to change someone's mind (e.g., the principal, the librarian, cafeteria workers, a city official) and effect change. Decide on an authentic topic—something students would really like to change—and write a class letter to model how it's done. Select recipients who may actually write a letter in response to the scaled-down copy of the letter students send, and perhaps make arrangements ahead of time with a local organization to write to the class or visit the classroom in response to the students' letter. Post the sample letter prominently in the classroom so that students can try writing their own letters during their writing time of day (see an example of a persuasive letter in the online resources at resources.corwin.com/literacycompanionk-2).

- As students write their own opinion pieces or persuasive letters, note problems they're experiencing and provide additional explicit instruction and practice. When students are having difficulty:

  o **introducing a topic and clearly stating an opinion,** share examples from books, articles, and samples of student writing; practice writing introductions together; give students multiple opportunities to try writing introductions that declare their opinions; and share their introductions with classmates.

- **stating reasons to support their opinions,** use a graphic organizer that prompts students to fully elaborate their reasons, brainstorm various reasons they might include in an opinion piece to convince or persuade someone to act differently, and challenge students to consider reasons that are based on observable facts. (Although K–2 students are not yet responsible for coming up with evidence-based reasons, conversations that can help them differentiate between reasons that are based on facts and those that are more subjective can begin in grade 1.)

- **using linking words to connect opinions and reasons,** draw students' attention to linking words (*and, because, also, second, next*) in samples of opinion pieces you've used with them, in both published materials and student writing, and highlight linking words with colored tape or markers in the opinion piece samples you've written together.

- **concluding an opinion piece or bringing it to closure,** refer students back to their statement of opinion in the introduction to make sure it matches the concluding statement, revisit the opinion piece samples you've shared with students to notice how they have been brought to a close, and give students opportunities to try writing concluding statements on their own. It's okay if the ending is a repeat of the opening statement; older students might restate it with different words, or add flourishes of voice (e.g., "I hope I have convinced you that dolphins are smart like people. If you don't believe me, *you* try learning all those water tricks!").

To teach students to write their opinions of books they've read:

- Recognize that the same structure that works for writing an opinion piece about a topic—that is, an introduction that states an opinion, reasons supporting the opinion, connecting words, and a conclusion—also works for writing an opinion about a book. Adapt some of the ideas listed above.

To help your English language learners, try this:

- Meet with students to discuss a book you've read aloud or a topic under investigation. Help students compose an opinion statement and write it on chart paper. Brainstorm and list reasons to support this opinion. Have students practice stating their opinions and reasons by using the reasons they've brainstormed. Have them use the following sentence stem when stating their opinions and reasons: "I think that _____ because _____." Make sure they understand the significance of the word *because*.

Developmental Debrief:

While our goal is to eventually have elementary students in the upper grades write opinion pieces based on verifiable evidence, most K–2 students start out by stating reasons based on personal experiences. We can move them toward more objective reasoning through lots of shared opinion writing and discussion. Base the writing on topics children know about, and think aloud as you draft and weed out lesser, personal reasons in favor of evidence. For example, here is how it might look: Upon asking, "Why do we need to save the whales?" you would nudge students to see that answers such as "Whale watches are fun" and "Whales are the biggest sea animals" are not strong, objective reasons. However, a response such as "If whales become extinct, many other sea creatures would die too" contains a valid reason. Over time, students understand that *valid* and *objective* reasons are those that could be embraced by many other people.

Write opinion pieces based on informational books you have read together, so that you can go back to the texts for facts and details that can be presented as reasons. For example, if you read a book about "taking care of our body," students might write about "why it's important to exercise" or "why it's important to eat healthy food" and use the book as a reference.

Academic Vocabulary: Key Words and Phrases

Analysis: This involves breaking up a complex idea or process into smaller parts (what it is, how it works, and what it is made from) to make it easier to understand.

Argument: Arguments are claims backed by reasons that are supported by evidence. Arguments have three objectives: to explain, to persuade, and to resolve conflicts between positions, readers, or ideas. Writers make their case by building their arguments with reasons and supporting evidence.

Claim: This is the statement that the writer is attempting to prove is true. An effective claim is short, precise, and clear and summarizes the writer's main point. It typically comes near the beginning of the piece and then is bolstered by a well-reasoned chain of evidence.

Closure: This comes at the end of an opinion piece, where the writer brings the argument to a close. Rather than ending an opinion piece with a more formal concluding statement or paragraph, kindergarten and first-grade writers might conclude by simply writing, "And that's why I liked the book." A second-grade student might write, "So now you have two good reasons why orcas should not be captured and kept in tanks. Think about it."

Concluding statement or section: This is where the writer circles back to restate his or her opinion and perhaps sum up the evidence in support of the argument being made. It's what brings closure to the piece.

Evidence: Evidence consists of the details the writer provides to support an argument or opinion. It might include facts, quotations, examples, photographs, expert opinions, and, when appropriate, personal experience. Evidence supports reasons that in turn support the argument or claim.

Linking words: These are words that connect one sentence, idea, or paragraph to another (e.g., *and, because, also, second, third, last, next*), allowing the writer to express an important relationship between opinion and reasons.

Opinion: This is a belief, conclusion, or judgment based on reasoning. In this standard, students need to base opinions on reasons and evidence, which can take the form of facts and details; the important thing is that they avoid relying on personal opinions to support their claims. That said, our youngest writers start with personal opinions and move on to more objective reasoning as they mature and gain experience.

Reasons/reasoning: Writers must base their claims and ideas on more than personal preferences or opinions when constructing arguments. The reasons students give to support their opinions or arguments must be based on evidence.

Substantive topics or texts: Writers are expected to write about compelling, important ideas or texts that examine big questions and challenge the reader. For K–2 students, this means writing opinions and responding to texts on age-appropriate topics, such as whether or not it's all right to capture wild orcas, keep them in tanks, and train them to perform in marine theme parks.

Notes

Linking words
claim/argument
reasons

Planning Page

Standard: _____

Purpose of Lesson/s:

Planning the Lesson/s	Questions to Ask

Differentiating Instruction	Thinking Beyond This Standard

The standards guide instruction; they do not dictate it. *So as you plan lessons remember you aren't teaching the standards, but instead are teaching students how to read, write, talk, and think through well-crafted lessons that draw from the pedagogy embedded within them. Engaging lessons often have several ELA standards within them and integrate reading, writing, speaking and listening, and language.*

Standard 2: Write informative/explanatory texts to examine and convey complex ideas and information clearly and accurately through the effective selection, organization, and analysis of content.

K Students use a combination of drawing, dictating, and writing to compose informative/explanatory texts in which they name what they are writing about and supply some information about the topic.

1 Students write informative/explanatory texts in which they name a topic, supply some facts about the topic, and provide some sense of closure.

2 Students write informative/explanatory texts in which they introduce a topic, use facts and definitions to develop points, and provide a concluding statement or section.

What the **Student** Does

K **Gist:** Using a combination of drawing, dictating, and writing, students compose informative/explanatory texts in which they name what they are writing about and supply some information about the topic.

They consider:

- What am I drawing or writing about?
- What two or three things do I most want my reader to know?
- What picture(s) will I draw to go with my words?
- What details can I add to the picture(s)?

1 **Gist:** Students write informative/explanatory texts in which they name a topic, supply some facts about the topic, and provide some sense of closure.

They consider:

- What is my topic?
- What facts will I include?
- How can I add pictures for extra information?
- What do I want to say last about my topic to make it sound like an ending?

2 **Gist:** Students write informative/explanatory texts in which they introduce a topic, use facts and definitions to develop points, and provide a concluding statement or section.

They consider:

- What do I want to explain about my topic?
- What details/facts will I include to give enough information?
- Is there an important word I have learned that I can define for my reader?
- What should I say first, second, and third so that I make a clear point about my topic?
- What ideas can I adapt from books (e.g., pictures with captions, labeled drawings, scale drawings) to help me illustrate my piece?
- When I think about my topic, what do I want to say as a final point or ending?

Note: Although the questions listed above are too difficult for most young students to internalize and apply on their own, we share them to give teachers a detailed sense of what their students should be striving toward as learners. K–2 students may not be able to ask these questions of themselves independently, but teachers can use them as a jumping-off point for lesson content and as prompts and reminders to share with students. Over time and with instruction, students will be able to pose these questions on their own.

What the **Teacher** Does

To introduce students to informative/explanatory texts:

- Begin by defining the terms. You might say something like, "*Informative* and *explanatory* are pretty fancy words, but let's make them simple. Informative texts *inform* and explanatory texts *explain*. They are very much alike in their purposes. For example, a newspaper informs us about today's news; I inform you about class rules. What do you do when you are teaching a friend how to play a game? You *explain* it, right? So as we read informative/explanatory texts, remember they are focused on *inform*ation, and *explain*ing it."

- Provide numerous examples of published informative/explanatory texts weeks before you ask students to write, calling attention to the introductions, key ideas or points, organization, graphics, and endings. This will give you opportunities to acquaint students with the features they will need to know when they plan and write in this genre.

- As you read texts aloud, ask students to determine the author's purpose. Make a chart (then post it and add to it throughout the year). For example, they might decide that Nicola Davies's purpose in *Big Blue Whale* is for readers to know how amazing blue whales are, or that Roma Gans wrote *Let's Go Rock Collecting* to encourage young readers to collect rocks on their own.

- As you discuss these texts, point out illustration techniques such as pictures (both illustrations and photographs), pictures with captions, maps, and diagrams. Give students the opportunity to recognize how each technique helps convey information.

To help students find a topic to write about:

- Observe students during reading time to see which topics they like. For example, if you notice students going for the books on sharks or space, gather texts on those topics. Put each collection (even three or four books and articles for starters) in a labeled plastic bag or book basket so students have access to these sets.

- Have students write informative/explanatory texts on science or social studies topics you're investigating. This helps to lighten one of the greatest challenges K–2 students face regarding nonfiction writing: they're typically unable to read the texts containing the information they'll need for their writing. By aligning the writing topics with books/topics you'll be reading aloud and using in shared reading, guided reading, online

resources, and field trips, you're building background knowledge they can access when writing.

To teach students to write an informative/explanatory text:

- Model writing an informative/explanatory piece with the entire class. This will help students envision what's expected of them. Provide instructions on how to do each of the following:

  - Introduce a topic and decide on the key points to include:
    - Gather informational texts on a variety of topics and have students notice how authors introduce their topics. Authors often try to hook readers by posing intriguing "Did you know . . . ?" or "Have you ever . . . ?" questions, by starting with an overview paragraph of subtopics the book addresses, or by asking a broad question such as "What is the solar system?"
    - Share examples of nicely narrowed topics to get across to students that "bite-size" topics (e.g., how kangaroos feed their young) make for more manageable writing. Have students work collaboratively on a nonfiction alphabet book using a topic about which students are passionate. After considerable brainstorming to identify concepts within the topic that fit with each letter of the alphabet, have each student volunteer to be responsible for writing a brief, several-sentence piece about a single letter/word. Assemble all 26 entries (with illustrations) into a class book.
    - Share with students a poster-size example of an informative/explanatory text. After they've identified the topic, have them point out (and mark with sticky notes) some of the key facts and details. Keep a class chart posted on the wall and record how authors communicate details through the use of sensory language, comparisons, bold print, and dates and numbers.

  - Use facts and definitions to develop points:
    - Give each student a piece of paper and have each list one important fact about his or her topic at the top. One at a time, call on students to share the facts they've written and try to say more about them. For example, if a student writes that beavers have sharp teeth, you might ask her what

beavers use their teeth for, or ask her to describe what the teeth look like. Explain to the class that this is the type of detail and elaboration they need to include in their writing.

o Call students' attention to how authors sometimes include definitions within the body of a text itself to explain important words or concepts. Such a definition is often explicitly stated within the same sentence as the important word—as a phrase alongside the word—or in the sentence directly following.

- Organize their writing:

o Provide students with 4-by-6-inch index cards and have them write *one* idea or point on each card. After students read over what they've written, they can rearrange the cards into an order that makes their information easier for the reader to follow and understand. Once they do this students often recognize that they've forgotten to include something important or that they need to more effectively introduce their topic or conclude the piece.

o Give students in grades 1 and 2 a sheet of copy paper that's been sectioned off into four quadrants. Have them write one sentence in each box about their topic as a whole or one key idea or point they're trying to make about the main topic. For example, if the main topic of a piece is the rain forest, a student might write four key ideas (one in each box) about the rain forest in general, or he might write details about one section of his piece, such as the emergent layer of the rain forest. Either way, this method allows students to review the order of their points, cut the boxes apart, and reorder them as needed. Grade 2 students might simply renumber the boxes instead of cutting and pasting.

- End their pieces:

o Share published writing with students so they can see how authors conclude their pieces. Have students practice writing a variety of conclusions for their texts.

o Create a list of ways authors conclude their pieces and have students choose from the list. Authors might try to enlist the help of the reader in working toward a cause, ask them to try an experiment at home, include a recipe for them to make, or encourage them to join an organization.

- Illustrate their texts effectively:

o After showing students their options for illustrating their informational/explanatory pieces—pictures (illustrations and photos), pictures with captions, diagrams, and maps—invite several students to share their writing with the class and discuss how they might illustrate various sections. Ask the student authors to read portions of their pieces aloud and state whether or not they plan to illustrate their texts and, if so, how. Encourage classmates to also offer suggestions. When possible, put the writing up on a whiteboard so that all students can see it easily.

To help your English language learners, try this:

- Allow students to draw or illustrate facts and details about their topics, and label them. Then provide predictable frames for them to continue adding details (e.g., "Elephants live . . . ," "Elephants eat . . . ," and so forth).

- Select three or four examples of informative/explanatory books or articles and flag particular pages that could serve as models or easy formats for students' entire pieces (e.g., "Five Fabulous Facts About _____"; question-and-answer formats; a single, detailed drawing with labels all around it; or cutout photographs and captions).

- Talk with students about how to "bookend" their work with an opening and closing sentence. Bring in actual bookends to illustrate what you mean.

Developmental Debrief:

When it comes to illustrating, kindergarten and first-grade students often draw a picture *before* they write. This helps them rehearse their ideas.

We strongly advise against having individual students (especially in kindergarten and grade 1) select different topics to write about, since it will be difficult for them to amass enough information on their own. It's better to have them, at least initially, write on a common shared topic.

The standards set the bar high for K–2, with descriptors like *introductions*, *development of points*, and *concluding sections*. These are worthy but advanced goals; keep working toward them, but accept all sorts of approximations along the way.

Academic Vocabulary: Key Words and Phrases

Closure: This comes at the end of an opinion piece, where the writer brings the piece to a close. Rather than ending an opinion piece with a more formal concluding statement or paragraph, kindergarten and first-grade writers might conclude by simply writing, "And that's why I liked the book." A second-grade student might write, "So now you have two good reasons why orcas should not be captured and kept in tanks. Think about it."

Complex ideas: Complex ideas involve analyzing the parts of something. To understand a plant, for example, we need to consider its color, its shape, its parts (leaves, roots, stem, flowers), how the parts work together, what it needs to survive, and how it fits into the larger ecosystem. Simple ideas, on the other hand, are those we can acquire only through a singular sensory experience. So in our plant analogy, a simple idea is that a cactus prickle is sharp.

Concluding statement or section: This is where the writer circles back to restate his or her opinion and perhaps sum up the evidence in support of the argument being made. This brings a sense of closure to the piece.

Convey information clearly and accurately: This means that writers choose the most important facts and details about a topic and organize and group them so that they're readily understood.

Informative/explanatory texts: These are texts written to give information or explanations about the natural world and other topics. They are defined by their objective to inform and explain about a topic using facts and an objective tone. They are generally written in the third person.

Points: These are the key ideas the author conveys to support the larger main idea.

Selection, organization, and analysis of content: Writers choose the most important facts and details about their topics and organize them to achieve their purpose. They also analyze what each detail contributes to the meaning of the text as a whole.

Notes

Planning Page

Standard: _____

Purpose of Lesson/s:

Planning the Lesson/s	Questions to Ask

Differentiating Instruction	Thinking Beyond This Standard

The standards guide instruction; they do not dictate it. So as you plan lessons remember you aren't teaching the standards, but instead are teaching students how to read, write, talk, and think through well-crafted lessons that draw from the pedagogy embedded within them. Engaging lessons often have several ELA standards within them and integrate reading, writing, speaking and listening, and language.

Standard 3: Write narratives to develop real or imagined experiences or events using effective technique, well-chosen details, and well-structured event sequences.

K Students use a combination of drawing, dictating, and writing to narrate a single event or several loosely linked events, tell about the events in the order in which they occurred, and provide a reaction to what happened.

1 Students write narratives in which they recount two or more appropriately sequenced events, include some details regarding what happened, use temporal words to signal event order, and provide some sense of closure.

2 Students write narratives in which they recount a well-elaborated event or short sequence of events, include details to describe actions, thoughts, and feelings, use temporal words to signal event order, and provide a sense of closure.

What the **Student** Does

K **Gist:** Using a combination of drawing, dictating, and writing, students tell the story of a single event or several loosely linked events, tell about the events in the order they happened, and tell what they think about what happened.

They consider:

- Do I want to tell about a real event that actually happened? Or do I want to make up a story?
- What happens? What happens first? Next? And then?
- How does it end?
- What do I think about what happened? Or, what do my characters feel?

1 **Gist:** Students write narratives in which they recount two or more appropriately sequenced events, include some details regarding what happened, use temporal words to signal event order, and provide some sense of closure.

They consider:

- What am I telling? Is it a real story about something that happened or one I imagine?
- What happens? And in what order do things happen?
- Have I added enough details so readers can understand?
- Have I used words such as *yesterday, today, first, next,* and *last* to make events clear?
- How does my story end?
- When I reread my story, does it make sense?

2 **Gist:** Students write narratives in which they recount a well-elaborated event or short sequence of events, include details to describe actions, thoughts, and feelings, use temporal words to signal event order, and provide a sense of closure.

They consider:

- What kind of story am I telling? Did it really happen or is it one I made up from my imagination?
- What happens? What is the main event? And in what order do things happen?
- Have I added details that describe people's actions, thoughts, and feelings?
- Have I used words such as *a long time ago, today, later, first, next, then,* and *last* to show the order of the events?
- How does my story end?
- When I reread my story, does it make sense? Have I made it clear how one event leads to another?

Note: Although the questions listed above are too difficult for most young students to internalize and apply on their own, we share them to give teachers a detailed sense of what their students should be striving toward as learners. K–2 students may not be able to ask these questions of themselves independently, but teachers can use them as a jumping-off point for lesson content and as prompts and reminders to share with students. Over time and with instruction, students will be able to pose these questions on their own.

What the **Teacher** Does

To have students narrate a single event (or several loosely linked events):

- Have students sit in a circle and give them opportunities to orally tell about events that really happened in their lives or made-up events. Be aware that it is often difficult for young students, especially kindergarten students, to differentiate between real events and those that are imagined. Also be aware that one student's true recount of the time he or she broke a leg will likely lead other students to relate similar, but imagined, narratives of their own, so you'll have to rein it in.

- Don't move too quickly from oral storytelling to having students write or draw their stories. Oral storytelling is an essential step for all K–2 students, but especially for those in kindergarten and first grade. Be sure to give other students in the class opportunities to respond to each teller's story.

- Explain to students that they will be writing stories about things that happened to them or something they make up. If it's several weeks into the school year, you're likely to find some examples of personal narratives in students' writing folders. Select a couple of students to share their narratives with the class. Then review with students several fictional stories that you've already read aloud to illustrate that stories in books are make-believe, as opposed to their classmates' stories, which really happened. Students need to understand the difference.

- Tell students that they are going to get to choose between writing about something that actually happened to them and making up a story using their imagination. Let each student tell what his or her story will be about before they start writing, and let kindergarten and first-grade students know that they might want to start by drawing a picture and then writing.

- Use prompts or storyboards to help students move from one part of their event to the next: One time _____. Next _____ _____. Then _____. Lastly _____. To make a storyboard, divide a blank sheet of paper into quadrants. At the top left-hand corner of each section, write one of the prompts in sequential order—*First, Next, Then,* and *Lastly.*

To have students use temporal words to signal event order:

- As you share big books or enlarged texts, call students' attention to the temporal words—such as *first, next, then, last, after, before,* and *during*—that help move the story along. Highlight these words with sticky notes, and then write them on a chart to remind students to include them in their written narratives.

To have students provide a sense of closure:

- Explain that readers like to know that the event they're reading about is coming to an end. Therefore, the writer needs to tell the reader how things turned out or how a problem was resolved. When you read narrative nonfiction (e.g., biographies, memoirs) and fiction books aloud, invite students to comment on the ending sentence or two. What do they notice about how the author ended the piece?

- When you read fictional narratives, point out endings that tie things up in a neat little bow, like "and they lived happily ever after," and endings that deliberately leave the door open a little, giving readers the feeling the story is done, but it's not quite over. For example, William Steig's *Spinky Sulks* ends with "too bad it couldn't last forever."

- Have students mark the beginnings and endings of their pieces with highlighter or sticky notes. If a student finds she has only a beginning and middle, this recognition should prompt her to add an ending.

To have students narrate two or more appropriately sequenced events, or a well-elaborated event or short sequence of events, in the order in which they occurred:

- Have each student select one real person from his or her life to write about. Explain that it should be someone the student finds interesting, funny, or provocative—someone who's "a real character." Give students time to consider who they might like to write about and share their reasoning with a partner. Do a brief brainstorming of character-revealing ideas: looks, clothing style, way of walking, favorite sayings, quirky habits, and so on. Then take the following steps:

  1. Have students draw their characters, thinking all along about what the characters are like and some

of the characteristic ways they have behaved in different situations.

2. Give each student an 8½-by-11-inch sheet of paper with two rectangular boxes on it, each taking up almost half of the page; the first box should be titled "One time" and the second "Another time" (see a sample in the online resources at resources.corwin.com/literacycompanionk-2). Have students draw in the two boxes the situations they will later describe in words. (Note that up to this point, students have only been illustrating their characters and scenes from their soon-to-be-written narratives.)

3. Give each student two pieces of lined paper and have them write about both events they just drew. The description of the first event should begin with "One time . . ." and the second with "Another time . . . ," and the writing should elaborate on the events in which the main character "showed his or her true colors."

4. After students have written their descriptions of these two events, have them write introductory and ending sentences or paragraphs.

5. Have students read their narratives out loud. As they read, call attention to the words the student authors use to illustrate their characters' most salient characteristics.

To help your English language learners, try this:

- Working in small groups, give students time and opportunities to tell and draw their stories before they write them. They can illustrate each part on a separate sheet of paper, write along the top or bottom what's happening, and rearrange the sections if the original event order does not accurately reflect what happened.

Developmental Debrief:

When working with kindergarten and first-grade students, students who struggle, and English language learners, it is essential to recognize the importance of giving students time and opportunities to tell their stories orally and illustrate them—as a rehearsal of sorts.

Some children may not have the fine motor skills or writing stamina yet to succeed in planning and drafting full introductory or ending paragraphs. Use your judgment and realize that in K–2, it can be sufficient if children's "paragraphs" are a sentence or two. Paragraphing is often something that begins to make sense in third grade. Probably the most important year-end goal is that students understand how their sentences connect and build on one another toward a conclusion.

Notes

Academic Vocabulary: Key Words and Phrases

Closure: This comes at the end of a narrative, where the writer brings his or her piece to a close by telling the reader how things turned out.

Event sequence: This is the order in which events occur in a story. Events that are well organized help the reader follow and understand the story.

Narrative: This is a story one tells, whether in prose or verse, a picture book or a play. A narrative can be fictional or grounded in fact, such as an autobiographical or historical narrative or simply a recount of a personal experience in one's life.

Real or imagined experience: Narratives that tell about real experiences are based on personal or historical records (memoirs, autobiographies). Narratives that tell about imagined experiences are fictional (picture-book stories, plays, poems, folktales). Although fiction writers may use some details from real life to imagine their stories, the stories are mostly made up.

Recount: This means to tell about events that occurred, what happened, or the story of something, in some detail.

Technique: Literary narratives are carefully crafted to affect readers emotionally; to study the technique is to study how the work affects the reader. With experience, writers combine many techniques to make their stories enjoyable to readers. Techniques include dialogue, word choice, the development of tension, and the use of contrasting characters.

Temporal words: These are words that signal the position of an event in time, and as such guide the reader through the story. Some examples of temporal words suitable for K–2 writers are *first, next, then, last, after, after that, before,* and *during.*

Notes

Planning Page

Standard: _____

Purpose of Lesson/s:	

Planning the Lesson/s	Questions to Ask

Differentiating Instruction	Thinking Beyond This Standard

The standards guide instruction; they do not dictate it. So as you plan lessons remember you aren't teaching the standards, but instead are teaching students how to read, write, talk, and think through well-crafted lessons that draw from the pedagogy embedded within them. Engaging lessons often have several ELA standards within them and integrate reading, writing, speaking and listening, and language.

Standard 5: Develop and strengthen writing as needed by planning, revising, editing, rewriting, or trying a new approach.

K With guidance and support from adults, students respond to questions and suggestions from peers and add details to strengthen writing as needed.

1 With guidance and support from adults, students focus on a topic, respond to questions and suggestions from peers, and add details to strengthen writing as needed.

2 With guidance and support from adults and peers, students focus on a topic and strengthen writing as needed by revising and editing.

What the **Student** Does

K **Gist:** With guidance and support from adults, students respond to feedback from the teacher and peers and add details to strengthen writing as needed.

They consider:

- Which comment do I find most helpful?
- Where can I add a detail or make a change?
- What other suggestions from my peers do I like?
- How can I fix that part?
- When I reread my writing now, do I like it more?

1 **Gist:** With guidance and support from adults, students focus on a topic, respond to questions and suggestions from peers, and add details to strengthen writing as needed.

They consider:

- What is the topic I'm writing about?
- Which question or suggestion do I think is a great idea that will make my piece better?
- What words and details can I add?
- When I reread my piece, is there something else I want to fix?
- How will I do that?

2 **Gist:** With guidance and support from adults and peers, students focus on a topic and strengthen writing as needed by revising and editing.

They consider:

- Am I clear about my topic? Is it too broad? Too narrow?
- Are my classmates' questions and suggestions helpful?
- What details and interesting words and phrases can I add to make my piece better?
- How can I use *like* and *because* to help me add more information to my sentences?
- Have I fixed up my spelling, punctuation, grammar, and so on so that the information is clear to my reader?
- When I reread my piece now, do I like it more? Are there other things I want to change?

Note: Although the questions listed above are too difficult for most young students to internalize and apply on their own, we share them to give teachers a detailed sense of what their students should be striving toward as learners. K–2 students may not be able to ask these questions of themselves independently, but teachers can use them as a jumping-off point for lesson content and as prompts and reminders to share with students. Over time and with instruction, students will be able to pose these questions on their own.

To help students respond to questions and suggestions from peers:

- Provide opportunities for students to receive feedback from classmates on their writing. In writing workshop classrooms, this is called the "writing share" and occurs at the end of the workshop. Several students read their pieces of writing as their classmates listen carefully; the classmates then ask thoughtful questions and make helpful comments. Students need to be taught how to give constructive feedback over many weeks and with considerable modeling from you. Teach students to first comment on what they like, ask questions that may help the writer to clarify meaning, and perhaps make a suggestion or two (see the "Developmental Debrief" section below).

- As students ask questions of each student author and make suggestions, record, on a special form, some of their key questions and suggestions for how to improve the piece (see a sample form at resources.corwin.com/ literacycompanionk-2). After the student author finishes sharing, give her the form to place in her folder so she will have it for reference when revising her piece. You will have to moderate how much you write for different students based on what the students are capable of reading back on their own.

To help students focus on a topic:

- Help students select topics for their stories, informative/ explanatory pieces, or poems that are broad enough that students will be able to round up sufficient information, but not so broad that the pieces cover everything under the sun. That said, in kindergarten and first grade, it is typical and acceptable for students to write bed-to-bed stories—that is, stories that relate everything that happened during a particular day, outing, or event. Or when writing nonfiction, they might write "All About" a particular animal, city, or holiday. As students move from first grade to second grade, and with explicit instruction and practice, they are more capable of understanding why—and how—to narrow their topics.

- Decide on a writing project that relates to a social studies topic, such as Eastern Woodland Indians. Divide the topic into subtopics (such as where the Eastern Woodland Indians lived, what their homes were like, what they ate) and stock the classroom with reference books and articles. Then assign each student to select one of those subtopics and write what he or she knows about it.

After students have completed the writing assignment, have all those who chose the same topic get together and read what they wrote to one another. Then allow students to add to their pieces the new information they learned from their classmates.

To help students add details to strengthen their writing:

- The term *details* is chameleonlike in grades K–2, given that children across this grade range are at vastly varied levels of literacy. In kindergarten, revising in general and adding details in particular is usually a matter of crossing out or adding a word or two—and maybe adding a sentence to the end or drawing a picture. Demonstrate how to add details to a piece of writing, and when you confer one-on-one with students, help them locate where they want to add words or facts. Most of all, helping students find topics that are neither too narrow nor too broad in turn helps them arrive at a good amount of detail for their pieces. For first and second grade, the advice is fairly similar. Assess what students can do and guide them to make just a few simple changes that will lift the quality of their writing. To move students toward writing more complex sentences, model how to use connecting words such as *like* and *because*. This scaffolds their ability to add more elaborate phrases.

To help students revise their pieces:

- Have students read their pieces to a small group of peers, receive suggestions from them, and then change their writing if the suggestions would improve the piece. For K–2 students we're not talking about heavy-duty revision: in kindergarten revision involves simply adding a word or two, maybe a sentence or two later in the year; and in first and second grade revision includes adding or changing a sentence or two, adding a definition to clarify a term, or including a more enticing opening or closing sentence.

To help students edit (proofread) their pieces:

- Begin making an editing checklist with students at the start of the school year, rather than posting a ready-made list with each item already accounted for. Add additional items as needed and as students' writing warrants. (An example of an editing checklist is provided in the online resources at resources.corwin .com/literacycompanionk-2.)

- Even though "rereading to make sense" sounds more like revising than an editing checklist item, it should actually be number one on any editing checklist, since the goal of both revising and editing is to make the piece more comprehensible.

To help your English language learners, try this:

- Meet with students in a small group either before or after your revision and editing lessons to give them a leg up on understanding what you'll be describing or a chance to process or practice what you've already taught.

- Choose a few selected teaching points to help students with during revision and editing. Base these few points on their proficiency levels in English. Students new to English may do very little revision and editing, whereas students with good face-to-face communication skills in English might need more help with academic language and formal English.

- Meet with students in a small group either before or after your revision lesson and help them think about the questions you or their peers are posing to help them strengthen their writing. Be careful to focus any one revision lesson on either content (e.g., topic, vocabulary) or conventions (e.g., grammar, punctuation) so as not to overwhelm your students learning English.

- Because vocabulary acquisition is key to improving English language learners' reading and writing skills, look for fun, creative ways to explore words, colloquialisms, figurative language, and idioms. All children benefit as readers and writers from such language play.

Developmental Debrief:

Although revision isn't reflected in the writing standards until second grade, it can begin as early as kindergarten and first grade if it's approached with a light touch. Of course, young writers won't be able to resee or reenvision their pieces and begin again, but they can read over what they've written to cross out sentences that don't add anything and insert sentences that do. As a teacher, approach all of writing and revision with these questions in mind: What's my gut telling me about *this* writer, *this* child? Will revising actually slow the child's progress or dampen his or her motivation to write at this particular juncture? Would it be more productive and instructive to let the child dive into a new piece he or she is eager to write?

Notes

Academic Vocabulary: Key Words and Phrases

Details to strengthen writing: Specificity via details, examples, and elaboration are what readers look for and expect from both informational and literary texts; details help satisfy the reader that the writer knows what he or she is talking about. It's not enough to make broad and general statements about ideas or events—authors need to provide details and specifics to flesh out the larger ideas and breathe life into them.

Editing: For K–2 students, editing involves fixing spelling, punctuation, and grammar errors. Editing and proofreading can take place throughout the composing process, not just at the end—particularly with more fluent readers.

New approach: At some point, the writer may feel the current approach—the voice, the style, the perspective, or the stance—is not effective, at which point it makes sense to write the whole piece over in some new style, in a different format, or from an alternative perspective to better convey the author's ideas to the audience on this occasion.

Planning: Students can do many things to plan. They can outline ideas, gather and generate ideas, use graphic organizers, and brainstorm to generate and make connections between ideas. Some make lists of what they need to do, read, or include.

Revising: Revision is *reseeing*, considering a piece of one's writing with an eye to making it clearer. For K–2 students, revision is best understood as rereading to make sense. Students can then make small adjustments. In kindergarten, crossing out or adding a word or two; in grades one and two, fixing a few sentences, using connecting words to make the sentences flow better, or rewriting beginnings and endings.

Rewriting: Sometimes used interchangeably with revising, this phase of the writing process involves not tweaking or polishing up what is there but replacing it with new ideas or language better suited to the audience, purpose, or occasion.

Strengthen: This is what revising does to writing: makes it stronger by tightening the wording, refining the argument, and removing what is unnecessary so that key ideas, reasoning, and evidence are emphasized.

Notes

Planning Page

Standard: _____

Purpose of Lesson/s:

Planning the Lesson/s	Questions to Ask

Differentiating Instruction	Thinking Beyond This Standard

The standards guide instruction; they do not dictate it. So as you *plan lessons remember you aren't teaching the standards, but instead are teaching students how to read, write, talk, and think through well-crafted lessons that draw from the pedagogy embedded within them. Engaging lessons often have several ELA standards within them and integrate reading, writing, speaking and listening, and language.*

Standard 6: Use technology, including the Internet, to produce and publish writing and to interact and collaborate with others.

K With guidance and support from adults, students explore a variety of digital tools to produce and publish writing, including in collaboration with peers.

1 With guidance and support from adults, students use a variety of digital tools to produce and publish writing, including in collaboration with peers.

2 With guidance and support from adults, students use a variety of digital tools to produce and publish writing, including in collaboration with peers.

What the **Student** Does

K **Gist:** With guidance and support from adults, students explore a variety of digital tools to produce and publish writing, and to interact and collaborate with peers.

They consider:

- What is my purpose for writing?
- Who is my audience? Who will read it?
- How can this digital tool help me share my message?
- How can my classmates and I use this tool to write together?
- How can this tool help me find and organize information to make story writing easier?
- How can it help me publish and present my writing?

1 **Gist:** With guidance and support from adults, students use a variety of digital tools to produce and publish writing, and to interact and collaborate with peers.

They consider:

- What is my purpose for writing?
- Who is my audience? Who will read it?
- How can this digital tool help me share my message?
- How can my classmates and I use this tool to write together?
- How can this tool make finding and organizing information and stories easier?
- How can it help us publish and present writing?

2 **Gist:** With guidance and support from adults, students use a variety of digital tools to produce and publish writing, and to interact and collaborate with peers.

They consider:

- What is my purpose for writing?
- Who is my audience? Who will read it?
- How can this digital tool help me share my message?
- How can my classmates and I use this tool to write together?
- How can this tool make finding and organizing information and stories easier?
- How can it help us publish and present writing?

Note: Although the questions listed above are too difficult for most young students to internalize and apply on their own, we share them to give teachers a detailed sense of what their students should be striving toward as learners. K–2 students may not be able to ask these questions of themselves independently, but teachers can use them as a jumping-off point for lesson content and as prompts and reminders to share with students. Over time and with instruction, students will be able to pose these questions on their own.

What the **Teacher** Does

To help students use digital tools to improve their writing:

- Impress upon students that technology is a powerful writing tool, much like crisp white paper and newly sharpened pencils. Show a few moments of an animated picture book or a great science presentation for kids on TeacherTube. Talk about what technology can offer that writing on paper can't, such as easy access to information, integration of sounds and images, color, and fancy fonts. Then make the point that it's easy to be dazzled by all these bells and whistles, but as writers, their job is to think about the messages they want to communicate to their readers. They need to ask themselves, *Am I giving my reader enough information about my topic? Enough words to tell a story?*

- Make digital tools a natural part of the classroom learning environment. Scaffold students' use of computers, tablets, and other technological tools by demonstrating and doing shared writing, as an entire class. This whole-class collaboration helps ensure that students who haven't had access to technology at home can learn to use various devices and tools. Likewise, have students work in small groups and pairs if you see that "tech savvy" can be peer-mentored. However, be careful that the more tech-savvy students don't dominate the devices. You might set a timer to make sure each student in a pair has equal screen time. Be prepared to work one-on-one with those students who need extra support.

- Delineate the functions of various writing tools so that students can choose from among them for one or more stages of writing and publishing: (1) researching information and visual images (Internet), (2) writing and drafting, (3) sharing (wikis), and (4) publishing (Keynote, PowerPoint).

To help students use digital tools to produce writing:

- Design a couple of lessons to help students access *quality* information on the Internet that's related to science or social studies topics. Have students spend five minutes, almost like a game, finding high-quality information online that correlates with or expands upon the information in textbooks. Provide a list of acceptable sources for information and have them bookmarked on the classroom computer.

- Look for ways to use technology—computers, tablets, displays, interactive whiteboards, document cameras—that are efficient, effective, and appropriate to the writing task and developmental stage of the writer.

- When working with first- and second-grade students, intentionally design writing assignments that contain small but meaningful opportunities for students to learn additional features of word processing (e.g., how to embed images, how to design a page so text flows around images, how to insert headers). Model how you accomplish these word-processing tasks for the whole class before students work independently. In addition, you might use kid-friendly apps, such as SpongeBob SquarePants Typing, to help orient students to keyboards through games and keyboarding drills.

- Differentiate instruction so that students who experience difficulty with various aspects of the writing process, such as getting and illustrating information or organizing their ideas, are matched with appropriate digital apps, such as Primary Writer (Grassroots Technologies), Sentence Maker (Grasshopper Apps), How to Write a Paragraph (Classroom Complete), and RealeWriter (RealeStudios).

To help students use digital tools to publish their writing:

- Before publishing student work online, carefully consider the implications of doing so, especially if the writing contains images or copyrighted materials. You may want to explore other options.

- Set up a class blog that's easy to maintain and monitor. Model its use and then make sure that all students get to contribute.

- When publishing, take those extra steps to ensure that the writing has been carefully edited for spelling, punctuation, and grammar. If students use spelling and grammar checkers on the computer, ask them to try to explain what the computer says is wrong. For example: "This 'sentence' has a green line under it; what does the computer say is wrong with the grammar? Can you find the problem? Can you fix it?"

To use technology to interact or collaborate:

- For grade 2 students, set up a group or collaborative space online (via Google Docs, a wiki site, or any other platform that allows users to create a password-protected space) where they can discuss and respond to each other's ideas and writing in or outside class.

- Gather useful links—to applications, primary source sites, exhibits, and other rich resources related to pieces students are writing—that students can explore together in class or at home as they gather and generate ideas for writing.

To help your English language learners, try this:

- Make sure students have ample opportunity to use technology to write and to share their writing with others.

- Meet with English language learners in small groups to plan their writing and plan how to use the technology to help them write in groups or individually.

Developmental Debrief:

In addition to being great fun, technology is a powerful way to help students gain information and share it with others. It also can motivate students to write more frequently, which is a key factor in their becoming better writers. That said, at least with K–2 writers, digital tools should never take the place of students getting their ideas down with pencil on paper. The fine motor skills involved in writing are part of how our brains are wired to learn information and to think. True enough, children today are using digital technology, including tablets and other computers, practically from birth, and this may in effect be changing their brain development in ways that research has yet to determine. But as teachers in K–2, we must still make a place for having students draft onto paper and learn the letter formations of the English language.

Notes

Academic Vocabulary: Key Words and Phrases

Collaborate: When students collaborate in writing, they work together to come up with ideas, work on pieces of writing or projects together, and respond to each other's writing projects, sometimes using features such as Comments in Google Docs.

Interact: Students interact with one another through written dialogues online, through chat groups, social media, e-mail, and other interactive platforms, to generate ideas about texts they are analyzing, papers they are writing, or topics they are exploring (prior to writing). Thus, they use technology to facilitate and extend discussions, generate ideas, provide feedback on peers' written pieces, or write and share their own writing with others for feedback or publication.

Produce: Producing writing involves using a range of technology tools—computers, applications, digital cameras to capture images and videos—to generate content and help students write.

Publish: This means that students use computers to publish and distribute quality materials around school, the community, or online.

Technology: For K–2 students, this refers to using computers and tablets to compose, revise, and edit writing. It also implies using applications to gather information to incorporate into the writing itself. Using technology also means writing with and for a range of forms and formats (e.g., interactive whiteboards, tablets, blogs, graphic displays, and video images) and publishing pieces for audiences to read.

Writing products: Given the emphasis here on the use of technology, writing products include the traditional pieces students write, but also such new and emerging forms as blogs, wikis, websites, presentations, and multimedia or hybrid texts.

Notes

Planning Page

Standard: _____

Purpose of Lesson/s:

Planning the Lesson/s	Questions to Ask

Differentiating Instruction	Thinking Beyond This Standard

The standards guide instruction; they do not dictate it. So as you plan lessons remember you aren't teaching the standards, but instead are teaching students how to read, write, talk, and think through well-crafted lessons that draw from the pedagogy embedded within them. Engaging lessons often have several ELA standards within them and integrate reading, writing, speaking and listening, and language.

Standard 7: Conduct short as well as more sustained research projects based on focused questions, demonstrating understanding of the subject under investigation.

K Students participate in shared research and writing projects (e.g., explore a number of books by a favorite author and express opinions about them).

1 Students participate in shared research and writing projects (e.g., explore a number of "how-to" books on a given topic and use them to write a sequence of instructions).

2 Students participate in shared research and writing projects (e.g., read a number of books on a single topic to produce a report; record science observations).

What the **Student** Does

K **Gist:** Students participate in shared research and writing projects.

They consider:

- What do I already know about the topic?
- What am I trying to find out about this topic?
- How am I going to get this information? What books can I look at?
- How can I study photos and pictures to make my writing piece stronger?

1 **Gist:** Students participate in shared research and writing projects.

They consider:

- What do I already know about the topic?
- What am I trying to find out about this topic?
- How am I going to get this information?
- How can I spot and flag new facts?
- How can I study photos and pictures to make my writing piece stronger?

2 **Gist:** Students participate in shared research and writing projects.

They consider:

- What do I already know about the topic?
- What am I trying to find out about this topic?
- What questions can I ask to help me get the information I need?
- How am I going to get this information?
- How can I spot and flag new facts?
- How can I take notes on new facts?
- How can I study photos and pictures to make my writing piece stronger?

Note: Although the questions listed above are too difficult for most young students to internalize and apply on their own, we share them to give teachers a detailed sense of what their students should be striving toward as learners. K–2 students may not be able to ask these questions of themselves independently, but teachers can use them as a jumping-off point for lesson content and as prompts and reminders to share with students. Over time and with instruction, students will be able to pose these questions on their own.

What the **Teacher** Does

To have students participate in shared research and writing projects:

- Organize your research and writing projects around science and social studies topics. With time at a premium, integrating reading, writing, and content areas makes sense.

- Plan to make the project part of a three- to four-week unit so that you have time to immerse students in explicit research and writing craft lessons, shared research experiences, and knowledge building before asking them to write. Decide what configuration will work best for your students: Small groups each collaborating on an aspect of a bigger topic? Partners? Individual work?

- Begin reading aloud on the topic or discussing what students already know at least a week prior to the official kickoff of your research/writing project. As you read aloud books on this topic (for example, weather or the human body) and discuss with students what you're learning, they will begin to acquire basic knowledge of the topic, which will eventually lead you and them to ask generative as opposed to dead-end questions. For example, "How do monarch butterflies travel so far during migration?" as opposed to "Are monarch butterflies and swallowtail butterflies the same size?" Or "How does the heart work with other parts of our body?" as opposed to "What are two ways our heart helps us survive?"

- If possible, write for a real audience—students in a grade level below, families, a school library display, a community organization, or a nonprofit organization (e.g., the National Wildlife Federation or a museum). Tweak the topic so that it's both manageable and motivating to students. For example, revamp the classic how-to writing assignment about how to eat an Oreo cookie by having kids write several how-tos and compile them in a booklet (how to make a fruit smoothie; how to take care of a pet).

- Give students access to a wide variety of information about the topic, author, or genre you're investigating. Bring in related books, photos, maps, puzzles, games, posters, poems, and artifacts; set up a display table for these items so that students have access to them during independent reading and writing times of day.

- Reinforce the concept that research requires outreach by engaging students in creating and conducting surveys, interviews, and so on.

- Allow students to use an ample amount of visual information to support their writing. Writing information-rich captions to accompany drawings or photographs, creating realistic drawings based on research, or making simple graphs that reflect facts about the topic can often be more productive and helpful in building writing skills than a project that requires a set amount of sentences or paragraphs.

- As you dig into this shared project and formulate questions that students find engaging and motivating, help them differentiate between "important" and "dead-end" questions. Important questions lead to a deeper understanding of a topic, a person, or an event. They make us think; they generate discussions and may even lead to differences of opinion. In contrast, dead-end questions converge on single or narrow answers, often yes or no, or produce isolated facts that are not part of a larger context.

- As you and your students gather information, try to chunk it into categories on separate pieces of chart paper. It's easier for students to get a handle on the information and report back orally or in writing when ideas and facts are clustered into categories.

- Teach students how to access information from texts by using tables of contents, indexes, and glossaries.

- Model for students how to identify key words in a passage and how to take notes when gathering information or observing an event. Have them practice this all-important skill throughout the day, even when they are not engaged in a formal research or writing project. It should be standard protocol for students to have access to clipboards, sticky notes, or notebooks whenever you read aloud or are engaged in a discussion, so that they can jot down notes, words, and sketches to help them identify and recall important information. Practice (with continued explicit instruction from you) does indeed make perfect.

- Provide students with graphic organizers to help them organize and record their thinking (see resources .corwin.com/literacycompanionk-2).

To help students recognize the variety of resources that are available to help them build knowledge about their research or writing topic:

- Gather multiple and related books about the topic, author, genre, or event for students to explore. Show them how to get information from the illustrations as well as from the text. Put the books into a large plastic storage bag or book basket that's labeled with the name of the topic, author, genre, or event.

- Provide students with links to websites they can go to for information. Send these links home so that families can work with students to help them build knowledge for their research or writing project.

To help your English language learners, try this:

- As often as possible, meet with students before working with the class as a whole or afterward to give them time to process and discuss what you're showing them.

- Focus on a strategy called preview-view-review. As often as possible, meet with students before working with the class as a whole to preview the topic, teaching information about the topic in students' primary language, if possible, to build students' prior knowledge (this is the "preview" part of the strategy). Then teach the lesson and engage students in writing in English (the "view" part of the strategy). Finally, afterward meet with students and discuss the lesson, the topic, and/or the subject to give students time to process and discuss what you've shown them (the "review" part of the strategy). If possible, facilitate this conversation in the students' primary language.

Developmental Debrief:

Although this standard, as rolled out for K–2 students, explicitly expresses the "shared" nature of research and writing projects, it's also possible for students to have a go at investigating a research topic or question on their own. The key to this is that students have multiple shared experiences where techniques and procedures are modeled for them in whole-class settings in which they participate, and that their individual attempts are viewed as approximations, typically crude at first but later moving on to more refined examples of the research/writing process.

Notes

Academic Vocabulary: Key Words and Phrases

Demonstrating understanding of the subject: Students show the depth of their knowledge and their research skills by gathering a range of high-quality information, data, evidence, and examples related to the problem, question, or topic they are investigating; they then demonstrate what they have learned by choosing the most salient details and examples and using those to support their claims in a coherent, logical manner throughout the piece.

Opinions: As used in this standard, this refers to students' personal views or attitudes about something, such as a picture book. In this context the opinion is subjective and most often not based on fact or objectivity. It's important not to confuse this standard's incidental use of the word *opinion* with the way it is used in Writing Standard 1, where writers of "opinion pieces" are directed to substantiate their claims with evidence found in the text.

Questions (focus): Researchers generate their own questions or investigate others' questions about a topic of substance; such questions are often the driving purpose of the research. Focused questions are questions that are not so broad that they are meaningless or so narrow that the students are unable to gather enough information.

Report: This is a type of informative/explanatory writing in which the goal is to communicate or enumerate information on a topic or recount events.

Research (short and more sustained): Students are engaged in research whenever they seek information about a question or subject. They're researching when they ask themselves or others questions about the causes, types, effects, meaning, and importance of anything they're studying for class or for their own interests. Short or brief inquiries might involve a student getting some background knowledge on an author, a book, or a time period; in science, a student is researching when he or she does something as simple as looking up a concrete fact or as involved as doing a hands-on experiment related to a topic; and in social studies, researching may be as quick as looking at a globe or as time-consuming as digging up primary sources on the topic or time period.

Subject under investigation: This refers to the topic, research question, or problem the student seeks to understand. This subject can come from students themselves or from a teacher.

Notes

Planning Page

Standard: _____

Purpose of Lesson/s:

Planning the Lesson/s	Questions to Ask

Differentiating Instruction	Thinking Beyond This Standard

The standards guide instruction; they do not dictate it. So as you *plan lessons remember you aren't teaching the standards, but instead are teaching students how to read, write, talk, and think through well-crafted lessons that draw from the pedagogy embedded within them. Engaging lessons often have several ELA standards within them and integrate reading, writing, speaking and listening, and language.*

Standard 8: Gather relevant information from multiple print and digital sources, assess the credibility and accuracy of each source, and integrate the information while avoiding plagiarism.

K With guidance and support from adults, students recall information from experiences or gather information from provided sources to answer a question.

1 With guidance and support from adults, students recall information from experiences or gather information from provided sources to answer a question.

2 Students recall information from experiences or gather information from provided sources to answer a question.

What the **Student** Does

K **Gist:** With guidance and support, students use information from print, digital sources, or experiences they've had to answer a question.

They consider:

- What question am I trying to answer?
- What do I already know about the topic that I can list to get me started?
- What book has the teacher read aloud that might help me?
- Were there facts or pictures we saw online that will help answer the question?

1 **Gist:** With guidance and support, students use information from print, digital sources, or experiences they've had to answer a question.

They consider:

- What question am I trying to answer?
- Do I have experience with the topic that I can list to get me started?
- What books has the teacher read aloud or put in the class library that might be useful? What have I read?
- Were there facts, pictures, or videos we saw online that I can see again to help me answer the question?

2 **Gist:** Students use information from print, digital sources, or experiences they've had to answer a question.

They consider:

- What question am I trying to answer?
- Have I experienced anything firsthand that I can use to get me started?
- What books has the teacher read aloud or put in the class library that might be useful? What have I read?
- What information have I/we gotten online that I/we can review?
- Have I experienced anything firsthand that might be helpful?

Note: Although the questions listed above are too difficult for most young students to internalize and apply on their own, we share them to give teachers a detailed sense of what their students should be striving toward as learners. K–2 students may not be able to ask these questions of themselves independently, but teachers can use them as a jumping-off point for lesson content and as prompts and reminders to share with students. Over time and with instruction, students will be able to pose these questions on their own.

What the **Teacher** Does

To help students recall information from print and digital sources to answer questions:

- Have students keep content-area notebooks to record ideas and information they're learning. These notebooks are most effective when the pages are unlined, so that students can draw or write wherever they choose on a page. Section these notebooks off as you begin a new topic and assign students tasks to do in them. For example, if students are working with partners to research a particular bird, have them draw a picture of their bird in its natural habitat, or draw and label the bird's food, or you might ask them to write all the things they already know about the bird before beginning the investigation.

- Write the focus question in large print on chart paper so students can continually refer back to it as they read, write, and discuss.

- Make sure all students understand the question they're trying to answer. Ask them to state the question in their own words and record it in their research notebooks.

- Ask students to paraphrase often. This is one of the most powerful techniques in content-area instruction because if students can state in their own words what they've heard you say or read, then they own the information in a way that wouldn't have been possible if they had simply copied your question or information from the board into their notebooks.

- Model for students how to recall and record notes on what they already know about a topic. Devise a simple graphic organizer to help them list and label what they know and want to know.

- Teach students how to take notes so they can do this as you read aloud or as they read texts. Create graphic organizers on which they can list important words or phrases they hear as you read aloud, with spaces alongside where they can write why they think the words or phrases are important. (For an example of such a graphic organizer, see the online resources at resources.corwin.com/literacycompanionk-2.)

- Demonstrate the power of images and place value on the pictures students draw to convey information they've gotten from print, digital sources, and firsthand experiences.

To help students recall information from experiences to answer a question:

- Plan experiences (field trips, guest speakers) that will give students more information about the topic under investigation.

- Inform students' families about the topic so that they can do their part to build students' knowledge. Suggest some experiences families might initiate that would help students gather more information.

To help students consider the credibility of the sources from which they get information:

- As you read aloud to students to gather information on a research topic, keep a list of the titles and authors on chart paper. Tell students that you're doing this to help you remember where you got the information and later give credit to these authors. This will model for students what they should, in later years, be able to do on their own.

- As you read aloud to students, pay attention to the degree of expertise the author has on the topic. If there are author notes, this information is often contained there. Share with students that an author's knowledge of his or her subject is something you always consider when reading informational text.

To help your English language learners, try this:

- Working with students in small groups, facilitate conversations with them about their knowledge and experience with a topic. Record their ideas on a chart, adding illustrations on the chart as necessary to ensure that all English language learners in the group comprehend the information. Additionally, work with the students in the group to look up information in books, articles, and multimedia texts to build and develop their knowledge about a topic. Add new information to the chart.

Developmental Debrief:

Researching at any age can be by turns exhilarating and overwhelming, so for students in K–2—who are still getting their sea legs with decoding and reading fluently, letter formation, and writing stamina—less is more.

Provide a *small* sampling of high-quality texts and bring students along slowly. Value the information students glean from visuals as much as the facts found in texts, and, similarly, encourage students to "note take" in pictures and simple paraphrases until you see they are ready for more elaborated reporting.

Notes

Academic Vocabulary: Key Words and Phrases

Accuracy: This means that the information used as evidence for a claim or support for a hypothesis is true, current, and precise.

Assess: This refers to students taking stock of all the information their searches yield or all the quotations and evidence they could include in their papers. Which should they use based on the criteria or research question?

Credibility: This is a measure of the believability of the source of information, based on how current, established, and relevant the source is, as well as the ethos of the writer and of any source cited. Established sources affiliated with recognized publishers, reputable universities, or respected authors are considered credible, authoritative sources.

Gather relevant information: Information is only relevant to the degree that it answers the research question or supports an argument the writer makes; all else should be left out or dismissed as irrelevant. If students have a carefully conceived, clear, and narrow research question or problem they are reading to answer or solve, they will be better equipped to know which information is most useful or relevant.

Integrate information into the text selectively: This means to weave relevant quotations, examples, details, and evidence into the paper through paraphrasing, indirect quotation, or direct quotation.

Multiple print and digital sources: Legitimate researchers consider an array of sources from different perspectives and media to be as thorough as possible in their analysis.

Plagiarism: This refers to including another's words as your own (without using quotation marks), whether those words are copied from a famous writer, a website, or a fellow student. It is *not* plagiarism to use another's words so long as you cite that person and put quotation marks around the words being quoted. When working with K–2 students, you needn't focus on plagiarism per se; however, when you see students lifting an author's words directly from a text, you need to gently remind them that these are words that the author worked very hard trying to get just right. Now it's their job to find and use their own just-right words in their research or writing project.

Source: Be mindful of the strengths and limitations of each source: some sources may have particularly good data about one issue but not another; when assessing or quoting sources, it is vital to be aware of the quality and reputation of each source on the subject at hand. Avoid overusing or relying exclusively on any one source: when researching a subject, students should not rely on a few select sources that conveniently offer them a wealth of quotations or evidence. They need to reference (and make use of) a variety of sources that represent different perspectives and stances on the issue or question they are researching if their observations, conclusions, and arguments are to be credible. Again, this applies to students in the upper elementary grades, and not so much K–2 students.

Notes

Planning Page

Standard: _____

Purpose of Lesson/s:

Planning the Lesson/s	Questions to Ask

Differentiating Instruction	Thinking Beyond This Standard

The standards guide instruction; they do not dictate it. So as you plan lessons remember you aren't teaching the standards, but instead are teaching students how to read, write, talk, and think through well-crafted lessons that draw from the pedagogy embedded within them. Engaging lessons often have several ELA standards within them and integrate reading, writing, speaking and listening, and language.

The Common Core State Standards

Speaking and Listening

College and Career Readiness Anchor Standards for

Speaking and Listening K–12

The K–2 speaking and listening standards outlined on the following pages define what students should understand and be able to do by the end of each grade. Here on this page we present the College and Career Readiness (CCR) anchor standards for K–12 so you can see how students in K–2 work toward the same goals as high school seniors: it's a universal, K–12 vision. The CCR anchor standards and the grade-specific standards correspond to one another by number (1–6). They are necessary complements: the former providing broad standards, the latter providing additional specificity. Together, they define the skills and understandings that all students must eventually demonstrate.

Comprehension and Collaboration

1. Prepare for and participate effectively in a range of conversations and collaborations with diverse partners, building on others' ideas and expressing their own clearly and persuasively.

2. Integrate and evaluate information presented in diverse media and formats, including visually, quantitatively, and orally.

3. Evaluate a speaker's point of view, reasoning, and use of evidence and rhetoric.

Presentation of Knowledge and Ideas

4. Present information, findings, and supporting evidence such that listeners can follow the line of reasoning and the organization, development, and style are appropriate to task, purpose, and audience.

5. Make strategic use of digital media and visual displays of data to express information and enhance understanding of presentations.

6. Adapt speech to a variety of contexts and communicative tasks, demonstrating command of formal English when indicated or appropriate.

Note on Range and Content of Student Speaking and Listening

To build a foundation for college and career readiness, students must have ample opportunities to take part in a variety of rich, structured conversations—as part of a whole class, in small groups, and with a partner. Being productive members of these conversations requires that students contribute accurate, relevant information; respond to and develop what others have said; make comparisons and contrasts; and analyze and synthesize a multitude of ideas in various domains.

New technologies have broadened and expanded the role that speaking and listening play in acquiring and sharing knowledge and have tightened their link to other forms of communication. Digital texts confront students with the potential for continually updated content and dynamically changing combinations of words, graphics, images, hyperlinks, and embedded video and audio.

College and Career Readiness Anchor Standards for

Speaking and Listening

The CCR anchor standards are the same for K–12. The guiding principle here is that the core speaking and listening skills should not change as students advance; rather, the level at which students learn and can perform these skills should increase in complexity as they move from one grade to the next. However, for grades K–2, we have to recognize that the standards were back mapped from the secondary level—that is, the authors envisioned what college students need and then wrote standards, working their way down the grades. Thus, as you use this book remember that children in K–2 can't just "jump over" developmental milestones in an ambitious attempt to achieve an anchor standard. There are certain life and learning experiences they need to have, and certain concepts they need to learn, before they are capable of handling many complex academic skills in a meaningful way. The anchor standards nonetheless are goalposts to work toward. As you read the "gist" of the standards below, remember they represent what our K–2 students will *grow into* during each year and deepen later in elementary, middle, and high school. The journey starts in K–2!

Comprehension and Collaboration

Discussion in one form or another is a vital, integral part of learning and classroom culture. To ensure students contribute substance, they are expected to read, write, or investigate as directed so they come to class ready to engage in the discussion of that topic or text with peers or the whole class. During these discussions, they learn to acknowledge and respond to others' ideas and incorporate those ideas, as well as others they discover through their research, as evidence to support their conclusions or claims. Students first evaluate details and evidence in various forms and from different sources and then select details and evidence as needed to use in their presentations. When listening to others speak, students learn to listen for key details and qualities so that they can evaluate the perspective, logic, evidence, and use of rhetoric in the other persons' presentations or speeches.

Presentation of Knowledge and Ideas

When giving presentations, students carefully select which details and evidence to use when supporting their ideas or findings, organizing this information in a clear, concise manner that ensures the audience understands. To that end, students focus on how to best organize and develop their ideas and supporting evidence according to their purpose, audience, occasion, and appointed task. When appropriate, they use digital media to enhance, amplify, or otherwise improve their presentations, adapting their language and delivery as needed to different contexts, tasks, or audiences.

Source: Adapted from Jim Burke, *The Common Core Companion: The Standards Decoded, Grades 6–8* (Thousand Oaks, CA: Corwin, 2013).

Standard 1: Prepare for and participate effectively in a range of conversations and collaborations with diverse partners, building on others' ideas and expressing their own clearly and persuasively.

K Students participate in collaborative conversations with diverse partners about *kindergarten topics and texts* with peers and adults in small and larger groups.

    a. Follow agreed-upon rules for discussions (e.g., listening to others and taking turns speaking about the topics and texts under discussion).

    b. Continue a conversation through multiple exchanges.

1 Students participate in collaborative conversations with diverse partners about *grade 1 topics and texts* with peers and adults in small and larger groups.

    a. Follow agreed-upon rules for discussions (e.g., listening to others with care, speaking one at a time about the topics and texts under discussion).

    b. Build on others' talk in conversations by responding to the comments of others through multiple exchanges.

    c. Ask questions to clear up any confusion about the topics and texts under discussion.

2 Students participate in collaborative conversations with diverse partners about *grade 2 topics and texts* with peers and adults in small and larger groups.

    a. Follow agreed-upon rules for discussions (e.g., gaining the floor in respectful ways, listening to others with care, speaking one at a time about the topics and texts under discussion).

    b. Build on others' talk in conversations by linking their comments to the remarks of others.

    c. Ask for clarification and further explanation as needed about the topics and texts under discussion.

What the **Student** Does

K **Gist:** Students have conversations with classmates and adults in large and small groups, follow class norms for discussions, and stay on topic throughout multiple exchanges.

They consider:

- Do I listen carefully to my classmates when they speak? Do I look directly at them so they can tell that I'm listening?
- Do I wait for a classmate to finish speaking before I share my ideas?
- Does what I have to say relate to what the rest of the class is talking about?
- Do I help the idea grow bigger by staying on topic?

1 **Gist:** Students have conversations with classmates and adults in large and small groups, follow class norms for discussions, build on one another's talk, and ask questions to clear up confusion.

They consider:

- Do I listen carefully to my classmates when they speak?
- Do I wait for a classmate to finish speaking before I share my ideas? Do I keep my hand down while a classmate is speaking?
- Does what I have to say relate to the text or topic my class is discussing?
- Do I respond to a question or comment made by a classmate?
- Do I ask questions when I'm confused?

2 **Gist:** Students have conversations with classmates and adults in large and small groups, follow class norms for discussions, build on one another's talk by linking comments to the remarks of others, and ask for clarification and explanations when needed.

They consider:

- Do I listen carefully to my classmates so I can really understand their comments?
- Do I wait for a classmate to finish speaking before I share my ideas? Do I keep my hand down while a classmate is speaking?
- Does what I have to say add something new to the discussion of the text or topic?
- Do I talk directly to the classmate who spoke last and try to build on her ideas? Do I give her the opportunity to respond? And then do I respond in turn to her?
- Do I allow other classmates to join the conversation?
- Do I ask classmates to explain what they mean when I don't understand?

Note: Although the questions listed above are too difficult for most young students to internalize and apply on their own, we share them to give teachers a detailed sense of what their students should be striving toward as learners. K–2 students may not be able to ask these questions of themselves independently, but teachers can use them as a jumping-off point for lesson content and as prompts and reminders to share with students. Over time and with instruction, students will be able to pose these questions on their own.

What the **Teacher** Does

To help students participate in conversations:

- Whenever possible, have students sit in a circle at the meeting area rather than audience-style, facing you. Although this may feel awkward at first, it helps students recognize that the goal is for them to talk *with* one another. In this instance, the form really does match the function—over time, you want students to look at and to one another to build ideas through discussion and rely on you less to "bless" their comments.

- Provide voluminous opportunities for students to practice their conversational skills by having them talk about what they're learning throughout the day. Bring back show-and-tell for kindergarten students who still need to connect home to school. Create "show-and-tell-ish" opportunities for first and second graders by having them bring in and discuss books, artifacts, and experiences that relate to content-area topics the class is studying. Be sure to provide a share time at the end of your reading and writing times of day so that students can talk with one another about what they did to become better readers and writers.

- Call attention to the times when good information and insights come from a student rather than from you or a text. For example, saying something like "Wow, Jeffrey! It's so interesting that you thought to say that. I never even considered that before" helps students recognize that they have important ideas to share and that they can learn from one another, not only from adults and texts. It's also important to refrain from commenting verbally or through facial expressions on each and every statement students make. Maintaining a poker face often motivates more students to offer ideas than when every comment is immediately deemed right or wrong. It's all right for misinformation to be verbalized and remain uncorrected for the time being, since part of the fun of learning is recognizing that while your initial idea was incorrect you now know a better answer.

- Teach students to come to group discussions prepared with ideas. For example, you may read aloud a picture book in the morning and explain that they will later gather to discuss their favorite parts. Allow time immediately after the read-aloud for students to jot down some notes in their notebooks or on sticky notes that they can later bring to the discussion to remind them of what they might want to contribute.

- Scaffold students' ownership of understanding fictional and informational texts and concepts by having

good, open-ended questions "in your back pocket" to get a discussion going. Begin with questions that are within students' grasp to motivate them to risk answers. Questions such as "Why do you say that?" and "Can you give me an example?"—and even "Why do you think I asked you this question?"—lie at the heart of critical thinking and will go a long way toward helping students explore complex issues and engage in discussions. Read up on modern Socratic method online and adapt it for your students and the content at hand.

To help students follow agreed-upon norms for conversation:

- Over the course of several weeks, co-construct with students a chart of speaking and listening norms they should try to follow. It's important that students help formulate these norms—rather than you posting a laminated list that's used from year to year—so that the ideas and phrasing are theirs. When students participate in setting norms, they understand why each item is important, how it applies to them, and that in following these norms they are learning lifelong skills. (For a sample chart, see the online resources at resources.corwin.com/literacycompanionk-2.)

- Teach explicitly what it means to be a good listener by modeling for students both an unacceptable listening scenario and an acceptable one. Call on two students to help demonstrate. In the first scenario the designated listener is looking around the room, playing with a shoelace, or waving his hand to speak while the designated speaker is still talking. In the second scenario the listener is looking directly at the speaker and making facial gestures (nodding, smiling) that indicate understanding. Remind students that this is playacting, and therefore more exaggerated than what they will experience in authentic classroom discussions.

To help students build on one another's talk and link their comments to those made by others:

- When establishing norms for class discussion, encourage students to respond to other students' comments before they offer any new comments of their own. For example, "Donnell, it got me thinking when you said _____. I also think that _____." While most kindergarten students will not be able to do this well or consistently, it's a worthwhile goal to strive for in first and second grade.

- Provide students with sentence templates that give them the language they need to enter a discussion (e.g., "I agree with what Maria said about _____, but disagree that _____"). Post some of these sentence templates on a class chart for easy reference (for a sample chart, see the online resources at resources.corwin.com/literacycompanionk-2).

- Introduce the idea of a follow-up or clarification question. For example, "Eva, you said that penguins aren't the only birds that can't fly. Can you give me another example?" Or "Where did you learn that?" Develop over time and post a list of follow-up questions students can use when asking classmates (or the teacher) to say more about an idea or comment they made in the course of a discussion.

- After a group discussion, ask students to reflect on how they did in terms of listening to others, participating in the conversation, staying on topic, including others, and linking their ideas to those of their classmates. It's helpful occasionally to videotape classroom discussions so that students can see themselves in action; as you review the tape together, have them comment on what went well and what didn't.

To help students ask for clarification when they don't understand:

- Celebrate when a student asks a question or asks for clarification. Students often think that asking questions indicates they are less smart than someone who seldom asks them. Help them understand that in reality, it's often quite the opposite. Students who ask questions or seek clarification show that they are engaged in the conversation and need additional information so they can continue their engagement. This is a good thing.

- When praising a student for asking a question, be specific about what he or she did well rather than giving empty praise by saying "Good question" or "Good job." Students need to hear precisely what they did well; for example, "You were able to identify the one thing that confused you and ask for help."

To help your English language learners, try this:

- Partner your English language learners together with other students who speak the same primary language so that they can talk in their primary language before you ask them to respond out loud. Buddying students up and encouraging them to talk in the language they are most comfortable with can help to reinforce their thinking and allows them to practice the best way to express their thoughts in English.

- Have the entire class write about a text or topic they will later discuss together or in small groups. Allow students who might be uncomfortable speaking extemporaneously to read what they wrote instead of speak it. Partner your English language learners with English speakers before you ask them to read their responses out loud so they can work through any vocabulary or structural problems of which the English language learners may be unaware.

Developmental Debrief:

It will likely take a lot of practice to help students understand that each of them is not the only person in class whose voice needs to be heard. As students mature they gradually move from an egocentric stance, where it's "all about me," to one that recognizes and is open to their classmates' perspectives. Be patient with students as they make this shift.

Notes

Academic Vocabulary: Key Words and Phrases

Collaborative conversations: These involve discussing ideas and working jointly with others to create new thinking. Students take the remarks of others and add details or further develop the thoughts.

Diverse partners: This refers to people and ideas from backgrounds, cultures, and perspectives that are different from a student's own. The idea is that students must know and be able to converse with all kinds of people.

Expressing: Students articulate and convey their own ideas instead of merely parroting back the ideas of classmates or authors.

Linking comments to the remarks of others: This is when students consider what their classmates have contributed to a discussion before adding their own ideas, and make reference to them as they comment themselves.

Multiple exchanges: This refers to discussions where an idea is considered and discussed by several persons, ideally growing richer and more complex as new ideas or examples are added, rather than the more typical question-answer, new question-answer pattern that is prevalent in many classrooms.

Notes

Planning Page

Standard: _____

Purpose of Lesson/s:

Planning the Lesson/s	Questions to Ask

Differentiating Instruction	Thinking Beyond This Standard

The standards guide instruction; they do not dictate it. So as you plan lessons remember you aren't teaching the standards, but instead are teaching students how to read, write, talk, and think through well-crafted lessons that draw from the pedagogy embedded within them. Engaging lessons often have several ELA standards within them and integrate reading, writing, speaking and listening, and language.

Standard 2: Integrate and evaluate information presented in diverse media and formats, including visually, quantitatively, and orally.

K Students confirm understanding of a text read aloud or information presented orally or through other media by asking and answering questions about key details and requesting clarification if something is not understood.

1 Students ask and answer questions about key details in a text read aloud or information presented orally or through other media.

2 Students recount or describe key ideas or details from a text read aloud or information presented orally or through other media.

What the **Student** Does

K **Gist:** Students show they understand the key details of a text that is read aloud or presented through other media by asking questions or requesting clarification.

They consider:

- Do I understand most of what is being read aloud or presented?
- Is there a part that confuses me?
- What do I want to ask?

1 **Gist:** Students ask and answer questions about key details in a text read aloud or information presented orally or through other media.

They consider:

- Do I understand what is being read aloud or presented?
- What are the most important details that I need to remember?
- Is there a part that I still don't understand?
- What questions might I ask that would help me understand better?
- What might I watch for or listen for during a rereading or a second viewing?

2 **Gist:** Students recount or describe key ideas or details from a text read aloud or information presented orally or through other media.

They consider:

- Do I understand what is being read aloud or presented?
- What are the most important ideas and details?
- What do I look for or listen for that signals important information?
- What questions might I ask that would help me understand better?
- What information should I include when telling someone the big ideas and details?

Note: Although the questions listed above are too difficult for most young students to internalize and apply on their own, we share them to give teachers a detailed sense of what their students should be striving toward as learners. K–2 students may not be able to ask these questions of themselves independently, but teachers can use them as a jumping-off point for lesson content and as prompts and reminders to share with students. Over time and with instruction, students will be able to pose these questions on their own.

What the **Teacher** Does

To have students ask and answer questions or request clarification about a text that is read aloud or presented visually or orally through other media:

- Cultivate a classroom environment where students feel free to pose questions and comments. People in general are tentative about putting ideas out there for fear of being judged or "wrong," so as teachers we have to model inquisitiveness, and always send the message that clarifying what we don't yet fully understand is an admirable and expected part of learning.

- Routinely help students differentiate between making a statement and asking a question by reminding them that a statement gives information and a question asks for information. After you've read aloud from a text or have given students time to examine a poster-size photograph, have students tell some of the things they learned as you list them on the board. Explain that these are statements of information. Looking over the list, challenge each student to select a statement that makes him or her wonder, or want clarification. Ask each student to pose a related question. For example, the statement "Penguins are waterbirds" might prompt "What is a waterbird?" This activity underscores for students that questions about a topic or statement can be used to get additional information or clarify current information.

- Harness the power of simple science experiments to make the function of asking and answering questions vivid for your students. Find simple hands-on demonstrations in books or online, present them, and ask: "What did you just notice [about the egg, the balloon, the magnet, or whatever]?" "What questions do you have about what might have caused this to happen?" "What do we need to investigate this topic/concept further?"

- Model for students how you ask and answer questions as you view, listen to, or read aloud a text by pausing periodically to pose a question. Let students know precisely which words or phrases prompted you to ask the question or required clarification by going back into the text or other media to locate the words or phrases. For example, when viewing a video on bears, you might say, "Let me pause this video for a moment because I think I heard the narrator say that black bears eat *both* plants and meat, and I always thought that black bears are plant eaters and that grizzlies and polar bears eat meat. Hmm. Now I'm confused. How can we find out which one is right?"

- Likewise, when students ask questions, begin in these very early grades to get them thinking of what exactly led them to ask the questions in the first place. Ask questions such as "What confused you?" and "What made you ask that?" Over time, this line of inquiry will help students recognize that questions don't just arise out of nowhere or pop into a person's head out of thin air. Instead, something they read, heard, or saw triggered their need to seek clarification.

To have students recount or describe key ideas and details from a text read aloud or presented through other media:

- Scaffold students' oral recounts and descriptions of key ideas and details by having them *illustrate* or *write* their ideas before asking them to present what they learned orally. You will likely need to differentiate even further by suggesting that kindergarten students draw detailed pictures of what they learned rather than write about it. Having this drawing/writing option serves as a welcome relief to students who have difficulty with writing and helps all students rehearse what they may want to communicate orally.

- Teach students how to take notes during read-aloud and other presentations so that they have something to work off of when reporting back to classmates about what they learned. This can begin as simply providing students with large sticky notes and asking them to draw or write one or two words in response to the information being presented. Then, as their writing skills improve, they can write or illustrate longer responses.

- In the context of interactive read-aloud, explicitly teach the ways in which good readers prick up their ears and train their eyes for cues to critical textual information. Cues from the presenter include pauses and words that are spoken softly or loudly, shifts in tone of voice, and speaker tags in dialogue. Students can be taught to use all their senses when watching videos, paying attention to visuals, scale, foreground and background, music, voice-overs, graphics and headings, and so on.

- As you present new information through read-aloud and other media, provide graphic organizers for students to record the main ideas and details (for a sample, see the online resources at resources.corwin.com/literacycompanionk-2). Then have them work with partners and restate in their own words what the text was about. In addition, give them opportunities to record on their graphic organizers what they learned from their partners.

- Read aloud or present information through other media. Then, with the students' help, formulate and record the key ideas and details in the material on a large chart. You might write the information as a narrative or as bullet points (with or without the student contributors' names alongside the pieces of information).

To help your English language learners, try this:

- Before asking students to share what they learned, allow them to read, hear, or view information several times.

- If possible, pair English language learners who speak the same primary language together so they can talk about their ideas before sharing with the group. This builds student confidence in responding to texts and other media.

- Organize groups for students to practice sharing their ideas in English. It is also essential to practice with your whole class how to give students learning English wait time so they can speak on their own, and how to encourage, not correct, when they are speaking in English.

- Show students a photograph (with or without a brief caption) that you found on the Internet related to a content-area topic they're investigating. Have them talk about what they see (and are learning) by looking closely at the photo from top to bottom and left to right. Record some of their observations on the chalkboard alongside the photo. Talk with them to decide which of the things they noticed are key ideas and details, and which are interesting but not key. Then ask students if they have any questions they wish they had answers to, and talk with them about how they might find the answers. Either work with them to get answers or pair them with peers to do so.

Developmental Debrief:

The ability to express in your own words ideas you've learned orally or from other media is difficult for young students; in fact, initially students may only be able to restate the author's words in their attempt to describe or retell what happened. Take comfort that with explicit instruction, scaffolding, and plenty of practice students will eventually be able to recall information and paraphrase on their own.

Notes

Academic Vocabulary: Key Words and Phrases

Diverse media: These include print, pictures and illustrations, video, and electronic and new media (e.g., Internet).

Evaluate: This means to determine the quality, value, use, or importance of data, details, or other forms of information one might include in a presentation as evidence to support one's position.

Formats: This refers to the ways in which information can be presented, including through narratives, numbers, charts, tables, slides, graphics, images, or mixed media—all of which allow the speaker to represent his or her ideas more fully and effectively.

Information presented orally or through other media: This simply refers to the fact that not all information involves print. There are other ways to convey information, such as orally (podcasts, read-aloud, guest speakers) or through still images, maps, charts, tables, and graphs.

Integrate: This means to join different sources of data into one cohesive body of evidence used to support one's claims.

Key ideas or details: These support the larger ideas the text develops over time and are used to advance the author's claims. Since not all details and ideas are equally important, students must learn to identify those that matter the most in the context of the text.

Recount: This means to give the key details of something: in a story it may be what happened in chronological order; in an informational piece it may involve stating the main ideas.

Visually, quantitatively, and orally: This refers to images, video, art, and graphics of any other sort intended to convey the ideas the speaker wants to communicate.

Notes

Planning Page

Standard: _____

Purpose of Lesson/s:

Planning the Lesson/s	Questions to Ask

Differentiating Instruction	Thinking Beyond This Standard

The standards guide instruction; they do not dictate it. So as you plan lessons remember you aren't teaching the standards, but instead are teaching students how to read, write, talk, and think through well-crafted lessons that draw from the pedagogy embedded within them. Engaging lessons often have several ELA standards within them and integrate reading, writing, speaking and listening, and language.

Standard 3: Evaluate a speaker's point of view, reasoning, and use of evidence and rhetoric.

K Students ask and answer questions in order to seek help, get information, or clarify something that is not understood.

1 Students ask and answer questions about what a speaker says in order to gather additional information or clarify something that is not understood.

2 Students ask and answer questions about what a speaker says in order to clarify comprehension, gather additional information, or deepen understanding of a topic or issue.

What the **Student** Does

K **Gist:** Students ask and answer questions in order to seek help, get information, or clarify something that is not understood.

They consider:

- What is the speaker telling about?
- What is one thing I found interesting?
- What question do I want to ask?

1 **Gist:** Students ask and answer questions about what a speaker says in order to gather additional information or clarify something that is not understood.

They consider:

- What is the topic?
- What do I already know about this topic?
- What are some things I learned from this speaker?
- What do I want to know more about?
- Did I follow agreed-upon norms for classroom discussion?

2 **Gist:** Students ask and answer questions about what a speaker says in order to clarify comprehension, gather additional information, or deepen understanding of a topic or issue.

They consider:

- What is the topic?
- What do I already know about this topic?
- Am I ready to listen and take notes?
- What are some things I learned from this speaker?
- Were there facts that surprised me or were the opposite of what I already know about the topic?
- How can I ask questions to clarify confusions?
- Did I contribute to the discussion by adding comments or elaborating on a classmate's remarks?

Note: Although the questions listed above are too difficult for most young students to internalize and apply on their own, we share them to give teachers a detailed sense of what their students should be striving toward as learners. K–2 students may not be able to ask these questions of themselves independently, but teachers can use them as a jumping-off point for lesson content and as prompts and reminders to share with students. Over time and with instruction, students will be able to pose these questions on their own.

What the **Teacher** Does

To give students practice asking relevant questions:

- Routinely help students differentiate between making a statement and asking a question by reminding them that a statement gives information and a question asks for information. Give students opportunities to try out their statement-making and question-asking skills in the context of real-life classroom situations. For example, at the end of reading and writing times of day, gather students and have individuals share pieces they wrote or talk about books they read, explaining in real time that the information and ideas the speakers are expressing are all *statements*. Next, give students the opportunity to ask the speakers questions about what they shared. Explain that their *questions* will prompt the speakers to give more information than they originally gave.

- Demonstrate an effective, brief presentation on a topic you know and care a lot about. Find online and real-life examples of passionate presenters (children's authors, who often have an online presence, are good sources; National Geographic and other organizations have free, short videos online). You want students to understand that generally speakers are experts who care about their topics, and it's their job to deliver information in a clear and engaging way. The flip side? It's students' job as listeners to get all they can out of the presentation, and use their smarts to think about whether the speaker has done an effective job.

- Before listening to a speaker, and to practice asking questions, help students understand how they can generate multiple questions based on one statement. For example, the statement "House spiders weave webs to catch flies" might start students wondering, How long does it takes a spider to build a web? How many flies does a spider catch each day? What else do spiders eat? Note that in the case of K–2 students, a "speaker" may be anyone from the science teacher to the music teacher, a classmate sharing something he brought in to share, or someone the students are interviewing.

- Acquaint students ahead of time with the topic the speaker will be presenting. Bring in books the speaker may have written or books, articles, and texts related to the speaker's topic. For example, if students plan to interview a zookeeper to learn about the job she performs, you might share books with students on zoos or various animals of interest that live in zoos.

- Have students brainstorm all the things they know about the topic. Then have them think of questions they hope the speaker will address or questions they might ask if the speaker doesn't address them in the initial presentation. They should write these questions down and bring them along when they listen to the speaker.

- Have students sit up close to the speaker so that the listening/question-asking experience feels more personal and intimate. Remind students of the speaking and listening protocol—that is, look directly at the person who is speaking, refrain from raising your hand while the person is speaking, allow others in class to ask questions and interact with the speaker, and make sure that someone hasn't already asked the question you want to ask. In addition, remind students to listen carefully to their classmates' questions so that they don't ask the same ones.

To ask and answer questions about what a speaker says in order to gather additional information, clarify something that is not understood, or deepen understanding of a topic or issue:

- Provide graphic organizers (see resources.corwin.com/literacycompanionk-2) for students to fill out with questions they have as they listen to a speaker, view a video clip, or hear a text read aloud. Although using such organizers is not appropriate for kindergarten students, first and second graders can get quite good at this skill over time and with practice.

- Provide a graphic organizer with spaces for students to indicate how well they understood segments of a presentation that's read aloud, viewed, or otherwise presented (for an example, see the online resources at resources.corwin.com/literacycompanionk-2). Students circle either a smiley face to show they understand something or a question mark to indicate that something confused them. Then they write a word, phrase, or sentence to show one thing they learned or what they didn't understand.

- Practice asking questions prior to listening to a speaker. Have students work with partners. Pose a question about the topic and have one student give a simple answer, and then have the partner continue to answer the question by adding details and elaboration. For example, you might ask them, "What is a mayor?" One student might simply say, "She runs the town." The second student would need to probe further with follow-up details; for example, "The mayor is voted to her job; the mayor goes to the parade; the mayor helps make rules for the town." These facts in turn would generate more questions that drill down deeper, such as "Who is our mayor?" and "Where is the mayor's office?"

To help your English language learners, try this:

- Take special care to make sure your English language learners can differentiate between statements and questions. Then help them ask and answer questions and generate questions from basic statements that you're certain they understand well and/or are especially meaningful to their lives.

- Meet with students in a small group to go over what a speaker will be presenting so they can plan a few questions ahead of time. Then, meet with them after the speaker finishes so they can talk about additional questions they might have.

Developmental Debrief:

Students in grades K–2 are going to need a lot of practice asking and answering questions. Differentiating between statements and questions and asking questions relevant to a given situation are difficult skills for students to acquire. Therefore, begin slowly and give students opportunities to ask and answer meaningful and authentic questions throughout the day.

Notes

Academic Vocabulary: Key Words and Phrases

Evaluate: In this instance, evaluate means to judge the credibility of a speaker and/or the information he or she presents.

Evidence: This consists of the data, details, or examples the speaker uses in the presentation; it also concerns how credible and accurate the information is.

Point of view: In this instance, point of view is the position a speaker takes in relation to the subject. A speaker may be representing his or her own point of view or that of another person. Either way, the audience needs to consider the speaker's point of view, as it may reveal a bias about the subject and undermine the credibility of the information being presented.

Reasoning: This is the logic of the speaker as it relates to the ideas presented—basically, do the speaker's conclusions make sense based on the evidence given?

Rhetoric: This refers to the devices, techniques, or strategies a speaker uses to persuade or influence how the listener or audience thinks, acts, or feels about the topic being addressed.

Notes

Planning Page

Standard: _____

Purpose of Lesson/s:

Planning the Lesson/s	Questions to Ask

Differentiating Instruction	Thinking Beyond This Standard

The standards guide instruction; they do not dictate it. So *as you plan lessons remember you aren't teaching the standards, but instead are teaching students how to read, write, talk, and think through well-crafted lessons that draw from the pedagogy embedded within them. Engaging lessons often have several ELA standards within them and integrate reading, writing, speaking and listening, and language.*

Standard 4: Present information, findings, and supporting evidence such that listeners can follow the line of reasoning and the organization, development, and style are appropriate to task, purpose, and audience.

K Students describe familiar people, places, things, and events and, with prompting and support, provide additional detail.

1 Students describe people, places, things, and events with relevant details, expressing ideas and feelings clearly.

2 Students tell a story or recount an experience with appropriate facts and relevant, descriptive details, speaking audibly in coherent sentences.

What the **Student** Does

K **Gist:** Students describe familiar people, places, things, and events and, with prompting and support, provide additional detail.

They consider:

- What person am I speaking about? Or, What place? What thing? What event?
- What is my favorite, most important detail about it?
- What else do I want to say?
- What are some details I can share?

1 **Gist:** Students describe people, places, things, and events with relevant details, expressing ideas and feelings clearly.

They consider:

- What person am I speaking about? Or, What place? What thing? What event?
- What is (are) the most important thing(s) I want my listeners to know?
- What are some related details?
- Will my audience get a good picture of this person (place, thing, event) from what I say?

2 **Gist:** Students tell a story or recount an experience with appropriate facts and relevant, descriptive details, speaking audibly in coherent sentences.

They consider:

- What is my story or experience about?
- What are some facts and details that will help describe or explain my story or experience?
- Am I addressing who, what, when, where, and why to make myself clear?
- Am I using my five senses to help me recount fully?
- Am I using a clear and loud enough voice so that I can easily be heard?
- Do all my sentences go together in a way that makes sense to a listener?

Note: Although the questions listed above are too difficult for most young students to internalize and apply on their own, we share them to give teachers a detailed sense of what their students should be striving toward as learners. K–2 students may not be able to ask these questions of themselves independently, but teachers can use them as a jumping-off point for lesson content and as prompts and reminders to share with students. Over time and with instruction, students will be able to pose these questions on their own.

What the **Teacher** Does

To help students describe familiar people, places, things, and events, and then provide additional/ relevant details:

- Allow students to bring in objects from home for show-and-tell. Rehearse with the sharers before they begin, going over the types of information to share, such as why a person associated with the object is important (person), where and when the sharer got the object and what makes it special (thing), where the sharer went and what it was like (place), and something interesting, fun, or exciting that happened in the sharer's life and what it was like (event).

- As you read fiction, informational text, and poetry, point out how authors use the five senses (taste, touch, smell, hearing, and sight) and the five Ws (who, what, when, where, and why). Make a poster-size chart showing a left hand and a right hand, complete with five spread-apart fingers on each. On each left-hand finger write one of the five senses, and on each right-hand finger write one of the five Ws. Remind students to refer to this chart as they read and write.

- Work with students in groups of three to help them talk about a photo that relates to a content-area topic they have studied. Have them list words that might be helpful in their description to classmates. As each group stands to present their information, the presenter should have a copy of the words to remind him or her what to cover.

- During shared writing, select a memorable school event so that all students can draw on their recollections. Get across to them that making a recount interesting to someone who wasn't at the event requires well-chosen details. But more important, you have to know how you felt about the experience first, so your details support your "take." Was it funny? Sad? Exciting? Why?

To help students tell a story or recount an experience with appropriate facts and relevant, descriptive details:

- Model how to tell a story or recount an experience with special attention to the introduction, key details and events, and conclusion. As you do, record information in note form on a poster-size graphic organizer (see the online resources at resources.corwin.com/ literacycompanionk-2), in the introduction box, the details and events box (list these in chronological order), and the conclusion box. Then have students volunteer to tell or recount their stories. As they do, the other students record notes on their own personal graphic organizers while you also record notes on another large organizer. Eventually give this experience over to the students and allow them to record notes on their own. Gradually move them from including basic information to elaborating on what happened.

- Focus on lighthearted, funny events and have students plan their recount using a simple structure, like a problem/solution hook. You might give them the prompt "The Big, Funny Mess" and think aloud about a mishap, such as a puppy wreaking havoc, soda spraying all over and how they cleaned it up, or a recipe gone awry.

- With a group of students, spend several days reading and rereading a wordless book (of which you have several copies), such as Tomie dePaola's *Pancakes for Breakfast*, Jerry Pinkney's *The Lion and the Mouse*, or Alexandra Day's *Good Dog, Carl*, inviting students to say what they think is happening. Allow them to work with partners and rehearse the story so they can later present a section of it to the class. Divide the class into however many sections there are students in the group. Each group will be the audience for one speaker/group member. Prompt the "listeners" to follow the story, tell the speaker their favorite part and why it's their favorite, and ask questions about the story.

To have students speak clearly, audibly, and logically:

- Make sure that after students have decided on what information they want to share, they also spend time working on their delivery. For K–2 students, this involves rehearsing with you or a partner to make sure that they are speaking clearly and loudly enough. A first big step is to remind students to avoid holding their papers in front of their faces as they speak. Little by little, and with practice, they'll realize that *how* you say something is quite often as important as *what* you say.

- Help students prepare a choral reading of a favorite poem that relates to a topic they're studying. For example, when learning about animals, students might select poems from Georgia Heard's *Creatures of Earth, Sea, and Sky: Animal Poems*. For students learning about weather, poems from Lee Bennett Hopkins's *Weather: Poems for All Seasons* would work well.

- Make Readers Theater a regular activity. Children need opportunities to prepare and present readings to improve their articulation, expression, and fluency. A vast number of tips and scripts for Readers Theater are available online.

To help your English language learners, try this:

- Meet with students in each stage of the process to help them plan and practice sharing information and ideas with partners, giving feedback as they share. Provide sentence starters to help them build a speech. For example, "My topic is _____. An important idea about this is _____ because _____. And another important idea is _____." Build on these starters depending on how fluent the students are in articulating in English.

- Have your English language learners work in a group and write about a text or topic they will later discuss together or in small groups. Allow students who might be uncomfortable speaking extemporaneously to read what they have written instead of speak it. Partner your English language learners with English language speakers before you ask them to read their responses out loud so they can work through any vocabulary or structural problems of which the English language learners may be unaware.

Developmental Debrief:

Young students often find it difficult to elaborate on information they want to express, whether orally or in writing. Therefore, we need to help supply the words. Sitting alongside students and having them rehearse their presentations will allow you to give feedback and help them fill in some missing pieces with appropriate and relevant details, vocabulary, and expressions.

Notes

Academic Vocabulary: Key Words and Phrases

Appropriate to the task, purpose, and audience: How one organizes, develops, and presents information varies depending on the objective, the actual purpose of the presentation, and the audience to whom one is speaking.

Findings: These are conclusions drawn from observations, investigations, experiments, or inquiries about questions or problems.

Line of reasoning: The speaker links a series of ideas in some meaningful and clear way as he or she speaks. This sort of connect-the-dots approach shows why the speaker thinks as he or she does and/or how the speaker arrived at a particular conclusion or argument.

Organization: An appropriate and effective structure is vital to a presentation's success. Whether the speaker's ideas are organized to show cause/effect or problem solution, are ordered from least to most important, or are arranged chronologically, a clear organizing structure is required so listeners can hear and process the ideas presented.

Present: A person who is merely *speaking* may be standing in front of an audience telling a story, explaining what a text means, or discussing what he or she learned from an experience. A person who is *presenting* has a more specific purpose, such as to persuade the audience to think or act in a certain way. To achieve this outcome, the presenter often uses evidence from a range of established sources and delivers the material using different media and/or software such as Keynote or PowerPoint.

Relevant, descriptive details: Students choose details that relate to the topic and provide description.

Speaking audibly in coherent sentences: This means that the speaker speaks loudly enough and clearly enough for the audience to more easily understand the ideas and information he or she is presenting and in a way that is pleasing to listeners. The information and ideas also need to be conveyed in sentences that are logical in and of themselves and that move reasonably from one idea to the next.

Notes

Planning Page

Standard: _____

Purpose of Lesson/s:

Planning the Lesson/s	Questions to Ask

Differentiating Instruction	Thinking Beyond This Standard

The standards guide instruction; they do not dictate it. So as you plan lessons remember you aren't teaching the standards, but instead are teaching students how to read, write, talk, and think through well-crafted lessons that draw from the pedagogy embedded within them. Engaging lessons often have several ELA standards within them and integrate reading, writing, speaking and listening, and language.

Standard 5: Make strategic use of digital media and visual displays of data to express information and enhance understanding of presentations.

K Students add drawings or other visual displays to descriptions as desired to provide additional detail.

1 Students add drawings or other visual displays to descriptions when appropriate to clarify ideas, thoughts, and feelings.

2 Students create audio recordings of stories or poems, and add drawings or other visual displays to stories or recounts of experiences when appropriate to clarify ideas, thoughts, and feelings.

What the **Student** Does

K **Gist:** Students add drawings or other visual displays to descriptions as desired to provide additional detail.

They consider:

- What can I draw that will help my audience better understand my presentation?
- Is there a photo or illustration from the Internet or a book I might include?
- What chart can I/we create that would add to the text?

1 **Gist:** Students add drawings or other visual displays to descriptions when appropriate to clarify ideas, thoughts, and feelings.

They consider:

- What can I draw that will make my presentation clearer?
- What details can I add to my drawing to give even more information?
- Is there a photo or illustration from the Internet or a book I might include?
- What chart can I/we create that would add to the text?

2 **Gist:** Students create audio recordings of stories or poems, and add drawings or other visual displays to stories or recounts of experiences when appropriate to clarify ideas, thoughts, and feelings.

They consider:

- How can I recite or retell this story/poem to reflect what the author intends?
- How can I read with expression and a pace that is right for the piece?
- What can I draw that will help my audience understand the story or poem?
- What details can I add to the picture to help make the message clearer?
- If I record the piece, are there sound effects I want to use to make my message clearer?

Note: Although the questions listed above are too difficult for most young students to internalize and apply on their own, we share them to give teachers a detailed sense of what their students should be striving toward as learners. K–2 students may not be able to ask these questions of themselves independently, but teachers can use them as a jumping-off point for lesson content and as prompts and reminders to share with students. Over time and with instruction, students will be able to pose these questions on their own.

What the **Teacher** Does

To help students add drawings or other visual displays to descriptions, stories, and recounts to provide additional detail and to clarify ideas, thoughts, and feelings:

- Model writing a short passage about a science or social concept with which students are familiar. Discuss with students what picture or visual might go with the text—that is, an image that would add more detail than just the text alone. Let students work alone or with partners on drawings of their own. Gather the students again to share and discuss the pictures they drew to accompany the text.

- Have students write short passages of their own—perhaps pieces that connect to a science or social studies topic, such as longhouses if they are learning about Eastern Woodland Indians. Have them read over their passages and identify their main messages and then illustrate their work in a way that best helps readers visualize the facts. Students can share their texts and visual images with partners or the class and explain how they go together.

- Gather a file of images from the Internet and from books that show contrast in the ways a subject can be portrayed. Elicit from students why one is more powerful than another. For example, a photograph of a whale far off in the ocean is going to clarify the subject and engage viewers less than a close-up of a whale blowing its spout, as will a cartoonish take on a honeybee versus a photo of bees in a honeycomb. The gist: you want students to understand that details, color, and clarity count.

- Guide students to make content-area museum displays as described in Ann Marie Corgill's *Of Primary Importance: What's Essential in Teaching Young Writers*. Although (and thankfully) regularly assigning students to make dioramas in response to reading is a thing of the past, this updated version, assigned sparingly in support of a content-area topic students are studying, helps blend visual representations with texts. Here students create museum displays out of shoe or craft boxes to characterize what one might see when visiting a museum. A study of animal habitats might lead students to make a display of ducks living in a pond or camels living in a desert, complete with a written plaque describing the habitat alongside it.

To help students hone their fluent and expressive reading skills to later create audio recordings of stories or poems:

- Provide models of strong, fluent reading. Read aloud often to students from a variety of materials and have them listen to audio recordings of stories and poems read by professional readers. Prompt them to consider what they liked about how a story or poem was read and explain how reading with expression helps listeners visualize what the author wants us to see.

- As part of modeling fluent and expressive reading, help students understand why you made particular read-aloud decisions. Put a copy of the text up on a whiteboard and point out which words, line breaks, and punctuation marks signaled you to read the text as you did.

- Provide choral reading experiences in which students collaborate on how to present a poem or short piece of prose to an audience effectively. Push students to explain their decisions. Check to make sure students can comprehend the text, as lack of understanding leads to difficulty with expressive reading. Sure, students can memorize and mimic our fluent reading, but it's best to provide texts they genuinely understand. Short, easy-to-learn selections often work best for choral reading, as do texts with rhyme, rhythm, and repeated phrases.

- Confer with students and listen to them read, providing specific feedback on what they do well and what needs improvement. When you sit alongside a student, point directly to the specific words and phrases in the text that she has read with appropriate inflection/pronunciation and those parts she needs to try again. Model by reading aloud how you would approach the text.

- Have students practice their oral reading frequently—for fluency, pace, and expression. This can be through partner reading or by having students read to buddies in a different grade or to volunteers in the classroom. Remember to keep attention to meaning front and center.

To help students create audio recordings of stories or poems:

- Help students choose appropriate stories or poems to record. Short, inviting texts such as Mary Ann Hoberman's *You Read to Me, I'll Read to You: Very Short Fables to Read Together* allow two students to work together to craft a presentation.

- Practice using websites and technology to record on. Have students listen to their recordings and rerecord if necessary. Share these recordings with larger audiences so that students receive feedback.

- Explore sound effects as ways to enhance presentations. Use bits of music and/or nature sounds (all available online), or have students devise effects that go with their stories or poems, à la old radio programs.

To help your English language learners, try this:

- When doing whole-class choral reading and recordings, meet with students ahead of time to make sure they can read the words accurately and well so that they don't stumble disproportionately to the rest of the class.

- Have your English language learners give presentations using pictures, realia, websites (Google Earth, for example), and other media. Allow them to use the media to share about their topic and reduce the amount of orally presented information.

Developmental Debrief:

In kindergarten and first grade, students most often draw before they write, or at least there's interplay between the illustrations and the words. Most kindergarten students start with drawings and then (and often only when prompted) add words. They may go back and forth between drawing and writing until they're done. In first grade some students begin by drawing, while others start with the words. It's important that in these early grades we don't discourage students from drawing, as this is a way for them to rehearse and think through what they may write and to complement and extend their written ideas.

Notes

Academic Vocabulary: Key Words and Phrases

Digital media: This includes presentation software applications such as PowerPoint, Keynote, and Google Presentation. It also refers to digital images, screen captures of online material, and stand-alone or embedded video, as well as audio and mixed media formats.

Enhance understanding: This refers to the use of all available media and methods—images, audio, multimedia, words, and graphs—in ways that make the abstract more concrete, more visual, more comprehensible. Through charts, images, graphs, and video, speakers illustrate the processes, concepts, or procedures they are discussing and help the audience *see* what they are saying.

Express information: This means to put forth, convey, or relate data, ideas, details, and content to the audience in the clearest way possible.

Visual displays to clarify information: These are tables, charts, graphs, and other infographics used to visually explain or otherwise convey an idea, especially one that is complicated or abstract.

Notes

Planning Page

Standard: _____

<table>
<tr><td colspan="2">Purpose of Lesson/s:

</td></tr>
<tr><td>Planning the Lesson/s</td><td>Questions to Ask</td></tr>
<tr><td>

</td><td></td></tr>
<tr><td>Differentiating Instruction</td><td>Thinking Beyond This Standard</td></tr>
<tr><td>

</td><td></td></tr>
</table>

The standards guide instruction; they do not dictate it. So as you plan lessons remember you aren't teaching the standards, but instead are teaching students how to read, write, talk, and think through well-crafted lessons that draw from the pedagogy embedded within them. Engaging lessons often have several ELA standards within them and integrate reading, writing, speaking and listening, and language.

Standard 6: Adapt speech to a variety of contexts and communicative tasks, demonstrating command of formal English when indicated or appropriate.

K Students speak audibly and express thoughts, feelings, and ideas clearly.

1 Students produce complete sentences when appropriate to task and situation. (See grade 1 Language standards 1 and 3 for specific expectations.)

2 Students produce complete sentences when appropriate to task and situation in order to provide requested detail or clarification. (See grade 2 Language standards 1 and 3 for specific expectations.)

What the **Student** Does

K **Gist:** Students speak audibly and express thoughts, feelings, and ideas clearly.

They consider:

- Am I speaking loudly enough to be heard (but not shouting)?
- Am I speaking clearly enough to be understood?

1 **Gist:** Students speak in complete sentences when appropriate to the task and situation.

They consider:

- What is my task?
- What am I trying to say or express?
- Am I using complete sentences?

2 **Gist:** Students speak in complete sentences when appropriate to the task and situation.

They consider:

- What is my task? Who is my audience?
- What am I trying to say or express?
- Am I using complete sentences?

Note: Although the questions listed above are too difficult for most young students to internalize and apply on their own, we share them to give teachers a detailed sense of what their students should be striving toward as learners. K–2 students may not be able to ask these questions of themselves independently, but teachers can use them as a jumping-off point for lesson content and as prompts and reminders to share with students. Over time and with instruction, students will be able to pose these questions on their own.

What the **Teacher** Does

To help students speak audibly and express thoughts, feelings, and ideas clearly:

- Speak clearly when talking with students. They need to hear what good articulation sounds like so they can emulate it.

- Give students authentic opportunities to speak throughout the day. Have them sit in a circle during meeting time or during reading or writing share time rather than audience-style facing you. This allows them to note facial cues or other indications that their audience understands them—or doesn't.

- Help students think about and/or rehearse what they want to say before speaking. Doing so will help their ideas come out more clearly. It often helps for students to have a prop to help them recall, such as a drawing, a note card with a couple of key words written down, or an artifact.

- Guide students to hold the paper or the book from which they're reading at waist or chest level. Remind them that blocking their faces makes it more difficult for the audience to hear them.

- Good posture often helps students speak more audibly. Insist that students stand or sit up straight and tall when addressing classmates or another audience.

- Remind students not to rush through their presentations, but rather take the time they need to deliver their messages effectively.

To help students speak in complete sentences when appropriate to the task and situation:

- Help students differentiate statements that are complete sentences and those that are not by sorting complete and incomplete sentences into categories.

- Teach students about linking words and phrases—such as *because*, *also*, and *then*—that can make their sentences more complete and complex.

- Provide students with opportunities to play sentence-building games such as sentence dominoes or online games such as Simple Sentences.

- Together with students, compile a list of questions that will help them find out things they'd like to know about one another, such as "Who is your favorite author?" and "What's your favorite sport?" Write each question on a separate 5-by-8-inch note card, and then have students select a card and answer the question it asks in a complete sentence. Encourage students to elaborate on the information they give. For example, if a student states simply, "My favorite sport is soccer," and then stops, ask the student to explain why soccer is her favorite or to give an example of a memorable event that happened at one of her games. Prompt students with words like *because* that help them make their answers more elaborate, complete, and complex.

- Play "Who? Did What?" Divide a large chart into two columns (with the left column narrower than the right). At the top of the left column write "Who?" and at the top of the right column write "Did What?" Have students list people or animals in the left column and then, in the right column, tell what they did. Return to this chart frequently to give students additional practice.

- Put students in authentic situations where they have to answer questions their classmates ask them. This might be after they've shared written pieces or at the end of reading time as they talk about books they enjoyed reading.

- Provide opportunities for students to answer questions orally. When students answer questions, prompt them to add more information by asking for examples, reasons to support their thinking, and so on.

To help your English language learners, try this:

- Spend time with students to help them think about what they want to say. Write down two or three sentences that express their ideas. Use sentence frames to help them practice. Allow them to read their sentences rather than speak them.

Developmental Debrief:

The ability to speak clearly is a skill that needs to be developed over time, and one that will have a great impact on a student's effectiveness in school and beyond. Meet with students' families to discuss the importance of oral language development and give them ideas of what they can do at home to help. For starters, families may simply need to recognize how important it is to routinely engage in conversations with their children and how easily they can accomplish this when they plan to do things together, such as preparing a meal or reading a book. In addition, families can borrow audiobooks from the library so that their children can listen to professional readers.

Notes

Academic Vocabulary: Key Words and Phrases

Adapt speech: This means to change the language, style of delivery, tone, or format of the presentation or speech as needed to suit the audience, purpose, and occasion.

Appropriate: Each presentation or talk has its own unique audience, and one must know which words, tone, and style to use when speaking on different occasions. What is appropriate in one situation, such as informal, colloquial speech to a group of people you know, may be inappropriate, or even offensive, at another time, when the occasion is formal and the audience has completely different expectations.

Command of formal English: This standard places a clear and consistent emphasis on a command of formal English—grammatically correct, clearly enunciated words delivered with good eye contact—as an essential ingredient in college or career success.

Communicative tasks: These include contributing to a discussion group in class, interviewing a guest who is visiting the classroom, asking questions when on a field trip, and presenting a topic to a group of students or families of classmates. Increasingly, and as students move up in the grades, these tasks and their related contexts will include, for example, conferring with people through online audio and video (or chat) platforms in order to collaborate, confer, and communicate.

Contexts: This refers to the place as much as to the purpose of any speaking event; examples include speaking in class, online, in small and larger groups, and to the full class or larger groups.

Indicated: One is sometimes asked to talk in a specific way to a group on a topic or occasion; thus one looks to the prompt, directions, adviser, teacher, or other source for indications about how to speak on a given occasion to a particular audience about a particular topic. In the event that it is not indicated, one must learn to determine for oneself what is the most appropriate way to speak in a given situation.

Speak audibly: This means to speak loudly enough to be heard but not so loudly that listeners feel they're being shouted at or that the message is in any way compromised.

Notes

Planning Page

Standard: _____

Purpose of Lesson/s:

Planning the Lesson/s	Questions to Ask

Differentiating Instruction	Thinking Beyond This Standard

The standards guide instruction; they do not dictate it. So as you plan lessons remember you aren't teaching the standards, but instead are teaching students how to read, write, talk, and think through well-crafted lessons that draw from the pedagogy embedded within them. Engaging lessons often have several ELA standards within them and integrate reading, writing, speaking and listening, and language.

The Common Core State Standards

Language

College and Career Readiness Anchor Standards for
Language K–12

Source:
Common Core
State Standards

The K–2 language standards outlined on the following pages define what students should understand and be able to do by the end of each grade. Here on this page we present the College and Career Readiness (CCR) anchor standards for K–12 so you can see how students in K–2 work toward the same goals as high school seniors: it's a universal, K–12 vision. The CCR anchor standards and the grade-specific standards correspond to one another by number (1–6). They are necessary complements, the former providing broad standards, the latter providing additional specificity. Together, they define the skills and understandings that all students must eventually demonstrate.

Conventions of Standard English

1. Demonstrate command of the conventions of standard English grammar and usage when writing or speaking.
2. Demonstrate command of the conventions of standard English capitalization, punctuation, and spelling when writing.

Knowledge of Language

3. Apply knowledge of language to understand how language functions in different contexts, to make effective choices for meaning or style, and to comprehend more fully when reading or listening.

Vocabulary Acquisition and Use

4. Determine or clarify the meaning of unknown and multiple-meaning words and phrases by using context clues, analyzing meaningful word parts, and consulting general and specialized reference materials, as appropriate.
5. Demonstrate understanding of figurative language, word relationships, and nuances in word meanings.
6. Acquire and use accurately a range of general academic and domain-specific words and phrases sufficient for reading, writing, speaking, and listening at the college and career readiness level; demonstrate independence in gathering vocabulary knowledge when encountering an unknown term important to comprehension or expression.

Note on Range and Content of Student Language Use

To build a foundation for college and career readiness in language, students must gain control over many conventions of standard English grammar, usage, and mechanics as well as learn other ways to use language to convey meaning effectively. They must also be able to determine or clarify the meaning of grade-appropriate words encountered through listening, reading, and media use; come to appreciate that words have nonliteral meanings, shadings of meaning, and relationships to other words; and expand their vocabulary in the course of studying content. The inclusion of Language standards in their own strand should not be taken as an indication that skills related to conventions, effective language use, and vocabulary are unimportant to reading, writing, speaking, and listening; indeed, they are inseparable from such contexts.

Source: Copyright © 2010. National Governors Association Center for Best Practices and Council of Chief State School Officers. All rights reserved.

College and Career Readiness Anchor Standards for

Language

The CCR anchor standards are the same for K–12. The guiding principle here is that the core language skills should not change as students advance; rather, the level at which students learn and can perform these skills should increase in complexity as they move from one grade to the next. However, for grades K–2, we have to recognize that the standards were back mapped from the secondary level—that is, the authors envisioned what college students need and then wrote standards, working their way down the grades. Thus, as you use this book remember that children in K–2 can't just "jump over" developmental milestones in an ambitious attempt to achieve an anchor standard. There are certain life and learning experiences they need to have, and certain concepts they need to learn, before they are capable of handling many complex academic skills in a meaningful way. The anchor standards nonetheless are goalposts to work toward. As you read the "gist" of the standards below, remember they represent what our K–2 students will *grow into* during each year and deepen later in elementary, middle, and high school. The journey starts in K–2!

Conventions of Standard English

Simply put, students should know and use the proper forms of English—spelling, grammar, usage, and conventions—when speaking or writing for public purposes or audiences such as at work or school. The emphasis here is on the crucial role that such attention to correctness plays in college and the workplace, where first impressions matter and the smallest error can cost customers or money. This becomes all the more important in light of social media trends, as businesses communicate more and more online, through social media, chat, and text messages.

Knowledge of Language

This standard not only recognizes the range of functions language plays in creating style, voice, and meaning but also emphasizes the importance of diction, syntax, and other factors as they relate to the writer's or speaker's ethos and general effect on the audience in a given context. One must, in other words, give serious thought to which words, which order, for which audience, and which purpose if one is to convey one's meaning with maximum effect.

Vocabulary Acquisition and Use

Vocabulary, so instrumental in reading, writing, and speaking/listening, is divided into several domains in these standards. First are those words that are unknown or have many possible meanings, the proper ones determined by the occasion or context in which they are used. An essential part of this standard involves using general and specialized reference materials in print or online to determine the etymology of words and learn more about their different meanings and usages. In addition to these words, students add to their word banks the ways in which language is used figuratively, as well as how word relationships suggest associations, connotations, or nuances depending on how they are used. Finally, students should pay most of their attention to those words that will help them understand or complete their assignments for school; this means learning those domain-specific words and phrases unique to each discipline that students routinely encounter when they read, write, speak, or listen. Over time, students should actively gather and work to grow their knowledge of and ability to use the words and phrases in each subject area to accommodate the increasing complexity of the texts and tasks they face at each subsequent grade level.

Source: Adapted from Jim Burke, *The Common Core Companion: The Standards Decoded, Grades 6–8* (Thousand Oaks, CA: Corwin, 2013).

Standard 1: Demonstrate command of the conventions of standard English grammar and usage when writing or speaking.

K Students demonstrate command of the conventions of standard English grammar and usage when writing or speaking.

    a. Print many upper- and lowercase letters.
    b. Use frequently occurring nouns and verbs.
    c. Form regular plural nouns orally by adding /s/ or /es/ (e.g., *dog, dogs*; *wish, wishes*).
    d. Understand and use question words (interrogatives) (e.g., *who, what, where, when, why, how*).
    e. Use the most frequently occurring prepositions (e.g., *to, from, in, out, on, off, for, of, by, with*).
    f. Produce and expand complete sentences in shared language activities.

1 Students demonstrate command of the conventions of standard English grammar and usage when writing or speaking.

    a. Print all upper- and lowercase letters.
    b. Use common, proper, and possessive nouns.
    c. Use singular and plural nouns with matching verbs in basic sentences (e.g., *He hops*; *We hop*).
    d. Use personal, possessive, and indefinite pronouns (e.g., *I, me, my*; *they, them, their*; *anyone, everything*).
    e. Use verbs to convey a sense of past, present, and future (e.g., *Yesterday I walked home*; *Today I walk home*; *Tomorrow I will walk home*).
    f. Use frequently occurring adjectives.
    g. Use frequently occurring conjunctions (e.g., *and, but, or, so, because*).
    h. Use determiners (e.g., articles, demonstratives).
    i. Use frequently occurring prepositions (e.g., *during, beyond, toward*).
    j. Produce and expand complete simple and compound declarative, interrogative, imperative, and exclamatory sentences in response to prompts.

2 Students demonstrate command of the conventions of standard English grammar and usage when writing or speaking.

    a. Use collective nouns (e.g., *group*).
    b. Form and use frequently occurring irregular plural nouns (e.g., *feet, children, teeth, mice, fish*).
    c. Use reflexive pronouns (e.g., *myself, ourselves*).
    d. Form and use the past tense of frequently occurring irregular verbs (e.g., *sat, hid, told*).
    e. Use adjectives and adverbs, and choose between them depending on what is to be modified.
    f. Produce, expand, and rearrange complete simple and compound sentences (e.g., *The boy watched the movie*; *The little boy watched the movie*; *The action movie was watched by the little boy*).

What the **Student** Does

K **Gist:** Students demonstrate command of the conventions of standard English grammar and usage when writing or speaking.

They consider:

- Do I print many upper- and lowercase letters?
- Do I use common, proper, and possessive nouns?
- Do I form regular plural nouns orally by adding /s/ or /es/ (*dog, dogs; wish, wishes*)?
- Do I understand and use question words (interrogatives) (e.g., *who, what, where, when, why, how*)?
- Do I use the most frequently occurring prepositions (e.g., *to, from, in, out, on, off, for, of, by, with*)?
- Do I produce and expand complete sentences in shared language activities?

1 **Gist:** Students demonstrate command of the conventions of standard English grammar and usage when writing or speaking.

They consider:

- Do I know how to print all upper- and lowercase letters? Do I apply this knowledge when I write?
- Do I use common, proper, and possessive nouns when I speak and write?
- Do I use singular and plural nouns with matching verbs in basic sentences (e.g., *He hops; We hop*)?
- Do I use personal, possessive, and indefinite pronouns (e.g., *I, me, my; they, them, their; anyone, everything*)?
- Do I use verbs to convey a sense of past, present, and future (e.g., *Yesterday I walked home; Today I walk home; Tomorrow I will walk home*)?
- Do I use frequently occurring adjectives?
- Do I use frequently occurring conjunctions (e.g., *and, but, or, so, because*)?
- Do I use determiners (e.g., articles, demonstratives)?
- Do I use frequently occurring prepositions (e.g., *during, beyond, toward*)?
- Do I produce and expand complete simple and compound declarative, interrogative, imperative, and exclamatory sentences in response to prompts?

2 **Gist:** Students demonstrate command of the conventions of standard English grammar and usage when writing or speaking.

They consider:

- Do I use collective nouns (e.g., *group*)?
- Do I form and use frequently occurring irregular plural nouns (e.g., *feet, children, teeth, mice, fish*)?
- Do I use reflexive pronouns (e.g., *myself, ourselves*)?
- Do I form and use the past tense of frequently occurring irregular verbs (e.g., *sat, hid, told*)?
- Do I use adjectives and adverbs, and choose between them depending on what is to be modified?
- Do I produce, expand, and rearrange complete simple and compound sentences (e.g., *The boy watched the movie; The little boy watched the movie; The action movie was watched by the little boy*)?

Note: Although the questions listed above are too difficult for most young students to internalize and apply on their own, we share them to give teachers a detailed sense of what their students should be striving toward as learners. K–2 students may not be able to ask these questions of themselves independently, but teachers can use them as a jumping-off point for lesson content and as prompts and reminders to share with students. Over time and with instruction, students will be able to pose these questions on their own.

What the **Teacher** Does

To help students demonstrate command of the conventions of standard English grammar and usage when writing or speaking:

- Cultivate an environment of respect and wonder relative to language, one that invites students into language instead of inspiring fear of it. You can do this by bringing in real-world writing that captures the power of language to entertain us, engage us, shape our thinking, and convey ideas.

- Model the virtue of correctness when addressing students orally and in writing. Every handout, every class e-mail, and every homework assignment should be an exemplar of clarity and correctness.

- Expose students daily to an array of texts in which language is used clearly and correctly. Put some of these texts on a chart or whiteboard so that students can see how published authors use grammar and conventions to their best effect. It's also fun to expose students to texts that drive home the importance of grammatical conventions in a playful and lighthearted way, as in Robin Pulver's *Nouns and Verbs Have a Field Day*.

- Consider these points when deciding or following through on a model for teaching grammar conventions:

  1. Keep a list of conventions you need to teach by the end of the year close at hand, and refer to it when planning lessons and at the start of each day.

  2. Recognize that one or two isolated lessons on any given convention will not lead to mastery. Look for multiple opportunities within each day and week to teach and reinforce language conventions in authentic, contextually sound ways.

  3. Recognize that language conventions are learned best when students experience them initially within the context of a text you're reading with them, so that they see firsthand their role in conveying meaning. Teach the conventions explicitly, and then design multiple lessons to reinforce or elaborate on the conventions.

  4. Give students opportunities to apply what they're learning about language conventions to their reading and written pieces. Acknowledge that neither explicit instruction nor independent practice alone does the job—students need both.

  5. If you're required to follow a specific language program or curriculum, also try to provide students with holistic and meaningful exposures to language conventions so that they recognize the relationship between the convention (the part) and the entire story, poem, passage, or other piece of writing (the whole).

- Look for evidence as you confer with students or observe them that they're transferring the language conventions you're teaching into their written and oral communication, and recognize that it will take multiple exposures over time and a great many opportunities for them to apply the conventions on their own. Teach and reteach as often as necessary.

- Provide students access to online grammar games that allow them to practice targeted language conventions.

- Read aloud books that focus on specific language conventions. For example, the Word Fun series by Michael Dahl (e.g., *If You Were a Noun, If You Were an Adjective*) provides enjoyable introductions to a range of grammar conventions.

To help your English language learners, try this:

- Confer regularly with students on their writing to both demonstrate the proper use of language conventions and assess how they're doing. Remember that students learning English will acquire the conventions at their own pace, and not in any given order that you teach them. However, consistent conferring about conventions will support students while they acquire English. Be sure to teach only one convention at a time, and then meet again to follow up.

Developmental Debrief:

Although this standard states that students will demonstrate a "command of the conventions" (in relation to those listed by grade), let's consider what this actually means for grades K–2. Realistically, during the early stages of students' development they will need to go through extended periods of making *approximations* in their independent use of language conventions before they can actually control those conventions in the strict sense of the word. View this as a necessary step in the right direction and a sign of progress, and not as a deficit that needs to be fixed immediately. As you teach and reteach conventions and as students have opportunities to incorporate these into their independent work, their approximations will more closely reflect standard English language conventions.

Notes

Academic Vocabulary: Key Words and Phrases

Adjectives: These are words that modify or describe a person or thing in a sentence. An adjective describes a noun and provides more information about the object signified.

Adverbs: These are words that usually modify verbs, but they can also modify adjectives or other adverbs. They change or qualify the meaning of these parts of speech. Adverbs often answer questions such as *how? in what way? when? where?* and *to what extent?*

Collective nouns: These are words that refer to collections of persons or things taken as a whole (*group, class*).

Common, proper, and possessive nouns: Common nouns are words that name persons, places, or things. Proper nouns refer to specific persons, places, or things and are capitalized (*Statue of Liberty, Paul*). Possessive nouns are used to show possession (*baby's* bottle or *dog's* collar).

Conjunctions: These are words that join together sentences, clauses, phrases, or words (*and, but, or, so, because*).

Conventions: These are the rules or norms of the English language that dictate generally accepted usage—that is, what's normal or typical.

Declarative, interrogative, imperative, and exclamatory sentences: Declarative sentences form statements. Interrogative sentences form questions. Imperative sentences make commands or requests. Exclamatory sentences show strong feelings or emotions.

Determiners: These are words that modify nouns, such as articles (*a, an, the*) and demonstratives, which are nouns, pronouns, or adjectives that point out specific persons or things (*this, that, them, those*).

Grammar: This is the study of words and their component parts and how they combine to form sentences; it encompasses the structural relationships in language that contribute to their meaning.

Irregular plural nouns: These are plural nouns that do not use the regular plural ending of -*s* or -*es* (e.g., *children, feet, women*).

Irregular verbs: These are verbs whose past tense and past participle are not formed by adding -*ed*, -*d*, or -*t* to the present tense.

Nouns: Simply put, nouns are words used to name persons, places, things, animals, or abstract ideas.

Personal, possessive, and indefinite pronouns: Personal pronouns refer to particular persons, places, or things. Possessive pronouns show ownership (*his, hers, theirs*). Indefinite pronouns are not specific in regard to which nouns they replace (*anyone, someone, few*).

Prepositions: These are words that link nouns, pronouns, and phrases to other words in a sentence.

Pronouns: These are words that can substitute for nouns (*I, she, they*).

Question words (interrogatives): These are words that typically indicate that a question is being asked (*who, what, where, when, why,* and *how*).

Reflexive pronouns: These are pronouns that are preceded by the nouns, adjectives, adverbs, or pronouns to which they refer (their antecedents) within clauses. Such a pronoun refers to the person or thing doing the action; for example, He bought *himself* a glass of milk.

Regular plural nouns: These are plural nouns that are made through the addition of -*s* or -*es* to the base words, sometimes with a few modifications to the base word, such as *wolf/wolves* and *fly/flies*.

Sentences: These are syntactical units, each of which conveys a complete thought or idea, that is, a statement, question, command, or wish.

Shared language activity: This refers to any language experience that students (or students and their teacher) engage in collectively.

Simple and compound sentences: Simple sentences (described by their structure) have one independent clause and no dependent clause. Compound sentences (also described by their structure) have two or more independent clauses and no dependent clause; the independent clauses can be joined by a conjunction (*for, and, nor, but, or, yet, so*), comma, or semicolon.

Singular and plural nouns with matching verbs: This refers to the "singularness" and "pluralness" of nouns and verbs, and whether or not they're in agreement. For example, *he* is a singular noun and *sits* is a singular verb, so they agree and go together ("he sits"); *we* is plural and *sit* is plural, so they're in agreement and go together ("we sit"). *He*, a singular noun, and *sit*, a plural verb, do not match, and using them together would be incorrect.

Usage: This refers to how one uses language—and if particular uses are permitted or approved.

Verbs: These are words that name actions or states of being; they change form to indicate tense, number, voice, or mood.

Planning Page

Standard: _____

Purpose of Lesson/s:

Planning the Lesson/s	Questions to Ask

Differentiating Instruction	Thinking Beyond This Standard

The standards guide instruction; they do not dictate it. *So as you plan lessons remember you aren't teaching the standards, but instead are teaching students how to read, write, talk, and think through well-crafted lessons that draw from the pedagogy embedded within them. Engaging lessons often have several ELA standards within them and integrate reading, writing, speaking and listening, and language.*

Standard 2: Demonstrate command of the conventions of standard English capitalization, punctuation, and spelling when writing.

K Students demonstrate command of the conventions of standard English capitalization, punctuation, and spelling when writing.

    a. Capitalize the first word in a sentence and the pronoun *I*.
    b. Recognize and name end punctuation.
    c. Write a letter or letters for most consonant and short-vowel sounds (phonemes).
    d. Spell simple words phonetically, drawing on knowledge of sound-letter relationships.

1 Students demonstrate command of the conventions of standard English capitalization, punctuation, and spelling when writing.

    a. Capitalize dates and names of people.
    b. Use end punctuation for sentences.
    c. Use commas in dates and to separate single words in a series.
    d. Use conventional spelling for words with common spelling patterns and for frequently occurring irregular words.
    e. Spell untaught words phonetically, drawing on phonemic awareness and spelling conventions.

2 Students demonstrate command of the conventions of standard English capitalization, punctuation, and spelling when writing.

    a. Capitalize holidays, product names, and geographic names.
    b. Use commas in greetings and closings of letters.
    c. Use an apostrophe to form contractions and frequently occurring possessives.
    d. Generalize learned spelling patterns when writing words (e.g., cage → badge; boy → boil).
    e. Consult reference materials, including beginning dictionaries, as needed to check and correct spellings.

What the **Student** Does

K **Gist:** Students demonstrate command of the conventions of standard English capitalization, punctuation, and spelling when writing.

They consider:

- Do I capitalize the first word in a sentence and the pronoun *I*?
- Do I recognize and name end punctuation?
- Do I write a letter or letters for most consonant and short-vowel sounds (phonemes)?
- Do I spell simple words phonetically, drawing on knowledge of sound-letter relationships?

1 **Gist:** Students demonstrate command of the conventions of standard English capitalization, punctuation, and spelling when writing.

They consider:

- Do I capitalize dates and names of people?
- Do I use end punctuation for sentences?
- Do I use commas in dates and to separate single words in a series?
- Do I use conventional spelling for words with common spelling patterns and for frequently occurring irregular words?
- Do I spell untaught words phonetically, drawing on phonemic awareness and spelling conventions?

2 **Gist:** Students demonstrate command of the conventions of standard English capitalization, punctuation, and spelling when writing.

They consider:

- Do I capitalize holidays, product names, and geographic names?
- Do I use commas in greetings and closings of letters?
- Do I use an apostrophe to form contractions and frequently occurring possessives?
- Do I generalize learned spelling patterns when writing words (e.g., cage → badge; boy → boil)?
- Do I consult reference materials, including beginning dictionaries, as needed to check and correct spellings?

Note: Although the questions listed above are too difficult for most young students to internalize and apply on their own, we share them to give teachers a detailed sense of what their students should be striving toward as learners. K–2 students may not be able to ask these questions of themselves independently, but teachers can use them as a jumping-off point for lesson content and as prompts and reminders to share with students. Over time and with instruction, students will be able to pose these questions on their own.

What the **Teacher** Does

To help students learn the conventions of standard English capitalization and punctuation when writing:

- Emphasize, reinforce, and teach students how to capitalize and punctuate within the context of your larger writing curriculum. For example, when doing shared writing, think aloud your punctuation and capitalization process, and when students contribute ideas, make checking and discussing punctuation and capitalization a natural thread of the conversation. Frame it as a matter of clarity rather than right and wrong so young students don't freeze up about writing.

- Share fiction and nonfiction picture books with students and examine how the authors use punctuation and capitalization to convey meaning. Think aloud about how all three—capitalization, punctuation, and meaning—go hand in hand.

- Have fun! Invent class charts of "Convention Bloopers" that students can contribute to when they spot mistakes; have parents be on the lookout for errors in newspapers, junk mail, and so on. As you read books aloud, chart what an upside-down world it would be if it was "mr. poppers penguin's" "Rosies Walk," and the like. Students will remember how to apply the conventions when they are taught in these multifaceted ways.

- Create a class editing checklist with students, rather than providing one that was created by classes of yesteryear. Make sure that you introduce only one convention at a time, and help students recognize that item's relationship to the written pieces they're producing. Provide students with personal-size copies of the checklist for their writing folders.

- Individualize your editing checklist by holding students accountable for the skills/items they can do somewhat consistently rather that insisting they assume responsibility for them all regardless of whether or not they're able. It makes little sense to hold a student accountable for beginning sentences with a capital letter and ending them with periods, exclamation points, and questions marks when that student does not yet have a working concept of what a sentence is. You will find that some students can easily apply all the checklist skills to their written pieces (and may need additional items to work on) while other students need more instruction and opportunities to practice just to master the basics.

- Occasionally create morning message-like texts that contain capitalization and punctuation errors so that students can try to identify and correct the mistakes.

- Engage students in interactive writing experiences in which each has a wipe-off board to use in trying to write a dictated sentence (or several) while one student attempts the same on chart paper. Students discuss how to correct any punctuation or capitalization errors and make adjustments to their own wipe-off board attempts.

- Teach capitalization and punctuation using this five-step approach: (1) As often as possible, have the convention you're teaching stem from what you've observed students doing or not doing in their writing. (2) Over the course of several days, provide direct instruction in the convention, explaining what it is, how it works, and why students should know and use it. (3) Create opportunities for students to practice using the targeted convention, which may be as simple as having them return to their seats and write. (4) Provide time at the end of writing for students to share how they've applied the convention you've taught. Here, access to a whiteboard comes in handy. (5) Recognize that you'll need to revisit this same convention many times throughout the course of the year to refresh students' understanding and ensure that they're applying it to their own writing.

- Confer with students on their writing, and, if necessary, reinforce a punctuation or capitalization skill you've taught directly. Through conferences and informal assessments, pull together groups of students who need more instruction on specific skills.

To help students learn the conventions of standard English spelling when writing:

- Provide students with abundant opportunities to write throughout the day, explaining that they should first concentrate on getting their ideas down on paper and then go back to correct the spelling of some words. This two-step process should not be interpreted to mean that "spelling doesn't count," but rather that it doesn't count so much *initially*.

- Help students learn basic sight words and remind them of why it's important to apply them to texts they write. (When students spell these high-frequency words incorrectly, the misspellings become habitual, and the habits are difficult to break.) Provide individual wordbooks that list these basic words (with spaces provided for students to write in additional words) or post words on the word wall for easy access.

- Target sight words by engaging students in the "look, say, cover, write, check" procedure, where you lead them to (1) *look* carefully at the focus word to notice letters, number of letters, and so on; (2) *say* the word slowly and carefully as they listen for the sounds (e.g., I hear *er* but see *or*); and (3) *cover* the word; then (4) call on a student to *write* the word on chart paper or a wipe-off board; and (5) uncover the word so students can *check* whether or not the word was spelled correctly.

- Recognize that for K–1 students, phonetic instruction and spelling instruction are largely one and the same. When students learn phonetic conventions, they are also learning to spell. For example, attention to rimes in phonics (e.g., the letters *–it* and *-op* that follow the initial consonant or consonant blend in one-syllable words, such as *sit* and *top*) also helps students expand the repertoire of words they can spell accurately and automatically.

To help your English language learners, try this:

- Engage students in interactive writing experiences in which each has a wipe-off board and they try their hands at writing a dictated sentence (or several) while one student attempts the same on chart paper. Do a think-aloud about how to correct any punctuation or capitalization errors, and have students make adjustments to their own wipe-off board attempts.

Developmental Debrief:

Although capitalization and punctuation are ultimately in the service of meaning and must be attended to, it's important not to focus on them too early or too stringently, because doing so may turn students off to writing for fear of making mistakes. Students need to experience the joy that comes from writing a silly story or sharing some really gross fact, such as how the horned lizard squirts blood from its eye onto an attacker. This is what motivates students to want to write more, and as they write more—and in conjunction with your instruction—they will learn the conventions.

Notes

Academic Vocabulary: Key Words and Phrases

Apostrophe: This is a punctuation mark used to stand in for omitted letters and to indicate possessives of nouns and pronouns.

Capitalization: This is the use of uppercase letters to signal where sentences begin and to indicate that words are proper nouns, such as in titles, people's names, and product or brand names. Learning the proper use of capitalization is especially important in light of the trend to ignore uppercasing in texting, a habit that is sometimes carried over into the workplace or classroom in the writing of more formal documents.

Commas: These are hardworking punctuation marks that are used for a variety of reasons. The basic tenet, however, is that commas are used to separate words or word groups.

Spelling conventions: These are the rules concerning the correct ways to spell words, the spellings one would find in a dictionary.

Irregular words: These are words that have uncommon letter-sound relationships and cannot be sounded out.

Phoneme: This is the smallest phonetic unit in a language that is capable of distinguishing the meaning of one word from another (*tip/tap* and *lake/bake*).

Phonemic awareness: This is the ability of students to hear, identify, and manipulate individual sounds in spoken words. It is based on a foundational understanding that spoken words are made up of individual sounds.

Phonetically (spell simple words): This means to sound words out, matching the sound with the letter or letters that make that sound.

Punctuation: This consists of all the marks—period, comma, colon, semicolon, dash, hyphen, quotation and question marks, parentheses, exclamation points, and others—that writers use to be clear, to make connections, and to create styles that suggest how their texts should be read. Punctuation is, as some say, what makes the music of the writing happen in ways similar to musical notations; it signals where, when, and how long to stop or speed up, where to pause, and what to emphasize.

Spelling patterns: These are common configurations of letters in several words with the same sound that are spelled in a particular way (*boy/toy/joy* and *name/game/blame*).

Notes

Planning Page

Standard: _____

Purpose of Lesson/s:

Planning the Lesson/s	Questions to Ask

Differentiating Instruction	Thinking Beyond This Standard

The standards guide instruction; they do not dictate it. So as you *plan lessons remember you aren't teaching the standards, but instead are teaching students how to read, write, talk, and think through well-crafted lessons that draw from the pedagogy embedded within them. Engaging lessons often have several ELA standards within them and integrate reading, writing, speaking and listening, and language.*

Standard 3: Apply knowledge of language to understand how language functions in different contexts, to make effective choices for meaning or style, and to comprehend more fully when reading or listening.

K (Begins in grade 2)

1 (Begins in grade 2)

2 Students use knowledge of language and its conventions when writing, speaking, reading, or listening.

    a. Compare formal and informal uses of English.

What the **Student** Does

K **Gist:** (Begins in grade 2)

1 **Gist:** (Begins in grade 2)

2 **Gist:** Students use knowledge of language and its conventions when writing, speaking, reading, or listening.

They consider:

- Do I understand the difference between formal and informal written and spoken language?
- Do I know whether to use formal or informal language when writing?
- Do I know whether to use formal or informal language when speaking?

Note: Although the questions listed above are too difficult for most young students to internalize and apply on their own, we share them to give teachers a detailed sense of what their students should be striving toward as learners. K–2 students may not be able to ask these questions of themselves independently, but teachers can use them as a jumping-off point for lesson content and as prompts and reminders to share with students. Over time and with instruction, students will be able to pose these questions on their own.

What the **Teacher** Does

To help students understand how formal and informal *written* language function and when to use each:

- First and foremost, expose students to a wide variety of texts in different styles, genres, and formats so students can learn from the authors the full range of formal and informal language choices they will need to make as writers. As you read these texts aloud, place sticky notes on pages that are good examples of formal and informal language to refer back to at a later time.

- Teach students some of the rules of formal written language and post them on chart paper for reference. These rules include avoiding the following: contractions, sentence fragments, clichés, and figurative language. Conversely, within the norms of informal written language, these kinds of things are acceptable.

- Select several anchor titles to familiarize students with informal written language. For example, you might use Dick King-Smith's *I Love Guinea Pigs*. After reading the book aloud several times for the wealth of information it so gently provides about caring for guinea pigs, go through it yet again and help students identify elements that contribute to its informal register. For example, the title itself hints that a friendly account will follow. Contractions are used throughout, and so are idioms ("as plain as the nose on your face") and colloquialisms ("they come in tons of different colors" and "as happy as can be").

- Show students examples of how poets digress from the conventions of grammar or language (poetic license) to create desired effects. For example, by simply putting one page of Bobbi Katz's *Pocket Poems* or one of Douglas Florian's poems (from *Insectlopedia* or another of his books) up on a whiteboard, you can expose your students to many of the ways poets alter language to fit their purposes.

- Expose students to texts that convey different *moods*— that is, the atmosphere that authors/illustrators create for readers through words and pictures. Reading a quiet, circular text like Philip C. Stead's *Bear Tells a Story* alongside Caralyn Buehner's energetic and bold *Superdog: The Heart of a Hero* will help students note the differences. Then have them examine the colors, words, and so on that are used to convey the story and mood. Get kids in the habit of saying, "That's a *happy* book" or "That's a *gentle* book," and then give some specific reasons why. Consistently advance the idea that authors use grammar, sentence structure, and vocabulary to set a mood.

- Have students find *patterns* in poems and in prose and help them understand that the author did this intentionally to achieve a certain informal effect. For example, Cynthia Rylant uses the pattern "When I was young in the mountains" to structure her picture book *When I Was Young in the Mountains* and the pattern "In November" for her text of the same title, which helps the reader have a cohesive experience of that chilly but cozy-inside month. Poets use repetition for a variety of reasons, such as to add rhythmic structure, to draw attention to a particular theme, or to make a point. This type of repetition works for informal written language but would not be found in formal language.

- Help students compose a personal e-mail to a friend, telling how a new toy broke after just hours of use. Then compose an e-mail to the toy company responsible for making and selling the toy. Compare the two letters for language, style, vocabulary, tone, and use of words. Repeat this activity several times with different topics (e.g., an e-mail to a friend about how sad it was to see photos in the news of oil-spill-slicked seabirds versus a letter to the oil company responsible for the spill; a thank-you note to a relative versus a thank-you letter to an organization that does charitable work). Chart what students notice about the two categories.

To help students understand how formal and informal *oral* language function:

- Help students differentiate between situations where formal English is more appropriate than informal English and vice versa. Using 3-by-5-inch notecards, write on each card one situation in which either formal or informal language is called for—for example, "phone a friend," "ask a teacher for help," "ask permission for a sleepover from a friend's mother," "share a joke," "order at a restaurant," "make a toast," or "introduce a guest at school." Have students select a card and decide whether formal or informal English would work best and role-play how it would sound.

- Audio record students talking to one another during a playful, informal time of day, such as during snack time or at recess. Allow students to listen to the recording several times, and then show on a whiteboard a transcript of a portion of the conversation. Read it with students and ask them to identify what makes the conversation informal and consider what they would have to do to make it more formal.

- Explain to students that colloquialisms are words or phrases used in informal conversation but not in formal speech or formal writing. Start a list of these, and add to the list throughout the year.

- Show students some informal sentences and ask them to reword them to make them formal. For example, they might reword "Can I go?" to "May I please be excused?"; "I'll catch up with you later" to "I will see you later"; "When are you com'n'?" to "What time are you going to arrive?" Do the same thing with formal sentences, rewording them to make them informal.

- Have students consider their audience to help them decide whether to use formal or informal English. For example, if you were speaking to a teacher, a neighbor, a classmate, a salesperson, a friend, or a friend's mom, would you use formal or informal English?

To help your English language learners, try this:

- Work with students on reading books of idioms. Marvin Terban's *In a Pickle, and Other Funny Idioms* contains many of the idioms students are likely to hear in conversations or encounter in texts, and each is illustrated and explained in kid-friendly terms. For example, the explanation of what "butterflies in the stomach" means begins like this: "A big spelling test is about to start. Or you're stepping up to bat. Or it's your turn to go onstage to sing. You're tense. You're scared. You feel a fluttery sensation in your stomach." Need we say more?

Developmental Debrief:

Second graders are on the cusp of a lifelong journey of knowing when to use formal and informal language, and you'll find that much of your teaching of this standard will center on helping them use correct grammar and conventions when writing. This demands some balancing on your part: while you want them to use correct, polite statements, commands, and questions when writing and speaking, you don't want to give the impression that writing can't sound conversational. The quality of voice in writing often comes from a writer who uses diction that is neither strictly "formal" nor "informal."

Notes

Academic Vocabulary: Key Words and Phrases

Conventions: These are the formal and informal agreed-upon ways of using both spoken and written language and refer to grammar and mechanics (spelling and punctuation).

Effective choices for meaning or style: Writers choose words and other elements such as punctuation, and then arrange them to serve some purpose (meaning) or effect (style).

Formal and informal uses of English: Formal English is more commonly used in writing (e.g., in textbooks, school reports, and essays) than in speaking situations. Formal English involves longer sentences and is frequently written in the passive voice. Informal English is used in everyday conversations and in personal letters, e-mails, and face-to-face school environments. It's likely to include idioms, contractions, and slang.

How language functions in different contexts: Specific types of texts are written for particular audiences, occasions, and purposes. How a text is written, the features or formats chosen, the words or sentence types included, the tone or style adopted—these all relate to the context in which the document is written and so must be considered by the writer, the speaker, the reader, and the listener.

Knowledge of language: This refers to an understanding of language in all its forms and functions, including vocabulary, grammar, usage, syntax, rhetoric, diction, and style.

Notes

Planning Page

Standard: _____

Purpose of Lesson/s:

Planning the Lesson/s	Questions to Ask

Differentiating Instruction	Thinking Beyond This Standard

The standards guide instruction; they do not dictate it. So as you plan lessons remember you aren't teaching the standards, but instead are teaching students how to read, write, talk, and think through well-crafted lessons that draw from the pedagogy embedded within them. Engaging lessons often have several ELA standards within them and integrate reading, writing, speaking and listening, and language.

Standard 4: Determine or clarify the meaning of unknown and multiple-meaning words and phrases by using context clues, analyzing meaningful word parts, and consulting general and specialized reference materials, as appropriate.

K Students determine or clarify the meaning of unknown and multiple-meaning words and phrases based on *kindergarten reading and content*.

    a. Identify new meanings for familiar words and apply them accurately (e.g., knowing *duck* is a bird and learning the verb *to duck*).

    b. Use the most frequently occurring inflections and affixes (e.g., *-ed, -s, re-, un-, pre-, -ful, -less*) as a clue to the meaning of an unknown word.

1 Students determine or clarify the meaning of unknown and multiple-meaning words and phrases based on *grade 1 reading and content*, choosing flexibly from an array of strategies.

    a. Use sentence-level context as a clue to the meaning of a word or phrase.

    b. Use frequently occurring affixes as a clue to the meaning of a word.

    c. Identify frequently occurring root words (e.g., *look*) and their inflectional forms (e.g., *looks, looked, looking*).

2 Students determine or clarify the meaning of unknown and multiple-meaning words and phrases based on *grade 2 reading and content*, choosing flexibly from an array of strategies.

    a. Use sentence-level context as a clue to the meaning of a word or phrase.

    b. Determine the meaning of the new word formed when a known prefix is added to a known word (e.g., *happy/unhappy, tell/retell*).

    c. Use a known root word as a clue to the meaning of an unknown word with the same root (e.g., *addition, additional*).

    d. Use knowledge of the meaning of individual words to predict the meaning of compound words (e.g., *birdhouse, lighthouse, housefly; bookshelf, notebook, bookmark*).

    e. Use glossaries and beginning dictionaries, both print and digital, to determine or clarify the meaning of words and phrases.

What the **Student** Does

K **Gist:** Students determine or clarify the meaning of unknown and multiple-meaning words and phrases based on *kindergarten reading and content.*

They consider:

- Do I recognize that words can have more than one meaning?
- When I read am I on the lookout for these differences in word meanings?
- Do I use word endings such as *-ed* and *-ing* to identify the main word and figure out what it means?
- Do I use prefixes (e.g., *re-* and *un-*) and suffixes (e.g., *-ful* and *-less*) to figure out the meaning of a word I don't know?

1 **Gist:** Students independently determine or clarify the meaning of unknown and multiple-meaning words and phrases based on *grade 1 reading and content,* choosing flexibly from an array of strategies.

They consider:

- Do I use surrounding words in a sentence to figure out the meaning of a word or phrase?
- Do I use prefixes and suffixes to figure out the meaning of a word?
- Do I identify root words and their inflectional forms (e.g., *looks, looked, looking*)?
- Do I have a variety of word-meaning strategies from which to choose when I don't know the meaning of a word?

2 **Gist:** Students independently determine or clarify the meaning of unknown and multiple-meaning words and phrases based on *grade 2 reading and content,* choosing flexibly from an array of strategies.

They consider:

- Do I use surrounding words in a sentence to figure out the meaning of a word or phrase?
- Do I use a known prefix to figure out the meaning of an unknown word (e.g., *happy/unhappy, tell/retell*)?
- Do I use a known root word to figure out the meaning of a word with the same root (e.g., *addition, additional*)?
- Do I use my knowledge of individual words to predict the meaning of compound words (e.g., *birdhouse, lighthouse, housefly*)?
- Do I use glossaries and beginning dictionaries to determine or clarify the meaning of words and phrases?
- Do I have a variety of word-meaning strategies from which to choose?

Note: Although the questions listed above are too difficult for most young students to internalize and apply on their own, we share them to give teachers a detailed sense of what their students should be striving toward as learners. K–2 students may not be able to ask these questions of themselves independently, but teachers can use them as a jumping-off point for lesson content and as prompts and reminders to share with students. Over time and with instruction, students will be able to pose these questions on their own.

What the **Teacher** Does

To help students determine or clarify the meaning of unknown and multiple-meaning words and phrases by using context clues:

- Model for students that the first step in handling unknown words when reading is to recognize that you don't know the meaning of a word that you consider essential to understanding the passage as a whole. Even if you don't stop to figure out the word at that moment, it's important that students hear you express the need to eventually know its meaning. As you work with students, begin to list the ways that readers figure out the meaning of words. Include the following in that list: (1) using context clues to figure out a word, (2) analyzing the word for its parts, and (3) referring to a dictionary or another resource for help.

- Engage students in a basic cloze procedure to help them recognize that they can use the context in which an unknown word appears—that is, the words around it—to *identify* the word. (In the next bulleted item we'll adapt this procedure to help readers determine what words *mean*.) Put up a sentence in which you have covered up or deleted a word or several words in a passage. Guide students to use the surrounding words to make informed guesses as to what the word is. Then unmask the word letter by letter so students can also use letter sounds to identify the word.

- Modify the basic cloze procedure described above to assist students in figuring out the *meaning* of words. Put up a passage in which you have deleted several vocabulary-type words. Have students read the passage and try to name the deleted words. For example, a student might make an educated guess that one word is *quiet*, but once all the deleted letters are revealed, she sees that the word is *still*, not *quiet*. This leads the student to recognize that the words *still* and *quiet* have similar meanings and both fit the sentence from the passage, "Be _____!"

- Model for students several ways to figure out the meaning of an unfamiliar word at the sentence level: (1) There may be a *synonym* in the sentence that hints at the unknown word; for example, "The puppy looked so *happy* and *content* all snuggled in his doggie bed." (2) There may be an *antonym*, such as in the sentence "My sister was *calm*, but I was *upset*." (3) Sometimes an *example* is given to help with the unknown word, such as "The children brought in all sorts of *containers* for their science project—*milk cartons, vases, bottles*—anything that would hold their collections." (4) Often explanations are given of what the unknown word means; for example, "We saw a video of how *predators* hunt and feed on other animals, their *prey*." Students also need to understand that there are times when context clues do not help with the meaning of a word.

To help students determine or clarify word meanings by analyzing word parts:

- Feature prefixes and suffixes on your vocabulary wall. Start by focusing on those that are the most common in printed school English. The most common prefixes are *re-, un-, dis-,* and *in- (im-, il-, ir-),* and the most common suffixes (note that inflectional endings are included here) are *-ed, -ing, -ly,* and *-s (-es).* Create classroom charts of grade-appropriate prefixes and suffixes.

- Provide picture books that teach students about prefixes and suffixes, such as *If You Were a Prefix* and *If You Were a Suffix* by Marcie Aboff (both from the Word Fun series) and Brian P. Cleary's *Pre- and Re-, Mis- and Dis-: What Is a Prefix?* and *-ful and -less, -er and -ness: What Is a Suffix?* (both from the Words Are Categorical series).

- Model how you go about analyzing words with affixes. Write a word, such as *unfriendly* or *speechless*, on a chart or whiteboard. Then look at its parts: What's the root and what does it mean? Is there a prefix and, if so, does that help me figure out what the word means? And last, is there a suffix and does that help?

- Provide a space on your vocabulary wall for words that have either a prefix or a suffix and words that have both. Write each word on a sentence strip card and highlight the affixes with wide highlighting tape. Keep adding to the wall as you study new words. Revisit the words frequently and have students make up sentences using the root word alone and sentences using the affixed words.

- Work with students to identify words that are related by their root to the word you are analyzing. Write the word in the center of a web and think through other words that share the same root. For example, the word *kind* is related to *kindness* and *kindly*; the word *fortune* is related to *fortunately* and *fortunate*. When working with K–2 students, you can include words with inflectional endings (e.g., *-s, -ed, -ing*).

To help students learn to consult general and specialized reference materials:

- Teach students to tag (with sticky notes) words whose meanings are unfamiliar so that they're reminded to consult reference materials after they've tried to figure out the meanings contextually or by analyzing the words' parts.

- Demonstrate how to access digital reference materials, especially picture dictionaries, beginning dictionaries, and thesauruses. Guide students through their use.

- Have a wide assortment of dictionaries, thesauruses, and vocabulary-related reference materials available to students in the classroom. It's better to give students access to several different titles than for them all to have copies of the same title. Teach students how to use these resources and provide opportunities to use them throughout the day. In addition, bookmark online dictionary and thesaurus sites for students to reference as they read and write.

To help students determine words and phrases with multiple meanings:

- Collect and chart words that are spelled the same but have more than one meaning (homographs). Purchase or make a blank big book in which students can write one homograph per page, along with a sentence to represent each of its meanings, and an illustration to accompany each meaning. Examples of homographs are *run*, *play*, *store*, *mouth*, *bill*, *record*, *tear*, *bark*, and *lead*.

- Help students recognize that some homographs are pronounced differently from one another, such as *sow* (a female pig) and *sow* (to plant seed), and other homographs are pronounced the same way, such as *bill* (beak on a duck) and *bill* (something that needs to be paid).

To help your English language learners, try this:

- Provide access to an appropriate language and picture-rich dictionary at school and at home.

- Dive into your units and mentor texts to develop a set of the most important words for your students to know in your class—and help them learn these words through discussion, pictures, and images from online searches and realia.

Developmental Debrief:

- Word learning is incremental. Transitioning from not knowing the meaning of a word to mastery is a slow process involving multiple exposures over time. True mastery is achieved when students can use a word as they speak and write and when they automatically understand what it means when they meet it in text. Research shows that we learn words that matter to us, and so while weekly decontextualized vocabulary lists may seem more structured, students are not likely to remember words unless we link word learning to meaningful, pleasurable, and personal experiences, such as word games, writing, and, of course, daily read-alouds.

Notes

Academic Vocabulary: Key Words and Phrases

Affixes: These are morphemes attached to the beginnings or endings of root words. They include prefixes and suffixes.

Compound words: These are words that are formed by the joining of two words. Both words in a compound word contribute to the meaning.

Determine and clarify the meaning of unknown and multiple-meaning words: Students cannot afford to ignore or not know many words in complex texts they read; lacking such knowledge, they cannot understand the texts they read, especially when these words appear in discipline-specific texts as specialized terms related to content-area topics.

Glossaries: These are lists of specialized words in a text, along with their definitions; they are often found at the backs of books.

Inflections: These are groups of letters added to the end of a word to change its meaning. Examples include *-s, -es, -ing,* and *-ed*.

Root: This refers to the base *unit* from which words are made through the addition of prefixes or suffixes, such as *dict* (to say) or *bio* (life). While roots are the basis for new words, they typically do not stand alone as words in and of themselves.

Root word: This is the base word when the affixes have been removed.

Sentence-level context clues: These clues enable a reader to make an informed guess at the meaning of an unknown word by looking at all the words around it and its place in the sentence.

Thesauruses: These are books that contain listings of words and their synonyms.

Notes

Planning Page

Standard: _____

Purpose of Lesson/s:

Planning the Lesson/s	Questions to Ask

Differentiating Instruction	Thinking Beyond This Standard

The standards guide instruction; they do not dictate it. So as you plan lessons remember you aren't teaching the standards, but instead are teaching students how to read, write, talk, and think through well-crafted lessons that draw from the pedagogy embedded within them. Engaging lessons often have several ELA standards within them and integrate reading, writing, speaking and listening, and language.

Standard 5: Demonstrate understanding of figurative language, word relationships, and nuances in word meanings.

K With guidance and support from adults, students explore word relationships and nuances in word meanings.

    a. Sort common objects into categories (e.g., shapes, foods) to gain a sense of the concepts the categories represent.

    b. Demonstrate understanding of frequently occurring verbs and adjectives by relating them to their opposites (antonyms).

    c. Identify real-life connections between words and their use (e.g., note places at school that are *colorful*).

    d. Distinguish shades of meaning among verbs describing the same general action (e.g., *walk, march, strut, prance*) by acting out the meanings.

1 With guidance and support from adults, students demonstrate understanding of word relationships and nuances in word meanings.

    a. Sort words into categories (e.g., colors, clothing) to gain a sense of the concepts the categories represent.

    b. Define words by category and by one or more key attributes (e.g., a *duck* is a bird that swims; a *tiger* is a large cat with stripes).

    c. Identify real-life connections between words and their use (e.g., note places at home that are *cozy*).

    d. Distinguish shades of meaning among verbs differing in manner (e.g., *look, peek, glance, stare, glare, scowl*) and adjectives differing in intensity (e.g., *large, gigantic*) by defining or choosing them or by acting out the meanings.

2 Students demonstrate understanding of word relationships and nuances in word meanings.

    a. Identify real-life connections between words and their use (e.g., describe foods that are *spicy* or *juicy*).

    b. Distinguish shades of meaning among closely related verbs (e.g., *toss, throw, hurl*) and closely related adjectives (e.g., *thin, slender, skinny, scrawny*).

What the **Student** Does

K **Gist:** With guidance and support from adults, students explore word relationships and nuances in word meanings.

They consider:

- Can I group objects into categories because they are similar in one or several ways?
- When I come across verbs and adjectives, can I come up their opposites to understand these words even more?
- Do I connect the words I am learning with my own life and experiences?
- Do I recognize the slight differences between the meanings of verbs that describe the same general action? Can I act out the meanings of these words?

1 **Gist:** With guidance and support from adults, students demonstrate understanding of word relationships and nuances in word meanings.

They consider:

- Can I sort or group words into categories because they are similar in one or several ways?
- Can I define words by category and by one or more key attributes?
- Do I connect the words I am learning with my own life and experiences?
- Do I recognize the slight differences in the meaning (and manner) of verbs and the intensity of adjectives? Do I recognize how those differences might change the meaning of a sentence or passage?

2 **Gist:** Students demonstrate understanding of word relationships and nuances in word meanings.

They consider:

- Do I connect the words I am learning with my own life and experiences?
- Do I recognize the slight differences in the meanings of closely related verbs and adjectives, and how those differences might change the meaning of a sentence or passage?

Note: Although the questions listed above are too difficult for most young students to internalize and apply on their own, we share them to give teachers a detailed sense of what their students should be striving toward as learners. K–2 students may not be able to ask these questions of themselves independently, but teachers can use them as a jumping-off point for lesson content and as prompts and reminders to share with students. Over time and with instruction, students will be able to pose these questions on their own.

What the **Teacher** Does

To help students sort and define words by category:

- Read aloud to the class (or to students in a small group) an informational text with discrete sections or chapters. Guide students to select words from that chapter or section because they "go together"—that is, they represent key information about the chapter's topic—and write them on chart paper or a whiteboard. For example, in "Baby Dolphins," a chapter from Sylvia M. James's *Dolphins*, students might choose the words *calf, underwater, milk,* and *mammal.* Invite students to compose sentences using two or more of the words. It's important for students to see words anchored in a category with other related words.

To help students identify real-life connections between words and their use:

- Identify verbs and adjectives, such as *avoid* or *fancy,* that students are likely to come across in their reading or as you read to or with them. Focus on two or three words at a time. Have students think about how the words relate to their lives and their experiences at home. For example, if a focus word is *avoid,* a student might say or write, "I tried to *avoid* going to bed on time by playing with my baby brother." If the word is *fancy,* a student might say or write, "My mother bought me a *fancy* skirt to wear, but I don't like it."

To help students understand the relationships between words:

- Designate a large portion of your bulletin board as the vocabulary wall. When teaching students to build semantic networks among words, it's important to have a wide variety of words readily accessible. This way you can more easily make connections between the words already on the vocabulary wall and new words you are introducing.

- Have students find examples of antonyms and share them. List them on your vocabulary wall or have students keep track of them in their reading notebooks. Come up with a fun way for students to remember that antonyms are opposites. For example, given that the prefix *anti-* comes from the Greek root *anti-,* meaning "opposite" or "against," students might devise a character and illustrate it, such as Auntie Antonym, who always says the opposite of what she means. If Auntie says, "The boat is *gigantic,*" she really means it's *tiny.*

- After reading a text to or with students, help them understand how the author chose his or her words carefully to help convey meaning to readers. For example, in *Down the Road,* Alice Schertle writes, "Hetty walked slowly down a *cluttered* aisle, looking *closely* at cans and cartons and bolts of fabric, just as if she might decide to buy something else." Call students' attention to the word *slowly* and have them consider its opposite (*quickly*) and do the same with *cluttered* (*organized*). Attending to an antonym helps students recognize that the author deliberately chose a word with an opposite meaning. What was her reason? Why did Alice walk *slowly*? Why was the aisle *cluttered* and not neatly organized?

- Design a graphic organizer for students to use as you help them consider antonyms and words that mean almost the same (synonyms). (For an example, see the online resources at resources.corwin.com/literacycompanionk-2.) Helping students see connections between words speeds up their vocabulary learning and gives them insight into the subtle word choices authors make.

- Check online sites for the most common English verbs (the same with adjectives). Identify words whose meanings you might want to help students understand. Words such as *confirm, create, produce, provide,* and *mention* are academic words that students are likely to meet in content-area studies, so they're good ones to focus on.

- Get to know TextProject (at http://textproject.org), the website where Elfrieda H. (Freddy) Hiebert provides a wealth of free vocabulary resources, including lists and lessons, banks of pictures that can help teach complex words, and help for English learners. You will also find good articles on word acquisition and text complexity on the site.

To help students distinguish shades of meaning between closely related verbs and adjectives:

- Select a passage from a book you've read aloud or a poem students are learning to post on a whiteboard. One example might be from Kathleen T. Pelley's *Magnus Maximus, a Marvelous Measurer*: "Together they walked down to the edge of the sea. They peeled off their shoes and socks and paddled in the water. Icy waves nibbled their toes as they shrieked and sang a silly song." Call attention to the verbs and adjectives the author uses—*walked, peeled off, paddled, nibbled, shrieked, icy,* and *silly.* For each word, have students come up with several words that mean almost the same, and consider whether or not any of those words would be good substitutes or how they might change the intended meaning of the passage.

- Write four or five words that have similar but different meanings, such as *pretty, gorgeous, attractive,* and *beautiful,* on individual cards. Have students discuss their meaning and arrange the cards on a continuum that moves from "less" to "more"—for example, from slowest to fastest, from least sad to most sad, or from happy to happiest. Have students give reasons for ranking the words as they did.

To help your English language learners, try this:

- Develop word banks in your classroom of descriptive words and refer to them in discussions about people, places, things, and information.

- Practice describing pictures or real items with your students, focusing on using a variety of words to describe clearly what the students are looking at.

- Create lists of "Dazzling Descriptive Words" and post the lists where students can easily access them during discussions and while writing. (This suggestion comes from Nancy Akhavan's 2007 book *Accelerated Vocabulary Instruction: Strategies for Closing the Achievement Gap for All Students.*)

- Take care to contextualize words when teaching them.

Developmental Debrief:

Whenever possible, and as naturally as possible, try to elaborate on the meanings of words you use with students. For example, if you say, "I cut my finger on this *jagged* edge," add, "See how *uneven* it is."

Notes

Academic Vocabulary: Key Words and Phrases

Antonyms: These are words that mean the opposite of other words. For example, *good/bad*, *up/down*, and *hot/cold* are opposites.

Category: This is a class or group of people, things, and so on having some quality or attribute in common.

Concepts (the categories represent): Concepts are mental representations or ideas. When we group words into categories we often do so because they represent the same or almost the same idea.

Distinguish shades of meaning: This refers to nuances in words with similar meanings. For example, while the meanings of *weep* and *cry* are similar, *weep* connotes intense sadness and grief, whereas *cry* suggests a loud expression of emotion.

Figurative language (figures of speech): When you describe something by comparing it to something else you are using figurative language. Similes and metaphors are two examples of figurative language found in texts for K–2 students. They compare things in ways that help readers see people, places, and things in interesting or surprising ways, and often help to convey deeper ideas or emotions.

Frequently occurring verbs and adjectives: These are verbs and adjectives that come up a lot in texts students read. And because they do, they're good ones to focus on when trying to build semantic networks or to help students identify their opposites.

Nuances in word meanings: These are the subtle meanings of some words as we use and come to know them. Readers learn to discern the implied meanings of words, and writers attend to the degrees of meaning as they select words to use in their pieces.

Real-life connections: This means that students connect what they're learning (in the case of this standard, words) to what they're experiencing in their lives.

Word relationships: These are the ways in which two or more words might be related grammatically, rhetorically, conceptually, or in some other meaningful way. Included in this category are figures of speech such as metaphors, analogies, and similes, which are based entirely on associations and relationships between words and ideas.

Notes

Planning Page

Standard: _____

Purpose of Lesson/s:

Planning the Lesson/s	Questions to Ask

Differentiating Instruction	Thinking Beyond This Standard

The standards guide instruction; they do not dictate it. So as you plan lessons remember you aren't teaching the standards, but instead are teaching students how to read, write, talk, and think through well-crafted lessons that draw from the pedagogy embedded within them. Engaging lessons often have several ELA standards within them and integrate reading, writing, speaking and listening, and language.

Standard 6: Acquire and use accurately a range of general academic and domain-specific words and phrases sufficient for reading, writing, speaking, and listening at the college and career readiness level; demonstrate independence in gathering vocabulary knowledge when encountering an unknown term **important to comprehension or expression.**

K Students use words and phrases acquired through conversations, reading and being read to, and responding to texts.

1 Students use words and phrases acquired through conversations, reading and being read to, and responding to texts, including using frequently occurring conjunctions to signal simple relationships (e.g., *because*).

2 Students use words and phrases acquired through conversations, reading and being read to, and responding to texts, including using adjectives and adverbs to describe (e.g., *When other kids are happy, that makes me happy*).

What the **Student** Does

K **Gist:** Students use words and phrases acquired through conversations, reading and being read to, and responding to texts.

They consider:

- Do I take note of and use words and phrases I hear used in conversations?
- Do I take note of and use interesting words and phrases I encounter when reading, being read to, and responding to texts?

1 **Gist:** Students use words and phrases acquired through conversations, reading and being read to, and responding to texts, including using frequently occurring conjunctions to signal simple relationships (e.g., *I named my hamster Nibblet because she nibbles too much*).

They consider:

- Do I take note of and use words and phrases I hear used in conversations?
- Do I take note of and use interesting words and phrases I encounter when reading, being read to, and responding to texts?
- Do I use words such as *and, but, because,* and *or* to express relationships?

2 **Gist:** Students use words and phrases acquired through conversations, reading and being read to, and responding to texts, including using adjectives and adverbs to describe (e.g., *When other kids are happy, that makes me happy*).

They consider:

- Do I take note of and use words and phrases I hear used in conversations?
- Do I take note of and use interesting words and phrases I encounter when reading, being read to, and responding to texts?
- Do I use adjectives and adverbs to describe people, things, and events?

Note: Although the questions listed above are too difficult for most young students to internalize and apply on their own, we share them to give teachers a detailed sense of what their students should be striving toward as learners. K–2 students may not be able to ask these questions of themselves independently, but teachers can use them as a jumping-off point for lesson content and as prompts and reminders to share with students. Over time and with instruction, students will be able to pose these questions on their own.

What the **Teacher** Does

To help students acquire and use academic and domain-specific words:

- Engage students in rich language experiences where they routinely participate in conversations and experiment with new vocabulary. Understanding that students learn vocabulary through multiple exposures over time will encourage you to create an environment where risk taking, as it applies to partially learned words, is valued and welcomed.

- Focus on what the Common Core and Isabel L. Beck, Margaret G. McKeown, and Linda Kucan (in *Bringing Words to Life*) call "Tier Two words." These are words that are likely to show up with high frequency in a mature language user's vocabulary. They include words such as *fortunate, exaggerate, determined,* and *harsh.* You might ask: Have you heard or seen the word before? Where? Have you heard it but don't know what it means? Do you know it (sort of) but are not sure you can explain or use it correctly? Do you know what it means and can use it as a reader, writer, listener, and speaker? Also consult Elfrieda Hiebert's TextProject website (http://textproject.org) for articles and resources on academic vocabulary teaching and learning.

- Select words to teach explicitly from a read-aloud or shared text with which the students are familiar. For each word selected, (1) locate and read the sentence that includes the target word, (2) state what the word means in student-friendly terms, and (3) use the word in a sentence and invite students to do the same. It's also helpful to have students express what the word means in their own words, orally or in writing.

- Engage students in a "Words Words Words" activity, in which they are on the lookout for the 10 to 15 words on the "active" list. (Words on the active list are those Tier Two words the teacher has selected from a recent read-aloud or shared text.) When students come across one of these words in their reading or use the word as they write, they can add tally marks alongside the word on the list. Once a word has a sufficient number of tally marks, the word is retired and replaced with a new word. This is most often done as a whole-class activity, in which a student is chosen to read the sentence in which he found one of the active words, omitting the word itself as he reads it to classmates. Then the student calls on a classmate to supply the missing word and explain why she thinks it's that word.

- When beginning a science or social studies unit, identify key domain-specific words that are likely to arise multiple times throughout a chapter or text. (Domain-specific words are the low-frequency Tier Three words that show up primarily in content-area studies but not in everyday conversations or general reading.) For example, in a unit on the body, you might select words such as *spine, skeleton, organ, lung,* and *muscle.* List the words and discuss them with students.

To help students become more independent in acquiring vocabulary knowledge:

- Encourage students to keep track of words they find interesting or puzzling by using sticky notes or writing the words in a notebook. Even though K–2 students may be unable, just yet, to determine independently what a word means, the practice of noting words of interest is an important first step.

To help your English language learners, try this:

- Check that students know essential academic terms—such as *describe, explain, compare, mean, different,* and *familiar*—that they're likely to meet as they work independently or complete assignments. Whenever possible, use cognates (words that are similar or the same in two languages), such as *realmente* for *really* and *especial* for *special,* to help explain what words mean. Check online for lists of Spanish-English cognates. (There are 20,000 of them!)

Developmental Debrief:

In K–2 classrooms, one of our primary responsibilities is to make learning words part and parcel of what we do each and every day. In addition to teaching words *implicitly* (as they surface in texts we read to and with students), we need to devote a part of each day to teaching words *explicitly* (deciding in advance what words are most essential for students to learn and then making deliberate moves *before, during,* and *after* reading to help students own them).

Notes

Academic Vocabulary: Key Words and Phrases

Acquire and use accurately: The emphasis here is on students adding words to their vocabularies so that they are eventually prepared for any text they might read or write about. To "acquire" words, students must attend to the words they see but do not know and then make an effort to both learn them and remember them for future use. The added emphasis on using words *accurately* reminds us that the difference between one word and another is often crucial to full and deeper comprehension.

College and career readiness level: Upon entering any postsecondary career or classroom, students immediately realize whether they are ready to meet the demands of that situation or not. Those not ready for the demands of college-level reading most often have to take one or more remedial classes, which costs time and money—and often momentum—for those trying to pursue college degrees.

Comprehension: This refers to students understanding what they read. In addition, full, robust comprehension demands that the reader take in *all* the details of a text and examine them in light of the occasion, purpose, and audience to see if there are other or deeper meanings to the text.

Conjunctions: Conjunctions are words that join other words, phrases, and clauses. The most common conjunctions are *but, and, or,* and *because.*

Expression: This involves students being able to use vocabulary they're acquiring to express themselves orally and in writing.

General academic and domain-specific words: Academic words are the general words students encounter in all subjects, such as *describe, compare, cooperate, ordinary, explain,* and *ignore.* Domain-specific words are the specialized vocabulary that students encounter as they study content-area topics. For example, when learning about weather, students are likely to meet and will need to know the meanings of terms such as *seasons, cycle, precipitation, climate,* and *evaporation.*

Independence in gathering vocabulary knowledge: To grow their vocabularies, students must take pains to figure out the meanings of unknown words by using context clues, analyzing words for their parts, or looking up words in reference materials so they can draw on them as they read and write. This independence comes from acquiring an appreciation for words and their meanings and involves students jotting down and looking up words that either interest or confuse them.

Words and phrases sufficient . . . for college level: This is similar to the entry above for "College and career readiness level"; however, the difference here is an emphasis on being able to use words and phrases appropriate to the college-level classroom. This means using refined, specific, and appropriate language when writing about or discussing a topic in a class.

Notes

Planning Page

Standard: _____

Purpose of Lesson/s:

Planning the Lesson/s	Questions to Ask

Differentiating Instruction	Thinking Beyond This Standard

The standards guide instruction; they do not dictate it. So as you plan lessons remember you aren't teaching the standards, but instead are teaching students how to read, write, talk, and think through well-crafted lessons that draw from the pedagogy embedded within them. Engaging lessons often have several ELA standards within them and integrate reading, writing, speaking and listening, and language.

Resources

Official Common Core State Standards K–1 Text Exemplars

Stories

Arnold, Tedd. *Hi! Fly Guy*
DePaola, Tomie. *Pancakes for Breakfast*
Eastman, P. D. *Are You My Mother?*
Lobel, Arnold. *Frog and Toad Together*
Lobel, Arnold. *Owl at Home*
Lopshire, Robert. *Put Me in the Zoo*
Minarik, Else Holmelund. *Little Bear*
Seuss, Dr. *Green Eggs and Ham.*

Poetry

Agee, Jon. "Two Tree Toads."
Anonymous. "As I Was Going to St. Ives."
Chute, Marchette. "Drinking Fountain."
Ciardi, John. "Wouldn't You?"
Fyleman, Rose. "Singing-Time."
Giovanni, Nikki. "Covers."
Greenfield, Eloise. "By Myself."
Hughes, Langston. "Poem."
Lopez, Alonzo. "Celebration."
Merriam, Eve. "It Fell in the City."
Milne, A. A. "Halfway Down."
Rossetti, Christina. "Mix a Pancake."
Wright, Richard. "Laughing Boy."

Read-Aloud Stories

Atwater, Richard and Florence. *Mr. Popper's Penguins*
Bang, Molly. *The Paper Crane*
Baum, L. Frank. *The Wonderful Wizard of Oz*
Garza, Carmen Lomas. *Family Pictures*
Haley, Gail E. *A Story, a Story*
Henkes, Kevin. *Kitten's First Full Moon*
Jansson, Tove. *Finn Family Moomintroll*
Mora, Pat. *Tomás and the Library Lady*

Wilder, Laura Ingalls. *Little House in the Big Woods*
Young, Ed. *Lon Po Po: A Red-Riding Hood Story From China*

Read-Aloud Poetry

Anonymous. "The Fox's Foray."
Hughes, Langston. "April Rain Song."
Langstaff, John. *Over in the Meadow.*
Lear, Edward. "The Owl and the Pussycat."
Moss, Lloyd. *Zin! Zin! Zin! A Violin*

Informational Texts

Aliki. *A Weed Is a Flower: The Life of George Washington Carver*
Aliki. *My Five Senses*
Bulla, Clyde Robert. *A Tree Is a Plant*
Crews, Donald. *Truck*
Hoban, Tana. *I Read Signs*
Hurd, Edith Thacher. *Starfish*
National Geographic Young Explorers. "Garden Helpers."
National Geographic Young Explorers. "Wind Power."
Reid, Mary Ebeltoft. *Let's Find Out About Ice Cream*

Read-Aloud Informational Texts

Dorros, Arthur. *Follow the Water From Brook to Ocean*
Gibbons, Gail. *Fire! Fire!*
Hodgkins, Fran, and True Kelley. *How People Learned to Fly*
Jenkins, Steve, and Robin Page. *What Do You Do With a Tail Like This?*
Llewellyn, Claire. *Earthworms*
Pfeffer, Wendy. *From Seed to Pumpkin*
Provensen, Alice and Martin. *The Year at Maple Hill Farm*
Rauzon, Mark, and Cynthia Overbeck Bix. *Water, Water Everywhere*
Thomson, Sarah L. *Amazing Whales!*

Stories

Averill, Esther. *The Fire Cat*

Cameron, Ann. *The Stories Julian Tells*

Gannett, Ruth Stiles. *My Father's Dragon.*

LaMarche, Jim. *The Raft*

MacLachlan, Patricia. *Sarah, Plain and Tall*

Osborne, Mary Pope. *The One-Eyed Giant* (Book One of Tales From the Odyssey)

Rylant, Cynthia. *Henry and Mudge: The First Book of Their Adventures*

Rylant, Cynthia. *Poppleton in Winter*

Rylant, Cynthia. *The Lighthouse Family: The Storm*

Shulevitz, Uri. *The Treasure*

Silverman, Erica. *Cowgirl Kate and Cocoa*

Steig, William. *Amos & Boris*

Stevens, Janet. *Tops and Bottoms*

Poetry

Dickinson, Emily. "Autumn."

Field, Rachel. "Something Told the Wild Geese."

Frost, Robert. "Stopping by Woods on a Snowy Evening."

Giovanni, Nikki. "Knoxville, Tennessee."

Hughes, Langston. "Grandpa's Stories."

Jarrell, Randall. "A Bat Is Born."

Merriam, Eve. "Weather."

Millay, Edna St. Vincent. "Afternoon on a Hill."

Rossetti, Christina. "Who Has Seen the Wind?"

Soto, Gary. "Eating While Reading."

Read-Aloud Stories

Babbitt, Natalie. *The Search for Delicious*

Curtis, Christopher Paul. *Bud, Not Buddy*

Kipling, Rudyard. "How the Camel Got His Hump."

Say, Allen. *The Sign Painter*

Selden, George. *The Cricket in Times Square*

Thurber, James. *The Thirteen Clocks*

White, E. B. *Charlotte's Web*

Read-Aloud Poetry

Browning, Robert. "The Pied Piper of Hamelin"

Eliot, T. S. "The Song of the Jellicles."

Fleischman, Paul. "Fireflies."

Johnson, Georgia Douglas. "Your World."

Lear, Edward. "The Jumblies."

Informational Texts

Aliki. *A Medieval Feast*

Beeler, Selby. *Throw Your Tooth on the Roof: Tooth Traditions Around the World*

Davies, Nicola. *Bat Loves the Night*

Einspruch, Andrew. *Crittercam*

Floca, Brian. *Moonshot: The Flight of Apollo 11*

Gibbons, Gail. *From Seed to Plant*

Kudlinski, Kathleen V. *Boy, Were We Wrong About Dinosaurs*

Leonard, Heather. *Art Around the World*

Milton, Joyce. *Bats: Creatures of the Night*

Ruffin, Frances E. *Martin Luther King and the March on Washington*

St. George, Judith. *So You Want to Be President?*

Thomson, Sarah L. *Where Do Polar Bears Live?*

Read-Aloud Informational Texts

Aliki. *Ah, Music!*

Arnosky, Jim. *Wild Tracks! A Guide to Nature's Footprints*

Coles, Robert. *The Story of Ruby Bridges*

D'Aluisio, Faith. *What the World Eats*

Deedy, Carmen Agra. *14 Cows for America*

Freedman, Russell. *Lincoln: A Photobiography*

Mark, Jan. *The Museum Book: A Guide to Strange and Wonderful Collections*

Smith, David J. *If the World Were a Village: A Book About the World's People*

Wick, Walter. *A Drop of Water: A Book of Science and Wonder*

Text Complexity Tool

Title:		Author:		Date:	
Appropriate Grade Level:		Length:		Text Type/Genre:	
		Too Simple	**Just Right**		**Too Complex**

QUANTITATIVE FACTORS			
Word Length			
☐ What is the average length of a word in this text? ☐ Do the words tend to have one or many meanings?			
Sentence Length			
☐ How long is the average sentence? ☐ Do sentences tend to be all the same length or vary as a function of style? ☐ Do the sentences have a range of syntactical complexity—or do they tend to follow the same pattern?			
Word Frequency			
☐ Which words are used frequently? ☐ Are these words known/familiar?			
Text Cohesion			
☐ How well does this text hold together or flow (thanks to signal words such as transitions)? ☐ Does the text use other techniques such as repetition or concrete language to improve cohesion? ☐ Does the text lack cohesion as a result of having no signal words?			
QUALITATIVE FACTORS			
Levels of Meaning or Purpose			
☐ If *literary*, does the text have more than one obvious meaning? ☐ If *informational*, is the purpose explicitly stated or implied? ☐ Does the text explore *more* than one substantial idea?			
Text Structure			
☐ Does the text use simple, predictable structures such as chronological order? ☐ Does the text use complex literary structures such as flashbacks or, if informational, sophisticated graphics and genre conventions? ☐ Does the text use other features—layout, color, graphics—in ways that might confuse or challenge some readers?			
Language Conventions and Clarity			
☐ Is the language literal, clear, modern, and conversational? ☐ Is the language figurative, ironic, ambiguous, archaic, specialized, or otherwise unfamiliar?			
Knowledge Demands			
☐ Does the text make few assumptions about what you have experienced or know about yourself, others, and the world? ☐ Does the text assume you know about this topic or text based on prior experience or study?			
READER AND TASK CONSIDERATIONS			
Motivation, Knowledge, and Experience			
☐ How motivated is this student to read this text? ☐ How much does this student know about this topic or text? ☐ How much experience does the student have with this task or text type?			
Purpose and Complexity of the Assigned Task			
☐ Is this student able to read and work at the assigned level? ☐ Are these questions the student will know how to answer? ☐ Is the student expected to do this work alone and without any support—or with others and guidance? ☐ Is this text or task appropriate for this student at this time? ☐ Is this text or task as, less, or more complex than the last one?			

Created by Jim Burke. Visit www.englishcompanion.com for more information.

Planning Calendar Templates

July Planning Calendar

Sunday	Monday	Tuesday	Wednesday	Thursday	Friday	Saturday

August Planning Calendar

Sunday	Monday	Tuesday	Wednesday	Thursday	Friday	Saturday

September Planning Calendar

Sunday	Monday	Tuesday	Wednesday	Thursday	Friday	Saturday

October Planning Calendar

Sunday	Monday	Tuesday	Wednesday	Thursday	Friday	Saturday

November Planning Calendar

Sunday	Monday	Tuesday	Wednesday	Thursday	Friday	Saturday

December Planning Calendar

Sunday	Monday	Tuesday	Wednesday	Thursday	Friday	Saturday

January Planning Calendar

Sunday	Monday	Tuesday	Wednesday	Thursday	Friday	Saturday

February Planning Calendar

Sunday	Monday	Tuesday	Wednesday	Thursday	Friday	Saturday

March Planning Calendar

Sunday	Monday	Tuesday	Wednesday	Thursday	Friday	Saturday

April Planning Calendar

Sunday	Monday	Tuesday	Wednesday	Thursday	Friday	Saturday

May Planning Calendar

Sunday	Monday	Tuesday	Wednesday	Thursday	Friday	Saturday

June Planning Calendar

Sunday	Monday	Tuesday	Wednesday	Thursday	Friday	Saturday

Teacher Notes

CORWIN LITERACY

STANDARDS-BASED TEACHING

The key to raising school- and district-wide achievement is purposeful, potent, standards-based instruction—all year long in every classroom. That's where the Your Literacy Standards Companion series can help. Series creator Jim Burke and an all-star team of authors walk you step by step through what the standards mean and how to teach them. Ensure that every student in your district has the critical skills they need to succeed on test day, in school, and in life.

Grades K–2
978-1-5063-8682-9

Grades 3–5
978-1-5063-8700-0

Grades 6–8
978-1-5063-8553-2

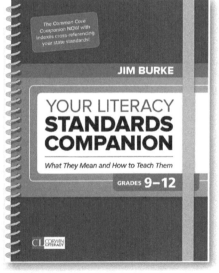

Grades 9–12
978-1-5063-8552-5

BECAUSE ALL TEACHERS ARE LEADERS

Douglas Fisher, Nancy Frey, John Hattie
Ensure students demonstrate more than a year's worth of learning during a school year by implementing the right literacy practice at the right moment.

Grades K–12
978-1-5063-3235-2

Douglas Fisher, Nancy Frey, John Hattie
High-impact strategies to use for all you teach—all in one place. Deliver sustained, comprehensive literacy experiences to K–5 learners each day.

Grades K–5
978-1-5063-3236-9

Wiley Blevins
Foremost phonics expert Wiley Blevins explains the 7 ingredients that lead to the greatest student gains, and includes common pitfalls, lessons, word lists, and routines.

Grades K–2
978-1-5063-2688-7

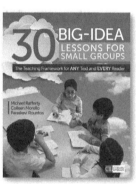

Michael Rafferty, Colleen Morello, Paraskevi Rountos
This amazing 4-part framework—Engaging, Discussing, Deep-See Thinking, and Connecting—gets students interacting with texts, developing their literal, inferential, evaluative, and analytical skills.

Grades 3–6
978-1-5063-3438-7

Gravity Goldberg
Let go of the default roles of assigner, monitor, and manager, and shift to a growth mindset. The 4Ms framework lightens your load by allowing students to direct their own reading lives.

Grades K–8
978-1-5063-1493-8

Nancy Boyles
Nancy Boyles delivers the playbook on close reading through lessons, assessment strategies, planning templates, online video, and more.

Grades K–2, 978-1-5063-2646-7
Grades 3–6, 978-1-4833-7567-0

CORWIN
A SAGE Publishing Company

CORWIN

A SAGE Publishing Company

CORWIN HAS ONE MISSION: to enhance education through intentional professional learning.

We build long-term relationships with our authors, educators, clients, and associations who partner with us to develop and continuously improve the best evidence-based practices that establish and support lifelong learning.